Governing the Economy

Europe and the International Order

Series Editor: Joel Krieger

Published

Joel Krieger, *Reagan, Thatcher and the Politics of Decline*

Forthcoming

Judith A. Hellman, *Journeys among Women*
Mark Kesselman, *The Fading Rose*
Andrei Markovits, *The West German Left: Red, Green and Beyond*
George Ross and Stanley Hoffmann, *The Mitterand Experiment*

Governing the Economy

The Politics of State Intervention in Britain and France

Peter A. Hall

OXFORD UNIVERSITY PRESS

New York   Oxford

Library of Congress Cataloging in Publication Data

Hall, Peter A.
  Governing the economy.
  Bibliography: p.
  Includes index.
  1. Great Britain—Economic policy—1945–
2. France—Economic policy—1945–   I.Title
HC256.5.H256   1986   338.941   86–8654
ISBN 0–19–520523–5
ISBN 0–19–520530–8 (pbk.)

10 9 8 7

Printed in the United States of America

Contents

Preface

One of Britain's more aristocratic Prime Ministers once said: "There are two problems in my life. The political ones are insoluble, and the economic ones are incomprehensible."[1] Many of his successors might agree; but the two sorts of problems are not always as separable as we imagine. This is a book about the political dimensions of economic management. It attempts to explain the direction that economic policy took in Britain and France over the post-war period; and one of its central contentions is that economic policy-making must be understood as an essentially political process. The effects of economic policy alter the welfare of millions, and its making is a process deeply conditioned by broader struggles between competing parties, ideologies, and social classes. To understand that process we need a model of the polity itself; and the case of economic policy-making in Britain and France suggests that our existing images of politics should be revised to incorporate a more complete account of the way in which policy is affected by an underlying institutional logic.

This book has had a long gestation. Some of its central ideas were first presented in a paper entitled "French étatism versus British pluralism," delivered to the Seminar on the State and Capitalism at Harvard University in 1978. Others were worked out in a number of previous articles, and I am grateful to their publishers for permission to present revised versions of some of the material appearing in them. Portions of chapter three appeared in *The Decline of the British Economy*, edited by Bernard Elbaum and William Lazonick, published by Oxford University Press. Chapters six and seven draw on articles in *Political Power and Social Theory*, vol. III, edited by Gosta Esping-Andersen, Roger Friedland and Maurice Zeitlin, published by Jai Press, and *State e Mercato* (April 1980) published by Il Mulino in Italy. Chapter eight appeared in a slightly different form in *Socialism, the State and Public Policy in France*, edited by Philip Cerny and Martin Schain, published by Frances Pinter; and portions of chapter nine draw on my article in *The State in Capitalist Europe*, edited by Stephen

Bornstein, David Held and·Joel Krieger, published by Allen and Unwin.

During the course of this work I have incurred many debts to friends and colleagues. Many years ago, Joel Krieger first suggested that I should consider the case of Britain and France in the context of theories of the state, and he later urged me to publish the results of that work. The scholarly and stimulating writings of Professor J E S Hayward, whom I have never met, provided the original impetus for my work on this comparison. Cosette Hall in Toronto and Wendy Hall in London were continuing sources of strength and hospitality. Throughout the project, Rosemary Taylor gave generously of her time and ideas, and without her inimitable support it could not have been completed.

For critical comments on portions of this volume I am most grateful to Barry Eichengreen, John Goodman, Peter Gourevitch, Hugh Heclo, Jane Jenson, Robert Keohane, Andrew Martin, Helen Milner, Harvey Rishikof, George Ross, Annalee Saxenian, Bruce Scott, and especially Raymond Vernon who has been a stringent critic over the years. Steven Hubbell, Sarah King, Mark Lilla and Melissa Williams gave me detailed editorial comments on much of the manuscript, and Thomas Ertman supplied important research assistance for the British chapters.

The Center for European Studies at Harvard University provided both the site for much of the work on this project and a great deal of its intellectual inspiration. It is difficult to imagine a more congenial or stimulating place to work, and I want to thank Abby Collins, its Assistant Director, for many kindnesses.

Finally, I am most indebted to four scholars who as teachers and friends first persuaded me, as they have many others, that European politics was worth a lifetime of study. Their wise counsel and unstinting criticism have profoundly shaped my ideas, and I dedicate this book to them: Samuel H. Beer, Suzanne Berger, Stanley Hoffmann, and Peter Lange.

Part I: The Intellectual Terrain

1

Economic Policy and the Paradigms of Politics

We live in an era of economic change. At this moment three generations of people who have had very different economic experiences live together in the industrialized democracies. The elderly came of age during a terrible economic depression. They will never forget the impact of mass unemployment in the 1930s. By contrast, their children grew up in a period of unprecedented prosperity. Freed from want by the long boom that followed World War Two, many of them learned to take economic well-being largely for granted. But the youngest generation has been born into another era of economic turmoil, characterized this time by the coincidence of inflation and a recession, a combination with much more uneven effects than the collective experience of the 1930s.

Economic problems pose political challenges, and many Western nations embarked on radical economic experiments in the wake of the 1979 oil crisis. On 3 May 1979 the British people elected Margaret Thatcher to lead a Conservative Government that repudiated the Keynesian consensus of the past three decades. On 10 May 1981 the French elected François Mitterrand to bring in a Socialist Government for the first time under the Fifth Republic. These Governments were asked to bring back the prosperity of the long boom, and their electorates have waited for the results with a mixture of hope and trepidation.

As they attempt to revive the economy, however, these states must also manage social conflict. Many of the economic policies undertaken to regenerate investment and growth have severe distributional consequences. Some industrial sectors win and others lose from economic triage. Some segments of the population find that their living standards are depressed, while others enjoy new tax benefits or higher levels of support. Therefore the problems of policy formation are not easy. Each state must respond to competing pressures and each policy must simultaneously accomplish multiple tasks.

In the face of these challenges, various nations have chosen different paths. Thatcher and Mitterrand were not the first leaders of Britain and France to embrace different economic philosophies. Immediately after World War Two the economic policies of these two nations began to diverge. By 1960 their people began to realize that they had embarked on separate economic trajectories. The French became fixated on economic growth, while the British pondered the prospects of economic decline.

How are we to explain why nations choose different policy paths and divergent political strategies to deal with similar economic problems? When those policies founder, can they be changed? At such points, what determines the course that economic policy will take? To what do the economic policies of the state respond?

These are the questions this volume addresses. They are important to all of us because state intervention has come to play an increasing role in our collective economic fate. But we know surprisingly little about the factors that influence economic policy. There are many bridges to be crossed.

To begin, we must move beyond the view of policy-making implicit in most economics texts. They tend to see policy primarily as a response to prevailing economic conditions, and policy-making as the resolution of technical issues. To some degree, of course, this idea is quite valid: policy does respond to economic conditions. But such a view is far too incomplete. Economic policy is also made by governments, and governments are political creatures. Unless economic policy-making is peculiarly immune from the sort of influences found in most other policy areas, we can expect political variables to have a decisive impact on the outcome. Economic policy-making must be seen as a highly political process.

Accordingly, this is a book about the political dimensions of economic management. It takes the view that political variables will have a definitive impact on the character and direction of economic policy. But if this is so, we face an even more perplexing set of issues: what kind of political variables are we talking about? How should we conceptualize the range of political factors that influence economic policy-making? Some analyses focus on the impact of electoral competition on economic outcomes. They suggest that governments pump up the economy somewhat inefficiently to secure re-election (cf. Tufte, 1979). But such analyses take altogether too narrow a view of political factors. Politics enters the policy process in multiple ways. Interested groups press for congenial policies; politicians and civil servants jockey for influence over the outcome; and political problems occur in the process of policy implementation. Indeed, the very definition of desirable policy is subject to political influence.

For reasons such as these, correctly conceptualizing the policy process so as to identify the political factors that most influence it is a major challenge. Economic policy constitutes one of the most important actions of the modern state; and there is serious contention about the concepts that should be used to explain state actions. To take a position on the determinants of economic policy is implicitly to endorse a particular understanding of politics. Any theory that is capable of explaining economic policies must be grounded in a broader view of the general determinants of state action.

Consequently, this book is also about contemporary models of politics. It examines the interaction of interests, institutions and ideas in the policy process; and it develops a conception of political action that puts particular stress on the critical role played by institutions in the definition and articulation of interests, the dissemination of ideas, the construction of market behavior, and the determination of policy. There are important respects in which the policy process remains open-ended: no human activity is ever fully determined. On the basis of the cases examined here, however, we can say that there is a certain institutional logic to the process of economic intervention in the industrialized democracies.

This claim challenges much of the existing literature. Several important lines of analysis have been developed to explain national economic policies; and each of them contains an implicit model of the polity. Behind contemporary analyses of economic policy we find competing functional, cultural, public choice, group-conflict, and state-centric models of politics. They are by no means entirely consistent with one another; and each claims to have the correct understanding of politics. Therefore our first task is to assess the viability of these models, especially for the purpose of explaining European economic policy. Each seems to suffer from some serious defects, and many of these derive from the neglect of institutional variables.

FUNCTIONALIST MODELS

Functionalist analyses usually begin from the assumption that political life should be understood as an organic whole. In David Easton's words, "each part of the larger political canvas does not stand alone but is related to each other part; or, to put it more positively, that the operation of no one part can be fully understood without reference to the way in which the whole itself operates" (1957: 383). On this view the actions of the state are explained by the functions they perform for the stability or survival of the political system as a whole. "The major descriptive task is to indicate what structures contribute to the satisfaction of what functionality requisites" (Holt, 1967: 86). The effects of a phenomenon essentially explain its existence.

There are both left- and right-wing variants of functional analysis. They are differentiated by their conceptions of the underlying system. Conservative analysts tend to view the political system as an analytically distinct arena, whereas Marxist analysts usually explain political action in terms of the functional requisites of a particular economic system (cf. Holloway and Picciotto, 1978; Gough, 1978; Parsons, 1951).

One of the fundamental problems with functionalist theories is that they are too robust. They suggest that the state can be expected to reproduce the economic system; and Marxist variants claim that the state will act in the interest of capital. But when we compare the experience of such European nations as Britain, France, and Germany, we find wide variation in the range of policies they have adopted and in the efficacy of these policies for economic reproduction or capital. In general, when these theories are confronted with the need to account for systematic variation among the policies of different nations, they explain too much.

In order to deal with this problem, some functionalists have suggested that certain policies can be construed as contradictory or dysfunctional within the terms of such a framework (cf. Godelier, 1974); but this does considerable violence to the initial concept of a "system." How are we to know when it will generate functional policies and when dysfunctional ones?

Similarly, the terms used to specify what functions a system must perform are usually quite vague. Some theorists speak of the state's need to perform "accumulation" and "legitimation" functions; others say the state performs "recruitment" or "interest articulation and aggregation" functions; but these terms are so open-ended that they fail to identify the policies or institutions that will perform such functions with any degree of specificity. Indeed, one systems analyst observed that "just as the same item may have multiple functions, so may the same function be fulfilled by alternative items" (Merton, 1957: 33–4). Many statements of function could be fulfilled by such a wide range of structures that they could accommodate almost anything, and so they explain nothing. The problem is magnified if the theory allows for dysfunctional structures and policies.[1]

Let us consider an example of functionalist analysis used to explain the economic policies of nations that include Britain and France. In an influential article, Bill Warren (1972) employs a "logical–historical" approach, reminiscent of systems analysis, to explain the development of planning over the course of the post-war period. He argues that "the logic of the move away from deflationary, indirect control of wages, dictated by the retrogressive effects of deflation on the long-run dynamism of the economy and by the successful resistance of the working class to such methods, led naturally towards attempts at longer-term planning" (1972: 5). Planning is explained as a necessary extension of full employment policies dictated by the nature of the capitalist system itself:

> In fact, it is precisely because the capitalist state is a class state that it operates full employment policy . . . both the political and economic motives inducing governments to intervene in new ways in the economy were designed directly to preserve the interests (and survival) of the imperialist system in general and individual capitalist states in particular, against their respective working classes, national rivals and the socialist countries. The state possesses no independence, but does exercise a genuine if relative autonomy, inherent in its own specific and creative functions (1972: 18, 29).

Warren's argument contains some important insights; but the appearance of full employment policies and planning cannot be derived in any definitive fashion from the functions associated with capitalism. In fact, others have derived almost precisely the opposite set of conclusions from similar functional observations. From similar assumptions, for instance, Kalecki has argued that state managers must induce periodic recessions precisely to avoid full employment and its deleterious consequences for the rate of profit and reproduction of capital (Kalecki, 1943; Boddy and Crotty, 1975). If the policy experiences of 1962–72 seemed to affirm Warren's analysis, those of 1972–82 seemed to affirm Kalecki's argument, in sum, confirming neither. This is the standard problem of functionalist analysis: the factors linking the system and its associated functions to actual policies remain underspecified; and in their absence, a transitory empirical correlation between the existence of capitalism and planning is hypostasized into a causal connection.

Many of these problems are largely attributable to the way in which functionalist analysts reverse the priority given to institutional structures. It might be possible to identify the functions of a given institutional structure, but it is virtually impossible to derive structure from function in a systematic and non-arbitrary way. It may well be that the polity and economy are a system, in some sense of the term, but if so, it is by virtue of the institutions that present individuals with a matrix of incentives which render them interdependent, and link their behavior to the nature of the system. Structural–functionalism only works if it gives causal priority to structure rather than to function.

CULTURAL ANALYSIS

'Culture' is a collective construct that is sometimes seen as one facet of a political system; but analyses of state action that identify political culture as the determinative variable provide us with a way of explaining political outcomes that need not entail the functional analysis common to most systems theory. Although cultural analyses share the emphasis of public choice theory on the role of individual action, the way in which they understand the bases of individual motivation sharply differs. Cultural analysts argue that the behavior of politicians and officials is strongly affected by the political culture into which they have been socialized and in which they operate.

"The political culture of a society consists of the system of empirical beliefs, expressive symbols, and values which defines the situation in which political action takes place. It provides the subjective orientation to politics" (Verba, 1965: 513). Thus defined, political culture can vary across classes, ethnic groups, or generations: but it is especially likely to vary across nations. Therefore we should be able to explain divergent national policies by reference to the different habits of mind of their citizens and officials.

In this tradition there is some excellent work directly focused on economic policy-making in Britain and France. Jack Hayward, for instance, has argued that the British remained shackled to incrementalist economic policies while the French state was able to reform its economy, largely because of culturally based differences in the political attitudes of civil servants and societal groups alike. In order to explain the success of French planning relative to British attempts, Hayward refers to "the operation of culturally-based dominant values that inhibit or preclude some kinds of government action and favour others" (1976: 341). In particular, he argues, the French "had acquired a style of authority that includes a capacity for crisis utilization for the purpose of imposing overdue changes. In Britain, the myth . . . of gradualist political development . . . has been a potent cultural constraint inhibiting any unprecedented response to a crisis" (1976: 351). As a result, "a reforming impetus coming from a French government is less likely to be impeded and more likely to be furthered by interest groups . . . than is the case in Britain" (1976: 341).

Hayward's formulation of the political problem and its cultural origins is powerful. No-one can fail to learn something of value about both nations from it. However, it suffers from two defects common to cultural analysis.

Because the contrast in national styles of policy-making is couched largely in cultural terms, it is often too sweeping to pinpoint and conceptually circumscribe the differences between them. For instance,

Britain's failure to develop a more forceful system of planning is blamed on the inertia and unpersuasiveness of British officials. But studies of other areas of policy-making, including those of social policy and public expenditure control, suggest that British officials can display considerable forcefulness and a real innovative capacity (Heclo, 1974; Heclo and Wildavsky, 1979; Nettl, 1965). Similarly, any reader of Crozier (1968), Peyrefitte (1980), Zysman (1977) or McArthur and Scott (1969) can find many instances when French officials failed to display the prescience, control, and forcefulness that Hayward tends to attribute to them. The cultural brush is too broad to capture the more limited differences between economic policy-making in the two nations.

Secondly, even when cultural analyses capture real divergence, they often still leave it unexplained. Culture is not inherited but learned, and learned anew with each passing generation. There must be vehicles for the creation and transmission of political culture; and cultural analysis must say more about those vehicles. In the absence of such an account we are left to wonder why such cultural differences occur and persist. The explanation is tantamount to saying: Britain is Britain and France is France. If functionalist analysts explain too much, cultural analyses often explain too little.

That points directly to the need for a more complete investigation of social and political institutions, for it is in the routines and rationalities imposed by a particular complex of institutions that a specific culture is born. The genesis of those institutions, in turn, can be traced to the events of a particular series of historical conjunctures, some contingent, others systematically tied to the distribution of power among social groups.

Similarly, events in one sphere of policy-making should not necessarily be associated with political culture as a whole. It may well be that policy is affected by more specific sub-cultures associated with a particular array of institutions. The "village life" that some scholars have observed in government departments may be conditioned as much by the institutional configuration of those departments and their clients as by broader cultural factors (see Heclo and Wildavsky, 1979).

Finally, some differences in behavior that we might be tempted to ascribe to distinctive cultures may be more directly attributable to the ways in which a particular institutional setting conditions the perceptions and expectations of those within it, by affecting the contingent matrix of incentives they face. That is to say, outside the confines of a particular organizational or institutional situation, the same people might act very differently. In that case their behavior should not be blamed on deeply ingrained cultural norms, but on the ways in which organizational context alters the calculations of rational actors. In the actions of a particular set of policy-makers, for instance, we may be seeing the operation of an institutional rationality rather than that of a cultural norm.

PUBLIC CHOICE THEORY

Public choice theorists apply the analytical techniques of economics to politics to develop a third model of the polity. In general, they are methodological individualists in that their principal unit of analysis is not whole systems but individuals, usually understood as rational actors. According to this view, politics is a competition among individuals whose goals are access to power or scarce resources, and whose means are rationally calculated to achieve those ends most efficiently. In Schumpeter's (1947) famous formulation, the principal actors are political entrepreneurs, in or out of office, seeking to maximize political support. Others analyze the bureaucracy as an aggregation of resource-maximizing agencies or individuals (Buchanan and Tullock, 1962; Breton, 1974; Niskanen, 1971). According to this approach, policies are best explained as the outcome of a game-like contest in which power-seeking individuals, or institutions acting like individuals, compete for resources and the support of electors who are also seeking to maximize their personal resources. Politicans become endogenous variables in models of the polity analogous to those of the economy.

The insights that such analyses can supply are well illustrated in the familiar model of the political business cycle. It specifies that vote-maximizing politicians, faced with a Phillips curve trade-off between inflation and unemployment and an electorate whose isopreference curves between these outcomes are convex and whose perceptions of economic performance are myopic, will take advantage of the time-lags between fiscal behavior and economic impact to deflate the economy shortly after an election and reflate it shortly before the next one, regardless of the appropriate response to the economic business cycle.

Nordhaus (1975) was able to show with some elegance that, under these conditions, rational political behavior would dictate an inflationary economic outcome. However, subsequent empirical work has not sustained these contentions as completely as the theory would lead one to expect (Lindberg and Maier, 1985; Whiteley, 1980; Alt and Chrystal, 1983). It seems that isopreference curves shift more rapidly than expected; politicians call elections on other issues; and economic variables are less amenable to political manipulation than the theory implies. The ruthless elegance of these models often seems to founder on the complexities of political motivation and economic behavior.

To take another example, Andrew Cowart (1978) has compared British and French economic policy using an approach heavily

influenced by public choice theory. Cowart employs a series of equations to model the economic policy behavior of European governments
on the assumption that they behave as rational actors, altering fiscal
and monetary policy in response to changes in the rates of inflation and
unemployment.[2] To test the model, he assesses its ability to postdict
quarterly variations in policy over a 25-year period in six European
nations. The results for Britain and France are especially interesting.
The models predict the course of British policy rather well, with total
R-squares around 0.60 (without the auto-regressive term), but they fail
to capture the determinants of French policy, where the R-squares
rarely reach 0.20. The technique reveals an interesting discrepancy
between policy-making in Britain and France; but we have to look
elsewhere for an explanation of it.

Institutional factors supply a good deal of the answer. Differences in
the organizational framework within which policy has been made in the
two nations alter the extent to which a simple rational actor model will
apply. While the British state relied on the sort of Keynesian demand
management that generates the results predicted by the model, the
French utilized planning institutions whose very operation tended to
militate against such results. In particular, the French were less willing
to employ fiscal or monetary policy against inflation because moderate
levels of inflation actually facilitated the operation of planning.[3] French
governments also had less reason to employ fiscal instruments in
response to unemployment because they were relying more heavily on
microeconomic intervention, through planning and an active industrial
policy.

Cowart finds his results for France "most counterintuitive" on the
grounds that the apparent unresponsiveness of macroeconomic policy
to changing economic conditions is inconsistent with the French state's
reputation for extensive intervention into economic life (1978: 310).
However, this reflects an overly simple conception of "intervention"
that could be dispelled if more attention were paid to institutional
variation between the two nations. Both the French and British states
intervened in the economy but with important differences in technique
that explain precisely this discrepancy. The British utilized a macroeconomic strategy built around Keynesianism (of the sort to show up in
Cowart's results) while the French relied on a microeconomic approach
(that replaced the demand management strategy tested by Cowart) to
achieve similar ends. We can correctly model state action and its effects
only in the context of an institutionalist analysis of modes of intervention.

These considerations bear on an issue that is central to the public
choice literature: namely, whether state intervention is helpful or
harmful to the efficient operation of the economy. Both sides of the

debate have their partisans, but the majority of public choice theorists tend to regard state actions as inherently less efficient than market operations (cf. Niskanen, 1971; Buchanan, 1967). They are undoubtedly influenced by the ability of neo-classical economics to demonstrate that Pareto efficiency can be achieved in some market settings (see Shepsle and Weingast, 1984).

However, such a view may neglect the institutional structure of markets themselves. Like public agencies, markets exist only within a certain organizational framework, and variation in that framework can profoundly affect their operation. Some studies recognize that barriers to entry, information and transaction costs, internal labor markets, oligolopolist positions, and the like can affect market operation. But many other facets of institutional setting can influence the behavior of market actors. The environment in which every manager operates is not simply composed of moving market parameters, specifying price, cost, and demand conditions. Diverse kinds of managerial hierarchies, financial networks, and workplace organizations are equally salient dimensions of his environment; yet few of these institutional factors are captured by traditional neo-classical analyses (cf. Elbaum and Lazonick, 1986; Chandler, 1962). Many public choice theorists may be guilty of juxtaposing an idealized conception of market operation to more institutionally nuanced views of government behavior.

In short, a more accurate assessment of the merits of state intervention must begin not only from an institutionalist understanding of the dimensions of state intervention but from a more explicitly institutionalist analysis of market behavior itself. When this is done, the often-rigid distinction between market-based and state-based styles of action can be called into question (cf. Williamson, 1975).

One branch of public choice theory that is already moving in a promising direction is organization theory (cf. Cyert and March, 1963; March and Olsen, 1984). Such theories attempt to combine rational actor models of behavior with a more complete understanding of the impact of organizational settings on such behavior. They suggest that policies are not the product of truly rational action, because the complexity of most problems and of most decision settings renders strategic action difficult (Simon, 1957). Instead, policies are seen as the product of a rationality that is "bounded" by the application of a more limited set of decision rules and by the effect of organizational aggregation of the sort found in many policy-making settings. Traces of incrementalism, for instance, have already been found in budgetary policy, and they are equally likely to exist in cases of broader economic policy-making (Padgett, 1981; Wildavsky, 1975).

To date, however, a great deal of organization theory has been devoted to the discovery of laws applicable to the operation of all organizations. More must be done to associate particular patterns of rationality with specific organizational attributes. However, this is a radical contention, for it implies that the notion of simple rationality is relatively meaningless as a description of motivation until it is given more content by a specification of the organizational conditions that identify the direction in which rational action is aimed and the means it is likely to apply.

In group theory the essential unit of analysis is not the political system as a whole or the individuals within it, but the social groups or classes who come into conflict within the polity. According to this model, policy is best explained as the direct product of group conflict. As one representative statement puts it:

> Interest is the primary propelling force and every action is based upon sharing of interest. Power configuration is basically the configuration of competing and struggling interests organized into groups. Ideology, values, the state, the formal organization of political decision-making, and the content of decisions are determined by a parallelogram of group forces (Macridis, 1977: 322).

Once again, there are important differences between left- and right-wing versions of the theory. In the 1950s and 1960s a group model became the basis for the pluralist analyses used to justify the constitutional arrangements of democracies and to explain their stability. Following in the footsteps of Arthur Bentley (1908), David Truman (1951) and others argued that the presence of many competing groups in the democratic polity and the capacity of such a polity to entertain the demands of all potential groups offered everyone access to political power, while the prevalence of overlapping memberships among groups reduced the likelihood of sectarian conflict.

On the left, others argued that the pertinent unit of analysis was not organized interest groups but social classes or class fractions whose underlying interests were rooted in the mode of production and more significant than those of other groups. These theorists argued that access to power in the liberal democracies was far less evenly distributed, and the potential for social conflict much higher than pluralists believed (Wolfe, 1977; Esping-Andersen et al., 1976; Gaventa, 1981).

We can find a nice illustration of the merits and limits of group models for the case of contemporary economic policy-making in an insightful study by Gosta Esping-Andersen and Roger Friedland (1982). They argue that "the current West European crisis reflects

changing political conflicts among classes over distribution and control
. . . [and] a critical factor in the making of a country's political economy is how social classes form alliances in the making of state policy"
(1982: 4–5). In their view, many European nations were governed for
most of the post-war period by an alliance between the petit bourgeoisie and either capital or labor. Each kind of alliance resulted in a
distinctive pattern of policy. Thus France can be contrasted to Scandinavia, while Britain represents a middle case where the working class is
powerful enough in the industrial arena to extract concessions from
employers and the state but not strong enough in the political arena to
impose a strategy of its own on capital. However, Esping-Andersen
and Friedland go on to argue that these longstanding class alliances
began to unravel under the impact of worsening economic performance
during the 1970s; and the path that each nation subsequently takes will
be "contingent upon a reordering of the relationship between labor and
capital . . . [to] be achieved through a change of existing class
alliances" (1982: 43).

The great virtue of this analysis is its insistence that coalitional
support must be found for any policy, and that the range of policy
alternatives will then be constrained by the relative balance of class
power. What is missing is a more extensive analysis of the basis for class
interest and class power; and such an analysis would entail a more
complete investigation of the organizations and institutional structures
that envelop social classes and the state. In a complex society, power is
mediated by organization and distributional conflict is conducted
through institutional structures that leave their imprint on the result.
Few would still agree with Arthur Bentley that: "The great task in the
study of any form of social life is the analysis of these groups. When the
groups are adequately stated, everything is stated" (1908: 208).

To some extent, even a group's self-understanding and interests can
be shaped by its patterns of organization and the organization of those
with whom it contends. If the interests and behavior of the working
class in Britain and France have often been somewhat different, for
example, those differences can be traced, at least in part, to historical
variations in class organizations.

Such factors become even more important when the outcome turns
on the class or group coalitions that are formed. For instance, the
formation of class compromises often depends on the nature of existing
interest organizations and the presence of appropriate institutional
brokers (see Przeworski and Wallerstein, 1982). The capacity of the
latter to generate common causes around which divergent interests can
unite or mechanisms for logrolling that obviate the need for common
causes can be the decisive factor in alliance formation (see Gourevitch,
1977a).

Moreover, policy-making in the contemporary state is almost always an incremental process in which many factors are aggregated. While the outcome may well be an implicit class coalition, the formulation of policy is often only obliquely related to the aspirations articulated by the spokesmen for social classes. We should not lose sight of the class interests at stake in economic policy-making; but to portray the policy process accurately, we should add to our outline of massive social groups a sketch of the institutional structures through which their demands are being shaped, their power is being determined, and their circumstances altered.

STATE-CENTRIC THEORIES

The political science literature has recently generated one other model of politics with important implications for the determination of policy. This is 'statist' or 'state-centric' theory. Against competing pluralist and Marxist models, state-centric theorists argue that policy is not primarily a reaction to pressure from interested social groups. Instead they suggest that the state should be seen as far more autonomous from societal pressure than previously imagined. In their view the state has interests and policy preferences of its own, as well as the capacity to impose these preferences against societal resistance.

Thus, Stephen Krasner (1980) argues that a conception of the "national interest" led American policy-makers to develop a foreign economic policy independently of domestic pressure. A review of British public policy leads Paul Sacks (1980: 350) to conclude that "states . . . are far more autonomous actors than was envisioned in earlier models of public choice." Eric Nordlinger (1981: 203) argues that "the democratic state is frequently autonomous in translating its own preferences into authoritative actions, and markedly autonomous in doing so even when they diverge from those held by the politically weightiest groups in civil society."

Although these authors occasionally exaggerate the extent to which earlier writers saw the state as the prisoner of private interests, their work provides an important corrective to models of the polity that underestimate the independence of the state. But it leaves us with a serious problem. Once societal explanations for the direction of public policy have been rejected, with what kind of explanation are we left? To say that policy is the product of state action, whether in the public interest or not, is hardly an explanation. As in an older style of systems theory, the state looms again as a black box, central to the explanation of political outcomes yet opaque.

The effort to illuminate the contents of this box has resulted in three prominent lines of theorizing. The first argues that policy-making can be seen as a process of "bureaucratic politics" (Allison, 1974; Halperin, 1974). Such an approach has the great virtue of reminding us that states are not unitary actors and policy may not be the result of a strategic rationality. But the model with which it replaced rational actor theory is so nebulous as to be virtually indeterminate when it comes to explaining or predicting the direction of policy. Policy-makers will "fight their corner" and "where they stand depends on where they sit." However, few guidelines are provided for predicting the specific interpretation that each player will put on his corner; and few guidelines are given for assessing the relative power of each player in the ensuing struggle. Policy-making remains a relatively indeterminate "war of all against all," only this time the contest takes place inside the state.

A second line of enquiry has been somewhat more productive. Building on the work of Deutsch (1963) and Heclo (1974), several analysts have argued that policy-making should be seen less as a struggle for power, and more as a process of social learning. On this view the formulation of policy is a process of solving the puzzles generated by the, often unintended, consequences of past policy. The form which new policies take is most influenced by the procedural legacy and political lessons of older policies in related fields. Although they are not state-centric theorists in other respects, Weir and Skocpol (1985), for instance, attribute Britain's reliance on social insurance, rather than reflation, to deal with the unemployment of the 1930s partly to the legacy of expertise and experience derived from prior social insurance programs. Similarly, John Ikenberry (1985) explains the American deregulation of oil prices in 1979 as the result of a process of social learning within the state.

It is undoubtedly an important insight to realize that policy-making can be a process of social learning; but this sort of theory is also problematic. How are we to know precisely what lessons will be learned from the past, and which are to be embodied in future policy? After all, lessons do not come unambiguously from history. Many different people have drawn widely divergent, and often contradictory, lessons from the Great Society programs that America implemented during the 1960s (cf. Aaron, 1979; Murray, 1984). In short, this approach can also be highly indeterminate.

Finally, we might use the notion of 'state capacities' to add an explanatory element to state-centric theories. Several theorists argue that a state's choice of policies will be heavily influenced by its existing capacities to carry out a range of policies. Those that require the costly development of new capacities are less likely to be pursued. Alternatively, the success or failure of a policy will depend largely on the institutional resources that the state has available to secure its implementation. Skocpol and Finegold (1983), for instance, argue that the success of the Agricultural Adjustment Act and the failure of the National Industrial Recovery Act in America during the 1930s are best explained by the presence or absence of longstanding institutional capacities within the American state.

This is a promising line of enquiry. To fully elaborate it, however, one must move toward a more complete consideration of state–society relations. The capacities of a state to implement a program tend to depend as much on the configuration of society as of the state. For instance, the effectiveness of French planning relied on the institutional configuration of the French financial system; just as the ability of a state to implement neo-corporatist incomes policies seems to depend on the centralization and density of its national union movement (Zysman, 1983; Schmitter and Lehmbruch, 1979).

In short, state-centric theory on its own does not provide much of an explanation for the behavior of the state; and the most promising attempts to provide better explanations all point to the particular importance of institutional variables. Paradoxically, it also becomes clear that the institutional networks affecting state action extend well into society, in such a way as to expose the state again to societal influences. The state appears as a network of institutions, deeply embedded within a constellation of ancillary institutions associated with society and the economic system. Contemporary states do not seem to be as autonomous from societal influence as state-centric theories imply.

For these reasons we must also be cautious about global distinctions between "strong" and "weak" states. The French state may be more resistant to some kinds of societal pressure than the British; but it remains vulnerable to other kinds that are less often observed, and any implication that the French state might be virtually independent of societal pressure would be wrong. The variations may be nuanced and policy-specific. As one of my colleagues says: "Strong states may simply be weak states about which we have less knowledge."[4] We must be careful not to search for, and even postulate, autonomy, when we should be sketching the institutional outlines and limits of societal influence.

AN INSTITUTIONAL APPROACH TO STATE–SOCIETY RELATIONS

Such a statement about the importance of societal influence might lead us back to an image of the state as a kind of billiard ball, pushed around by competing interest groups. For several reasons, however, that kind of image is problematic. On the one hand there is evidence that pressure group influence over economic policy has not been very great

(Marsh and Grant, 1977; Wilson, 1983). On the other, such an image of the polity implies that policy is a relatively contingent outcome, varying with the shifting impact of interest representations; whereas the strong continuities present in national patterns of economic policy belie this view.

Precisely these continuities suggest where we might look for an alternative approach to the determinants of state action. There are likely to be structural consistencies behind the persistence of distinctive national patterns of policy. The problem is to locate and specify them; that entails an institutional analysis of the polity and economy.

Such an analysis is suggested, in embryonic form at least, by a recent line of thought that situates politics within a broader framework of state–society relations. Initially, some of the most important work in this field was done by neo-Marxist scholars who became particularly interested in the role that the state plays in the reproduction of a capitalist economic system.[5] In most cases they were principally interested in explaining why states could be said to pursue policies that are in the interests of capital. The most innovative of these theorists began to argue that the behavior of 'state managers' was heavily influenced by the organization of the polity and economy (Block, 1977; Poulantzas, 1976; Miliband, 1977; Jessop, 1977; Offe, 1984, 1985).

By revealing the organizational incentives that state managers face by virtue of their institutional position within a democratic state presiding over a capitalist economy, for instance, Fred Block (1977) was able to explain why it might make sense to see state managers as "relatively autonomous" from the capitalist class. He argued that the government's organizational position within the political system gave it a broader perspective than most capitalists, and some ability to resist pressure from individual segments of business; but its dependence on "business confidence" in order to secure economic prosperity and re-election also limited the degree to which its policies could diverge from business interests (cf. Krieger and Held, 1978; Lindblom, 1977).

Most neo-Marxist analysts have been interested in the common characteristics of 'the capitalist state,' but their line of enquiry can be extended to organizational variations among capitalist states. Here the analyses of another group of scholars, also working within a state–society framework, have been fruitful (Katzenstein, 1978; Skocpol, 1979; Gourevitch, 1978; Skowronek, 1982). Katzenstein (1978: 308), for instance, attributes the persistence of longstanding foreign economic policies in the Western nations to the importance of certain 'policy networks' in each of those countries. Although his precise specification may be contentious, those policy networks are clearly a function of the organization of the state and society. That, in turn, is the cumulative product of political struggles at a series of crucial historical conjunctures.

Building on this work we can construct an institutionalist analysis of politics that is capable of explaining historical continuities and cross-national variations in policy. It emphasizes the institutional relationships, both formal and conventional, that bind the components of the state together and structure its relations with society. While those relationships are subject to incremental change, and more radical change at critical conjunctures, they provide the context in which most normal politics is conducted.[6]

The concept of institutions is used here to refer to the formal rules, compliance procedures, and standard operating practices that structure the relationship between individuals in various units of the polity and economy. As such, they have a more formal status than cultural norms but one that does not necessarily derive from legal, as opposed to conventional, standing. Throughout, the emphasis is on the relational character of institutions; that is to say, on the way in which they structure the interactions of individuals. In this sense it is the organizational qualities of institutions that are being emphasized; and the term 'organization' will be used here as a virtual synonym for 'institution.'

The outlines and implications of an institutionalist analysis will be elaborated more fully in the chapters that follow; but some comments about the general relevance of institutional factors for politics and for our understanding of the political process would be apposite here.

Institutional factors play two fundamental roles in this model. On the one hand, the organization of policy-making affects the degree of power that any one set of actors has over the policy outcomes. As Weber (1958) noted, that should be particularly true in the modern era, when politics and administration have become increasingly organized activities. On the other hand, organizational position also influences an actor's definition of his own interests, by establishing his institutional responsibilities and relationship to other actors. In this way, organizational factors affect both the degree of pressure an actor can bring to bear on policy and the likely direction of that pressure. Such an analysis can be applied both inside and outside the state.

With an institutionalist model we can see policy as more than the sum of countervailing pressure from social groups. That pressure is mediated by an organizational dynamic that imprints its own image on the outcome. Because policy-making in the modern state is always a collective process, the configuration of the institutions that aggregate the opinions of individual contributors into a set of policies can have its own effect on policy outputs.[7] Even the degree to which that thinking is incremental rather than strategic is affected by the nature of the process, as the contrast between British and French approaches to industrial policy-making readily suggests.

Those with long memories of political studies in an earlier era might view this argument with some irony. After all, the study of institutions was once seen as the principal subject-matter of political science (cf. Dyson, 1982; Easton, 1953). Contemporary analysts might read with profit the works of an era when the principal texts in political science still had titles like *The State* (Wilson, 1908). Does this argument simply reflect a return to an earlier institutional focus? This is not a trivial point because most of the models of the polity reviewed here were initially constructed precisely to escape the emphasis on institutions that dominated political science during the first half of the century.

Although we can still learn from earlier forms of institutionalism, the approach being suggested here is fundamentally different. Earlier works concentrated on the institutions associated with a country's constitution and formal political practices (cf. Lowell, 1908; Laski, 1938; March and Olsen, 1984). By contrast, the approach proposed here ranges more widely to consider the role of institutions located within society and the economy, as well as less formal organizational networks, in the determination of policy. Whereas the earlier institutionalism militated against cross-national comparisons, this approach utilizes them to identify the most salient institutional determinants of policy.

Similarly, this kind of analysis should also be distinguished from some kinds of organization theory. Although we have much to learn from organization theorists, many of their works are designed to discover principles that apply to all or most organizational behavior. By contrast, this enterprise is focused more directly on the effects of historically specific patterns of organization. There is a natural affinity between the two enterprises that should be encouraged; but this approach bridges something of a gap in the organization literature between microlevel studies of individual operating units and macrotheoretical arguments applied across all kinds of organizations.

THE PLAN OF THE BOOK

The chapters that follow are designed to fulfill multiple purposes. At the most basic level they contain an account of economic policy-making and the course of economic policy in Britain and France over the postwar period, which can be read for its own sake. The principal purpose of the book, however, is to explain the direction that economic policy has taken in these nations, and by so doing to illuminate the political dimensions of economic management. The volume's fundamental contention is that the direction of policy was determined, not simply by prevailing economic conditions, but also by a political dynamic. That dynamic has multiple features, but one of the most central is the role that the organization of capital, labor, and the state play in the determination of policy. Accordingly, the book develops an institutional approach to the explanation of policy outcomes that may have wider applicability in the political sphere.

The volume is organized around a comparison of economic policy-making in Britain and France. For centuries these two nations have been eyeing each other's political and economic institutions. In the face of similar economic challenges during the post-war period they moved along rather different policy paths; and the problem of explaining the divergence in paths is one of the principal puzzles addressed here. To this end the book is divided into four parts. This chapter, reviewing the theoretical terrain, comprises the first part.

Part II is devoted to the political economy of Britain. Its first chapter takes a slightly more historical approach to the principal policy preoccupation of the post-war period: what are the factors that account for British economic decline? In keeping with the overall emphasis this chapter argues that we must undertake an institutional analysis of markets and market behavior in order to identify the causes of decline. When this is done there is a good deal of evidence to suggest that, in the first instance at least, Britain's economic problems resulted from the short-comings of British markets rather than public policy.

Chapter three takes up the question of why the British state did not step in to correct the defects of British markets. To answer it, the chapter attempts to identify broad patterns within British economic policy and to account for their persistence in the face of continuing economic problems.

Chapter four considers some of the more dynamic qualities of British economic policy-making, through an examination of the evolution of Keynesianism over the post-war period. The economic experiment of the Conservative Government under Margaret Thatcher is the current culmination of that evolution, and chapter five examines it in some detail. As usual the emphasis is on the political factors associated with economic policy-making and the implications of the Thatcher experiment for state–society relations.

Part III turns to the political economy of France. Since the primary feature of French economic policies has been a system of national economic planning, chapter six outlines the basic operation of planning. It argues that the character and functioning of the French Plans can only be understood if they are seen as instruments for coping with political as well as economic problems.

Chapter seven considers the evolution of the French planning process from its inception during the 1940s to deplanification in the 1970s.

The object of the chapter is to explain the changes that took place in planning relative to the broader dynamic of state–society relations.

Chapter eight examines the Socialist economic experiment undertaken in France under President François Mitterand. It is very different from the experiment of Margaret Thatcher, and we can draw some implicit conclusions about the austerity of the left and the right from a comparison of the cases. Once again the chapter argues that the economic policies of the Mitterrand Government can be understood only within their political context.

Part IV turns directly to a comparison of economic policy-making in the two nations. Chapter nine employs a comparison of the broad patterns of macroeconomic, industrial and incomes policy in Britain, France, and Germany over the post-war period to outline the institutional logic behind economic policy more completely. Germany is added to the analysis here in order to gain more comparative leverage over the issues at hand. Finally, chapter ten returns to the Anglo-French comparison to summarize the dynamic elements in state–society relations that affect economic policy. It is particularly concerned with the interaction of interests, institutions, and ideas in the policy process.

PART II: The Political Economy of Britain

2

Markets and the State in British Economic Decline

The decline of the British economy is one of the great puzzles in contemporary political economy. How did the economic success story of the nineteenth century become a tale of economic failure during the twentieth century? Why did the nation with Europe's highest per capita national product in 1945 end up on the lower end of the European scale in 1985? These are the questions which any survey of British economic policy cannot avoid.

They are historical questions. Britain's economic problems began in the late nineteenth century (table 4.1). Her rate of economic growth declined from 2.6 percent a year in 1800–60 to 2.0 percent in 1856–1913 and 1.1 percent in 1913–37, only to rise again to 2.4 percent in 1937–73 (Matthews et al., 1982: 498).[1] Compared with this record, Britain's post-war economic performance has been relatively good. In international terms, however, Britain has fared poorly since 1945. Between 1950 and 1976 the British economy grew only two-thirds as fast as the largest sixteen Western economies (Aldcroft, 1982: 34). The UK share of world exports of manufactures fell from 25.5 percent in 1950 to 7.5 percent in 1985 (table 4.2). In short, British industry coasted to moderate rates of growth on a post-war wave of international prosperity, but failed to secure as many advanges from the world-wide boom as France and Germany whose rate of growth were almost twice as great as those of the United Kingdom.

In the United Kingdom these developments have been greeted with dismay and a certain amount of collective soul-searching. As on the Orient Express, everyone has been implicated: obstructionist trade unions, myopic public officials, aficionados of the tea-break, poor engineering professors, the foppish scions of the Third Generation, and outward-looking financiers. Indeed, public pronouncements on the subject have contributed as much to the general gloom as the facts themselves.

Table 2.1 British rates of economic growth in comparative perspective (percentages)

Period	UK	US	Sweden	France	Germany	Italy	Japan
Annual percentage growth rates							
1873–99	1.2	1.9	1.5	1.3	1.5	0.3	1.1
1899–1913	0.5	1.3	2.1	1.6	1.5	2.5	1.8
1913–24	0.3	1.7	0.3	0.8	−0.9	−0.1	3.2
1924–37	1.0	1.4	1.7	1.4	3.0	1.8	2.7
1937–51	1.0	2.3	2.6	1.7	1.0	1.4	−1.3
1951–64	2.3	2.5	3.3	4.3	5.1	5.6	7.6
1964–73	2.6	1.6	2.7	4.6	4.4	5.0	8.4
1873–51	0.9	1.7	1.7	1.4	1.3	1.3	1.4
1951–73	2.4	2.3	3.0	4.4	4.8	5.5	7.9
1873–73	1.2	1.8	1.9	2.0	2.0	2.4	2.6

Source: Matthews et al. (1982), table 2.5, p. 31.

Table 2.2 Britain's share of world exports of manufactures (percentages based on values in US $ at current prices)

Year	UK	US	Germany	Italy	France	Japan	Sweden
1881–85	43.0	6.0	16.0	2.0	15.0	0.0	1.0
1899	34.5	12.1	16.6	3.8	14.9	1.6	0.9
1913	31.8	13.7	19.9	3.5	12.8	2.5	1.5
1929	23.8	21.7	15.5	3.9	11.6	4.1	1.8
1937	22.3	20.5	16.5	3.7	6.2	7.4	2.8
1950	24.6	26.6	7.0	3.6	9.6	3.4	2.8
1964	14.0	20.1	19.5	6.2	8.5	8.3	3.4
1973	9.1	15.1	22.3	6.7	9.3	13.1	3.3

Source: Matthews et al. (1982), p. 435.

Therefore it is important to observe that a good deal of the discrepancy between British and continental rates of growth over the post-war period is probably attributable to factors beyond the control of British producers or policy-makers. Edward Denison (1967) has pointed out that total growth of GNP can be decomposed into two separate components: the growth of factor inputs, such as labor and capital, and the growth of the productivity of those inputs. Since the availability of labor is heavily affected by population growth in the absence of immigration, economic growth over the post-war period was naturally more constrained in Britain than in the five continental nations with higher rates of growth of labor supply. This crucial economic input was less available, and consequently 'often more expensive, in Britain. Total productivity growth in post-war Britain was also restricted by factors beyond national control. Kindleberger (1964) and Kaldor (1966) have argued that a major portion of the productivity increase in the continental nations resulted from the movement of their workforce from self-employment or the agricultural sector, whose productivity is generally low, to the industrial sector, whose productivity is usually much higher. Because Britain industrialized in the nineteenth century this source of productivity increase no longer remained available in the late twentieth century. By 1950 only 5 percent of the British labor force was in agriculture, compared with 25 percent in West Germany, 29 percent in France and 43 percent in Italy. For this reason alone, Britain's rate of growth was bound to be lower than that of her rivals. Denison (1968) has calculated that up to 30 percent of the difference in annual rates of growth between Britain and France and 15 percent of the difference between Britain and West Germany over the 1950–62 period may be attributed to this factor alone.

Similarly, many of the most dramatic gains in productivity during the twentieth century were achieved through the introduction of mass-production techniques associated with Fordism and the use of larger plants to secure economies of scale (Piore and Sabel, 1984; Boyer and Mistral, 1983). In many sectors, full use of these methods was made in the continental nations only after World War Two. By contrast, Britain secured many of the initial productivity gains to be achieved through this transformation during the inter-war period. By 1950 she already had the highest percentage of manufacturing plants of minimum efficient size in the world after the United States (Bain, 1966).

On the export side, Britain's fate was also at least partially fore-ordained. Even if British levels of exports grew at a stable rate, the nations of Europe and the Third World would have made inroads into her share of world exports, as their own industrialization process proceeded. As new industrializers, many of these nations could take advantage of lower wage rates and recent technology more readily than the British (Kaldor, 1966, 1977; cf. Peacock, 1980; Krause, 1969).

In short, perhaps half of the shortfall between British rates of economic growth in the post-war period and European rates of growth may be attributable to factors largely beyond British control. Some gnashing of teeth could be avoided if British performance were seen more often in this perspective.

Even when these factors are taken into account, however, there remains a gap that cannot easily be justified between British rates of growth and productivity increase in the post-war period and those of her rivals. For instance, Denison (1968) calculates that, after making allowance for all factors beyond the nation's control, the British economy still grew at a rate 1.6 percent per annum slower than that of West Germany and 1 percent per annum below that of France or Italy in the 1950s and early 1960s.

The British economy does not utilize the resources available to it as efficiently as its overseas competitors. In 1978, for instance, 10.9 man-hours were needed to produce a ton of steel in Britain, compared to 6.4 hours in France and 4.8 hours in Luxembourg (Pollard, 1982: 11). The British automobile industry could produce only 5.1 vehicles per employee in 1973 versus 6.8 in France and Italy, 7.3 in Germany, 12.2 in Japan, and 14.9 in the United States (Central Policy Review Staff, 1975: 80; cf. Caves, 1980: 136). How is this to be explained?

Within the literature a partial consensus has emerged concerning the role of three factors that might be seen as the proximate causes of poor economic performance. First, British rates of investment have often lagged behind those of her competitors. In the post-war period especially, aggregate industrial investment has been proportionately lower than in Europe. Secondly, the rate of industrial adaptation in British industry has frequently been surpassed by that of competing nations. Britain has often been slow to reallocate resources towards new and fast-growing sectors; and within many industries new technology has not been introduced as rapidly as elsewhere. Finally, the organization of work in Britain seems to be less efficient than in many other nations, as demonstrated by the work-time requirements cited above. These factors appear again and again in most analyses of Britain's productivity (cf. Kirby, 1981); but they are proximate factors whose occurrence must itself be explained. Why does British industry seem to suffer from these defects?

In response to this question, many analysts identify the growth of state intervention, misguided macroeconomic policies, or the peculiarities of British culture as the culprit. These are three of the most popular explanations for British decline. Therefore, let us review each of these explanations in the light of data from the post-war period, when the decline that is to be explained became most acute.

THE SIZE OF THE STATE

The expansion of the British state is often adduced to explain Britain's relatively slow rate of growth in the recent period. Some analysts suggest that the growth of the public sector diverted critical resources from more productive pursuits in the private sector (Bacon and Eltis, 1976; Eltis, 1979). As Margaret Thatcher put it in 1975:

> The private sector creates the goods and services we need both to export to pay for our imports and the revenue to finance public services. So one

must not overload it. Every man switched away from industry and into government will reduce the productive sector and increase the burden on it at the same time (cited in Bacon and Eltis, 1978: 32).

Others argue that the growth of public spending, especially on the welfare state, and correlative increases in taxation impaired growth by reducing the incentives of private sector actors to put more effort and investment into the economy (Jones, 1978; Joseph, 1976). A third view maintains that the rising public sector borrowing requirement (PSBR or budget deficit) associated with increased levels of public expenditure began to "crowd out" private investment over the past two decades (Chrystal, 1979: ch. 9; Congdon, 1978; Carlson and Spencer, 1975).

All of these positions begin from the incontrovertible fact that the share of national resources being channelled through the public sector has increased dramatically in the period since World War Two. In Britain, public expenditure as a share of GNP rose from 32 percent in 1950 to 45 percent in 1980. The annual public sector borrowing requirement (PSBR), which hovered around 4 percent in the 1950s, reached 8 percent of GNP in the 1970s before falling in the recent period. The critical issue, however, is one of causation. Did the expansion of public activity itself limit the growth of the private sector in Britain?

Despite the jeremiads of recent years, there is little evidence to support the theory of a causal connection between public sector growth and economic decline. First, the timing of the two occurrences is not coincident. The performance of the British economy relative to that of her trading partners began to decline at least 50 years before the public sector began to grow appreciably. In absolute terms, British growth rates actually improved during the period when most public sector expansion took place. This implies that the growth of the welfare state may have enhanced economic performance.

Comparative analysis also suggests that the growth of the public sector had little to do with Britain's relatively poor economic performance. In many European nations whose rates of growth exceeded that of Britain over the post-war period, including Germany, France, Sweden, Norway, the Netherlands, and Austria, government spending as a portion of GNP was equal to or higher than the British level. Recent studies have found a significant positive correlation between the expansion of the public sector and rates of growth during this era (Kohl, 1981; Smith, 1975; Cameron, 1982).

In 1976 Bacon and Eltis argued in a flamboyant and rather physiocratic way, that the growth of public spending and employment on "unproductive" pursuits was squeezing out the number of "productive" workers in manufacturing who were ultimately the nation's only means of support because they alone produced real value-added. However, subsequent attempts to analyze the causal relation between public sector expansion and economic performance in the UK itself have produced negative results. Hadjimatheou and Skouras (1979) call into question both the premises and empirical data of Bacon and Eltis (1976). The contention that public sector activity is "unproductive" neglects the contribution that health policy, education, and infrastructure make to national well-being; and the argument that public sector growth in the 1970s squeezed the manpower resources available to the private sector seems implausible given the high levels of unemployment during much of the period.

Comparative analyses also cast doubt on the view that the costs of the welfare state impaired British economic performance. In all the faster-growing nations cited above, taxes consumed a substantially greater portion of GNP than they did in the UK, and the marginal tax rates of many of these high-growth nations were also higher at most income levels (Ward and Neild, 1978: 102). Empirical studies of the impact of personal taxation on work effort are inconclusive (Stern, 1976; Fiegehen, 1980) and the incidence of corporate taxation in Britain actually fell over the post-war period (King, 1975; Moore and Rhodes, 1976).

Finally, although Britain's institutional investors are currently putting a rather high proportion of their capital into government gilt rather than industry, no satisfactory evidence has been found to link a high PSBR with lower levels of private investment. Most studies suggest that government borrowing has not squeezed the funds available to industry (HM Treasury, 1977), and that investment in the UK responds much more strongly to expectations of demand and profitability than to changes in the interest rate induced by the PSBR (Savage, 1978). Public sector deficits still seem more likely to expand investment through their impact on demand than to restrict it via their monetary effects.

THE IMPACT OF MACROECONOMIC POLICY

Another group of critics blame Britain's post-war decline on the macroeconomic policies of successive governments. They argue that erratic attempts at demand management disrupted the investment plans of industry, and the unwarranted defense of an overvalued exchange rate impaired the competitiveness of British exports (Pollard, 1982; Blank, 1978; Strange, 1971). In Sidney Pollard's words:

> while Montagu Norman had only 11 years . . . to damage the British economy, the Treasury have had over 30 years since the end of the last war. In that period, they have transformed the strongest, the technologically most advanced and most promising of European industrialized economies into the weakest, poorest and most backward. It is an

achievement of economic mismanagement unparalleled in the annals of the civilised world (cited in Aldcroft, 1982: 41).

Essentially there are four respects in which macroeconomic policy may have impaired the performance of the British economy. First, the timing or intensity of demand management in the post-war period may have been destabilizing for the economy (Dow, 1964; Hansen, 1968; Caves et al., 1968). Second, the particular monetary instruments on which the government relied for demand management in the post-war decades, and the frequency with which they were applied, may have been especially disruptive to investment (Aldcroft, 1982: 43; Channon, 1973: 47). Third, failure to devalue the pound may have impaired the competitiveness of British products on world markets (Beckerman, 1972; Posner and Steer, 1978). Finally, the broad stance of British policy over the period may have been more deflationary than necessary, thus needlessly inhibiting the growth of investment, output, and productivity (Hansen, 1968; Pollard, 1982).

A debate has raged over the potentially destabilizing effects of British demand management. Although British policy remained the least stabilizing of seven major nations in a recent econometric study, further evidence (Boltho, 1982; OECD, 1973) suggests that post-war policy was positively destabilizing only if the investment of public enterprise is considered a component of policy. Policy was also more correctly timed in the years after 1965. In comparative terms, overall variations around the trend of output and investment, including the impact of demand management, have not been as great in Britain as in many nations with faster growth; and one finds numerous instances of destabilizing policy in such nations (Bispham and Boltho, 1982; Whiting, 1976; Surrey, 1982; Price, 1978).

Similarly, the contention that British reliance on certain monetary instruments for demand management had an adverse effect on industry is contradicted by recent studies that have failed to find any convincing evidence of a relationship between interest rates and the level of investment in the UK (Savage, 1978). Many industrialists have testified that short-run changes in monetary policy had no effect on their long-term investment plans; and it now seems likely that post-war controls on bank lending did not effectively restrict the money supply (Radcliffe Report, 1954; Goodhart, 1975; Smethurst, 1979). Although nominal interest rates have been slightly higher in the UK than in most other industrialized nations over the post-war period, the real rate of interest on long-term loans seems to have been lower. In these terms British monetary policy has not been unduly restrictive.

The consequences of Britain's high exchange rate policies have also been widely debated. Many commentators argued that devaluation should have been considered between 1949 and 1967 when Britain's international competitiveness fell steadily. But the post-1968 experience must render one less sanguine about the advantages of such a move (Cambridge Economic Policy Group, 1978; Stout, 1979). The case for devaluation rests on an optimistic reading of four parameters: the price elasticities for British exports and foreign imports in Britain, the propensity of British exporters to utilize price advantages for profit-taking versus reorganization and higher volume production, and the rapidity with which real wages adjust to the domestic price inflation that devaluation entails (Posner and Steer, 1978). Although there is a possibility that these parameters were more favorable in earlier years, recent experience suggests that there are few grounds to assume that developments on any of these fronts would make devaluation effective

In particular, the apparent absence of "money illusion" among British unions means that wage costs rise rapidly in the wake of a devaluation (Tarling and Wilkinson, 1977; Ball et al., 1977; Henry et al., 1976). Partly as a result, the price advantages which British industry received from the 1967 devaluation had disappeared by 1971 (Tew, 1978). If the export price advantages of devaluation last only until lagging real wages adjust, a series of devaluations would have been necessary to maintain competitiveness over the post-war period. When this policy was pursued in 1972–79, Britain's share of world exports did increase after falling by 7 percent in the preceding 13 years, but the increase was marginal and by no means did it eliminate balance of payments problems or render deflation unnecessary.

Moreover, one might question any such strategy which depends on depressing real wages, on the grounds that the more fundamental problem is lower levels of productivity growth which have made British goods less competitive on world markets and turned Britain into a low wage economy. Devaluation simply limits the impact of low productivity on exports – it does not remedy the causes of the problem. The long-term effect of the strategy would have been to render Britain even more dependent on low-wage industries and low productivity for its national income at a time when most industrialized nations prospered by exploiting their comparative advantage in high wage and high value-added industries, in the face of increased competition from the developing world. The increasing role of quality considerations in export competitiveness also indicates that it would have been particularly short-sighted for Britain to pursue a strategy focused on price competitiveness (Kravis and Lipsey, 1971; Stout, 1977; Panic, 1975). In short, while devaluation in the early 1920s or 1960s might have made a short-term contribution to the competitiveness of British industry, it was unlikely to be a panacea for the underlying problems.

It is more difficult to assess the contention that British macroeconomic policy has been overly deflationary in the post-war period. The gap between actual GDP and potential GDP (assuming full factor use) between 1955 and 1973 was only slightly higher in Britain than the European average and the average in nations that achieved much higher rates of growth, such as Germany, Austria, Belgium and the Netherlands (Bispham and Boltho, 1982: 305). Similarly, the net impact of British budgetary policy on demand was low by European standards but only slightly less than in France, Sweden, and Belgium over the 1955–77 period (Hansen, 1968; OECD, 1978). Britain's macro-economic stance was not greatly out of line with those of many high-growth nations, and given the underlying buoyancy of consumption and employment, there may have been little room for more expansionary policy (Paish, 1970; Matthews, 1968).

A highly reflationary policy would have been possible only if, as a by-product, it altered the relatively high income-elasticity for imports and low trend-rate of productivity growth in Britain which rapidly imposed balance of payments constraints on expansion (Thirlwall, 1978; Panic, 1975). Even those who argue that expansion should be used for this purpose, therefore, admit that it would have to be accompanied by stringent controls on imports and incomes (Cambridge Economic Policy Group, 1978; Singh, 1979). Such a strategy runs serious risks, beyond the possibility of foreign retaliation. Protection could fuel domestic inflation and shift resources into the least efficient sectors of the economy without forcing them to rationalize, as the tariff of 1932 seems to have done (Corden et al., 1978).

In short, these results suggest that more frequent devaluation or further expansion would have had a marginal impact at best on British rates of growth. To blame Britain's problems primarily on her macro-economic policies is to mistake the source of the problem; and to look to better macroeconomic management alone for the solution is to overestimate the impact that alternative policies could have had on a stagnant economic base (Brown and Stout, 1979).

THE ROLE OF CULTURE

A third set of authors attribute Britain's economic decline primarily to factors associated with the culture of the nation and the structure of its industrial classes (Anderson, 1966; Allen, 1976; Wiener, 1981; Nairn, 1977). Perry Anderson, one of the earliest and most eloquent exponents of this view (1966: 47), suggests that:

> The present crisis is a general malady of the whole society, infrastructure and superstructure – not a sudden breakdown, but a slow, sickening entropy. . . . The industrial bourgeoisie which in its prime merged with the landed aristocracy has in their union become infected and corroded with the vices of the latter. . . . The world-conquering entrepreneurs of

the mid-nineteenth century had become flaccid administrators in the mid-twentieth.

According to such views, either the continuing cultural hegemony of the British aristocracy drew talent, resources, and ultimately entrepreneurs themselves away from intensive industrial activity toward less productive pursuits, or the cultural 'bloody-mindedness' of British trade unionists began to interfere with industrial reorganization. It is very difficult to assess the independent impact of culture on the economic performance of Britain. In this case, "culture" refers to the attitudes of the British people to their work and associated industrial questions. Some observers stress the decline of an "industrial spirit" among the middle classes since the Victorian period. Others emphasize the laziness or obstructionism of the British workforce. However, both lines of explanation have difficulty explaining why attitudes that were presumably conducive to economic growth in the heyday of British industrialization gave way to less productive states of mind; and no theory of national attitudes can effectively account for the discrepancy between those parts of British industry that perform particularly well and those that do not.

Most important, cultural theories of decline suffer from a heuristic problem. Unless they can account for the origins of national attitudes by reference to the institutions that generate and reproduce them, they do little more than summon up a *deus ex machina* that is itself unexplainable and thus somewhat suspect. When such theories are grounded in a theory about evolving British institutions, however, they are no longer purely cultural. Indeed, the most intriguing lines of argument are those that point to the institutions associated with the management of Empire or the development of the British educational system to explain the transition from a culture oriented towards entrepreneurial activity to one that attaches higher value to public service or the landed life (cf. Warwick, 1985; Nairn, 1977; Roderick and Stephens, 1982).[2] Even these, however, are generally unable to explain why the many British businessmen and laborers who have exerted a great deal of occupational effort are still unable to produce as much as their continental counterparts, or why some sectors of British industry have performed well by international standards while others have not.

TOWARDS AN ALTERNATIVE EXPLANATION

All of these theories look beyond the market system to explain economic decline. Each identifies an exogenous variable, whether the state and its policies or culture, as the principal problem. Such an approach, intentionally or not, fits well with neo-classical economic theory. The neo-classical view sees markets as ideal allocators of resources. When not interfered with, market mechanisms can be expected to allocate resources in such a way as to maximize social welfare and economic growth. On such a view Britain's deviation to a less-than-optimal growth path must be attributable to exogenous variables, such as public policy, that interfere with the operation of British markets rather than to the nature of those markets themselves.

However, Britain's relative economic decline has been an extensive process, stretching through many periods of policy and cultural fashion over 100 years. When the full dimensions of decline are observed it seems much more likely that they might be related more directly to the operation of the economy, and indeed have something to do with the characteristics of market mechanisms in Britain.

After all, Britain has had one of the most unconstrained market systems in the industrial world. From the Poor Law Reform Act of 1834 and the repeal of the Corn Laws in 1846, her governments embraced the self-regulating market economy, an international regime of laissez-faire, and Keynesian demand management successively, so as to avoid more direct intervention into the affairs of industry (Polanyi, 1944; Kenwood and Lougheed, 1983; Shonfield, 1969). In a nation where market mechanisms were given particularly free rein, we should look first to the operation of such mechanisms for the sources of economic decline.

To do so, however, requires a prior analytic step. We must move beyond neo-classical conceptions of markets and market behavior.[3] In general, neo-classical analyses are still based on an ideal-typical conception of markets that makes little allowance for the impact of institutional variation on market behavior. Although microeconomists have shown that factors related to barriers to entry, information costs, firm concentration, and X-efficiency can affect the way in which markets clear, the range of institutional variation admitted into most macroeconomic analyses is still limited. As a result, traditional neo-classical models are often highly idealized portraits of reality. They cannot capture many forms of systematic variation across nations in the operation of market mechanisms. Accordingly, they miss many of the most fundamental sources of economic decline.

To rectify such models we must recognize that markets are themselves institutions. In short, the market setting in which entrepreneurs and workers operate is a complex of interrelated institutions whose character is historically determined and whose configuration fundamentally affects the incentives the market actors face. Three important implications follow from this formulation.

First, the institutional configuration of markets can be fundamentally different across nations. That applies in the first instance to the most crucial markets that a firm faces, and those that feature in most analyses of corporate behavior: financial markets affecting the supply of capital, product markets determining the demand for the goods a firm produces, and labor markets bearing on the supply of the most critical factor of production, manpower. This has been one of the fundamental insights of the new economic history (see McCloskey and Floud, 1981; Sandberg, 1974).

However, the new economic history is still strongly rooted in a neo-classical tradition that focuses on the traditional features of demand and supply associated with market character. We must go farther, as Elbaum and Lazonick (1986) have recently done, to recognize that these facets of market setting do not exhaust the range of relevant institutional variation. The mix of costs and benefits that bears on corporate decisions is also likely to be affected by institutional factors intrinsic to the operation of the firm, such as the organization of the work process or the managerial structure of the firm, and by institutional dimensions of the broader social setting in which the firm is located, such as the nature of the educational system (which affects the training and skill levels of managers and workers) or the nature of the housing system (which can affect labor mobility).

Third, institutions structure and integrate national production in a complexly interdependent way (see Lipietz, 1984; Boyer and Mistral, 1983). It is a particular combination of institutional factors that accounts for the style of decision-making within the system and its co-ordinating abilities. Because there are many jointly necessary conditions associated with each set of economic outcomes, alterations in one particular institutional factor, such as the educational system or the shopfloor position of the union movement, may not transform the operation of the entire system or may not do so in the predicted direction. Even when the configuration of labor or product markets changed, for instance, British firms might not always have been ready to take advantage of the shifts because the behavior of their managers and workers was still being shaped by another set of institutional practices inherited from an earlier era.

In short, the incentives inherent in a market setting tend to lead firms into certain kinds of activities and away from others, by altering the terms of the implicit the cost-benefit analysis that managers and workers undertake. Even if we regard firms as strategic actors we must recognize that their most rational course of behavior cannot be derived *a priori*. It will be determined, in large measure, by the set of inducements that confront them within a particular complex of market institutions. Market rationality is a historically specific form of rationality.

It should be apparent that this analysis owes a great deal to the work of Alfred Chandler (1962, 1974) and his students on managerial hierarchy and corporate strategy; but it departs from Chandler's thinking in an important way. Perhaps by virtue of studying the organizational breakthroughs that enabled brilliant entrepreneurs to make much better use of the productive resources at their disposal, Chandler tends to see managers as the masters of their environment. By contrast, this argument stresses that there are many factors which managers take for granted as largely beyond their control. If structure usually follows strategy, in Chandler's view, this analysis suggests that strategy follows structure much more often.

In part, this difference of view arises because the principal topic of Chandler's work is managerial structure, whereas this argument is about a much broader range of structures, many of which Chandler himself admits are beyond the control of managers. In part, the reformers of corporate structure whom Chandler sees as typical managers are viewed here as more exceptional. Although institutional structures can be manipulated to some extent, their alteration is neither easy nor costless; and change may have to be incremental or associated with a measure of uncontrolled disruption.

EARLY INDUSTRIALIZATION, EMPIRE, AND THE SHAPE OF BRITISH MARKETS

This suggests that we should look more closely at the particular institutional setting of the markets facing British firms. Here the experiences of early industrialization and empire become especially important to the analysis. As Gerschenkron (1962) observed some years ago, the timing of a nation's industrialization tends to affect the pattern of its institutional development. Britain was the world's first industrializer; and later she became the manger of a vast overseas empire. Both experiences shaped the institutional setting of British markets so fundamentally in some cases that their legacy has lasted right to the post-war period.

In the first instance we might consider the impact of early industrialization on the factor endowments of British industry and the effect of its timing, in combination with subsequent developments overseas, on the structure of demand for British products. These variables began to affect corporate behavior adversely in the late nineteenth century; and the actions taken then had consequences for the subsequent periods. A national economy is not constructed overnight; and the institutions that structure its activities cumulate in response to changing market conditions over many years.

In addition, these historical experiences left British firms with certain kinds of organization on the shopfloor and in the boardroom; and they placed firms in specific institutional positions *vis-à-vis* other social entities of importance to them, such as the banks, the state, and the educational system.

We can break down the legacy of Britain's historical experience into four separate components: those associated with the structure of financial markets, those linked to the nature of product markets, those related to managerial structures and education, and those associated with labor markets and shopfloor organization. In each case it is possible to see how the institutional setting induced managers and workers to take the kind of decisions that led to the decline of the British economy.

The industry–finance nexus

Let us begin with the organizational relationship between British industry and the banks. Great Britain began to industrialize in the late eighteenth century around textiles. Since start-up costs were relatively low and entrepreneurs could build on an existing proto-industry, labelled the "putting out" system, the structure of the industry was characterized by many small, competing firms. It was not difficult for firms to finance investment through retained earnings or the solicitation of funds from family and friends that eventually gave rise to joint-stock forms of corporate organization and the development of an important stock market.

As a result, British firms came to depend heavily on internally generated funds and issues of equity for finance. In this context a particular kind of banking system developed. First, the banks that provided industrial capital in nineteenth-century Britain were principally regional entities, located near the sectors with which they did business and designed to serve the small family firms that early industrialization had produced. But these regional banks were not large or nationally integrated enough to serve as major sources for finance for industrial conglomerates of the sort that began to dominate international commerce in the latter part of the century. Partly as a result, many of them disappeared, and Britain was left without the kind of national industrial banks that later industrialization generated on the continent (Gerschenkron, 1962; Cottrell, 1980).

Secondly, since Britain's small firms did not initially rely on the banks for industrial finance, the latter developed a practice of lending to industry in relatively small amounts at a time, and primarily on a short-term basis or one that could be rolled over to ease temporary liquidity problems. For this reason the banks generally saw no need to take an equity share in firms or to play an active role in their management.

The French and German cases provide an appropriate comparison. Partly because those nations industrialized later around iron and steel, when start-up costs were high, their industries came to depend much more heavily on long-term loans from massive investment banks for industrial finance. As long-term lenders, those banks, in turn, acquired a greater interest in the future prosperity of their creditors which led them to take an equity position and more active management role in these firms. Over the years they used this influence to orchestrate new investment programs or rationalization schemes within an industry (Hall, 1983b; Zysman, 1983).

By contrast, the relationship between finance capital and industry remained different in Britain. As short-term lenders, the banks never acquired the interest or influence over industry necessary to lead them to orchestrate its periodic reorganization. This is important because it reduced the number of "visible hands" in Britain. Initiatives for the rationalization of industrial sectors would have to come spontaneously from the firms themselves or from the state, if they came at all.

The traditional separation between the banks and industry in Britain also had implications for firm behavior. Since British firms remained dependent on earnings and the favor of the stock exchange for industrial finance, short-term considerations of profitability probably also played a greater role in corporate calculations than they did on the continent (see Abernathy and Hayes, 1980). These were likely to deter some firms from forgoing current income for the sake of long-term rationalization. Many of the small, often family-owned, firms in Britain consciously resisted expansion even at the cost of relatively low rates of profit in order to avoid relinquishing control to the banks or other creditors during the inter-war period (Hannah, 1976).

There is some evidence that these factors were still at work after 1945. British industry's dependence on internally generated funds and the stock market for finance continued into the 1970s. The Wilson Committee (1977: ii) found that 70 percent of the funds available to industry over the past decade had come from retained earnings; and the standard practice of British banks, through the 1950s and 1960s, was not to lend funds for terms of over 2 years for the purchase of capital equipment (Williams et al., 1983: 69). Not surprisingly, apart from a few rescue operations mounted by the Bank of England and affiliated bodies, the banks do not seem to have initiated any sizeable amount of industrial restructuring during the post-war period.

In this context the international role of the City appears to be a less important factor than might be expected. Some have suggested that British industry was starved of capital at critical moments of development because British bankers were biased against British industry in favor of overseas business. For instance, those who see low levels of investment as the principal problem of British industry often identify the massive exports of British capital in the late nineteenth century as one of the factors behind Britain's initial decline. By 1913 the value of British assets abroad reached £4 billion, up from £235 million only 50 years earlier (Cottrell, 1980: 13).[4] At the same time, investment in British industry lagged: the United States was utilizing twice as much capital per worker as was Britain by 1907 (Mathias, 1969: 425). Perhaps partly as a result, British manufacturers lost markets to America and Germany during this period, particularly in capital-intensive industries (Kennedy, 1974; Crafts and McCloskey, 1979).

However, capital exports on this scale cannot be attributed simply to the international bias of the City, or to the exigencies of empire. Once again, the structure of market incentives was far more important. Edelstein (1976) has shown that foreign rates of return were generally substantially higher than domestic rates; and the government bonds into which many British investors shifted their assets were generally seen as more secure than investments in domestic industry. Perfectly rational market behavior took capital out of the country just as British industry needed to retool to meet rising German and American competition.

Product markets and the structure of industry

The industrial structure and relative weight of many British sectors was further reinforced by the nature of British product markets in the nineteenth century. Since the textile and metal-working industries of Britain developed early, firms were initially organized around specialized products; and each industry spawned a multitude of small firms. An industrial structure based on many small suppliers organized around segments of the product market survived well into the twentieth century, when overseas competitors were able to capture world markets with vertically integrated conglomerates and standardized products, taking more advantage of economies of scale.

Studies by Saul and Byatt (in Aldcroft, 1968) confirm the impact of market setting on the British mechanical and electrical engineering industries in the Victorian period. Britain's imperial role had already given her industrialists a foothold and interest in the semi-industrialized nations of the world. Strong demand there for the products of Britain's older engineering branches (such as locomotives, boilers, and heavy machine tools) drew investment to these sectors and away from more modern sectors, such as light machine tools, where home demand was weak.

Similarly, while Britain did generate some electrical engineering firms in the 1880s, the longstanding dependence of industry on steam-power and gas (itself a product of early industrialization) initially limited demand for their electrical products. Even the English branch of Siemens, a German producer, did badly right up to 1914. Uninhibited by such extensive domestic commitments to other sources of power, however, the electrical firms of Germany and America flourished at the turn of the century; and when Britain did move toward electrical power, foreign companies were already the more advanced producers.

When Germany and America began to industrialize rapidly in the late nineteenth century, their home markets for producer goods began to rise much more rapidly than those in Britain. In this case, too, lateness was an advantage. Because of tariff barriers, British engineering firms could not take full advantage of demand in these nations. Faced with less rapid domestic demand, they grew more slowly than overseas competitors in the early years of this century. British growth tended to rely much more substantially on the consumer goods industries.

Since the rate of technological change was faster in industries that were underrepresented in Britain, and slower in industries overrepresented there, it is not surprising that total factor productivity growth in Britain was slower than that in America or Germany in the Edwardian period (Matthews et al., 1982). The origins of this divergence can be traced back to Britain's early industrialization and the industrial structure it engendered.

Demand factors often had a long-lasting impact on industrial structures in Britain. Consider the iron and steel industry during the late nineteenth century. Although the Bessemer process for steelmaking was invented in England, domestic demand for steel rails, the product for which the new technology was best suited, grew slowly in the 1880s and 1890s because the era of railway construction was already over in Britain. At the same time, the appearance of smaller open-hearth furnaces allowed small and medium-sized producers to meet the growing demand for tinplate steel with less capital-intensive forms of production. Hence, the British steel industry also remained fragmented and relatively under-capitalized into the twentieth century, while German and American firms were developing highly integrated conglomerates that would ultimately compete more successfully on world markets (Elbaum and Wilkinson, 1979).

Developments such as these, which left British industry with a certain set of strengths and weaknesses, combined with the structure of international demand to lead Britain away from growing European markets and to give Germany a comparative advantage there at the turn of the century. At this time the needs of the less-industrialized nations of Africa, Asia, and South America were actually more complementary to the capacities of British industry; and they provided a buoyant demand for British textiles, locomotives, simple machine tools, and electrical equipment in the period preceding World War One. By 1913 about half of all British exports went to such nations (Saul, 1960). The cultural and political ties fostered by the British Empire, of course, also drew British industry toward these markets rather than those of the more industrialized nations of Europe.

This orientation toward semi-industrialized markets remained a feature of numerous British industries well into the post-war period (cf. Pratten, 1976). By then, however, it had become something of a handicap. In the 1950s and 1960s Japan and the United States made significant inroads into these markets; Britain lost 27 percent of her market share in the overseas sterling countries between 1959 and 1966 alone (Krause, 1969). The greatest marketing opportunities were opening up in Europe, where British factor endowments at last seemed to provide a better chance for maintaining comparative advantage. But Britain's early failure to seek membership in the European Economic Community shut her out of many continental markets for another 20 crucial years; and Britain's share of world exports declined steadily in the post-war period.

Firm organization and performance

As this discussion indicates, Britain left the industrial revolution still a nation of small firms. Although there were notable giants in some British industries, most sectors were divided between small firms, often with a highly specialized range of products, well into the inter-war period.

More important, many of the advantages to be gained in the inter-war period were economies of organization, in the sense that with improved forms of managerial control, a firm could make better use of existing factors or markets to grow without any loss of managerial control or efficiency. As a result of the pioneering work of Alfred Chandler (1962, 1974), most analysts regard the development of a multidivisional form of corporate organization as the source of significant economic advantages. With the notable exceptions of ICI, and Unilever, however, British firms were slow to move in this direction. As late as 1950 only a handful of British firms were organized in this way (Channon, 1973).

Similarly, although there were many mergers in Britain in the inter-war and post-war eras, there is a good deal of evidence to suggest that full advantage was not taken of them (Hannah, 1976). After merger or acquisition, the new British conglomerates did not usually reintegrate their production units so as to achieve optimal economies of scale and integration. In that respect Britain failed to reap many of the fruits of conglomeration despite the increasing concentration of industry. Here, too, the influence of old institutional practices remained strong, despite superficial change; and the persistence of other organizational factors interacted with the changes that did take place to limit their import. The continuing organizational strength of the trade unions, for instance, probably made it difficult for many newly merged firms to reintegrate their production units fully.

Several other aspects of early business practice also handicapped British firms as they entered the era of organized capitalism. There is some evidence that the organization of British production in the metalworking industries, around a 'consulting engineer' system designed to produce one-of-a-kind products to the specifications of individual customers, limited the introduction of large-batch manufacturing techniques in these industries during the early years of this century. The traditional reliance of British firms on merchant middlemen to market their products in the overseas colonies also meant that many businesses did not develop extensive distribution networks or innovate marketing techniques as early as their international competitors (Payne in Aldcroft, 1968).

These examples suggest that firm organization is often slow to change; and even after the formal institutions change, the traditional attitudes of a generation or two of managers socialized under the older scheme may persist. Moreover, institutions like the educational system and the managerial hierarchy interact; and change in one may not be followed by change in another crucial link in the institutional network for many years.

Lazonick (1986) has also shown how the structure of the educational system interacts with the structure of management to limit the efficiency of British firms. He argues that managerial efficiency can be improved by high levels of mobility and information exchange within the firm. As a consequence of early industrialization, however, Britain developed highly segmented forms of firm organization. This problem was then compounded by the nature of management education in Britain. In his words "Britain developed a highly-segmented university system that produced bureaucratic personnel for highly-segmented managerial structures." Most engineers were still educated through apprenticeship programs that put a great deal of distance between them and the Oxbridge graduates who were preferred management candidates. That inhibited the ability of engineers and other technical specialists to move into management, and segmented the flow of information in the firm. Moreover, until the 1960s Britain failed to develop any full-time graduate schools of management that might have provided a conduit around this segmentation.

These characteristics in the educational system can again be traced back to the effects of an industrializing process which created many small firms whose demand for managerial and technical personnel was much more restricted than that in America or Germany, where larger conglomerates were actively funding business education and seeking its graduates (Lazonick, 1986: 24). There may be respects in which British managers have had to hobble towards efficiency, chained to outmoded systems of education or inefficient managerial hierarchies.

The structure of the labor market and shopfloor power

Finally, the organization of work and the nature of the labor market are also distinctive to Britain in ways that are related to early industrialization. Because Britain industrialized when the influence of craft traditions was still strong, the productive process in many industries was organized around skilled laborers who often controlled the pace of production, the work of other laborers, and their own wage rates. Several consequences followed from this.

First, in the presence of a large pool of skilled labor it was often more profitable, in the short-term at least, for firms to rely on traditional methods of production rather than introduce technological innovations that made greater use of unskilled operatives. In several sectors this consideration seems to have delayed the rationalization of the industrial process. Sandberg (1969) and Lazonick (1981, 1983), for instance, have shown that the relative abundance and low cost of skilled labor in Britain, traceable to the experience of early industrialization, rendered the introduction of ring-spinning unprofitable in the textile industry for all finer grades of cotton yarn. High levels of firm fragmentation in Britain also prevented the use of ring-spinning and automated looms for coarse grades of yarn. Thus, industrial organization and the character of the labor market led British textile producers to act in a way that ultimately hastened the industry's decline.

Secondly, the pivotal position that skilled workers enjoyed in the production process of many industries made it relatively easy for them to organize trade unions to protect their wages and exert control over the shopfloor. As a result, Britain developed one of the strongest and most fragmented trade union movements in the Western world. A substantial segment of it was organized along craft lines, and the center of power in the British union movement remained on the shopfloor. National unions, let alone a centralized confederation, never really captured full control over the behavior of rank-and-file unionists.

These developments contributed to the type of incentives that British industrialists faced. In particular, management often encountered strong shopfloor resistance to the introduction of new technology and forms of work organization that might entail some deterioration in the wages, working conditions, or shopfloor control of their workforce. As early as 1897 the engineering employers had to utilize a lockout in order to force the Amalgamated Society of Engineers to accept new technology and piece-rate systems of payment. In spite of this move the ASE was soon able to reassert its power on the shopfloor.

Trade union defiance was rendered even more onerous by the presence of competing unions in many plants. Throughout the post-war period numerous industries were hit by wildcat strikes by groups of workers defending wage differentials or particular payments systems and forms of work organization advantageous to their members. Partly for this reason, the piece-rate payment systems, which were utilized in many other countries to improve worker productivity, in Britain often became mechanisms whereby shop stewards consolidated their influence over the workforce and extracted higher wages without conceding corresponding increases in productivity (Daniel and Milward, 1983; Brown, 1981; Maitland, 1983). It is not surprising that overmanning has been a problem in British industry. Even when Taylorist and Fordist methods of production which employed deskilling and assembly lines to manufacture standardized products more efficiently were introduced in Britain, the efficiency gains they promised were often never fully realized, because powerful unions were able to retain a considerable degree of control over work practices and manning levels.

As Britain moved close to full employment in the post-war period, the shopfloor power of the trade unions increased substantially over inter-war levels. Hence it became even more difficult and costly for British manufacturers to introduce labor-saving forms of technology. This became one of the principal preoccupations of the Donovan Commission on industrial relations. Union resistance was likely to be fierce as British workers, quite reasonably, used their available power to protect their jobs and work pace. Therefore, British managers faced fewer incentives than many of their foreign competitors to innovate.

CONCLUSION

The foregoing analysis suggests that the principal factors behind Britain's economic decline may be related to the institutional structure of British markets: there is no need to implicate the state immediately. The incentives and disincentives implicit in the structure of British markets and firms alone were sufficient to account for low levels of investment, lagging industrial adjustment, and outmoded work practices. In this light it also seems unfair to blame economic decline on the quality of British entrepreneurs or on the bloody-mindedness of British unions. The actions of British managers can be seen as perfectly reasonable in the light of existing market incentives. In that respect this argument finds common cause with the cliometricians who respond to the question "why did Victorian Britain fail?" with the answer "British entrepreneurs did as well as anyone could be expected to in the circumstances" (cf. McCloskey, 1981). Similarly, the organization of British unions and of work gave rank-and-file unionists, too, a particular set of incentives to behave as they did. It channelled natural defense of their wages and working conditions in a particular direction. Each set of actors sought to maximize their returns within the context of a particular institutional setting.

The result, however, was economic decline. Post-war Britain fell into a particularly vicious circle. In a nation such as Britain during the 1950s and 1960s, when labor is already fully employed and the capital-labor ratio is therefore rising, the appearance of diminishing returns means that the capital to output ratio will also increase, generating lower profit levels, unless new forms of capital-saving technology are introduced. But British managers faced an array of disincentives that made it especially difficult for them to introduce such technology or utilize it fully. Thus it is not surprising that British rates of profit continued to fall to particularly low levels; and low levels of profit inhibit further investment and innovation. In such a situation it is also rational for investors to send their funds abroad where a higher return is on offer, as they are currently doing, rendering industrial expansion even more difficult.

Although further work needs to be done to substantiate this argument fully, Britain seems to have suffered from a historical paradox. Her very success at industrializing first, and then at achieving full employment in the post-war era, sowed the seeds of industrial decline. These accomplishments, and subsequent developments that were heavily influenced by them, left the British market setting with a particular institutional configuration that militated against spectacular economic success.

Hence, any search for the causes of British economic decline should not turn too quickly to the state. It should begin instead with an analysis which regards markets as themselves institutions. They have a particular organizational configuration that structures the relations between economic actors; and they are embedded in an ancillary set of institutions, ranging from the managerial organization of the firm and the organization of work practices to national systems of education and housing, which also profoundly affect the behavior of market actors. Within this context the behavior of British managers and workers was perfectly reasonable. Individuals were responding to the incentives they faced; but the economy suffered in the long run from the actions of individuals who were doing the best they could.

Neo-classical economic models tend to suggest that markets provide a coordination mechanism capable of ensuring that the welfare-maximizing efforts of individuals will also conduce to an outcome that can provide the greatest possible benefit for all. The principal exception occurs in the case of 'public goods'. These are goods whose value cannot be captured by their producers; hence they will not automatically be produced by the market. However, the analysis in this chapter indicates that our understanding of markets, and their role for social welfare, must be considerably more nuanced. Because of the particular structure of British markets, the 'invisible hand' failed to transform the efforts of individuals to maximize their own welfare into long-term benefits for all. Instead, market incentives led managers and workers to make decisions that brought slow rates of growth and a deepening circle of economic decline. In the context of British markets at least, rapid economic growth turned out to be a public good.

3

Patterns of British Economic Policy

The previous chapter suggested that we should not move too quickly to blame the state for British economic decline. Britain has had one of the most unconstrained market systems in the industrial world; and economic decline must be seen, in the first instance, as one of the central consequences of the institutional structure of British' markets. If the state is absolved of principal responsibility for decline, however, it is not totally unimplicated in the outcome.

Political theories of both the left and right expect the state to rectify the institutional factors responsible for slow economic growth. Marxists have traditionally seen the state as the 'executive committee of the bourgeoisie' or the 'ideal collective capitalist' which manages the direction of a capitalist economy in a more prescient way than individual capitalists could themselves (Jessop, 1977; Miliband, 1969). Recent analyses of the "relative autonomy of the state" have been elaborated to explain precisely why it is able to do this (Poulantzas, 1976; Block, 1977; Therborn, 1978). If economic decline was the result of market failure, many public choice analysts can also be interpreted to imply that the British state should have taken steps to rectify the conditions associated with slow growth. In their view the principal role of the state is to supply public goods and to correct the external diseconomies generated by a market economy (Head, 1962; Buchanan and Tullock, 1962; Niskanen, 1971).

Therefore we might well ask why the British state did not take more active steps to alter the institutional conditions that fostered slow rates of growth. As John Zysman (1983) has pointed out, comparative economic advantage can be an artefact of public policy. National industrial strategies can alter the comparative advantage of a nation (cf. Scott, 1982). In Britain, however, both macroeconomic policy and industrial policy seem to have done little to improve the nation's economic performance over the past century.

Let us look more closely at the basic patterns of British policy to see why this was so. The first problem is to characterize the continuing features of British economic policy and the second is to explain why they took a particular form. Accordingly, the following sections attempt to identify the broad patterns of British macroeconomic and industrial policy since World War One. The presence of relatively consistent patterns over a period of political flux is itself a striking finding. It suggests that the roots of policy, like those of economic decline, may lie in institutional rigidities characteristic of the British state and society. These are examined in the concluding sections of the chapter.

THE PATTERN OF MACROECONOMIC POLICY

From 1918 to the floating of the pound in 1972 macroeconomic policy in Britain was dominated by a concern to maintain the value of sterling on the foreign exchanges. This is now a truism of the economic literature, and it is borne out by the economic history.

From 1918 to 1925 the direction of fiscal and monetary policy was largely influenced by the government's determination to return to the gold standard at pre-war parity ($4.86 to the pound). As a result the bank rate was raised to 7 percent and monetary policy remained tight throughout the 1920s, despite a rate of unemployment that never fell below 10 percent during the period (Aldcroft, 1970). The single relaxation of 1922 coincided with a strengthening of sterling across the foreign exchanges. Public spending was also slashed in accordance with the recommendations of the Geddes Committee in order to deliver a budget surplus and retire the national debt. As a consequence, Britain failed to recover from the recession of 1920–21 with the speed of most other nations, but Winston Churchill was able to announce a return to the gold standard in April 1925 (Pollard, 1969).

Most analysts now agree with Keynes that this move overvalued the pound by about 10 percent (Keynes, 1925; Kirby, 1981: 39). Thus, the return to pre-war parity virtually dictated an entire constellation of policies. In order to retain foreign confidence the budget had to be balanced and interest rates raised by international standards (Pollard, 1969: 218 ff). Moreover, the need to reduce British wage rates in order to maintain international competitiveness in the face of an overvalued exchange rate led directly to the wage cuts and General Strike of 1926. These deflationary monetary and fiscal policies almost certainly depressed the rate of economic growth and handicapped British industry at a time when her European counterparts were using the boom of the 1920s to rebuild and reallocate resources (Lewis, 1949; Howson, 1975; Moggridge, 1972). Britain was pinned to a cross of gold until 1931.

Despite the urging of Keynes, the Liberals, and many trade unionists, the Labour government of 1929 refused to abandon the deflationary policies recommended by the Treasury and City in favor of the public works programs pursued in Sweden, Germany, and the United States (Gourevitch, 1984; Skidelsky, 1967). However, in what Chamberlain called "one of the landmarks of the strange and eventful history of the race," the Labour government was turned out of office and Britain forced off gold in 1931 (Capie, 1984: 139). The new coalition lowered the bank rate to 2 percent for the next 7 years; but it did so specifically to lower the carrying costs of the public debt rather than to inspire industrial expansion, and fiscal policy remained tight until rearmament in the late 1930s. The recommendations of the May Committee, rather than those of the Macmillan Committee, guided policy through the 1930s (Youngson, 1960: 83–92; Richardson, 1967).

By the end of World War Two a profound transformation had taken place in the economic philosophy guiding British policy-makers. They began to embrace a variant of Keynesianism which suggested that higher levels of investment and employment could be sustained through the management of aggregate demand. Policy was to be aimed at a new goal, the achievement of full employment, and manipulation of fiscal and monetary policy was to be used to attain it (Employment Policy, 1944; Dow, 1964). Despite this development, however, the maintenance of a high exchange rate remained an overriding priority for successive Governments. When aggregate demand was expanded, rising levels of consumption sucked in imports and produced a deficit in the balance of payments. Rather than devalue the exchange rate to correct this imbalance, British Governments chose to deflate the domestic economy. Hence each period of expansion was followed by an abrupt deflation that generated a famous series of 'stop–go' cycles. The timing of these "stops" indicates that they were not the result of Keynesian attempts to moderate the fluctuations of the business cycle, but rather a direct consequence of attempts to correct the balance of payments so as to avoid devaluation (Hansen, 1968; Mosley, 1976). The formulation of policy was still ultimately determined by exchange rate considerations.

On Treasury advice, the post-war Labour government imposed severe import re.trictions in 1947–48 to avoid a devaluation that was nonetheless forced on them in the following year. The year 1951 again brought deflation, followed by a slight expansion in 1953–54 under the new Conservative Government. However, when speculation mounted against sterling, deflation was imposed in the winter of 1955–56. A brief expansion under Harold Macmillan in the spring of 1957 ended with another speculative run on sterling and deflation that autumn, marked by a rise in the bank rate to 7 percent and the reductions in capital investment that generally characterized such episodes. A reflationary budget prior to the 1959 election was followed by deflation in 1960–61, and the "Maudling boom" of 1962–63. Although the Labour Government of 1964 under Harold Wilson had promised to "reforge Britain in the white heat of the scientific revolution" it decided against devaluation to counter an inherited balance of payments deficit and was forced into a series of deflationary measures, both before and after the involuntary devaluation of November 1967 (Brittan, 1970; Beckerman, 1972; Wilson, 1971). Only in 1972, after America left the gold standard, did a Conservative government under Edward Heath decide to let the exchange rate "float" rather than interrupt the expansion of 1972–73. Unfortunately, the oil crisis of 1974 brought that boom to an end, and attempts at reflation under Labour in 1974–75 foundered when the balance of payments crisis of 1976 forced Britain to the International Monetary Fund (IMF) (Coates, 1980; Stewart, 1977; Fay and Young, 1977). The Callaghan government decided to let the exchange rate rise again in the autumn of 1977 rather than allow the domestic money supply to expand. That administration reflated during 1978–79 in the hope that North Sea oil would loosen the balance of payments constraint; but just as this took place the nation elected a Conservative Government under Margaret Thatcher, that repudiated Keynesianism itself and encouraged the exchange rate to rise in 1980–81 so as to weed the less competitive portions of British industry out of the economy (Stephenson, 1981; Keegan, 1984).

As shown, British macroeconomic policy, both before and after the war, was dominated by the pursuit of a relatively high exchange rate and was consequently more deflationary than it might otherwise have been. Although monetary policy was loosened in the 1930s with salutary results, the government felt able to do this only after devaluation had been forced on them, and fiscal policy remained tight. After 1972 the Government adopted a more flexible attitude to the exchange rate but speculation against sterling again forced the government to implement deflationary policies in 1976–77. The years of Thatcher governance have been marked once more by relatively deflationary policies and a brief flirtation with high exchange rates.

THE PATTERN OF INDUSTRIAL POLICY

The preceding chapter, however, indicates that our attention should be focused even more directly on policies that transform the nature of industrial activity. Only in conjunction with an activist industrial policy could more expansionary macroeconomic policies have begun to address the underlying problems of the economy. Yet industrial policy remains a neglected feature of most analyses. All too often it is viewed as no more than a set of funding programs for industry. Every industrial policy, nonetheless, contains three components: the volume of funds it channels to industry; the set of criteria that governs the choice of sectors, firms, and projects to be supported; and the degree of government pressure that is brought to bear on the reorganization and reallocation of resources within industry. Since 1918, British policy has followed a pattern that is distinctive in each of these respects.

The amount of money that British Governments were willing to spend on industry was negligible until the 1960s. Despite some advances under the Trade Facilities Act of 1921, the Treasury kept a tight hold on the public purse strings during the interwar period. Instead, tariffs were used to augment the public coffers and protect the private sector (Grove, 1967: 245). By contrast, Sweden, Japan, Germany, and even the United States spent considerable sums on guaranteed loans, industrial subsidies, and public works in this period (Lewis, 1949). As late as 1961, the British state spent over £270 million on aid to agriculture and less than £50 million on industry and employment (Grove, 1967: 265). Modest tax allowances were the principal investment incentive for business. In the 1960s, however, subsidies replaced tax allowances, and they increased during the 1970s as successive governments began to rescue firms hit by the post-1974 recession. Between 1971 and 1979 the government spent £9290 million on subsidies to the private sector, as well as large sums on the nationalized industries (*British Business*, 8 February 1980). By the 1970s, therefore, Britain was spending almost the same percentage of GDP on industrial grants as France or Germany (Dechery, 1980).

The set of criteria that guide British industrial support remained more distinctive. A substantial portion of British aid has been devoted to regional development programs whose object is not to promote specific firms or sectors but to transfer resources to the depressed regions of the country. Britain was a pioneer of such policies, implementing the Special Areas Act in 1934, the Town and Country Planning Act in 1947, the Regional Employment Premium of 1968, and the Industry Acts of 1972 and 1975 (McCrone, 1969; MacLennan and Parr, 1979). Regional policy was not notably successful until the 1960s, and even then its effect was more to shift the location of investment than to stimulate new investment or rationalization (Moore and Rhodes, 1973; Ashcroft, 1979). Many British legislators favored this form of policy precisely because it was voluntary, non-selective among firms, and likely to have little impact on the structure of industry (Grant, 1982). In 1979 the portion of public expenditure devoted to regional aid was twice as great in Britain as in most other European nations (Nicol and Yuill, 1982: 435).

British policy also emphasized research and development, which has consumed almost 50 percent of public spending on industry since 1970.

Although the program is seemingly analogous to continental efforts, British funds were put to far more restricted uses. Since the 1960s well over 70 percent of state spending on R&D has gone to the aircraft, aerospace, and nuclear sectors (Grove, 1967: 268; Whiting, 1976b). By contrast Germany, France, and Japan spent equivalent sums on a broader spectrum of promising industries, including chemicals, electrical goods, transportation, and machine tools (Freeman and Young, 1965; Channon, 1973: 33).

Finally, the British criteria have tended to channel the remaining selective aid to unprofitable firms and declining sectors (Young and Lowe, 1974). For instance, over £500 million of the £600 million allocated to the National Enterprise Board, which the Labour government established in 1975 to rejuvenate British industry, was spent to rescue a few large firms such as British Leyland, Rolls Royce, Ferranti, and Alfred Herbert (Fleming, 1980: 149). At first glance this seems eminently reasonable: unprofitable firms most need support. In a few cases the policy enabled a sound firm to survive. In most cases it sent vast resources to firms or sectors where Britain's prospects for success on world markets could never have been promising. While most nations began some rescue operations after the 1974 recession, France, Japan, and Germany have been more inclined to focus aid on profitable firms in sectors targeted for long-term growth (Vernon, 1974).

The third component of industrial policy involves the degree of state pressure employed to hasten rationalization within manufacturing sectors. The object of such pressure is generally to consolidate existing firms into units of the most efficient size, to improve the level of investment or technology, to alter work practices or product specialization, and to reallocate resources within and between industrial sectors. State intervention of this sort can take many different forms, however, and it is important to distinguish those in which the government compels compliance from particular firms or industries and those in which state-supported schemes are essentially directed by the private sector. The striking feature of British intervention has been its reliance on the latter. With the exception of an occasional nationalization, compulsory schemes have been avoided in favor of a highly consensual or "quasi-corporatist" approach, to use Samuel Beer's (1969: 297) term.

Since 1918, industries in Britain have essentially been asked to rationalize themselves. The government initially encouraged sectors to form trade associations so as to provide the state with a bargaining partner (Blank, 1973). When a sector seemed in need of reorganization the government authorized these associations to establish common pricing policies, mergers, production quotas, and investment or marketing schemes; in order to facilitate such schemes it made public resources available, either in the form of tariff protection during the 1930s or in the form of subsidies, tax concessions or import quotas during the post-war period. While these revenues were often presented as inducements they were rarely used as sanctions; and the government's role in reorganization remained limited. Such a consensual approach to industrial policy stands in striking contrast to the more dirigiste policies of Japan or France, where sectoral plans were drawn up by the state rather than industry, where individual firms were the direct object of numerous programs, and where a host of public sanctions was employed to enforce implementation (Shonfield, 1969; Warnecke and Suleiman, 1975; Zysman, 1983; Magaziner, 1979; Johnson, 1982).

The case of the coal industry was representative of British policy during the interwar period. After nationalization was rejected in 1919, the Mining Industry Act of 1926 authorized the Railways and Canal Commission to amalgamate neighboring collieries, but the initiative was left with industry and few results followed (Kirby, 1973). The 1930 Coal Mines Act created a cartel in the sector, mandated improvements in wages and working conditions, and established a Coal Mines Reorganization Commission to undertake amalgamation; however, amendments that might have given the Commission power to enforce rationalization were defeated by industry opposition in the House of Lords in 1930 and again in 1936 (Youngson, 1960: 66). As a consequence little changed, and the British watched coal output per manshift rise by barely 10 percent in 1913–36 versus 117 percent in Holland, 81 percent in Germany, 50 percent in Belgium, and 25 percent in France (Pollard, 1969: 111). This pattern was repeated in one sector after another, including steel, shipbuilding, and cotton (Pollard, 1969; Elbaum and Lazonick, 1986; Allen, 1951). The Economist (15 June 1940, cited by Harris, 1972) described inter-war industrial policy as:

> a set of notions that sees its ideal of an economic system in an orderly organization of industries, each ruled feudally from above by the business firms already established in it, linked in associations and confederations and, at the top, meeting on terms of sovereign equality with such other Estates of the Realm as the Bank of England and the Government. Each British industry, faithful to the prescription, has spent the past decade in delimiting its fief, in organising its baronial courts, in securing and entrenching its holdings and administering the legal powers of self-government conferred on it by a tolerant State.

By 1956 over 2550 agreements restricting trade had been made public, and many others undoubtedly remained underground (Channon, 1973: 26).

Collusive practices were viewed less benevolently in the 1950s, but the general thrust of policy did not change. The Industrial Development and Organization Act of 1947, which might have begun a process of active economic planning in Britain, left the initiative to form Development Councils up to private sector actors with the result that only four were ever established (Blank, 1973: 85; Grove, 1967: 291). Apart from belated action on restrictive practices and the introduction of investment allowances, the impact of which was marginal at best, the Government's principal effort was on regional development (Caves, 1969: 61). In 1962 the Conservatives established a National Economic Development Council (nicknamed "Neddy") to discuss economic policy with the Trades Union Congress and Federation of British Industries. Although some policy-makers hoped the Council would become a vehicle for economic planning on the French model, it never assembled the sanctions that put teeth into the French plans. Neddy remained a body for tripartite consultation between government and industry (Budd, 1978; Leruez, 1975; Opie, 1972).

The Labour Government of 1964–70 tried to introduce a more dirigiste industrial policy by establishing a Department of Economic Affairs to formulate national plans, a Ministry of Technology to foster research and development, the Industrial Reconstruction Corporation to facilitate mergers and modernization in the private sector, and a National Prices and Incomes Board to encourage productivity agreements between industry and labor (Beckerman, 1972; Shanks, 1977; Hague and Wilkinson, 1983; Young and Lowe, 1974). However, the DEA failed in the face of Treasury resistance; and the other institutions did not begin to move beyond consensualism until the last 18 months of their existence (Graham, 1972; Brown, 1970). Although these programs represented a brief attempt to improve upon the existing patterns of policy, they supplied too little too late.

Under the Conservatives in 1970–74 and Labour in 1974–79, industrial policy reverted to its normal course, marked only by larger expenditures on aid for declining sectors. After an abortive switch to investment allowances, the Industry Act of 1972 restored a system of subsidies, but almost all went to regional development grants or the industrial bailouts of British Leyland, Rolls Royce, and Cammel Laird (Young and Lowe, 1974). The industrial policies of the Labour Government were very similar. Only one of the "planning agreements" that the 1973 program advertised as a scheme for imposing investment plans on industry was ever negotiated; and the National Enterprise Board became little more than a source of capital for ailing firms whose redundancies the government was unwilling to tolerate (Wilks, 1981; Grant, 1982). The "new industrial strategy" of November 1975 created 39 Sectoral Working Parties (SWPs) operating by consensus at the sectoral level, much like the state-sponsored cartels of the 1930s.

What were the effects of this pattern of industrial policy? In political terms the answer is clear. Despite the growth of the state apparatus and the nominal extension of intervention, British policy tended to reinforce the power of the private sector *vis-à-vis* the government. The result was "less the domination of public over private powers than their interpenetration leading to the creation of a broad area of shared authority" (Beer, in Blank, 1973: xi). The principal effect of the SWPs, for instance, was to strengthen the ability of industrial actors to lobby the government for various forms of protection (Grant, 1982). This underscores the importance of distinguishing between different forms of "state intervention". The form of state involvement in the economy that emerged in Britain was fundamentally different from that in France, and it had different consequences. In particular it was characterized more by the growth of bargaining between the government and the two sides of industry than by the growth of unilateral state control (cf. Winkler, 1976).

The economic effects of industrial policies are harder to assess. On balance, British policy seems to have reinforced the ability of existing firms to resist market pressure for reorganization. By providing subsidies, authorization for price fixing, production quotas, or import protection to these sectors, without at the same time bringing sufficient pressure in favor of rationalization to bear on the individual firms in an industry, British policy tended to enhance rather than reduce the structural rigidities of many markets. This is reflected in the mediocre results that have followed from such schemes. For instance, the tariffs and state-sponsored cartelization of the 1930s kept prices high in many sectors, but did little to remedy the underlying inefficiency of the firms (Elbaum and Lazonick, 1986; Singh, 1979: 96). By contrast, the more activist policies of Germany contributed to the dramatic improvement of its manufacturing base, from an even worse situation (Lewis, 1949).

Similarly, most studies of post-war industrial policy conclude that insufficient resources were devoted to the problem (Clarke, 1973), that policy was not sustained enough to produce adequate results (Hague and Wilkinson, 1983; Broadway, 1969) or that these programs had very little impact on the investment and allocation decisions of private sector actors (Imberg and Northcott, 1981; Mottershead, 1978). Although British policy cushioned the impact of contraction in declining sectors, it seems to have had a minimal effect on the most serious problem underlying poor economic performance, namely, on low levels of productivity (Caves and Krause, 1980: 185). Only during the one period when industrial policy veered towards dirigisme, under the Labour Government of 1964–70, did the growth of the capital–labor ratio and output per person begin to approach continental levels. The experiences of other nations, such as France and Japan, suggest that in order to tackle underlying productivity problems Britain would have needed an industrial policy based less on voluntarism and more on rationalization enforced directly by the state.

THE ROOTS OF POLICY

These patterns in British policy present us with a double problem. On the one hand the persistence of consistent patterns of policy in a world of flux demands explanation. On the other hand most contemporary theories of the state would lead us to expect British Governments to adopt policies to remedy the nation's economic problems; yet the British state did not pursue effective strategies for restoring the profitability, productivity, and growth of the British economy. This, too, should be explained.

To arrive at an answer we must abandon the idea that the actions of all states, even within industrialized societies, are driven by the same set of functional exigencies. Most regimes, especially of a democratic character, confront a similar set of imperatives associated with the maintenance of power (cf. Levy, 1980; Block, 1977; Jessop, 1977; Tufte, 1979). However, the nature of their response is subject to wide variation, and the precise form it takes is strongly influenced by the institutional setting within which the state finds itself. In other words, the state is an endogenous variable within a particular social, economic, and international system. The constraints on its action are not specified simply by a given mode of production or form of government: within both of these broader frameworks there is a great deal of relevant institutional variation. British policy was different from the policies of other capitalist democracies in large part because of the institutional peculiarities of the British environment.

There are four aspects to the structural setting of the British state that had an important influence over policy: the position of Britain within the international system, the organizational configuration of British society, the institutional structure of the state itself, and the nature of the wider political system, understood as the network of political parties and interest intermediaries that seek to influence policy. Each of these variables affected the likelihood that the government would be willing to formulate a particular policy or the chances that it would be able to implement such a policy. Together they pushed policy-makers in a particular direction by altering the balance of perceived costs and benefits that accrued to any one policy.

Like British markets, the British political setting was shaped by two of the formative experiences in British history: early industrialization and empire. Britain's experiences as the first industrializer and an imperial power left her with a peculiar set of international relations, financial institutions, producers' organizations, and governmental structures that were transformed in the ensuing two centuries but never entirely replaced (Hobsbawm, 1968; Kurth, 1979).

Britain's international position

Although Britain's macroeconomic stance had only a limited impact on her relative economic performance, the government's persistent defense of the pound drew attention and resources away from the problems of the domestic economy. This approach to policy was rooted in the experience of empire. During the inter-war period a clear-cut set of international concerns and obligations pressed policy-makers to return to the gold standard (Moggridge, 1972). Even after British hegemony had declined, however, the imperial legacy continued to influence policy.

One aspect of this legacy was an overhang of foreign sterling balances. The net holdings in sterling and short-term sterling assets of foreigners grew to a considerable size because a major portion of world trade was once conducted in sterling. These balances continued to average £3.5 billion for most of the post-war period, rising at times to as much as £6 billion (Caves, 1969; Tew, 1978). They intensified the possibility that any weakening in the exchange rate, or balance of payments deficit, could lead to massive sales of sterling and a precipitous drop in the value of the currency. This heightened the pressure on policy-makers to respond with deflation to any balance of payments crisis; and the latter became a kind of hair-trigger inducing the periodic 'stop–go' cycles of macroeconomic management (Blank, 1978; Brittan, 1970).

Along with this financial legacy came a diplomatic one. Most of the overseas balances were held in the official reserves of nations who once belonged to the old sterling area. Any fall in the British exchange rate would reduce the value of these reserves and have serious diplomatic repercussions. As a result British policy-makers were inclined to see devaluation as a form of default on Britain's international obligations, a consideration which influenced civil servants and politicians alike. Although the Bank of England is often portrayed as the only agency resisting devaluation, the Bank itself suggested a floating exchange rate in 1952. The scheme, known as 'Operation Robot', might have left Britain with a more advantageous parity at a critical time in her post-war recovery. However, it was vetoed by the Cabinet on the grounds that any drop in the exchange rate would mean abdication of Britain's duty to the overseas holders of sterling (Butler, 1971: 159; Brittan, 1970; Roseveare, 1969).

Similarly, overseas spending to meet Britain's extensive military and diplomatic obligations intensified pressure on the balance of payments. For most of the post-war period private sector transactions across the external account were in surplus, but the public sector ran a sufficient deficit to throw the entire balance of payments off and trigger periodic "stop–go" cycles (Pollard, 1981; Manser, 1971).

Because Britain had been one of the principal suppliers of capital to the rest of the world, her governments also became accustomed to relying on a surplus in the invisible account, derived primarily from repatriated profits and shipping fees, to make up for a growing deficit in traded goods (Manser, 1971). When exports began to decline during the inter-war period this cushion reduced the pressure on the state for action to revive manufacturing. Moreover, when Britain was deprived of the surplus by World War Two (in which she lost overseas assets worth £100 million a year to the balance of payments while acquiring significant external liabilities) the nation was bound to face recurring balance of payments problems (Caves, 1969: 153). A series of post-war Governments had to face the consequences of relying for too long on the financial advantages of imperial power.

Finally, the experience of empire left Britain with financial institutions that were heavily oriented toward overseas lending (Clarke, 1967). Therefore the City became a powerful lobby against devaluation (which was widely expected to weaken international confidence in British financial markets) and a proponent of deflation in the face of balance of payments crises (Thomas, 1968; Blank, 1978; Cairncross and McRae, 1974). By contrast, in Germany, the banks' equity position in domestic industry and their less-developed international role gave them a stronger interest in policies that would expand German industry and exports; and the German financial sector agitated successfully to keep the deutschmark undervalued on the world exchanges (Kreile, 1978; Joint Economic Committee, 1981).

Societal structure

There are those who discount the effect that society can have on public policy because they point, quite properly, to the ability of the state to resist societal pressure (Nordlinger, 1981). However, this view neglects the fact that, in the era of the managed economy (Beer, 1969), public policy is implemented to a great extent through societal rather than state organizations. Differences in the organization of society may affect both the problems with which states are forced to deal and their capacity to implement policies to address these problems. In these respects, two features of British society had profound consequences for economic policy.

The nature of British financial institutions and their relationship to industrial capital was one such feature. As we have seen, because the nation industrialized during the textile era when start-up costs were low, British manufacturers came to depend primarily on internally generated funds and public issues of equity for finance (Kurth, 1979; Cottrell, 1980). Britain did not develop large investment banks interested in industrial modernization, capable of financing it, and influential enough to enforce it on recalcitrant firms (Hall, 1983b; Zysman, 1983). Consequently, the tasks facing the British state were greater than those in many other nations.

In addition, the organization of British financial markets limited the state's ability to control the flows of funds in the banking system in order to finance or induce compliance with a more aggressive industrial policy. Industry was relatively independent from the banks because it borrowed only over the short term and relatively sparingly; and the banks themselves were insulated from government control by the powerful Bank of England. Even after nationalization in 1949 the Bank used its quasi-autonomous status to resist any reforms that might adversely affect the City (Sayers, 1976; House of Commons, 1970). Its sponsorships of the Bankers Industrial Development Company in 1930, the Industrial and Commercial Finance Corporation in 1945, and the Finance Corporation for Industry in 1946 were all undertaken to forestall the more radical attempts of a Labour government to establish public investment banks (Grove, 1967: 247, 449).[1]

The form of organization of British labor and employers placed another set of constraints on state economic policy. Britain had developed a strong labor movement by 1918, when over four million people were affiliated with a trade union, and by 1975 union membership covered 50 percent of the workforce. Since large portions of labor were organized along craft lines, however, the Trades Union Congress remained a loose federation without much central control over its members (Martin, 1980). Employers' associations took a similar form: organization was extensive but most national associations were merely loose confederations of smaller units.

The organizational strength of the unions forced the government into negotiating with them to secure industrial peace, initially during World War One and then in the inter-war period. The Ministry of Labour expanded more than any other agency in this era, and these early attempts to bargain with the representatives of labor and capital set a pattern for subsequent policies in the industrial arena. The British state passed up unilateral action in favor of negotiations with organized labor and capital (Middlemas, 1979).

If the strength of the unions vis-à-vis the government initially pressed the state into a particular pattern of policy formulation based on bargaining, however, the internal weakness of union and employer organizations, vis-à-vis their membership, limited the options facing the government for policy implementation. In particular it prevented the state from using these associations to impose industrial reorganization on their members, as nations with more corporatist arrangements were able to do (Schmitter and Lehmbruch, 1979, 1982). Thus the

Mond-Turner talks of 1928, several agreements with the CBI, and a series of incomes policies broke down in the face of rank-and-file defections. The organizational features of Britain's unions and employer associations rendered them more effective as veto groups than as positive contributors to an active industrial policy (cf. Olson, 1982).

State structure

Finally, Britain was governed throughout this period by a state whose particular institutional structure imparted a consistent bias to policy. Just as the configuration of a market influences the behavior of individuals in it, so the structure of the state affects the incentives, balance of power, and flow of information facing individuals at different positions within it. This, in turn, influences the kind of policies they are likely to implement. Because policy is the product of a collective process, the particular form of aggregation implicit in each state influences the outcome.

The British state contained a particularly powerful central bank which was a private corporation until 1949 and even afterwards retained the right to hire its own staff, deal directly with the Prime Minister, and take public positions at variance with government policy (Sayers, 1976; Keegan and Pennant-Rae, 1979). As the only public repository of expertise on monetary matters the Bank of England was able to dominate decision-making in this area. It "deliberately cultivated a mystique that at best befuddled discussion and at worst intimidated those who had to take political responsibility" (Sayers, 1976, II: 387). The Chief Economic Advisor to the Treasury, for instance, did not learn about the 1957 increase in Bank Rate until after it had been implemented; and even when political leaders suspected there might be viable alternatives to the Bank's advice, they usually followed the Bank for fear that no-one else could accurately assess the monetary options (Hall, 1982b: ch. 7; Chapman, 1968).

Because Bank officials saw themselves as spokesmen for an internationally oriented financial community, custodians of the exchange rate, and financiers for the public debt, they tended to oppose devaluation, alterations to the financial system, and expansionary measures that might lead to higher borrowing or balance of payments difficulties (Grove, 1967: 449; Moggridge, 1972; Wilson, 1971; Brittan, 1970). Therefore, they acted as a powerful force for fiscal conservatism in both the inter-war and post-war periods.

The other institution at the heart of British policy apparatus has been HM Treasury. For many years it supervised all departmental promotions, and it still vets every spending proposal submitted to the Cabinet

(Roseveare, 1969). As a result the 'Treasury view' exercised a pervasive influence throughout the civil service. One Minister of Labour, for instance, complained that his departmental staff lacked "the necessary audacity of imagining schemes which they felt would certainly be frowned on by the Treasury" (Lowe, 1978: 283).

The Treasury emerged from the nineteenth century as an institution dedicated to the control of public expenditure. Until a few changes were made in 1975 its officials had virtually no familiarity with, or direct concern for, the progress of British industry. Therefore they were far more likely to suggest reductions rather than expansion in the funds spent on industry (Beer, 1959: 77). Just as the Treasury opposed granting spending powers to the industrial commissions of the 1930s, so it opposed the National Enterprise Board in 1975 (Middlemas, 1979: 229; Marsh and Locksley, 1983: 53). Moreover, Gladstone co-existed uneasily with Keynes. The Treasury rejected fiscal expansion in the 1920s and 1930s in order to protect the exchange rate and public debt; and many post-war officials, with one eye on rising expenditure totals, were relieved to be able to use balance of payments problems as an excuse for reducing public spending (Winch, 1969; Roseveare, 1969; Heclo and Wildavsky, 1974). As late as 1962 there were still no more than a dozen economists in the Treasury: its chief focus remained the control of expenditure, yet it has continued to dominate economic policy-making (Grove, 1962: 113; Heclo and Wildavsky, 1979). The British case stands in contrast to that of France or Germany, where one of the principal preoccupations of the Ministry of Finance and Economics has been the economic conditions facing industry, or that of Japan where the Ministry of International Trade and Industry is far more powerful in such matters than the Ministry of Finance (Katzenstein, 1978; Johnson, 1982).

The organization of the British civil service also reduces the state's capacity to pursue innovative economic policies (Hall, 1983a). Its upper echelons are staffed almost exclusively with personnel who spent their life in the service; information and advice is channelled to political leaders through a few individuals at the top of the hierarchy; and, until recently, promotion was dependent on the approval of these civil servants rather than that of elected officials. Most economic decisions are made in great secrecy, and few official documents are ever exposed to public scrutiny. As a result the access of political leaders to alternative sources of advice is limited; power is concentrated in the hands of those with the greatest interest in longstanding approaches to policy (Roseveare, 1969: 271; Benn, 1980; Thomas, 1968). The character of the civil service system and the politics–administration nexus in Britain may thus contribute to the extraordinary continuity that has characterized her economic and industrial policies.

The political system

In many nations a coalition of social groups, forged by political elites around a new set of priorities, has been the agency for a major shift in policy (Gourevitch, 1984; Ferguson, 1984). Why did we not see the emergence of such a coalition dedicated to a more activist industrial policy in Britain? To answer this question we must consider the institutional features of the wider political system, including both the political parties and interest intermediaries in Britain who would have had to organize such a coalition.

In the first place, the nature of the constituent groups which form the building blocks of such coalitions was different in Britain than in many other nations. Early commercialization of agriculture, marked by widespread enclosures, and rapid industrialization reduced the independent farmers remaining in the country to very small numbers by 1918 (Moore, 1966; Kemp, 1969). Unlike the Social Democrats in Sweden and the Democrats in the United States, therefore, the Labour Party in Britain lacked the option of forming a workers–farmers alliance around farm supports and reflationary policies (Gourevitch, 1984). Similarly, the pronounced divisions between industrial entrepreneurs and the financial sector in Britain meant that business pressure on both parties was more heavily weighted toward the concerns of international finance than in many other nations.

If a new social coalition were to take power in Britain, it would also have to do so through the party system. However, party organizations develop deeply rooted doctrines which become central to their existence and resistant to change. In Britain these doctrines tended to militate against more coercive state intervention. In addition, the close ties that British parties developed with particular interest groups also limited their range of action.

Within the Conservative Party, two strains of thought existed uneasily side by side. One segment, associated with the Tory democracy of Disraeli, was prepared to condone a measure of intervention, in the form of regulations or transfer programs to limit the effects of the market on the populace (Gilmour, 1977). In the 1930s, for instance, a small group of MPs associated with Harold Macmillan agitated for industrial reorganization, but they sought statutory authority only for schemes that had the support of a substantial majority of the firms in a given industry (Macmillan, 1934). During the post-war period these ideas were pressed most strongly by a group of MPs around R. A. Butler, who persuaded the party to accept the basic programs of the welfare state (Beer, 1969: ch. 11). However, in the industrial sphere the most they were willing to advocate were consultative mechanisms such as those mentioned in the Industrial Charter of 1947 (Harris,

1972).

Even these proposals encountered opposition from the other strain of thought that ran through party doctrine. Its proponents defended the unimpeded operation of market mechanisms and opposed most forms of state intervention altogether (Joseph, 1976; Greenleaf, 1984). Their influence within the party can be traced to the laissez-faire sentiments that many businessmen defecting from the Liberals brought to the party at the turn of the century; but they became particularly powerful in the mid-1950s and again after Margaret Thatcher assumed the leadership in 1975 (Harris, 1972; Behrens, 1980). Neither stream of Conservative thought condoned state intervention of the sort that right-wing governments in France frequently practiced. Moreover, the proposals of Tory democrats were always susceptible to defeat within the party by a coalition of free market ideologists and the business leaders who were respected advisors to the party on such issues. Macmillan's schemes for industrial reorganization in the 1930s lost to just such a coalition.

In some respects the Labour Party seems a more appropriate vehicle for an activist industrial policy. Its post-war program of nationalization certainly reflected a clear-cut willingness to intervene. However, the longstanding ideology of the party centered on precisely this – nationalization – not on how the state might be used to revive private industry. Labour MPs hesitated to use public funds for schemes that raised profits; they were more interested in reducing unemployment in declining sectors. For instance, Labour members attacked the British Sugar (Subsidies) Bill of 1924 on the grounds that it was inappropriate for the government to subsidize any private industry (Hansard, 18 December 1924: 1300). In a mixed economy, however, an efficient industrial policy must often direct funds away from declining sectors to more promising, and perhaps already profitable, industries and firms. The highly effective and interventionist industrial policies of France and Japan were conducted during long periods of conservative rule. In Sweden and Austria, socialist governments were careful to adapt their programs to a mixed economy (Muller, 1983; Martin, 1979).

The close ties between British parties and particular interest intermediaries also constrained their action. It is often observed that Britain has a "strong" state, that is, one that is relatively impervious to direct pressure from organized interest groups (Katzenstein, 1978). However, while it is true that the British executive dominates the legislature, employs a highly insulated bureaucracy, and concentrates power in the hands of the Cabinet, British political parties have enjoyed no such insulation. The trade unions pay 80 percent of the Labour Party's expenses and dominate its annual conference (Minkin, 1978; Allen,

1960). Many Conservative MPs not only depend on business interests for their electoral funds but continue to devote a substantial portion of their time to employment in the City or industry while in office (Mellors, 1978; Ramsden, 1979). Therefore, while both parties have a degree of independence that derives from their need to appeal to a broad cross-section of society, their policies have been heavily influenced by the groups on whom they depend for finance, advice, and personnel. These groups were also inclined to oppose state intervention in the industrial area.

In contrast to many socialist parties in Europe, which embraced Marxism and interventionist doctrine before they formed an alliance with the trade unions, the Labour Party was created to defend the independence of the labor movement (Drucker, 1979; Miliband, 1961). The formative experiences of the British trade unions, which pitted them against a state attempting to break their power, left them staunch opponents of any policies that seemed to limit their autonomy to determine wages and working conditions through collective bargaining (Pelling, 1976; Fenley, 1980). The lessons of Taff Vale and the Osborne decision lived on in the memories of many trade unionists. So the Labour Governments that came to power in the inter-war period strove not so much to revive British manufacturing as to protect the industrial power of the unions. This goal lent their economic policies a non-interventionist cast.

In the post-war era, Labour's approach to industry was again primarily consultative. Representatives who urged more activist policies at the annual conference often met stiff opposition from a coalition of party leaders (influenced by the structural constraints of Government or electoral appeal) and trade unionists who saw such policies as a threat to their autonomy in the workplace (cf. Minkin, 1978; Hatfield, 1976; Coates, 1975).

Within the Conservative Party the influence of City interests, concerned about international confidence rather than industrial modernization, has been particularly strong. Even the employers' associations remained defenders of the status quo structure of industry. In contrast to the French CNPF, they did not become the agents for a rationalizing alliance between the most dynamic sections of capital and the state (Blank, 1978; chapter seven). Although a few businessmen, such as Sir Alfred Mond, were willing to consider such an alliance, the British employers' associations were rarely prepared to endorse an interventionist policy. Because they were trying to assemble a broad membership, which was ever ready to desert to competing associations, they usually refrained from any action that might disturb the vested interests of their members (Grant and Marsh, 1978). Consequently, just as the unions waged bitter battles against industrial relations legislation in 1968 and 1971 the employers fought to remove selective inducements from the Coal Mines (Reorganization) Act of 1930, the Industrial Organization and Development Bill of 1954, and the Industry Act of 1972 (Jenkins, 1970; Crouch, 1977; Harris, 1972; Mowatt, 1955).

The two post-war conjunctures

The inertia of the political system became most important during the critical conjunctures that followed the two world wars. Many European nations utilized these periods of dislocation to change direction. Although Britain did not suffer the trauma that accompanied defeat, these were periods of widespread disillusionment with the old order and rising aspirations for the future. The extension of intervention during the war also provided a precedent on which the state might have built a new industrial policy. Why did the political system not respond?

The prospects for change after World War One depended heavily on the possibility that an interventionist coalition might emerge around Lloyd George. As Minister of Munitions and Prime Minister during the war, Lloyd George masterminded Britain's first serious steps toward state direction of industrial resources. He drew to his side Winston Churchill and the most interventionist of the Conservatives, such as Austen Chamberlain, Lord Birkenhead, Arthur Balfour, and Stanley Salvadge; and it was widely believed that they might form a Fusion Party (Middlemas, 1979: 169; Cook, 1976). Drawing on the intellectual legacy of Joseph Chamberlain and Randolph Churchill, such a party might have built a program around the extension of tariffs, the welfare state, and the enforced rationalization of industry.

However, Lloyd George was viewed by the Conservatives as a dangerous maverick, and the chances for fusion faded when Bonar Law's followers threw their support to the Tories rather than the unpredictable Welshman (Mowatt, 1955: 135 ff). Adroit maneuvering by Stanley Baldwin, which committed the Conservative Party to protection before Lloyd George could draw support on that issue, sealed the fate of the Fusionists. Britain's future would lie with the Conservatives or Labour.

At a second critical conjuncture, after World War Two, Labour secured a majority in Parliament and inherited a system of physical controls that might have been adapted, as in France, to industrial planning (cf. Cohen, 1977a). After implementing the nationalization proposals of its 1945 manifesto, however, the Government did little else to influence the direction of industry. Precisely the sort of factors outlined above inhibited further action. The trade unions opposed any extension of manpower planning, and opposition from business associations scuttled Stafford Cripps's attempt to establish tripartite

Development Councils in most industries. The desperate state of the balance of payments preoccupied economic policy-makers and inhibited any attempts to reorganize the financial sector. With one eye on the export earnings of insurance, for instance, the Treasury opposed Aneurin Bevan's plans to nationalize the industrial assurance companies; and the nationalization of the Bank of England remained a technical exercise. The Bank retained control of the Bank Rate, and the rest of the financial sector remained untouched (Morgan, 1984; Eatwell, 1979; Rogow, 1955). Despite the reforms in other areas the post-war Labour Government missed its opportunity to take control over the domestic flows of capital within the financial sector. The French case suggests that such a move would have been necessary if a more active industrial policy or effective system of planning were to be implemented (cf. Zysman, 1983).

Instead, the remaining energies of the Labour Government went into the creation of social programs, such as unemployment insurance, superannuation, and the National Health Service, that we now associate with the welfare state. They were a remarkable achievement and one around which support could be rallied within both the Party and an electorate more interested in social reform than in socialism. On the economic side of its platform the Party desperately needed a plank that seemed to make full employment possible. Party leaders were gradually won over to the view that a version of Keynesianism, based on the management of aggregate demand, could accomplish this task (cf. Crosland, 1956). This was an important step. Since Keynesianism seemed to provide a technique for achieving full employment without the need for more detailed intervention into the decisions of industrial sectors, it was instrumental in persuading both parties that they could abandon economic planning without sacrificing economic performance (Skidelsky, 1979; Schott, 1982). As such, Keynesianism played a major role in the victory of the "revisionists" within the Labour Party, and contributed to the convergence in party politics known as "Butskellism" (cf. Crosland, 1956; Butler, 1971). The nation that most avidly embraced Keynesianism also adopted the most arm's-length industrial policy in Europe. In that respect, while Keynes's doctrine solved many of the parties' political problems, it by no means solved Britain's economic problems.

CONCLUSION

This analysis suggests that the state is not primarily responsible for Britain's economic decline. However, it has not been an innocent bystander. If the principal causes of economic decline lie elsewhere, successive British Governments did little to address them. There were alternatives. The French experience in the post-war period suggests that a state can transform the operation of its economic system, but first it must transform itself (cf. Hoffmann, 1978). The British have found this process difficult because institutional rigidities limited the actions of the British state, just as such rigidities influenced the operation of the British economy (cf. Shepsle and Weingast, 1984). The structure of Britain's international position, state, and society pushed policy-makers in a particular direction by influencing the perceived costs and benefits that accrued to any one policy.

This observation has important implications for contemporary theories of the state. None of the main theoretical alternatives quite fits the British case. Those who explain state action as a response to the dictates of capital or the functional imperatives of capitalism cannot explain the inadequacies of British policy from the point of view of capital or the great variation in policies across capitalist nations (cf. Jessop, 1977; Poulantzas, 1976). Pluralists who view the state as a respondent to the concerns of competing social groups miss the fact that policy-makers had interests and inclinations of their own, and that the biases inherent in their institutional setting precluded an equal response to all groups (cf. Truman, 1951). The more recent group of state-centric theorists who view the state as a free-floating actor, generating its preferences in relative autonomy from the rest of society, miss many of the respects in which the very structure of that society conditions its preferences (cf. Nordlinger, 1981). They imply that the policy choices of the state are relatively unaffected by the configuration of society; yet if there is one lesson to be learned from the course of British economic policy, it is that policy is not made from a tabula rasa; policy-makers are profoundly influenced by the labyrinth of institutionalized relations that are history's legacy to every society.

4

The Evolution of Keynesianism

As we have seen, the pattern of British macroeconomic and industrial policies displays broad continuities since World War One whose roots lie in persisting features of Britain's international position, state, society, and political system. Within these parameters, however, we can also discern some evolution in British policy. No nation has an entirely static policy position. We will find a similar mixture of continuity and change in French economic policy.

In this context one of the central analytic problems is to explain how change and continuity can coexist. What factors act as forces for change in the policy arena? What constraints condition new initiatives in such a way as to draw many of them back towards older patterns of policy? That is the subject of this chapter, which concentrates on a more detailed analysis of British economic policy during the post-war period.

This was an era when Britain turned towards Keynesian economics. In itself that marked a break with the past. But, as we shall see, the structural features of Britain's economic and political setting transmuted Keynesianism into a pattern of policy that was not as different from past practice as one might have expected. In subsequent years Keynesianism also went through a series of stages. To a large extent the history of post-war economic policy in Britain can be seen as a story about the development and ultimate collapse of Keynesian patterns of policy-making (cf. Martin, 1979; Longstreth, 1983).[1]

As any economist would suggest, the evolution in policy was partly a reaction to underlying economic developments. However, the most important changes in policy were also a response to the political consequences of past policy. The economic and political conditions that followed from each stage of policy established the terms in which successive stages of policy would be defined.

The course that economic policy took in post-war Britain was also quite different from that in France; and one of the purposes of this chapter is to describe and account for these differences. Here, too, we find that divergent political contexts, closely related to the distribution of power among social classes in each nation, go some way toward explaining the outcomes. The most critical decisions, setting each nation on diverging economic trajectories, were made just after World War Two.

THE POST-WAR SETTLEMENT, 1945–51

The years immediately following the war were a critical conjuncture for the British polity. At such moments social institutions become more elastic, and longstanding patterns of policy are especially subject to change. Widespread hardship through 5 years of fighting had left the British populace disillusioned with past policies and eager to create a better world. Partly for this reason, they gave Labour a sweeping victory in the election of July 1945, with 393 seats to 210 for the Conservatives and 12 Liberals. As Michael Foot later said, "No socialist who saw it will forget the blissful dawn of July 1945. The great war in Europe had ended; the lesser war in Asia might be ending soon. This background to the scene in Britain naturally deepened the sense of release and breath-taking opportunity" (Foot, 1974: 17).

In many respects the 1945 Government's program was the most radical of any administration before or since. It was built on three pillars: nationalization of several leading economic sectors and institutions; the foundation of a welfare state that would provide minimum levels of housing, health care, education, and social security to all members of society; and a commitment to the achievement of full employment through public management of the economy.

Perhaps curiously, the Government's nationalization program, while the most controversial of its policies, was also the least significant over the long term. With considerable legislative efficiency, Labour nationalized the Bank of England; the telecommunications concern, Cable and Wireless; the British Overseas Airways Corporation; the railways; the remainder of the electricity sector; the coal and gas industries; most large trucking concerns; and the iron and steel industry. In many cases the long-delayed rationalization of these sectors was then accomplished. However, public ownership was not to be the vehicle for subsequent moves toward workers' control; and the state shied away from utilizing the nationalized industries to inspire further rationalization within the private sector.

Enthusiasm for nationalization within the Government itself began petering out in 1949 when dissension arose over the question of including subsequent proposals in the next electoral manifesto (Morgan,

1984: 400). Over the ensuing decade, power within the Party gradually shifted toward those who argued that a socialist economic policy could be built around Keynesian demand management rather than further nationalization (Crosland, 1956). Although these revisionists did not succeed in removing Clause 4 calling for the common ownership of the means of production, distribution and exchange from the Party constitution, they were to dominate the Party for another 30 years (Beer, 1969: ch. 7).

As a result the Government's moves toward Keynesianism and the welfare state became far more important policy precedents. Although the British state had mandated workmen's compensation in 1893, old age pensions in 1908, and unemployment insurance in 1911, the famous Beveridge Report of 1942 recommended that a universal system of social security and a national health service should be established after the war. Accordingly, family allowances, payable to all mothers for child support, were authorized in 1945; a system of national insurance benefits payable to the sick and unemployed was established in 1946–48; and a national health service, providing free care for all individuals, was set up by Aneurin Bevan in 1948. These measures were notable for their universality and generosity in a time of economic scarcity. All were accepted by subsequent Conservative Governments. John Strachey could observe that

> British capitalism has been compelled, by the sheer pressure of the British people, acting through our effective democratic institutions, to do what we used to say it would never, by definition, do; it has been forced to devote its productive resources to raising the standard of life of the population as a whole (Warde, 1982: 26).

With respect to the economy, by far the most striking feature of the 1945 Government's policy was its commitment to full employment. With the possible exception of Sweden, no other Western government made employment the centerpiece of post-war policy. A concern to avoid the dole queues of the inter-war era led the Coalition Government to publish a pathbreaking White Paper of Employment Policy in 1944. Its first sentence read: "The Government accepts as one of their primary aims and responsibilities the maintenance of a high and stable level of employment after the war." That bipartisan statement became the basis for both Labour and Conservative policy until the end of the 1970s.

Despite memories of the Great Depression, however, such a declaration would not have become the basis for public policy without the economic theories of John Maynard Keynes. Neo-classical doctrine, on which the pre-war 'Treasury view' was based, maintained that the state could not directly reduce unemployment; and a government would have been foolish to take responsibility for an aggregate it could not influence. However, Keynes (1936) argued that the government could alter the level of economic activity and employment by manipulating the budgetary deficit and associated monetary instruments. In short, it could virtually eliminate unemployment.

Keynesian ideas were first employed in Kingsley Wood's budget of 1941, which raised taxes so as to dampen domestic demand in the face of wartime spending. That action took place within the context of wartime controls that rendered budgetary policy a simple supplement to direct resource planning. After the war, however, the British Treasury began to accept the idea that the manipulation of budgetary policy alone might be sufficient to moderate incipient fluctuations in the economy (Schott, 1982; Dow, 1970). By varying the level of public spending or taxation the government could alter the spending power of consumers and thus the investment plans and employment levels of industry. In later years changes in hire purchase controls and the bank rate were also used to affect these variables.

The acceptance of Keynesian doctrine had immense political significance. On the one hand it led the government to accept responsibility for the level of unemployment. On the other hand it meant that public officials could expect to attain full employment without having to utilize direct controls on industrial inputs or outputs. That made an implicit class compromise possible.

Up to this point, working-class political parties and the spokesmen for capital had been locked in a virtually irreconcilable conflict. Labour argued that the working-class goals of full employment and a reasonable distribution of income could be attained only through nationalization of the means of production. The supporters of private capital, of course, opposed any arrangement that would have deprived them of ownership and control over the means of production. The programs of the post-war welfare state went some distance toward resolving the problem of income redistribution; but it was only the advent of Keynesianism that resolved the conflict over full employment. If Keynesian policies worked, the working class could be guaranteed full employment through the management of aggregate demand, without depriving capitalists of ownership and control over the investment and resource allocation decisions of industry (Przeworski and Wallerstein, 1982). Labour and Conservative politicians alike saw this as a formula on which they could base a cross-class appeal. Not surprisingly, both parties accepted it during the 1950s.

The acceptance of Keynesianism, however, had important implications for the evolution of economic planning in Britain. During the 1940s and 1950s politicians were gradually persuaded that detailed supervision over the activities of industrial sectors was no longer necessary to attain full employment. Therefore the Government began to dismantle the unpopular system of controls used to supervise the flow of goods and funds within the economy during the war. Although some forms of rationing were not lifted until the late 1950s, Harold Wilson at the Board of Trade lit the first 'bonfire of controls' in 1948–49.

These moves were significant because the industrial controls assembled during the war were powerful instruments that might have put teeth into a system of economic planning. Without them, economic plans were likely to be little more than public relations exercises. Despite the rhetoric about economic planning of the 1945 Labour Government, the state was actually dismantling the institutions that might have allowed it to reorganize British industry. As we have seen, the contrast between Britain and France in this period rests partly on a divergence of goals: the British attached far more importance to the maintenance of full employment than to industrial reorganization *per se*. However, the failure to develop or retain appropriate institutions in the immediate post-war period meant that, even when the British began to seek industrial reorganization in the 1960s, the state would find itself without readily available instruments to implement such a policy.

The Bank of England was nationalized in 1945, partly in revenge for the trouble Montagu Norman had caused the Labour Government of 1931; but very few of the senior personnel in the Bank were replaced, and the institution remained virtually as independent from the government as it had been in the pre-war period (Morgan, 1984: 100). Moreover, in contrast to the French case, the Government did not go on to nationalize any of the other major British banks. It therefore forfeited one of the principal means for control over the flows of funds to industry within the financial system.

Instead, the Government relied on the Capital Issues Committee, established by the Conservatives in 1939, to oversee major share issues and long-term loans, and on a National Investment Council, established in 1946, to coordinate the private sector's investment and savings policy. However, both bodies were dominated by appointees from the private sector and neither became a significant instrument of policy (Leruez, 1975: 42–3). Similarly, two investment banks, created by the Bank of England to ward off further demands for bank nationalization (the Industrial and Commercial Finance Corporation and the Finance Corporation for Industry) remained under private control.

At the national level the Cabinet rejected the idea of setting up an autonomous planning body in favor of a small Central Economic Planning Staff reporting to its Economic Committee. The Prime Minister's concern to make all crucial decisions at Cabinet level virtually assured that no amount of detailed economic planning could take place. Instead, annual Economic Surveys discussed the appropriate allocation of resources for each succeeding year but did nothing to enforce them. The only longer-term plan, drawn up to meet the conditions of Marshall Plan aid in 1947, was virtually ignored. As a contemporary observer put it: "operational planning is felt by the Economic Planning Staff either not to be necessary at all or at best something that will take care of itself more or less spontaneously once the proper analyses of needs have been made" (cited in Leruez, 1975: 49).

Attempts at sectoral-level planning were largely toothless. Stafford Cripps appointed sectoral working parties for 17 major industries in 1945–47, each composed of four industrialists, trade unionists, and Board of Trade officials; but these were purely consultative bodies. The Industrial Organization and Development Act of 1947 mandated the establishment of tripartite Development Councils for major industries; but only four were ever created – in cotton, silverware, clothing, and furniture. With the exception of the Cotton Board, which was really a re-named trade association, the others foundered in the face of employer opposition.

Here as elsewhere, the Government relied heavily on tripartite institutions, composed of representatives from employers' federations and the trade unions, to formulate and implement policy. The planning process as a whole was supervised by an Economic Planning Board on which employers and unionists were well represented. Each of the regulatory commissions in the financial and industrial arenas was dominated by such private sector representatives. It was not unusual for key allocation decisions to be made entirely by private officials of the relevant trade associations (Rogow, 1955: 59 ff). Since they usually favored the existing firms within a sector it is not surprising that the system tended to perpetuate, rather than eliminate, the structural defects of British industry.

To explain this pattern of behavior we might look first to the organization of British society. Of paramount importance here was the organizational strength of the British union movement. Trade union leaders had gained considerable influence within Whitehall during the war; and they retained much of their power during the post-war Labour Government. A total of 120 Labour MPs were themselves sponsored by a trade union. Moreover, post-war manpower shortages enhanced the industrial power of the unions which already had nine million members by 1949. Eager to make use of this bargaining power to recoup wartime sacrifices of earnings, union leaders were hostile to the continuance of industrial controls that might interfere with collective bargaining or the rising living standards of their members (Morgan, 1984: 125, 133, 371; Schott, 1982: 308; Beer, 1969). Particular vehemence was reserved for wage and manpower restrictions but many unionists saw a threat in the extension of any controls, and they pressed this position on the new Labour Government.

The role of employers was also important at this critical conjuncture. In both Britain and France they opposed planning systems that seemed to infringe on the ability of private managers to control the flow of resources. In France, however, the most powerful trade associations had been discredited as a result of collaboration with the Vichy regime. Their public credibility and political power was at an all-time low just after the war. In Britain, by contrast, the power and respectability of industrialists had been enhanced by their active participation in the war effort. Labour, as well as Conservative, Ministers had relied on them to run the economy during the war. In 1945 Whitehall was still full of officials on secondment from the private sector. Unilever alone, for instance, had 90 employees at the Ministry of Food (Rogow, 1955: 62).

Therefore, British industrialists were in no mood to roll over for a Labour Government. They lobbied steadily, from inside and outside the state, for the abolition of controls; and, when faced with official intransigence, they mounted major public relations campaigns against the Government's policies. Aims for Industry was founded in this period to fight the nationalization of iron and steel; and 'Mr. Cube' was invented by Tate and Lyle to carry its campaign against nationalization of the sugar industry to the people. Employer opposition effectively blocked the use of Development Councils for industrial reorganization.

In short, the British state faced a society whose producer groups were often hostile to the extension of state control and far more powerful than their French counterparts (see Beer, 1969; Kuisel, 1981). However, this is not an entirely sufficient explanation for the British outcome. Armed with a firm electoral mandate the Labour Government had been able to push through a national health service and substantial nationalization program against considerable opposition, and there is little doubt that it could have gone further than it did to enforce industrial reconstruction on the private sector. The explanation must depend partly on the weakness of pressures for such action from within the political system itself.

As we have seen, the dominant components of Labour Party ideology did not really mandate such action. The Party's policy toward industry had always been dominated by the notion that nationalization was to be the principal tool for industrial rejuvenation. This left the question of policy toward the remainder of private industry up in the air. It was not a subject to which the policy-making organs of the Party had given much thought in the inter-war period. The idea that the state might be used to render private industry even more profitable was anathema to many Labourites; and, as we have seen, many proposals for private sector planning could run afoul of the trade unions' traditional concern for maintaining the independence of collective bargaining.

Therefore, discussion of such questions within the labor movement had generally taken the form of a debate between those who favored more extensive use of nationalizations and those who wanted to limit the scope of the nationalization program out of a concern for business confidence. Except for the occasional reference to an investment board or national investment bank, the issue of control over the private sector had been largely defined out of the terms of discussion. Nationalization of the banks and insurance companies was the one openly debated measure that might have gone some distance in this direction; and this proposal ultimately foundered on the electoral ambitions of the Party leadership, who saw it as an issue that might arouse more opposition than support within the electorate. Although the 1932 Conference passed a motion from the floor calling for nationalization of the joint-stock banks, the proposal was quietly dropped by the leadership in subsequent years (Pollard, 1979).

The principal concern of the 1945–51 Labour government, then, was not so much the reorganization of industry, as it had been in France, as the achievement of full employment. For this purpose the Government moved away from direct industrial intervention toward Keynesian principles, which suggested that full employment could be attained through the management of aggregate demand without interfering in the allocation and investment decisions of private industry. In the boom that followed the war, full employment was successfully achieved. However, the structure of private industry was not greatly altered, and Britain began to fall farther and farther behind her industrial competitors on the continent.

THE FIRST PHASE OF KEYNESIANISM: DEMAND MANAGEMENT

In October 1951 the Conservatives began 13 years in office. They denationalized the iron and steel industry but otherwise accepted virtually all the economic policies that Labour had left them. The die was cast in 1948 when R. A. Butler persuaded the Party to accept an Industrial Charter that ratified the goal of full employment, the welfare state programs, and the Keynesian approach of the preceding regime. His policies were so similar to those of Hugh Gaitskell, the last Labour Chancellor, that commentators began to describe the economic policies of the 1950s as 'Butskellism'.

The defining characteristic of British policy was a growing acceptance of Keynesian demand management. Budget deficits were used to stimulate consumption and investment when the economy appeared to be stagnating; and hire purchase controls, increases in the bank rate, and spending cuts (often in the investment programs of the nationalized industries) were used to reduce demand when rapid growth seemed likely to bring inflation or a balance of payments deficit. In essence this was Keynesian; but several features of Britain's international position and domestic organization imparted a peculiar quality to the policy.

To be exact, Keynes envisioned that demand management would be used to moderate the fluctuations that endemic shocks generated in the economy. On such a view, budgetary policy would be used primarily in response to changing levels of growth and unemployment (Keynes, 1936: 378). To an unusual extent, however, budgetary policy in Britain came to be dictated by incipient balance of payments crises. While expansionary policy was still undertaken largely in response to rising levels of unemployment, deflationary policy was pursued whenever a serious balance of payments crisis arose; and such crises struck the British economy frequently in the 1950s and 1960s.

In the first instance the origins of this deviation from simple Keynesianism can be traced to the peculiar international position of Britain, outlined in the previous chapter. Since sterling had become the principal reserve currency for much of the world during the period of British empire, overseas governments and traders held massive stocks of the currency, which they were occasionally anxious to redeem for dollars or another currency. To meet such demands it was estimated that Britain needed to run a surplus on the balance of payments of roughly £350 million a year (Radcliffe Report, 1959). However, the British economy was barely capable of exporting enough goods and services to run an average surplus of half this amount. Therefore Treasury and Bank of England officials lived in a state of perpetual anxiety about anything that might spark a run on the nation's very limited reserves of foreign exchange.[2] Their response was to recommend deflation whenever an exchange rate crisis loomed on the horizon.

The problem was rendered more intense by the Bank of England's 1962 decision to allow foreign securities denominated in foreign currency to be issued in London. Coupled with a policy of providing cheap foreign exchange cover, the object was to revive London's position as an international financial center; and the ultimate effect was to turn the City into the world's leading Eurodollar market. New Eurobond issues in London rose from $134 million in 1963 to $3368 million in 1968 (Strange, 1971: 205). The move certainly improved the invisible earnings of the City, but it also led to massive short-term capital inflows and outflows. As the size and volatility of such flows increased, the Bank of England had increasing difficulty defending the exchange rate. The slightest rumor could lead to massive speculation against the pound, as investors sought to protect their investments in sterling. The peculiar financial position of London, therefore, made it difficult for the government to ignore minor balance of payments deficits of a sort that would not bother most other countries.

By the 1960s the other factor which put pressure on sterling and on macroeconomic policy-makers was the Government's insistence on maintaining the exchange rate at a relatively high level (Krause, 1968). A high exchange rate inhibited exports, which were the principal source of foreign exchange, by raising their price abroad, and it increased the amount of foreign reserves required to cover sterling liabilities. At the same time it encouraged speculation against the pound.

The British state's opposition to devaluation in the 1960s is often blamed on the influence of the City of London, and there is no doubt that City figures were pressing their opposition to such a move on the government. However, one should not overemphasize the role here of direct pressure from the City. Successive Governments knew that the balance of payments depended on the City for from £200 to £400 million in annual earnings that might have been threatened by devaluation. They were even more mindful that devaluation would represent default to the many Commonwealth nations that held sterling reserves. Once again the structual features of Britian's international position, rather than the operation of a pluralist mechanism, constituted the more effective constraint on policy-makers' decisions (see Strange, 1971).

Macroeconomic policy soon fell into a set of 'stop–go' cycles. Expansion was pursued at the first sign of rising unemployment, and deflation followed from any run on the reserves (Brittan, 1964: 288). Rearmament for the Korean War in 1950–51 led to a massive balance of payments deficit in 1951 and budgetary retrenchment in 1951–52. The Conservative Chancellor, R. A. Butler, then initiated a reflation in 1953–54, which gave way to another external deficit in 1955 and consequent deflation in 1956 when Harold Macmillan became Chancellor (Macmillan, 1971: 6). When he became Prime Minister in 1957 the new Chancellor, Peter Thorneycroft, first introduced a moderately expansionary budget in April, and then a package of deflationary measures in September following another run on the pound. Derek Heathcoat Amory, who became Chancellor on Thorneycroft's resignation in 1958, introduced the most expansionary budget yet on 8 April 1959 in response to a rise in the unemployment figures. The resulting balance of payments deficit brought another 'stop' in July 1961 under yet another Chancellor, Selwyn Lloyd. The Prime Minister's memoirs paint the usual picture:

At the end of July 1961 the Treasury, supported or instigated by the Bank of England, had become seriously alarmed at the continued signs of inflation now reflected in an unfavourable balance of payments for the third year in succession. Although I was tempermentally opposed to some of the deflationary proposals which the 'authorities' seemed to think necessary, I was forced to agree to certain further measures of restriction. These involved new economies in public expenditure and more rigorous exchange controls as well as deflationary steps calculated to curtail consumption, including the temporary raising of the Bank Rate to seven per cent (Macmillan, 1973: 35)

After this episode the new Chancellor, Reginald Maudling, instituted another reflation in 1962–63.

The Labour Government under Harold Wilson, which took office in October 1964, faced almost immediate pressure on the pound as a result of the Maudling boom, and embarked on a series of deflationary measures rather than lower the exchange rate. Wilson's controversial decision not to devalue in the opening months of his administration was justified in terms of Britain's international obligations, but seems to have been equally motivated by a concern for its political consequences in the face of an impending election (Wilson, 1971: 27). Deflationary measures in April and July 1965 – and again in February, May, and July 1966 – failed to stem the tide of speculation against sterling. However, they completely undermined the new Government's commitment to secure a 4 percent rate of economic growth. Devaluation of sterling from $2.80 to $2.40 was ultimately forced on the Government in November 1967, along with recourse to borrowing from the International Monetary Fund (IMF) and a sustained period of further deflation under the new Chancellor, Roy Jenkins. The Government's refusal to devalue upon taking office condemned the nation to a series of balance of payments crises and deflationary packages, which undoubtedly contributed to its electoral defeat in 1970.

However, one salutary effect followed from the 1967 devaluation. Both financiers and policy-makers soon discovered that it had not seriously impaired the international operations of the City of London. As a result, when America left the gold standard in the summer of 1971 the City was willing to contemplate a floating rate of exchange and further devaluation in June 1972.

For several more years macroeconomic policy remained resolutely Keynesian. Concern for rising levels of unemployment inspired reflation in 1972–73, and again in 1974–75, after another Labour Government under Harold Wilson had been elected to cope with the effects of the oil price shock and miners' strike of autumn 1973. By the time James Callaghan became Prime Minister in 1976, however, it was apparent that no feasible demand stimulus was going to be adequate to stop the rising tide which took unemployment from 500,000 in 1973 to 1.6 million in 1977. The PSBR had already been increased to an unprecedented 11 percent of GDP, and public expenditure as a whole had reached 50 percent of GDP.

In the autumn of 1976 another dramatic run on sterling forced the Government to make radical cuts in public spending for 1977–78 in return for a loan from the IMF. The state stood helplessly by as unemployment continued to increase in Britain, as in the rest of Europe. For all intents and purposes the Keynesian era was over in Britain. It ended as it had begun, dominated as much by the balance of payments constraint as by the goal of full employment.

THE SECOND PHASE OF KEYNESIANISM: INCOMES POLICY

Although full employment remained the principal goal of British Governments from the war to 1979 the era of 'pure' Keynesianism lasted only through the 1950s. During this decade the Government relied almost exclusively on aggregate demand management to attain its economic goals. In a sense that was a golden age when Keynesianism seemed to fulfill its promise of providing steady levels of growth and employment without any need for direct interference in the affairs of industry or labor.

By the end of the 1950s, however, one of the intrinsic defects in Keynesianism became apparent. It proved to be an excellent technique for stimulating employment; after all, that was the problem for which *The General Theory* had originally been designed. But it contained no mechanism for coping with rising levels of inflation. With A. W. Phillips's discovery in the late 1950s of a stable trade-off between inflation and unemployment, Keynesianism was somewhat revised: demand management was focused on the two targets so as to aim at an acceptable point on the Phillips curve. However, a nation committed to the achievement of full employment was impatient with such compromises; and as Britain moved into the 1970s even this trade-off seemed to become unstable. Therefore successive Governments began to search for a mechanism with which to control the level of inflation directly.

The mechanism to which they turned was an incomes policy, understood in this case as voluntary or compulsory controls on the rate of growth of wages and, to a lesser extent, prices. The post-war Labour Government had already experimented with such a step when it negotiated voluntary wage and price restraints with the principal producers groups in 1948 (Beer, 1969: 205). However, subsequent Conservative Governments hoped to avoid conflict with the unions on this point. As a result they pursued a policy of "industrial appeasement even at the cost of highly inflationary wage settlements" (Butler, 1971: 164). Macmillan remarked that "in the long run, and for the common good, the umpire is better than the duel" (Middlemas, 1979: 400). He went only so far as to appoint a three-man Council on Prices, Productivity, and Incomes, under Lord Cohen in 1957, to advise the nation on the appropriateness of wage and price settlements.

By the end of the decade, however, many individuals were beginning to see incomes policy as something of a panacea for Britain's problems. Treasury economists believed that they might be able to move off the Phillips curve and avoid compromising their full employment goals if an incomes policy were used to restrain inflation directly. The Bank of England saw incomes policies as the kind of measure that might forestall further speculation against the pound by reducing the rate of inflation. Both were enthusiastic about a policy that increased their room for maneuver but was the responsibility of others to implement (Brittan, 1970: 256 ff). While Conservative politicians were not anxious to engage in such direct intervention into the economy, they were persuaded by advisors, such as Lord Robbins, who blamed Britain's poor economic performance on the overly rapid growth of income and consumption (Robbins, 1971; Paish, 1966).

Accordingly, Selwyn Lloyd announced the first of many incomes policies in July 1961. Government employees were to experience a 'pay pause' until the following year, when a White Paper was published suggesting that money incomes should rise by no more than $2\frac{1}{2}$ percent a year for the foreseeable future. Despite union opposition, a National Incomes Commission was established in July 1962 to supervise the operation of this 'guiding light'. Like most of its successors the policy was distinguished by two features. Its principal object was wage rather than price restraint; and the Commission was given no powers of compulsion. It was hoped that, by publicizing excessive wage settlements, the weight of public opinion could be brought to bear against them. Not surprisingly the policy was largely a failure. Workers in the electricity industry successfully violated the initial pay pause; London busmen and postal workers, among others, received settlements well above the norm. Public opinion was little influenced by NIC reports that appeared 6 months to a year after the initial settlements.

The 1964–70 Labour Government followed suit with an almost continuous succession of incomes policies, beginning with the establishment of a National Board for Prices and Incomes in early 1965. Once again the Board was able to consider only a small number of wage and price cases, and it could do no more than delay their implementation. Instead of attempting to enforce an incomes policy, the Labour Government relied on its amicable relations with the trade unions to secure a measure of voluntary restraint. The unions were willing to cooperate in part because they perceived Britain's economic situation as perilous, and in part because they were anxious to keep a Labour

Government in power. The TUC General Council agreed to establish a small committee that was to vet all major wage settlements over the ensuing 5 years. Apart from a 12-month wage freeze imposed during the sterling crisis of July 1966, these remained the principal incomes policy measures of the Labour Government. Although the Government took on statutory powers to suspend wage increases during the freeze, it used these only seven times to affect no more than 36,000 workers in all.

The subsequent Conservative Government under Edward Heath took a slightly different approach to the problem. Initially Heath hoped to rely exclusively on a tough line toward public sector wage settlements. When this failed to reduce the rate of inflation below 11 percent and was broken by the National Union of Mineworkers in early 1972, the Government moved to statutory control. A 5-month pay freeze from November 1972 was followed by two additional stages that, while nominally restrictive, saw hourly wages grow by approximately 13 percent a year. A Pay Board with nominal power to disallow settlements and fine offenders was not established until November 1973, barely 3 months before the end of the Government, by which time Heath had become locked in a desperate struggle over wages with the miners.

The 1974–79 Labour Government initially relied on a voluntary Social Contract negotiated with the union, according to which wages were not to exceed increases in the cost of living. In return the Government was to take several measures to restore union power at the workplace and to provide increases in the 'social wage' going to pensioners, the unemployed, and the low-paid. As the rate of inflation rose above 20 percent, however, the obvious failure of this policy pressed the Government and TUC into negotiating a more restrictive policy based on a flat £6 weekly increase for the year from July 1975. The agreement was renewed for another year of roughly 5 percent increases in July 1976; but TUC enthusiasm for the policy began to wane rapidly in the face of severe public spending cuts, rising unemployment, and rank-and-file dissent. Although the Government appealed for a 10 percent wage norm in 1977, the TUC agreed only to the principle that settlements should run for at least 12 months; and in July 1978 the Congress rejected Prime Minister Callaghan's attempt to impose a 5 percent norm on wages.

For much of this period the Government held in reserve a set of *ad hoc* sanctions to be used, if necessary, against firms granting exorbitant wage increases. This threat was helpful in securing restraint during 1975–76, but little use was ever made of the sanctions. Although effective enough to depress real income in 1976–77, the incomes policy ended in disarray during the winter of 1978–79 when a series of strikes hit vital services within the public sector.

The extensive use which Britain made of incomes policies in this period was largely inspired by the organizational strength of labor. By the 1960s British trade unions were generally powerful enough to ensure that their members secured continuing real wage gains, despite changing levels of inflation or devaluation. To reflect this fact the traditional wage equations in most macroeconomic models of the British economy were replaced by an exogenous variable based on a simple mark-up over domestic inflation (Ormerod, 1979; Posner, 1978). Similarly, the Phillips curve trade-off between wage increases and unemployment began to disappear.

The characteristic path that British incomes policies followed was also heavily conditioned by the structure of the labor movement. In the initial stage the Government's calls for voluntary restraint would go unheeded, as individual unions quite rationally attempted to protect their wage differentials in the face of accelerating inflation. A severe balance of payments crisis would then force the state into a sterner position, often marked by a brief pay freeze, followed by a hard-won agreement with the TUC on continuing restraint. That agreement would hold for a year or two, often with more success under Labour, until rank-and-file discontent over the distortion of differentials and declining real incomes forced the trade union leaders into repudiating further restraint. In the subsequent free-for-all, many unions would make up the losses their members had suffered over the preceding years.

In other words, the Trades Union Congress had just enough authority over its 112 member-unions to persuade them to accept a period of restraint in the face of a serious economic crisis. However, it did not have enough control over the rank-and-file to prevent serious challenges from eroding the policy within a year or two. A powerful layer of shop stewards facilitated unofficial work stoppages; and the presence of over 100 competing unions gave the individual unions more incentives and power to break from the policy so as to protect wage differentials. Contrast the British case with the more centralized union movements of Austria or Sweden. In those nations the organizational opportunities for rank-and-file dissent were less substantial; and top union leaders were more likely to trade restraint for governmental concessions. Since their membership encompassed most of the workforce they could be reasonably certain that the benefits of the policy would flow to their members; and they had less chance to free-ride. Broader macroeconomic questions were likely to take greater precedence on union agendas than the wage differential issues that preoccupied the fragmented

British unions. For these reasons incomes policies have generally been more effective and long-lasting in these nations (Lange, 1985; Cameron, 1985).

The economic effects of incomes policy in Britain remain a point of contention. Although Britain experienced consistently higher rates of inflation than France or Germany over this period, the policies' supporters maintain that inflation would have been even worse without them. During the brief periods of absolute freeze, at least, wage inflation did slow; and the 1975–78 years saw wage increases fall below the rate of price inflation. By contrast, the critics argue that wage norms soon became minima which tended to raise the pay of weakly organized workers more than they restrained the settlements of the strong – for an aggregate increase in inflation. At best the policy can be said to have had a mixed and rather weak impact on the economy (Blackaby, 1979; Clegg, 1971; Fels, 1972; Smith, 1968).

Far more important were the policies' political effects. The resort to incomes policies vitiated an important component of the Keynesian promise to provide economic management without direct interference in the affairs of the private sector. The impact on employers was not substantial. Private capital retained most of its authority over investment and resource allocation decisions, as the post-war class compromise envisioned. However, the policy interfered directly with the autonomy of the trade unions over their principal preoccupation, wage determination. One unintentional effect of incomes policy was to turn the unions into public antagonists with the state.

A second unintentional effect was of even greater importance. Although incomes policies were designed to integrate the unions into a national system of wage determination, they actually accelerated a trend toward the organizational disintegration of the unions themselves. That trend entailed growth in the numbers of shop stewards within British plants and an increase in their influence over wage determination at the expense of central union leaders. Incomes policies tended to immobilize the union leadership for lengthy periods of time and encouraged the spread of productivity agreements and plant bargaining, as part of the wage drift associated with a national norm. Both developments increased the numbers and authority of local stewards (Brown, 1981; Daniel and Milward, 1983; Clegg, 1979).

Paradoxically, much of that growth occurred in the decade after the Donovan Commission had identified the shop steward movement as one of the principal sources of disorder within the British industrial relations system. Hence the incomes policies of the British state, designed for one purpose, were frustrating corollary attempts to develop more centralized systems of wage determination. Once again, through short-term policies, the state was inspiring societal reorganization of a sort at odds with its long-term goals (see Tolliday and Zeitlin,

1985). The British state and society, then, cannot be analyzed as separate spheres. They are constantly acting on each other; and the unintended political or organizational consequences of policy were often even more significant than its immediate economic objectives.

Nevertheless, the consequences of incomes policy were probably even more severe for the British state than for the unions. For two decades it became embroiled in the most difficult and complex of negotiations over the determination of recompense and relative income differentials within the economy. Convoys of politicians and trade union leaders, trundling back and forth between Congress House and Downing Street, became a familiar sight for the British populace. At stake were some of the most rudimentary and intractable issues of social justice (Goldthorpe, 1974). To many of the questions which these negotiators were asked to decide, there were no consensual answers. Therefore, as often as not, the Government had to put its authority on the line to enforce a series of wage settlements about which there was substantial social conflict. It is not surprising, then, that the very process began to erode the authority of the state in the eyes of both the unions and the electorate.

A succession of Governments were defeated at the polls, at least partly because they seemed unable to stem a rising tide of industrial conflict for which they had taken responsibility by embarking on an incomes policy. Simple regressions indicate that an 'industrial relations cycle' may have become just as important to a Government's electoral success as the traditional 'political business cycle.'[3] The appearance of industrial conflict just prior to an election seemed to play a major role in the defeat of the government in 1970, 1974, and 1979 (Butler and Kavanaugh, 1975, 1981).

THE THIRD PHASE OF KEYNESIANISM: INDUSTRIAL INTERVENTION

The British state also began to embark on a more active industrial policy in the early 1960s. This was not a necessary concomitant of Keynesianism so much as an attempt to remedy its deficiencies within the British economic context. Throughout the 1950s Keynesian demand management contributed to the maintenance of full employment in Britain.[4] However, it did not inspire a great deal of reorganization within British industry. The effect of a demand stimulus was to encourage the full utilization of existing factor inputs; but many impediments to faster economic growth remained embedded in the institutional structure of British production. In fact, since Keynesian doctrine was instrumental in persuading both political parties that they could do without an active industrial policy, it actually postponed deliberate attempts to rationalize the economy.

Once the issue of sterling convertibility was resolved in 1958, however, public attention shifted increasingly toward the problems of economic growth. All of a sudden the British realized that, although the economy was growing faster than it had since the 1870s, the nation's performance was still lagging behind that of her European competitors. A number of publications, such as Andrew Shonfield's *British Economic Policy since the War* (1958) and Michael Shanks's *The Stagnant Society* (1960) began to draw attention to the nation's relative economic decline. To explain the outcome, these authors began to point to the low levels of investment, outmoded work practices, and overmanning of British industry. In search of solutions, organizations such as Political and Economic Planning, and the National Institute of Economic and Social Research, spoke of the virtues of economic planning *à la française* (PEP, 1960). Therefore the attention of both trade associations and the government shifted toward the kind of microeconomic concerns that demand management had not been able to address. They began to consider supplementing Keynesian techniques with a measure of economic planning.

It is significant that the initiative came from the private sector. The British state was still not organized in such a way as to render microeconomic issues one of the central concerns of its policy-making organs. As late as 1957 there was still only one economist in a Treasury dominated by administrators whose interest and expertise lay in public expenditure control. While the Treasury was gradually acquiring a capacity for demand management, marked by the establishment of a National Economy group in 1962 it had little expertise in industrial matters. The Board of Trade, which knew something about industry, remained on the sidelines of economic policy-making.

Therefore the Federation of British Industry led the way. Inspired by a few industrialists such as Hugh Weeks, Sir Hugh Beaver, and Reay Geddes, the FBI held a conference at Brighton in November 1960 to consider Britain's economic prospects; this Conference endorsed proposals for closer cooperation between government and industry in the formulation of longer-term economic plans. Treasury officials were lukewarm to the idea; but they were preoccupied with how to secure an incomes policy, and gradually came to believe that a planning organ might be used to this end. Selwyn Lloyd sold the idea to Prime Minister Macmillan; and in the summer of 1961 he invited the FBI and TUC to participate in the establishment of a planning body. The FBI accepted immediately, but the TUC hesitated until guarantees were given that the new body would not be linked to the incomes policy that the Government had just announced.

In early 1962 the National Economic Development Council was established as a tripartite forum for consultation between the government and industry. Its 20 members were appointed in roughly equal numbers by the Government, FBI, and TUC. A National Economic Development Office, with about 75 staff members responsible to the Council and the Chancellor, was established to examine Britain's economic problems and contribute to the formulation of longer-term plans. The NEDC was to become a central fixture of British politics for the next 20 years (Blank, 1973; Leruez, 1975).

It was designed to be the central planning institution for the British economy; as such its form and mode of operation were highly revealing. First and foremost it was a tripartite forum for consultation between government, employers, and unions rather than an arm of the state charged with the preparation of an economic plan. NEDC recommendations were to be the outcome of bargains struck between three parties, among whom the government was simply a co-equal negotiator. Thus, the Council perpetuated a voluntaristic tradition according to which the state left matters of industrial reorganization largely up to the private sector rather than try to impose its own plans.

Despite superficial similarities, therefore, the NEDC was fundamentally different from the French Planning Commission. The latter had close links to the rest of the state apparatus and more tenuous connections to the private sector. By contrast the NEDC was not well-integrated into the economic policy-making process. Control over policy remained in the hands of a Treasury already suspicious of the NEDC and unlikely to be overly influenced by its recommendations. Even if the NEDC had wanted to press for implementation of a detailed national plan, it was not well placed to do so.

The Economic Development Committees (or little Neddies) which the NEDC subsequently set up at the sectoral level followed the same tripartite pattern: 45 percent of their members were employer representatives; 20 percent were drawn from the unions; 12 percent came from the state; and the rest were independent experts (Leruez, 1975: 148). The 21 EDCs were almost exclusively consultative bodies for the exchange of information within the industry rather than agents for the implementation of reform.

Not surprisingly, the principal contribution which the NEDC made to the British economy in the following years was to provide a forum for the negotiation of incomes policies. The reports prepared by NEDC staff on the state of the British economy were frequently insightful documents; but they seem to have had little impact on economic policy-making. More often than not the Economic Development Committees became institutions which industry used to lobby the government for special subsidies or protection, rather than instigators of fundamental microeconomic change.

After the election of 1964 it was up to a Labour Government to carry these initiatives one step further. Labour's campaign had been built around Harold Wilson's promise to "reforge Britain in the white hot heat of the scientific revolution". After a decade of struggle the Labour Party had embraced a rather technocratic vision of socialism which blamed Britain's economic problems on the Tories' outmoded Edwardian mentality and implied that socialists were much better placed to harness the energies of science and meritocracy (see Warde, 1982: ch. 3). Planning occupied a prominent place in this vision; therefore Wilson immediately established a new Department of Economic Affairs to draw up a National Plan and take on responsibility for long-term economic performance. He created a Ministry of Technology (Mintech) to administer some £200 million of research and development funds annually and supervise four high-technology industries: machine tools, computers, telecommunications, and electronics. At the end of 1966 he appointed an Industrial Reconstruction Corporation, with a capitalization of £150 million, to assist in the rationalization of British industry.

Both the Department of Economic Affairs and the National Plan were dismal failures, partly because they were never equipped with the tools required to enforce their proposals, and partly because unremitting pressure on sterling forced the Government into a series of deflationary measures that vitiated their overly optimistic plans. If the Government had devalued and deflated upon taking office, it might have pre-empted some of the balance of payments problems that continued to stymie its plans for growth. However, the DEA would still have lacked the means to implement its plans, since it had no microeconomic instruments of its own and was locked in battle with a Treasury that continued to control the direction of macroeconomic policy (Wilson, 1971: 893). The National Plan itself entailed no more than the promulgation of hastily conceived and wildly ambitious targets for growth that bore little relation to the actual trajectory of industrial sectors.

The operations of Mintech and the IRC proved to be a more important step in the development of policy. They initiated a measure of direct intervention into industrial affairs that was to remain a hallmark of subsequent policy. The IRC was specifically designed to promote mergers among British companies; and it ultimately supported or financed 50 such deals involving 150 companies. While some of the hybrids, such as British Leyland and Kent-Cambridge, subsequently performed poorly, a number succeeded in giving Britain viable firms in growth sectors (Hague and Wilkinson, 1983). From a comparative point of view the IRC suffered from two handicaps. It was a relatively small program, affecting only 50 of the 3400 mergers that took place in Britain while it was in operation; and an exclusive focus on mergers meant that it could not address many more fundamental problems of British industry (Young and Lowe, 1974: pt. II).

The Ministry of Technology became the central actor in a series of selective interventions sponsored by the Labour Government. It renationalized 14 steel companies in 1967, established a Shipbuilding Industry Board to support that industry, created International Computers Limited to lead the computer sector, and promoted a series of schemes for machine tools through the National Research Development Corporation (Young and Lowe, 1974: ch. 1). At the same time the National Board for Prices and Incomes was focusing national attention on the problem of achieving higher levels of productivity through the reform of work practices. In the words of the Prime Minister, the object was to take British industry "by the scruff of the neck and drag it kicking and screaming into the twentieth century" (Fry, 1975: 14).

Even in this period, which was the high-water mark of industrial intervention in Britain, however, the funds devoted to selective intervention were dwarfed by programs of regional aid and those whose subsidies were granted automatically to any firm undertaking certain kinds of investment. Over £300 million, for instance, was spent on regional aid in 1969–70. In France, at this time, these priorities were reversed; the bulk of industrial aid was selective, and only £15 million was spent on regional policy (Leruez, 1975: 188). Even under the Wilson Government in Britain, the largest portion of aid came in the form of tax breaks rather than subsidies. This concentration on non-selective aid was significant because it limited the extent to which the British state brought direct pressure to bear on industry to reorganize and rationalize its operations. Most firms could benefit from government subsidies without undertaking such action. The contrast with France is striking.

Under the Conservative Government of 1970–74 and the Labour Government of 1974–79 the pattern continued. Regional concerns and non-selective investment incentives continued to dominate policy. The Heath Government initially attempted to disengage the state from industrial intervention. The NBPI, IRC, and Ministry of Technology were abolished, and tax incentives again replaced investment grants. In the face of rising unemployment, however, a new Industry Act was passed in 1972 which provided for large industrial subsidies. Nevertheless, almost three-quarters of the funds spent under this Act went to non-selecive aid for the development areas.

In the 1970s the British state did begin to spend greater sums on selective aid to industry, as did all Western nations. However, the great bulk of these funds went to failing firms in the declining sectors of the economy. As such they were more a rearguard action than a frontal assault on the problems of the economy. Industrial bail-outs began with the state-sponsored formation of Upper Clyde Shipbuilders in 1967 and continued with aid to the Mersey Docks and Harbours Board, Birmingham Small Arms, Rolls Royce, Cammell Laird, and UCS under the Conservatives. Labour stepped in with massive subsidies to British Leyland, Chrysler, Rolls Royce, Alfred Herbert, Ferranti, and a variety of other firms. Over half of the initial £1 billion capitalization of the National Enterprise Board, the successor to the IRC, went to Rolls Royce and British Leyland. By contrast, the NEB's purchase of shares in 66 other firms was a minor matter.

It is noteworthy that the four planks in Labour's 1973 program that might have entailed direct intervention into the affairs of private industry were never implemented. Plans for a national investment bank to take a controlling interest in the top 25 British firms were replaced by the National Enterprise Board, modelled on the IRC, whose operation was to be considerably more circumspect and focused on failing enterprises. The proposal that all major firms should be forced to sign planning agreements with the state specifying their investment and modernization plans was never implemented. The recommendations of the Bullock Report that workers should be given one-third of the seats on the Board of Directors of firms with over 2000 employees were ultimately ignored. The opportunities available under the Industry Act of 1975 for the Secretary of State to obtain information from, and issue directives to, the private sector also went unused after Tony Benn was replaced as Secretary of State for Industry in June 1975.

Instead, the Government announced a "new industrial strategy" in November 1975 that was, once again, tripartite and resolutely voluntarist. The relevant White Paper observed that "The government must take the initiative in developing the industrial strategy, but the main task of seeing that it brings higher productivity in British industry must fall on unions and management" (Grant, 1980: 4). Under NEDC auspices, Sectoral Working Parties, composed mainly of employer and trade union representatives, were established in 39 industrial sectors. Their task was to stimulate industrial reorganization in order to achieve greater productivity, much as the EDCs had been asked to do before them. The outcome was very similar. In some cases the SWPs effectively lobbied the government for additional industrial aid; but in the few instances where their efforts resulted in new investment plans, most of the firms involved indicated they would have undertaken the investment regardless of SWP assistance. A careful review of the exercise indicates that it had very little impact on industrial reorganization, and concludes that "if a similar strategy is to be attempted in future, it will have to rely less on simple persuasion and more on modifying the behavior of key actors through the use of incentives and penalties" (Grant, 1980: 20).

In short, British industrial policy seems to have done little to modify the organization or work practices of British industry. It consistently left the initiative for rationalization up to private sector actors them-selves, and, faced with a relatively unchanged set of market incentives, they clung to traditional practices. Even where the government offered financial incentives for investment and the introduction of new tech-nology, its offers were only occasionally taken up. By 1978–79 over a quarter of the available funds for modernization remained unspent because the private sector had been unwilling to take advantage of the schemes (Grant, 1980: 10). An authoritative review concluded that, in Britain, "industrial policies seem limited to a peripheral role of tidying up the edges of the economy, rather than providing any central thrust to alter and improve industry's performance and that of the economy as a whole" (Mottershead, 1978: 483).

How can we account for this pattern of policy? Some argue that it derives from the British attachment to voluntaristic values that militate against state intervention in the economy (cf. Greenleaf, 1984). There may be some truth to this. A century of laissez-faire policies may have left a mark on the British political psyche; but the extensive interven-tion that we find even under nineteenth-century governments and the ease with which a post-war Labour Government nationalized large segments of industry seem to belie this view. We might find more tangible reasons in the longstanding doctrines of political parties, the organization of the state, and the balance of power in British society.

Political parties are the agents of collective purpose in a democracy (see Beer, 1969). As such they distill the multiple strands of social sentiment into concrete programs backed up by a particular moral vision. In Britain especially, these programs are not invented *de novo* every 5 years; rather they build on an accumulation of ideas, sifted by the party over decades into an electoral appeal. Although every few decades brings some strikingly innovative ideas, often designed to reforge the party's electoral coalition, even these tend to be founded on some set of longstanding partisan sentiments. Therefore it is instructive to consider the continuities in Britain's party platforms.

In so far as economic policy is concerned, we find that the two main British parties have offered the electorate a choice, but one limited to two rather specific packages. Those packages pose a hidden dilemma for industrial policy. On the one hand the Conservative Party has been concerned about the profitability of British industry but reluctant to countenance extensive state intervention into its affairs. Even the most radical economic policies that Conservative leaders have been willing to endorse in the post-war period – Keynesian demand management, social security transfers and regional development grants – have entailed no more than an arm's length relationship between the state and industry. On the other hand the Labour Party has been willing to consider interventionist policy, as its nationalization program indicates, but is far less enthusiastic about employing interventionist policy to increase the profitability of the private sector. Expressed in such blunt terms the dilemma may be slightly exaggerated, but there is a kernel of truth in it. Therefore the British electorate has never been offered the option taken up by the French or Japanese: a policy whereby the state employs an extensive array of sanctions and incentives to enforce modernization on industry so as to favor its most profitable and growing segments.

However, these terms also draw our attention to another set of limitations implicit in the organization of state–society relations. As we will see, the French state employs a panoply of sanctions to enforce its industrial strategy. The most potent of these stem from its control over the flows of funds in the financial system. This sort of instrument has not been available to the British state, partly because successive Governments have shied away from the nationalization of the banks, and partly because the Bank of England, which has some influence in this sector, retains considerable independence from the Government. Neither of these are immutable conditions. However, a Government does not embark casually on nationalization within the financial sector. It is the kind of policy for which a strong electoral coalition must be built; and the task was not accomplished at the opportune juncture immediately following the war. Therefore the absence of control over the flow of private investment has stood in the way of a more dirigiste industrial policy.

A third set of obstacles are present in the entrenched position of British producer groups. All the relevant studies suggest that the CBI does not have enough power to prevent a government from implementing measures to which it is clearly committed (Grant and Marsh, 1977; Blank, 1973). As one Cabinet Minister told William Keegan: "Whoever went to the country on the issue of how well they got on with the CBI?" (Keegan and Pennant-Rae, 1979: 128). However, the CBI's campaigns against even semi-interventionist measures, such as the 1972 Industry Act, Tony Benn's pursuit of planning agreements, and the recommendations of the Bullock Report, may have been of some significance to the outcome (Bruce-Gardyne, 1974; Coates, 1980: ch. 3; Hatfield, 1976). In particular, they shaped the climate of opinion within which all Governments weighed the economic benefits of potential policies against their electoral costs (see Crossman, 1975: II, 455).

The trade unions proved to be more important political actors. Since the persistence of traditional work practices seemed to be a significant component of Britain's poor economic performance, measures to improve the flexibility of industrial relations might well have merited a place on the political agenda. Time and time again, however, opposition from the trade union movement was sufficient to block alterations to the industrial relations system. Barbara Castle's attempt to implement some of the suggestions of the Donovan Commission on industrial relations in 1968–69 was effectively crushed by the unions, who feared that the proposals, outlined in a White Paper entitled "In Place of Strife," would erode their traditional autonomy in collective bargaining (Jenkins, 1970). Jack Jones, the powerful leader of the Transport and General Workers Union, told the Cabinet: "Let us face the reality. The question isn't whether our scheme works or your scheme works. It is the fact that our people won't accept Government intervention" (Castle, 1984: 661). He went on to explain that a rank-and-file revolt was entirely possible. The trade unions' influence over the Labour Party itself was decisive. A Cabinet colleague noted: "We spelt out to [Castle] what the situation was, how we couldn't possibly get the Bill through the Party and that this would mean that if we didn't withdraw it in time the Party would reject it" (Crossman, 1975: III, 519).

In 1971–74 the industrial strength of the unions alone was sufficient to prevent the Heath Government from implementing an Industrial Relations Act intended to enhance the authority of the trade union leadership *vis-à-vis* the rank-and-file, and to bring collective bargaining within a legal framework (Moran, 1977; Crouch, 1977; Holmes, 1982: ch. 2). Several dockers went to jail rather than obey the Act, and British employers proved reluctant to utilize its provisions for fear of the resulting industrial disruption. In the midst of a bitter conflict with the miners' union the Heath Government ultimately lost an election fought over "who rules Britain." However dubious the merits of these pieces of legislation, their failure went some way to explain why successive Governments were unwilling or unable to intervene forcefully in the sphere of industrial relations.

In the face of such powerfully organized producers' groups it is not surprising that British Governments should have attempted to negotiate industrial reorganization through tripartite arrangements. Whereas such negotiations were at best an adjunct to policy in France, they were central to the British pattern. The state lacked the capacities to proceed readily in any other way; and it faced the prospect of much stiffer opposition.

THE COLLAPSE OF THE KEYNESIAN CONSENSUS

The complex of policies described here as Keynesianism was devised, and then revised, in order to solve both economic and political problems. In Britain the Keynesian era came to a close when these policies proved increasingly inadequate to the economic challenges facing the nation and more productive of political problems than solutions. In the end the political dynamic which Keynesianism set in motion was decisive.

The beginning of the end came in the fall of 1973. The oil embargo and massive OPEC price increase that followed the Arab-Israeli war plunged the world into a prolonged recession. One nation after another attempted to revive its economy with a demand stimulus, only to find that unilateral expansion could not be sustained in an increasingly interdependent world. In medium-sized, open economies, such as Britain's, a stimulus brought inflation and an influx of imports that generated immediate balance of payments problems and an exchange rate crisis severe enough to force deflation again on the government.

The new Labour Government reflated in 1974–75 but largely through increases in social spending and public sector wages. As a result the cost of the oil price increase to the nation was borne primarily by the corporate sector, which received no tax relief until November 1975. Accordingly, consumer spending rose, but investment remained stagnant. Moreover the reflation temporarily started the economy growing again, but only at the cost of an inflation rate that reached 25 percent in the spring of 1975. The populace began to see inflation as a more serious problem than unemployment; and that endangered the postwar settlement which committed the government above all else to the maintenance of full employment.

In any case the Government was unable to prevent unemployment from rising. British economists discovered that the "multiplier" effect, which was supposed to magnify the impact of budgetary changes on consumer spending and national production, had fallen. Their attempts to revive the economy led to a massive balance of payments crisis in 1976, which forced policy-makers to choose between a radically protectionist strategy or recourse to the IMF. The Labour Government found itself unprepared to embark on a radical new strategy in the midst of an immediate crisis when the only officials with a detailed knowledge of the situation were urging a more cautious course. As a result an agreement was reached with the IMF in December 1976, which forced the state to make sweeping public expenditure cuts in 1977–78. That effectively eliminated any further scope for reflation. The Keynesians were like motorists repeatedly trying to start a car that had run out of gas.

In the ensuing 2 years, exchange-rate concerns, and their commitment to the IMF, forced the Government to pay increasing attention to the growth of the monetary aggregates at the expense of unemployment. While the popular view saw the power of the unions climbing in this period, the power of the financial sector actually grew more dramatically. The state's money supply targets were like hostages to fortune, forcing officials to take deflationary action whenever the City noticed a deviation from trend (Hall, 1982a).

Prime Minister James Callaghan delivered a speech to the 1976 Labour Party Conference that might well have been the obituary for Keynesianism in Britain:

> We used to think that you could spend your way out of a recession and increase employment by cutting taxes and boosting government spending. I tell you in all candour that that option no longer exists. . . . The cosy world we were told would go on forever, where full employment would be guaranteed by a stroke of the Chancellor's pen, cutting taxes, deficit spending, that cosy world is gone (Labour Party, 1976: 188).

In the face of global recession, growing rigidities in the domestic economy, and international economic interdependence, the scope for demand management in Britain, while perhaps not exhausted, seemed far more limited than before.

The second fateful development in fall 1973 came when the Heath Government entered into a bitter confrontation with the National Union of Mineworkers. Rather than meet their demand for a 30 percent wage increase, well above the existing incomes policy guidelines, Heath decided to try to outlast a strike, putting the nation on a 3-day workweek in December, and ultimately calling an election on the issue for February 1974. He lost that election narrowly, and the new Labour Government met the union demands; but the experience helped to turn both the Conservative Party and much of the electorate into critics of the political power of the trade unions.

The 1975 crisis was sufficiently evident to inspire the Labour Government and trade unions to agree on a serious incomes policy. However, the Government spent the next 4 years attempting to claw back the increases in public expenditure it had blithely authorized in 1974–75; and partly for this reason, it remained unable to prevent unemployment from rising inexorably. Therefore it could offer the unions no real *quid pro quo* for wage restraint and, as the immediate crisis passed, they were bound to become increasingly disillusioned with the fruits of the social contract. Two decades of conflict between the unions and the state over incomes policy culminated in a 'winter of discontent' during 1978–79, when several public sector unions openly defied the incomes policy. For a period they shut down the hospitals, graveyards, and garbage collections across England. These moves intensified growing public reaction against neo-corporatism in Britain. By 1979, 79 percent of the electorate and over 50 percent of trade unionists themselves believed that the trade unions had too much power in Britain.

As a result many people began to search for a way of managing the economy that did not entail repeated industrial conflict and a constant series of tripartite negotiations with producers groups. In part they wanted to restore the authority of the state. Its power over the economy seemed to have been diminished by the unions at home and the central bankers abroad. Many of those casting about for an alternative began to see advantages in a set of economic doctrines associated with 'monetarism'.

The central contention of monetarist economics was that the rate of inflation could be controlled if the government maintained a reasonably low rate of growth of the money supply. Since the latter was supposed to be directly linked to the size of the PSBR, the doctrine implied that budgetary deficits should not generally be used to stimulate the economy. In any case, that was unnecessary because monetarists saw the economy as inherently stable (in striking contrast to Keynes) and unemployment as the result of overly high wages rather than a deficiency of demand (see Chrystal, 1979; Cuthbertson, 1979).

The policy implications were clear. There was no need for the government to employ demand management to stabilize the economy. It could not reduce unemployment by doing so in any case. Discretionary policy should be replaced by adherence to a few simple rules that dictated the appropriate rate of growth of the money supply. If these rules were apparent to all, they would warn the unions off excessive pay settlements because, with restricted monetary growth, those would only result in rising unemployment. At the same time the exchange rate, which was quite sensitive to relative rates of national monetary growth, would be stabilized, and Britain's need for foreign borrowing reduced.

Although they were supported by a considerable technical apparatus, the monetarist ideas were simple. In fact they were very similar to the neo-classical doctrines that Keynes had argued against and replaced. Because the Keynesian and monetarist economic paradigms depended on quite different assumptions, however, they were largely incommensurable. That is to say, their validity could not be fully established by econometric simulations (Hall, 1982b). Acceptance was largely a matter of faith.

Partly for that reason, monetarist doctrine made little headway among professional economists in Britain. A few prominent figures at Manchester University, the London School of Economics, the London Business School, and Liverpool became advocates of monetarism. But the vast majority of British economists, including virtually the entire upper echelons of the Treasury, remained resolute Keynesians throughout the 1970s. This might be attributable in part to the centrality of forecasting within Treasury procedures. Policy-making, by this time, revolved around econometric simulations on a Keynesian model for which there were no good monetarist substitutes.

In such a situation, as perhaps with the case of Keynesianism 40 years before, those who accepted monetarism were primarily those with an interest in its prescriptions. Most prominent among these were City economists who found monetarist analyses helpful for understanding the relationships they had to predict between the monetary aggregates. However, many others in the City also found monetarist prescriptions conveniently congruent with their existing preferences for restrictive monetary policy and firmly anti-inflationary measures. One prominent stockbroker described the subsequent diffusion of monetarist ideas in these terms:

> It is monetarism as a fashion rather than as an economic theory which has gripped the City. We are businessmen and solicitors, not economists, and 'controlling the money supply' has the same intuitive appeal today that 'priming the pump' had in the heyday of Keynesianism, twenty years ago (Hall, 1982a: 469).

As the official most sensitive to City concerns, the Governor of the Bank of England was the first major policy-maker to accept monetarist ideas, at a time when the Bank's own economic department remained largely Keynesian. He attributed this to "the layman's apparently intuitive perception of the broad relationship between monetary growth and inflation – perhaps clearer to him than to the professional who knows all the necessary qualifications" (*Bank of England Quarterly Bulletin*, March 1978: 34). Beginning in 1976 he became an influential advocate for monetary control within the state.

Monetarism was embraced most avidly of all by a group of Conservative politicians who were seeking a weapon against the neo-corporatism of recent years. The Conservatives had always been divided between old Tories, who saw nothing wrong with some state intervention, and those who held a more laissez-faire set of beliefs. The former had led the Party for most the post-war period; but in 1975 Margaret Thatcher defeated Edward Heath for the leadership, and the balance within the Party shifted. Thatcher's views on policy were not a major issue in the leadership campaign; she was the beneficiary of dissatisfaction with Heath that became apparent too late for several others to mount a successful challenge (Behrens, 1980; Stephenson, 1980). However, with the help of Sir Keith Joseph she wasted no time in pulling the Party toward a monetarist point of view.

For the Conservatives, monetarism was a godsend. It seemed to confirm and justify what many had always believed: optimal economic performance could be achieved with a minimum of intervention in the economy. "Rules rule" was the graffiti scribbled in one City toilet. The doctrine was aimed most directly at inflation – the aggregate that captured center-stage in the 1970s. More important yet, it seemed to suggest that inflation could be reduced without any need to bargain with the trade unions. Their influence over policy and the economy could be minimized. Many Conservative spokesmen suggested that by adhering to a strict rule for monetary growth the rate of inflation would fall regardless of the unions' actions. One school of monetarists, who attributed 'rational expectations' to economic actors, assumed that the unions would automatically limit their wage claims in the face of a monetary rule because they know that unemployment would otherwise result. The prospect of lower inflation without rising unemployment was the magic that monetarism seemed to promise. Others realized that wage claims would be reduced only after unemployment had risen, but were perfectly willing to see such an outcome. Either seemed a more desirable alternative to tripartism, and a method for breaking the power of the trade unions.

The movement of the Conservative Party toward monetarism was ultimately the most significant factor in the collapse of the Keynesian consensus. In 1979 Thatcher was to form a Government and embark on a determined monetarist experiment. But even on the left, the Keynesian consensus was breaking down.

The Labour Party found itself caught in a political pincer. As inflation became a more serious problem, Labour Governments had come under increasing pressure to come up with a viable anti-inflationary policy. They had settled on a negotiated incomes policy as the solution. In keeping with this the Party gradually began to base a larger portion of its electoral appeal on the ability to secure industrial peace and a viable accommodation with the trade unions (Panitch, 1975). However, several developments during the 1970s undermined this strategy. The unions became progressively more hostile to such a policy, as they saw what it entailed. The right to participate in the kind of constrained policy-making that seemed possible in the recession of the 1970s was not particularly attractive to union leaders; and their followers, whose acquiescence was vital to the success of any incomes policy, were increasingly unwilling to trade tangible wage gains for more nebulous concessions on the macroeconomic front.

One solution might have been to give the unions greater leverage over investment decisions in the economy and policy-making in return for their assent to an incomes policy. That was the Swedish path (Martin, 1979); but two factors militated against such a solution. The fragmented organization of the British union movement made it unlikely that union leaders could enforce wage restraint in return for this concession; and the electorate was growing more hostile to the prospect of greater union power over the direction of the economy. The Labour Party was caught in a serious bind.

In the face of such dilemmas the Party divided into two camps. One, most represented within the Parliamentary Labour Party, continued to advocate an incomes policy and was ready to contemplate the use of sanctions to enforce one. The other, led from the constituencies, accused the 1974–79 Labour Government of retreating from the interventionist industrial policies of the 1973 program and imposing an arbitrary wages policy on the unions. This group sought a more protectionist strategy of reflation behind tariff barriers coupled with an aggressive industrial policy, which they hoped would make an incomes policy unnecessary. As Michael Foot, the new Party leader, presided helplessly, the two sides began to clash at the 1977–78 Party Conferences over issues of internal party democracy; and many of those on the right ultimately broke away to form a new Social Democratic Party in 1981 (see Kogan and Kogan, 1983). From that point forward the Conservatives benefited from a seriously divided opposition.

It should be clear that Keynesianism ultimately collapsed in Britain as much for political as economic reasons. Since demand management alone was not effective against inflation, an incomes policy became the indispensable supplement to Keynesianism. Given the organization of the British labor movement, however, the implementation of an incomes policy was bound to be conflictual and short-lived. Instead of enhancing the effectiveness of the state, Britain's fitful experience with neo-corporatism gradually undermined its authority. Once again, the political disadvantages of a policy were more fateful than its economic benefits.

Similarly, monetarism triumphed in Britain, not as economic science, but as a political ideology. Its validity could not be proven in scientific terms, but to those who were seeking some way to restore the authority of the state it seemed to offer a solution. Rules would replace discretion and endless negotiation. It was also a doctrine designed to justify an attack on the power of the unions. At best they would have to accommodate themselves to a more deflationary macroeconomic policy. At worst it rationalized the use of rising unemployment as a weapon of labor discipline. In British politics that marked the end of an era based upon the Beveridge Report and the post-war settlement. It is to the new era that we now turn.

5

The Conservative Experiment of Margaret Thatcher

On 3 May 1979 the British people initiated a national economic experiment by electing a Conservative Government under Margaret Thatcher. The Conservatives came into office on a platform repudiating the Keynesian consensus that had underpinned British policy-making since the war. Sir Keith Joseph initiated the rethinking of party policy with a wide-ranging attack on the policies of the defeated Heath Government at Preston on 4 September 1974; and over the next 5 years, Margaret Thatcher turned his ideas into party policy, as she consolidated her grip on the leadership (Joseph, 1976).[1] The Party's new position combined a political critique of growing state intervention based on theories of 'political overload' with an economic critique of Keynesianism founded on monetarist conceptions of the economy (Thatcher, 1980).

Tapping a longstanding strain in Conservative thinking, Thatcher argued that the British state had grown too large. As its involvement in the economy had increased, the efficiency of state activity had diminished. In the industrial arena especially, the government was undertaking too many projects that could be accomplished more effectively by the private sector. To fund a welfare state that the nation could not afford, past Governments had raised taxes to a level that were sapping the work incentives of many Britons. Therefore, public expenditure and the scale of government activity had to be reduced to make room for reductions in taxation; and many traditional state activities should be returned to the private sector. That entailed selling off many of the nationalized industries, contracting-out services currently performed by public employees, and reducing the stock of public housing by selling council houses and encouraging private rather than public ownership of housing.

Inspired by the work of monetarist economists, Thatcher went on to argue that rising levels of inflation were caused primarily by inordinate increases in the money supply that followed from excessive public sector deficits. Keynesian attempts to sustain economic growth through the management of aggregate demand had failed. They simply raised public deficits and the rate of inflation, fostering uncertainty and low levels of investment rather than growth. Therefore growth without inflation was most likely to be obtained if the government adhered to rigid targets for monetary growth and maintained a low public sector borrowing requirement (PSBR) whatever the state of the economy.

For these reasons Thatcher also believed that the incomes policies that had accompanied Keynesian economic management were unlikely to reduce the rate of inflation. They simply reinforced the power of the trade unions; and trade union power itself was one of the principal sources of Britain's economic decline because it inhibited economic innovation and maintained wages at internationally uncompetitive levels. Therefore one of the Government's principal objects should be to reduce the bargaining power of the trade unions in both the industrial and political arenas. That entailed a retreat from neo-corporatist arrangements for bargaining with producers groups, and legislation to limit the facility with which trade unions could mount strike action.

On rational expectations grounds, several analysts argued that the promulgation of a credible monetary target would lead workers to reduce their wage demands automatically out of the knowledge that to do otherwise would price them out of a job in a tight monetary environment. The result was a set of policies that seemed to solve many problems at once.

Monetary control could be presented as a method for reducing inflation that need not entail any sacrifice of growth or higher levels of unemployment. In 1980 one of Thatcher's most influential advisors told a House of Commons Committee that "on the assumption that policies are properly understood when they are announced and implemented, the disturbance to output and employment from reduction in the money supply and in the PSBR will be minimal" (House of Commons, 1980: 142). The strategy could also be seen as a method for disciplining the workforce that did not require extensive bargains or agonizing rounds of strikes of the sort that had been threatening the authority of the state. On the contrary, there was a nice sense of automatic justice to the operation of monetarism, as originally presented. In the face of a tight monetary constraint, the adverse consequences of excessive wage settlements were supposed to fall on precisely those who had perpetrated them. As Sir Geoffrey Howe, the Government's initial Chancellor of the Exchequer, put it: "if workers and their representatives take pay decisions which are unwise because they seek too much, they will find they have crippled their employers and gravely harmed themselves by destroying their own jobs" (Holmes, 1985: 98).

Although the vast majority of British economists did not subscribe to these views, the platform had a great deal of electoral appeal: lower taxes, the termination of incomes policies, and council house sales were popular with the electorate (Crewe, 1980). Moreover, by merging the sophisticated arguments of economic theorists into the political prescriptions of neo-conservative thought, the program seemed to display a coherence and credibility that no other critique of Keynesianism had yet attained. Margaret Thatcher sounded authoritative when she said: "Some say I preach merely the homilies of housekeeping or the parables of the parlour. But I do not repent. Those parables would have saved many a financier from failure and many a country from crisis" (Riddell, 1983: 7).

After three decades of convergence in political programs the British party system again functioned as an agency of innovation. Following a palace coup within the Conservative Party the electorate faced a clear choice in 1979; and 5 years of mediocre economic performance under Labour, culminating in the "winter of discontent," persuaded them to take a chance on a radical break with the past. Six years into the experiment we can now ask: to what degree have the Conservatives been able to implement the policies they intended, and what political and economic consequences have followed?

MACROECONOMIC POLICY, 1979–86

Thatcher came into office with an ambitious macroeconomic program. Her principal goals were: to limit the rate of growth of the money supply, to reduce the size of the public sector deficit, to cut total public spending, and to lower levels of taxation. However, none of these is an easy task, and it is often particularly difficult to attain multiple goals simultaneously. As a result the Government made slow progress, and soon found that it had to establish an order of priority among these goals.

When updated Treasury estimates became available to the new government in 1979, Ministers discovered that public spending was rising much more rapidly than anticipated. As a result the maximum spending cuts feasible in the short term would not make room for substantial reductions in total taxation and the PSBR at the same time. Therefore the Prime Minister decided to give priority to reductions in the PSBR by balancing income tax reductions with corresponding increases in expenditure taxes.

The June 1979 budget lowered the tax rate on higher incomes from 83 to 60 percent and the standard rate of income tax from 33 to 30 percent; but it increased the value-added tax (VAT) on consumer expenditure from 8 to 15 percent and allowed the nationalized industries to charge substantially more for their products. Public spending was to be cut by 2 percent (£1.5 billion) in 1979–80 and by 6 percent (£4.2 billion) in 1980–81. As a result the PSBR fell from 5.5 percent of GDP in 1978–79 to 4.8 percent in 1979–80. That represented a tightening of the fiscal stance. Monetary policy was even more contractionary. The Minimum Lending Rate was raised from 12 to 14 percent when the Government took office, and it was raised again to a record high of 17 percent in November 1979.

Despite deteriorating economic conditions the Government held fast to its strategy through the budget of March 1980. Once again, fiscal and monetary policy remained contractionary so that the PSBR and rate of growth of the monetary aggregates could be reduced. The centerpiece of policy was a document setting out the Government's Medium-Term Financial Strategy (MTFS). It proposed further increases in taxation and reductions in spending so that the PSBR could be reduced from 3.8 percent of GDP in 1980–81 to 1.5 percent of GDP in 1983–84 regardless of the underlying state of the economy (see table's 5.1 and 5.2). The Government's goal was to make deep cuts in public spending early on in its term, so that tax reductions could follow just before the next election. Publication of the MTFS was designed to demonstrate the Government's determination to stick to its promised course and therby influence the expectations of private sector actors. Certainty about the Government's plans was supposed to encourage businessmen to invest and to discourage workers from making excessive wage demands

It should be apparent that the government was no longer taking a Keynesian approach to economic management. Keynesians vary the fiscal and monetary stance over the short term in response to fluctuations in the underlying rate of growth of output. By contrast, this Government was adhering to rigid monetary and fiscal targets regardless of the deteriorating state of the real economy. As one Bank of England official put it: "It was after that [1980] budget that I began to take them seriously. They meant it. They were concentrating on intermediate targets and variables like M3 and the PSBR, and not, like every other government since the war, on output and employment" (quoted in Keegan, 1984: 145).

Moreover, the Conservative strategy was beginning to depart radically from the neo-conservative policies of the Reagan administration in America. Initially the two regimes seemed to have similar approaches to the economy. Their electoral platforms both argued for monetary restraint and cuts in public expenditure and taxation. However, both soon discovered that reductions in social spending were difficult to achieve. At that point President Reagan made cuts in taxation his first priority, and accepted record increases in the public sector deficit to make room for these and higher levels of military spending. Margaret Thatcher chose to forgo tax cuts in order to lower the public sector

Table 5.1   Public spending, public borrowing and taxation as a percentage of GDP, 1974–84

Financial year	Public Spending (% of GDP)	General government borrowing requirement (% of GDP)	Taxation and National Insurance contributions (% of GDP)
1974–75	50.1	8.2	35.6
1975–76	50.6	9.0	36.2
1976–77	48.8	5.6	35.8
1977–78	44.5	3.3	34.6
1978–79	45.0	5.2	33.7
1979–80	44.6	5.0	34.9
1980–81	47.4	5.8	35.9
1981–82	47.6	3.3	38.7
1982–83	48.0	3.6	38.5
1983–84	47.6	3.3	38.3
1984–85	47.0	2.9	39.0
Average 1974–79	47.8	6.3	35.2
Average 1979–85	47.0	4.0	37.6

Sources: Central Statistical Office, *Economic Trends* (Aug. 1985).

Table 5.2   The 1980 Medium-term financial strategy compared with out-turns (% of GDP)

Financial year	General government expenditure		General government receipts		PSBR	
	Plan	Out-turn	Plan	Out-turn	Plan	Out-turn
1980–81	46.6	45.8	42.2	40.1	3.8	5.4
1981–82	43.8	46.2	40.5	43.0	3.0	3.3
1982–83	45.6	47.2	43.0	43.4	2.3	3.2
1983–84	42.3	45.7	40.5	42.1	1.5	3.2

Sources: Gavyn Davies, "The macroeconomic record of the Conservatives". Paper presented at the Center for European Studies, Harvard University, 1985; CSO, *Economic Trends*, various issues.

deficit. While America experienced a Keynesian stimulus under the guise of 'supply-side economics', the British Government pursued much more austere economic policies.

By the end of 1980, however, it became apparent that the British economy was experiencing a severe recession. The rate of unemployment doubled between 1979 and 1981. GDP fell by 2.2 percent in 1980 and 1.1 percent in 1981. In particular the rapid appreciation of sterling on the foreign exchanges was undermining the competitiveness of British industry. The effective exchange rate of sterling rose by 10 percent between 1979 and 1981 and British competitiveness declined by 16 percent. The best available estimates suggest that about one-tenth of that increase can be attributed to the effects of North Sea oil production (Buiter and Miller, 1983: 319; cf. Alt, 1985). International confidence in the Thatcher Government may also account for some of the rise; but it is likely that the high level of interest rates in Britain was responsible for much of it (Davies, 1985: 13). Indeed, the Thatcher Government initially encouraged the appreciation of sterling in the hope that it would reduce domestic inflation. 'International' monetarists, among whom the Government's new Chief Economic Advisor was prominent, believed that a rising exchange rate was the principal mechanism whereby a tight monetary policy would reduce inflation (cf. Conservative Party, 1977).

At the same time the Government was finding it far more difficult than they had expected to control the rate of monetary growth. Despite penal interest rates and targets for the growth of sterling M3 of 7–11 percent in 1980–81 and 6–10 percent in 1981–82, that aggregate grew by 17.7 percent in 1980–81 and 14.1 percent in 1981–82. This did not reflect a loose monetary policy. By conventional measures the supply of money remained quite restricted. Instead, the demand for money was rising as businesses, suffering a severe liquidity squeeze in the face of rising wage rates and falling competitiveness, desperately sought bank loans to stay afloat. But the rise in the monetary aggregates caused consternation within the Government. Thatcher pressed the Bank of England to come up with new mechanisms for monetary control, since the traditional 'corset' on bank lending had been lifted in 1980; and a host of new measures for the money supply were devised.

Meanwhile the Confederation of British Industry began to express serious concern about the state of manufacturing. In October 1980 its Director-General threatened the Government with a "bare-knuckle fight" unless interest rates were lowered and the economy expanded (Keegan, 1984: 155). Even the Chairman of ICI, one of the Prime Minister's favorite companies, went to No. 10 Downing Street to warn the Government about the losses the firm was sustaining. More important, perhaps, the Prime Minister's new economics advisor, Alan Walters, argued that monetary policy was too tight.

As a result policy changed slightly, beginning in 1981. Officials decided that the exchange rate should be encouraged to fall, and that a more flexible monetary policy would be conducive to this end. Accordingly, the Government accommodated the existing rates of monetary growth by promulgating new targets from higher base points and in 1982 began to employ a mixed set of indicators rather than a single monetary aggregate as the target variable. Monetary policy remained restrictive, but the exchange rate was eased down. Even this small shift in emphasis was important to a Government whose economic philosophy had been built around monetary control.

At the same time the Chancellor argued that fiscal policy had to remain contractionary in order to permit some relaxation of monetary policy. The 1981 budget reduced MLR from 14 to 12 percent but raised the personal tax burden by failing to adjust tax thresholds upwards in line with inflation, as recent governments had done. The 1981–82 PSBR was expected to be £10.5 billion, itself a contractionary stance in the midst of recession; but government departments, anxious to stay within the new cash limits on their expenditure, failed to spend as much as planned so that the PSBR ultimately came in £1.5 billion below target.

By the spring of 1981, Margaret Thatcher's insistence on a contractionary fiscal stance in the face of continuing recession finally provoked a small revolt within the Cabinet. Her failure to secure all the public spending cuts she sought forced the Government to announce that expenditure totals for 1982–83 would be £5 billion more than originally planned. But Thatcher took revenge by dismissing several moderates (or 'wets' as *The Times* had called them) and promoting Ministers known to be loyal monetarists, in September 1981. The 1982 budget again accepted some overshooting of the monetary targets but stuck to a tight fiscal stance.

As the rate of price inflation fell below the rate of wage increases and consumers began to spend a greater proportion of their income, domestic economic activity began to pick up in 1983. Anticipating an election, the Chancellor also included a modest series of tax cuts in the budget of March 1983 that loosened the fiscal stance by raising tax thresholds and allowances slightly more than necessary to match inflation. By no means was this a repudiation of prior policy. The Government simply took advantage of the room for maneuver gained from stringent policy in 1979–82 to undertake a very limited expansion. Some commentators have argued that the modest growth of the British economy in 1983–84 is largely attributable to this loosening of policy (Davies, 1985: 6).

Despite an improvement in the rate of growth, however, unemployment continued to rise in 1984–85. Nigel Lawson, the new Chancellor of the Exchequer, was concerned about this problem but refused to accept the Keynesian view that it could be rectified by expansionary macroeconomic policy. Instead, he told the nation that rising levels of unemployment resulted from real wages that were too high and rigidities in the labor market. On this view unemployment could not be addressed by macroeconomic policy. It would fall only when workers accepted lower real wages and when microeconomic measures were taken to eliminate the labor market rigidities (such as union power) that fostered high wages (Lawson, 1984).

Table 5.3   The British fiscal stance, 1974–84

Change from previous year in % potential GDP	Structural budget balance			Inflation-adjusted structural budget balance		
	UK	EEC	OECD	UK	EEC	OECD
1974	0.1	0.5	−0.3	−1.7	−1.0	−1.1
1975	−0.5	1.3	1.6	−3.7	0.8	1.5
1976	0.2	−0.5	−0.5	3.0	−0.1	−0.2
1977	−1.7	−0.9	−0.2	−1.3	0.8	−0.4
1978	2.1	1.2	0.6	5.7	−2.5	1.0
1979	−0.6	0.1	−0.2	−2.7	−0.8	−0.7
1980	−2.0	−0.8	−0.1	−3.4	−1.8	−0.7
1981	−3.0	0.4	−0.4	−0.4	1.0	0.0
1982	−1.5	−0.7	0.3	−0.1	−0.3	0.7
1983	1.7	−0.5	0.1	3.0	0.0	0.4
1984	−0.3	−0.7	−0.2	−0.3	−0.3	−0.1
Cumulative						
1974–78	0.2	1.6	0.2	2.0	−2.0	0.8
1979–84	−5.7	−2.2	−0.5	−3.9	−2.2	−0.4

Sources: Gavyn Davies, "The macroeconomic record of the Conservatives". Paper presented to a Conference on the Thatcher Government and British Political Economy, Harvard University, 19 April 1985; Richard Price and Patrice Muller, "Structural budget indicators and the interpretation of fiscal stance in OECD economies", *OECD Economic Studies* (Autumn 1984).

Note: Negative numbers indicate fiscal tightening.

Therefore the fiscal stance of the 1984 and 1985 budgets remained slightly contractionary and interest rates remained high (table 5.3). Macroeconomic policy was still driven by concerns about inflation on the premise that lower wage rates were the only viable route toward long-term growth. To deal with unemployment, the 1984 and 1985 budgets concentrated on manpower programs and tax changes designed to encourage employers to hire additional staff. Corporate taxes and employers' national insurance charges were reduced; and tax allowances that favoured capital investment over labor force increases were repealed. The Government's employment policy was activist but decidedly microeconomic.

INDUSTRIAL RELATIONS POLICY

As we have seen, most post-war British Governments dealt with inflation by entering into an intricate series of negotiations with the trade
unions. In return for a measure of wage restraint the state traded
economic policy concessions designed to reduce the level of unemployment, raise the social wage, and strengthen the unions' bargaining
position on the shopfloor. Although they were usually short-lived and
not always successful, neo-corporatist attempts to bargain with the
unions became a feature of Britain's full employment economy.

When Margaret Thatcher came to office the full employment conditions that had underpinned this system of bargaining were already in
decay. In the wake of the 1974 recession the Government was no longer
able to deliver full employment in return for wage restraint; and further
extensions of the social wage could be financed only by higher taxes on
precisely those who were being asked to exercise wage restraint. Both
the electorate and the negotiating parties were becoming disillusioned
with neo-corporatist practice.

However, Thatcher repudiated the system directly: "No Government
should bind itself by an agreement with a minority sectoral interest so as
to lose its freedom of action on matters affecting all the people of the
land" (Kahn, 1985: 27). One of the principal objectives of her administration was to reduce the power of the trade unions in both industrial
and political arenas.

Partly because some Ministers believed that a tight monetary policy
alone might discipline the unions, the Government took few direct steps
to counteract inflationary wage claims during its first year in office. To
honor an electoral promise, Thatcher even granted the large public
sector pay increases that the Clegg Commission had recommended
before she came to office. As a result the public sector wage bill
increased by 25 percent in 1979 and the rate of inflation hit 22 percent in
the spring of 1980. That, in turn, induced a sharp change in Government
policy. While continuing to reject tripartite bargaining, Thatcher
resolved to resist public sector wage demands and industrial action on
lay-offs more vigorously.

The Iron and Steel Trades Confederation were the first to suffer from
this policy. After a bitter strike in 1980 they were forced to accept a cut
in real wages and a reorganization scheme that allowed British Steel to
reduce its workforce from 209,000 to 81,000 over a period of 5 years.
The general civil service unions then lost an extended dispute in 1981,
although the government retreated before resistance from the National
Union of Mineworkers to a plan for extensive pit closures. In 1982,
however, the government successfully fought lengthy battles with the
National Union of Railwaymen and National Health Service employ-

ees. By 1984 it felt sufficiently strong to resist an all-out strike by the National Union of Mineworkers against another pit closure scheme; and after a year of bitter industrial action that brought daily clashes between picketing miners and brigades of police, the NUM gave in, reluctantly accepting a scheme that was supposed to eliminate 70,000 jobs by 1988. The Government's policy of active resistance to public sector pay disputes had been remarkably successful.

One of the factors behind its success was undoubtedly the rising rate of unemployment. Although the promulgation of a monetary target itself seems to have had no discernible impact on union expectations, the government's tight fiscal and monetary policies contributed to a recession which raised the number of jobless from 1.2 million in 1979 to over 4 million in 1984. Just as the classic literature on the subject predicted, rising levels of unemployment weakened the bargaining power of the unions dramatically. The Trades Union Congress lost 17 percent of its members in 5 years, mainly to the ranks of the unemployed; and even the outgoing Permanent Secretary of the Treasury was prompted to observe that "What has emerged in shop-floor behavior through fear and anxiety is much greater than I think could have been achieved by more cooperative methods" (*The Times*, 31 March 1983).

The third prong of the Government's strategy against the unions was a series of legislative acts designed to weaken the unions *vis-à-vis* employers, and to increase the influence of rank and file sentiment over union leaders. The Employment Acts of 1980 and 1982 eliminated the workers' right to picket beyond their own place of work, rendered it more difficult for unions to secure closed-shop agreements, significantly limited the number of workers eligible to appeal dismissal to labor tribunals, outlawed the practice of letting contracts only to unionized firms, and rendered the unions liable for damages of up to £250,000 for each breach of these laws. In effect these Acts annulled many of the legal immunities that the union movement had acquired under the Trades Disputes Act of 1906.

Under this legislation and the 1984 Trade Union Act, the unions were also compelled to seek majority approval from a secret ballot of rank-and-file members before holding a strike or contributing to a political fund; and they were required to elect their leadership through secret ballot of the membership. These measures were designed to render the trade unions more democratic; but the Government also hoped that the membership would prove more moderate than existing union leaders on most questions, and thus less likely to challenge employers or the state. Although hotly contested by the unions, and perhaps less important than the rising level of unemployment, these measures certainly contributed to the erosion of trade union power in Britain.

INDUSTRIAL POLICY

In Opposition, many Conservatives had been very critical of British industrial policy. They argued that government intervention in industry was almost invariably inefficient and should be rolled back. Public funds could be saved and industry rendered more competitive if the nationalized industries were forced to make a profit or reprivatized, and grants to 'lame ducks' in the private sector were abolished (Conservative Party, 1977; Joseph, 1976). The Party's basic approach to industry seemed to herald a return to the policies of laissez-faire pursued in the latter half of the nineteenth century; and the appointment of Sir Keith Joseph as Secretary of State for Industry in 1979 confirmed the priority that Thatcher gave to this goal.

In practice, however, Thatcher's industrial policy has been a good deal more complicated. There are really two sides to it. On one hand, the Government has made a remarkable attempt to reduce government intervention in the economy by selling off many of the nationalized industries and reducing the funds available to the private sector. On the other hand, in those areas where the Government remains involved in industry, its actions have been much more selective and directed than the policies of its predecessors. After rejecting macroeconomic manipulation as a solution to Britain's economic problems, the Thatcher Government began to show renewed interest in microeconomic measures designed to reinvigorate the economy.

The most striking component of industrial policy is the reprivatization program. By the end of 1985 at least 50 percent of the shares in over a dozen companies formerly under state ownership had been sold to the private sector. The list includes: British Aerospace, Cable and Wireless, Amersham International, the National Freight Company, Britoil, Associated British Ports, International Aeradio, British Rail Hotels, Enterprise Oil, Sealink, Jaguar, British Gas Onshore Oil, and British Telecom. To date, 400,000 jobs have been transferred to the private sector and another eight firms are to be sold before 1988, taking a total of 600,000 jobs off the public rolls. If this program is fully accomplished the share of state industries in total national production will have fallen from 10.5 percent in 1979 to 6.5 percent by 1988.

Reprivatization serves multiple purposes. The Government raised over £7 billion between 1979 and 1985 from these sales; without them its macroeconomic strategy would have necessitated further tax increases or public spending cuts. And it hopes to raise another £10 billion before 1988, much of it from the sale of British Gas. Of course, Ministers also hope that these firms will be more efficient under private ownership. In view of the fact that shareholders tend to vote Conservative, they are also interested in broadening the number of shareholders in the British population beyond the present 3 percent (compared with 20 percent in the United States). The Financial Secretary in charge of reprivatization announced that it "will produce an irreversible shift in attitudes and achievement which will bring lasting benefits to the United Kingdom" and Margaret Thatcher herself has said that "We need to create a mood where it is everywhere thought morally right for as many people as possible to acquire capital" (*The Economist*, 19 October 1985: 70; McFadyean and Renn, 1984: 15).

However, there are some residual problems with reprivatization. Many of the companies are doing quite well under private ownership, but these are mostly firms that were also profitable under state management. The state has also now lost the revenues they might have brought to the public coffers in the coming years. Moreover, the sales do not seem to have broadened the pattern of share ownership in Britain substantially. Many of the individuals who initially bought British Telecom shares, for instance, have sold them to large institutional investors. Most important, many of the privatized firms, like British Telecom, British Gas, the British Airports Authority, and the Thames Water Authority, hold natural monopolies over critical areas of the economic infrastructure. Attempts to open up these fields to further competition may well prove counterproductive, and there is a danger that their monopoly position may be exploited unduly for private gain. Although the activities of such firms will be regulated, it is not clear that regulation is any more efficient in these areas than nationalization.

It will be some years before the consequences of reprivatization can be assessed fully. We can probably assume that these firms will be at least as efficient under private ownership as under state management; and preceding governments rarely employed the nationalized industries for broader social purposes. In that sense the program is likely to bring a net gain to the British economy. In areas of natural monopoly, however, privatization may well redistribute income from consumers to private shareholders.

In a similar vein the Thatcher Government has also loosened the regulatory framework within which the private sector operates. It has reduced the amount of statistical material that firms are required to supply to the government, albeit at the cost of losing some aggregate economic information. For the first time in many years, competition was allowed in long-distance bus services, apparently to the benefit of both producers and consumers. Small businesses, in particular, have also been relieved of many planning restrictions. Twenty-four urban areas have been declared 'enterprise zones', in which planning restrictions have been lifted and tax relief granted to businesses that relocate there. In their first 17 months about 4500 new jobs were created in these zones; but critics charge that these are jobs drawn away from neighboring areas rather than new positions (cf. Riddell, 1983: 184).

If these measures alone comprised the Conservative Government's industrial policy, we might well see it as an exercise in laissez-faire. However, there has also been an important interventionist component to policy. That was most evident in the Government's approach to the nationalized industries. In 1979–81 Sir Keith Joseph channelled large sums of money to the unprofitable public enterprises. British Leyland, the British Steel Corporation, and British Shipbuilders all received substantial infusions of capital; and several private firms were rescued with public funds, taking Department of Industry expenditure from £1 billion in 1978–79 to £2 billion in 1981–82. Initially it looked as if the nation's most prominent critic of 'lame ducks' had become, like his predecessors, another patron of handicapped waterfowl.

However, it soon became apparent that this Government's strategy was different. Thatcher put a set of ruthless industrialists in charge of the nationalized industries and instructed them to render the firms profitable at any cost in terms of lost employment or forgone capital investment. Sir Michael Edwardes at British Leyland, Ian MacGregor at British Steel and then the National Coal Board, and Sir John King at British Airways, among others, took this mandate seriously. Their relations with the government were not without friction, as Ministers attempted to impose strict financial limits on the capital expenditure programs of these firms while their managers argued for greater freedom of action and investment in longer-term growth (Edwardes, 1983; *Financial Times*, 5 May 1983; Riddell, 1983: 170 ff). However, the Government proved willing to fight a bitter series of strikes in order to back up its strategy. As a result, reorganization schemes, involving the loss of over 250,000 jobs between 1979 and 1985, were implemented in steel, coal, the national airline, automobiles, the railways, and shipbuilding (Riddell, 1983: 167; Holmes, 1985: 161 ff). All of those industries were more efficient, if much smaller, as a result of this experience. It is arguable that the Conservatives proved to be better managers of the public enterprises than the Labour Governments that initially nationalized them. At the very least, Thatcher was able to achieve the kind of industrial reorganization in these sectors that had eluded preceding regimes.

Other facets of the Government's policy toward the private sector have been equally interventionist (cf. Henderson, 1983). In particular, officials have moved away from the rule-based programs that traditionally dominated public spending in this area to more selective forms of intervention, aimed especially at high-technology industries. The Government has severely reduced the public resources going to regional development. Ministers argued that if investment in the assisted areas was efficient, it would be made anyway; and if it were not, it should not be subsidized. They reduced the size of the assisted areas from those covering 44 percent of the population to ones covering only 27 percent. A larger proportion of the funds were to be spent on a selective basis; and automatic grants were limited to £10,000 per job created. The level of expenditure planned for regional aid between 1984 and 1988 was halved to £400 million; and some of the savings were redirected toward assistance for research and development.

In general, funding for research and development has not been cut as heavily as other programs; and the Government has introduced a series of programs designed to encourage the growth of high-technology sectors. The National Enterprise Board was instructed to sell most of its industrial holdings and transformed into the British Technology Group with the more limited task of fostering scientific contacts between industry and the universities. A new Minister for Information Technology was appointed to superintend schemes assisting research and development in microelectronics, fibre optics, information technology, and outer space. Funding for the basic program in these areas was raised from £50 million in 1978–79 to £250 million in 1983–84. The Government has also directed departments to favor British contractors over foreign firms in high-technology areas, such as computers and radar. Although assistance to these sectors actually forms a small component of the overall industrial budget, and one that is dwarfed by equivalent French expenditures, the Thatcher Government has been openly interventionist in this area.

As unemployment rose the Government also developed a substantial manpower training program. Under the Youth Opportunities Programme it paid minimal wages to school-leavers employed in industry-based training schemes; and under the Young Workers Scheme it offered employers subsidies to employ youngsters at less than £40 a week. The Community Enterprise Programme made it possible for local councils to utilize the unemployed on a variety of public works. The Job Release Scheme subsidized those who took early retirement to make a job available for unemployed youths. Along with the Temporary Short Time Working Compensation Scheme and Community Industry, these programs offered places to about 647,000 people in 1984–85, in some cases at a cost of £5355 per job (Williams, 1983: 86). By 1983–84 these schemes were costing the Exchequer over £2 billion a year.

One of the Government's obvious objects was to reduce the numbers of those officially counted as unemployed; but Margaret Thatcher also hoped to up-grade the skills of young people who could not find a job and to lower wage costs at the bottom end of the labor market (cf. McFadyean and Renn, 1984: 21). These programs reflected the monetarists' general view that Britain's high levels of unemployment were the result of mismatches and overly high wages in the labor market rather than deficiencies in the general level of demand. In the short term they certainly provided a source of income and some socialization into the labor market for young people who might otherwise go through their teens and twenties without ever finding a job. However, many trainees left the programs without any prospect of further employment, partly because it was difficult to forecast which kind of skills would be in demand, and partly because low vacancy rates meant that few skills were in demand at all. Moreover, one Manpower Services Commission report suggested that three out of four of the people being subsidized by such schemes would have been employed anyway, or were taking jobs that would have gone to others.

This microeconomic approach was somewhat at odds with the Government's initial stance against state intervention in the market system; but it differed from the emphasis of previous administrations on macroeconomic stimulation, rule-based grants heavily oriented towards regional policy, industrial bail-outs, or tripartite consultation to revive British industry. The Thatcher policies gave policy-makers a great deal of discretion over the allocation of funds and tried with some degree of success to avoid subsidizing industrial losers, in favor of already profitable enterprises in the emerging sectors. The principal beneficiaries of discretionary government grants in the 1981–84 period included: GEC, Ferranti, STC, Lucas, Plessey, BICC, Ford, Metal Box, ICI, Trafalgar House, Courtaulds, Vickers, Unilever, and Philips (*New Statesman*, 21 May 1985: 21). If the analysis in chapter one is correct, there is a great deal to be said for such a strategy: it is more likely to lead to the reorganization of British industry than the industrial bail-outs of yesteryear.

Ironically, however, the Conservative Government has been unwilling to make such intervention its principal priority. Pride of place has gone to the privatization program; and the effectiveness of its microeconomic measures has been limited by the paucity of resources devoted to them. In particular, the Government's fixation on reducing total public expenditure has seriously handicapped its ability to make full use of selective industrial instruments. While preliminary indications are that the support for microelectronics, for instance, has been quite productive, the sums devoted to that area are far too small to have a major impact on the industry (Policy Studies Institute, 1985). Funding for microelectronics has been increased five-fold under Thatcher but to only £250 million a year. Similarly, the Government's reasons for diminishing the automatic component in regional development grants were sound – a more selective program might well employ the funds more efficiently – but any effects will be seriously undermined by the massive reductions in total funding for the program. In the coming years industrial policy is one of the principal areas in which Thatcher hopes to achieve substantial economies. Despite some industrial initiatives, most Ministers are still putting their faith in the ability of British markets to revive themselves.

OBJECTIVES AND PERFORMANCE

Any assessment of the Thatcher years should begin with performance relative to its own objectives. As we have seen, the Government's principal goals were to cut public expenditure and levels of taxation so as to reduce both the PSBR and the share of national resources being channelled through the state. A lower PSBR was supposed to lower the rate of growth of the money supply and bring down the rate of inflation. In these terms performance has been mixed. Margaret Thatcher avoided the U-turn that drew most preceding administrations away from their initial objectives. The minor loosening of fiscal and monetary policy in 1983–85 was far from a return to Keynesianism. However, the Government has fallen somewhat short of reaching its own goals.

Public expenditure was supposed to fall from 43.8 percent of GDP in 1978–79 to 42.3 percent in 1983–84; instead, it rose to 45.7 percent of GDP (see table 5.1). In volume terms total public spending rose by about 2.2 percent a year between 1979 and 1985, compared with 1 percent a year in 1974–79 and 3.3 percent in 1951–79 (Judge, 1982: 28; Thompson, 1986). In short, the Thatcher Government held the growth of public spending substantially below average post-war rates, but it did not depress spending as successfully as the preceding Labour administration. Why? Four factors loom large in the outcome.

Despite her attack on 'big government', Thatcher was unwilling to dismantle any of the major programs associated with the welfare state in Britain. Public opinion polls showed that even avid critics of government inefficiency did not want to see substantial cuts in the National Health Service, primary education, unemployment insurance, or old age pensions. Although the Conservatives chipped away at the edges of these programs they could not effect major savings without dismantling major portions of them; and, together, these programs account for almost half of total public expenditure (table 5.4).

Second, the economic recession of 1980–82 and rising levels of unemployment automatically increased outlays on social security and supplementary benefits, some of the state's largest spending programs. Despite some attempts to cut the level of benefits, each jobless person cost the Exchequer about £6300 a year in transfer payments and lost revenue for a total of £20 billion in 1984 (Fraser and Sinfield, 1985).

Table 5.4 Percentage change in British public expenditure programs, 1974–85

	Percentage change in program in real terms	
	1974–75 to 1978–79	*1979–80 to 1984–85*
Defense	+1.4	+22.8
Overseas aid	+44.5	−19.0
Agriculture	−59.3	+38.1
Industry, energy, trade, and employment	−33.8	+17.8
Transport	−19.0	−4.3
Housing	−19.1	−54.6
Other environmental services	−4.1	−6.3
Law and order	+11.0	+29.1
Education, science, art, and libraries	−0.2	+1.8
Health	+8.7	+16.7
Social security	+24.2	+28.4
Total public expenditure (planning total)	+1.5	+9.4

Sources: Expenditure White Paper 1979 (Cmnd 7439); *Expenditure White Paper 1985* (Cmnd 9428).

The recession increased the public funding needs of the nationalized industries; and substantial cuts in other programs could not fully compensate for increases in the social security, health service or industry and employment budgets of 28, 17, and 18 percent respectively in real terms between 1979–80 and 1984–85. In a period of faster overall economic growth, public spending might have grown at 2 percent a year and still fallen as a proportion of GDP; recession eliminated that possibility. The high public spending to GDP ratios reflect a sluggish denominator as well as a rising numerator.

Third, the Government deliberately increased expenditure on such traditional Conservative priorities as defense, law and order, and agriculture. Although Thatcher did not embark on a military build-up of the scale undertaken by President Reagan, she ensured that Britain was one of the few nations to adhere to the NATO directive seeking a 3 percent real increase in annual military expenditure. In addition, the Falklands War and garrison were estimated to cost £3.2 billion over 10 years. Projections for the years from 1986 suggest that defense spending should level off, at the cost of some reduction in conventional forces to pay for the Trident nuclear system, but expenditure on the police will continue to increase as part of the Conservative response to recent inner-city riots.

Finally, the Government's initial hope that massive savings could be effected with no loss in services, by increasing the efficiency of the civil service, has not been fully realized. Sir Derek Rayner, a leading businessman, was appointed to No. 10 Downing Street in 1979 to eliminate waste in government departments. The 135 efficiency reviews conducted between 1979 and 1982 produced actual and potential savings of about £300 million at some cost in terms of reduced services, and the number of civil servants fell by 11 percent between 1979 and 1983; but there seems to be little further scope for savings without substantial cuts in public services (Riddell, 1983: 122).

Similarly, the Government extended the system of cash limits on departmental spending, originally developed in 1976, to the entire gamut of public spending, and devised new external financing limits for the nationalized industries. These frightened departmental administrators into considerable underspending in 1981–84 and seem to have improved fiscal control over public enterprise. However, Thatcher's attempts to impose similar limits on the local authorities, who account for over 25 percent of public spending, have been less successful. Although local capital expenditure has fallen dramatically, current spending remained 6–8 percent above target levels in 1979–83, especially under Labour-controlled Councils (Jones and Stewart, 1983).

The Government's tax policies have been largely determined by its record on public spending and its policy toward the public sector deficit. Once Thatcher decided to reduce the size of the PSBR at all costs, she could not reduce the aggregate tax burden because she had not cut public spending as much as anticipated. As a result, total government revenue rose from 38.4 percent of GDP in 1978–79 to 42.1 percent in 1983–84. More than any other, this Government has benefited from North Sea oil and large-scale sales of public assets. Between 1979 and 1985 it received almost £40 billion from North Sea oil, £12 billion from the sale of council houses and land, and £7 billion from the sale of the nationalized industries. Without these once-for-all gains, the tax burden or PSBR would have been even higher.

The administration's most startling experience, however, came in the sphere of monetary policy. As table 5.5 indicates, the monetary aggregates grew considerably faster than intended in the 1979–84 period. Despite high interest rates, the monetary aggregates were increased by a surge in bank lending to companies desperate for funds with which to weather the recession (cf. Kaldor, 1984). After lifting the 'corset' on bank liabilities only to consider and reject a monetary base system of control, the authorities had trouble adhering to rigid monetary targets. Only when the economy began to pick up again, and the Government agreed to accommodate existing monetary growth in 1984–85, were the target ranges achieved.

It seems that the money supply is much harder to control than monetarists originally thought; but this was only a superficial defeat for

Table 5.5 British monetary growth compared with target rates, 1977–85

| | Percentage increase in sterling M3 | |
	Target	Outcome
Apr. 1976–Apr. 1977	9.0–13.0	7.8
Apr. 1977– Apr.1978	9.0–13.0	14.9
Apr. 1978– Apr.1979	8.0–12.0	10.9
Oct. 1978– Oct.1979	8.0–12.0	13.4
June 1979– Apr.1980	7.0–11.0	9.7
Feb. 1980– Apr.1981	7.0–11.0	19.9
Feb. 1981– Apr.1982	6.0–10.0	13.6
Feb. 1982– Apr.1983	8.0–12.0	10.8
Feb. 1983– Apr.1984	7.0–11.0	8.6
Feb. 1984– Apr.1985	6.0–10.0	9.5

Sources: *OECD Economic Studies* (Autumn 1984), p. 35; Central Statistical Office, *Financial Statistics*, various issues.

the Government. It did manage to implement a tight monetary policy in the 1979–83 period, even if not precisely as intended; and, after a regrettable resurgence in 1979–80, the British rate of inflation fell from 13.4 percent in 1979 to 5 percent in 1985. That drop may well owe more to changing international conditions, rising unemployment and a tough stand against the unions than to monetary policy; but by whatever means, the Government achieved its principal economic objective (cf. Beckerman, 1985; Buiter and Miller, 1983).

Even for the Thatcher Government, however, these more immediate goals were only a means toward the broader end of regenerating British industry and securing long-term economic growth. Ultimately it is by such measures that the Thatcher Government's economic performance will be judged. Let us turn to them.

MACROECONOMIC PERFORMANCE UNDER THATCHER

It is difficult to evaluate Britain's economic performance under Thatcher – in part, because a significant component of her strategy is aimed at the longer term, which we have yet to see, and in part because she has held office during a period when world-wide economic performance has been inferior to that in the first three decades after the war. Fortunately, there is one appropriate case against which the Conservative episode might be compared. That is the period from 1974 to 1979 when a Labour Government attempted to cope with an oil shock and global recession similar to that of 1979. Since the instincts of the Labour Government remained decidedly Keynesian (although they were briefly forced into more contractionary policies), this provides us with an opportunity to compare the effect of Keynesian and monetarist approaches to similar economic problems.[2]

Moreover, such a comparison takes on added significance in the contemporary conjuncture. Since 1974 politicians in the Western world have faced a new economic situation. The exhaustion of the Fordist model, coupled with two severe oil shocks, brought an end to three decades of widespread economic prosperity. Both the Labour administration of 1974–79 and its Conservative successor elected in 1979 have had to cope with rising levels of unemployment and inflation in a situation of slower growth. Whereas previous administrations could distribute the fruits of economic growth, these Governments have often had to apportion economic sacrifice. They were called upon to depress state or consumer spending so as to make room for investment, distribute the costs of the oil price increase, or restrain inflation.

As a result both the Labour and Conservative Governments instituted more austere economic policies; and some commentators have begun to argue that there is little difference between austerity as administered by the left and the right. Those who argue that political parties (or politics) do not have a major impact on economic outcomes have secured another round of ammunition (Rose, 1984; McCormick, 1985; cf. Castles, 1982). Convergence theories based on economic growth have given way to new convergence theories based on economic decline. In such a context it is particularly appropriate to ask if there have been any important differences in the consequences that followed from Labour and Conservative policies since 1974.

In broad macroeconomic terms the results do not favor Thatcher. Over the entire decade, British performance was below the average of the industrialized world; but on almost all measures the performance of the British economy was superior under the Labour Government than it was under the Conservatives, despite the advantages that North Sea oil revenues offered in the later period.

Gross domestic product grew more slowly than the OECD average in both periods, but the ratio of British to OECD growth was 0.56 under Labour compared with 0.48 under the Conservatives (see table 5.6). Industrial production fell dramatically in 1980 and 1981 under the impact of a rising exchange rate, and it has yet to recover as strongly as it did under Labour.

As a by-product, the rate of unemployment has risen far more dramatically under Thatcher than under Callaghan. Jobless levels in Britain have been creeping upwards for almost two decades; but in

Table 5.6   British economic performance under Labour and the Conservatives in international perspective

	Real GDP growth (% change p.a.)	Industrial production (% volume change p.a.)	Unemployment* (% p.a.)	Consumer prices (% change p.a.)	Investment (GFCF as % of GDP)
1974	−1.1	−2.8	3.1	16.0	20.6
1975	−0.7	−6.1	4.6	24.2	20.1
1976	3.8	3.3	6.0	16.5	19.5
1977	1.0	5.3	6.4	15.8	18.6
1978	3.6	3.0	6.3	8.3	18.6
1979	2.1	3.9	5.6	13.4	18.8
UK average, 1974–79	1.5	1.1	5.3	15.7	19.4
EEC average, 1974–79	2.4	–	4.9	10.4	21.1
OECD average, 1974–79	2.7	2.4	4.9†	10.0	21.9
1979	2.1	3.9	5.6	13.4	18.8
1980	−2.2	−6.5	6.9	18.0	18.1
1981	−1.1	−4.0	10.6	11.9	16.5
1982	2.3	3.1	12.3	8.6	16.6
1983	3.1	3.0	13.1	4.6	16.5
1984	2.4	1.0	13.2	5.0	–
UK average, 1979–84	1.1	0.08	10.3	10.3	17.3
EEC average, 1979–84	1.4	–	8.3	9.3	20.0
OECD average, 1979–84	2.3	1.9	7.1†	8.6	21.1

Sources: OECD, *Economic Outlook* (June 1985); *National Institute Economic Review* (Feb. 1984, Feb. 1985, Aug. 1985).
* OECD standardized definition.
† Fifteen OECD countries only.

1974–79 they rose only slightly faster in Britain than elsewhere in the OECD. By contrast, almost half of the British increase since 1979 seems attributable to distinctively British factors, and the most likely candidate is government policy. When the official figures are corrected to include the jobless who cannot claim unemployment benefit, over 4 million people are unemployed in Britain today, compared with roughly 1.5 million in 1979 (see table 5.6).

The manufacturing sector has been shrinking in Britain for decades, but manufacturing as a share of total output or employment has fallen much more steeply since 1979 than before. The consequences are only partially hidden by the effects of North Sea oil. A 59 percent increase in the volume of British energy exports since 1979, for instance, hides the fact that manufacturing exports have risen by only 3 percent since 1979 compared with an 11 percent increase in the preceding 5 years (see table 5.7). In the same period manufacturing imports have risen by 30 percent in volume. In other words, the Thatcher policies seem to have hastened the deindustrialization of the British economy far more substantially than those of Labour.

Table 5.7   British foreign trade performance, 1974–84

	Export volume (% change p.a.)	Manufacturing export volume (% change p.a.)	Import volume (% change p.a.)	Current balance (£ million)	UK share of world manufacturing exports
1974	5.2	5.1	0.4	−3278	8.8
1975	−2.2	−3.4	−8.6	−1523	9.3
1976	8.6	8.1	6.5	−846	8.8
1977	8.4	7.5	1.8	+53	9.4
1978	2.8	0	6.7	+1162	9.5
1979	3.8	−1.0	8.4	−525	9.7
1979	3.8	−1.0	8.4	−525	9.7
1980	0.8	1.0	−3.8	+3477	9.7
1981	−1.1	−6.0	−3.9	+6930	8.6
1982	2.7	1.1	4.2	+4881	8.5
1983	0.6	−2.1	7.7	+2294	8.0
1984	8.7	9.7	9.5	+196	7.6
Average, 1974–79	4.4	2.7	2.5	−826	9.3
Average, 1979–84	2.6	0.5	3.7	+2876	8.7

Sources: National Institute Economic Review (Nov. 1981, Feb. 1985, Aug. 1985); OECD, Economic Surveys: United Kingdom (July 1981, Jan. 1985).

What remains of British manufacturing, however, has grown considerably more efficient under the Conservatives. The cold bath into which they plunged British industry reduced overmanning. Output per worker has risen by a dramatic 22 percent compared with a 7 percent increase over the preceding 5 years. In these terms, British industry as a whole is now more efficient; but it remains to be seen if a shrunken industrial base can expand before the oil runs out. Further efficiency gains might well depend on entirely different factors, such as greater levels of investment and technical innovation; and this picture is not rosy. Levels of investment in manufacturing were barely higher in 1979 than in 1974, and since then, they have fallen by 30 percent (see table 5.8). The volume of total British investment, including housing, rose by only 5 percent under Labour and by 3 percent in 5 years under the Conservatives. These are hardly levels adequate to rebuild British industry.

Table 5.8   The British manufacturing sector, 1974–84

	Selected indicators of manufacturing performance				
	Output (% vol. change	*Employ- ment (% change)*	*Investment (% change)*	*Productivity (% change output/man- hour)*	*Unit labor costs (% change)*
1974	−1.5	0.3	9.9	−1.3	22.0
1975	−6.9	−4.5	−10.0	−2.6	30.0
1976	2.0	−3.1	−3.3	5.3	11.5
1977	1.9	−3.0	4.6	1.6	8.6
1978	0.5	−0.5	6.8	1.1	12.7
1979	−0.3	−1.1	3.6	1.5	15.5
1979	−0.3	−1.1	3.6	1.5	15.5
1980	−8.5	−5.8	−13.7	−3.7	22.0
1981	−6.3	−9.8	−25.0	3.1	9.0
1982	0	−5.2	−3.5	6.4	5.5
1983	2.5	−4.1	−1.4	7.4	0.9
1984	2.0*	−1.6	15.3	4.7	3.4
Average, 1974–79	−0.7	−2.0	1.9	0.9	16.7
Average, 1979–84	−1.8	−4.6	−4.1	3.2	9.4

Sources: National Institute Economic Review (Nov. 1981, Feb. 1984, Feb. 1985, Aug. 1985); OECD, *Economic Surveys: United Kingdom* (Mar. 1978, Feb. 1980, July 1981, Feb. 1983, Jan. 1985).
*Treasury estimate.

Moreover, the aggregate figures mask an important discrepancy between trends in public and private investment. In order to secure public spending cuts, both Governments have found it easier to cut capital, rather than current, expenditure. As a result the level of annual public investment has fallen by 31 percent since 1974. The slight increase in total investment is attributable entirely to a 38 percent increase in private investment over the decade. In effect, the public sector has been most responsible for the rundown in British levels of investment.

THE DISTRIBUTIONAL CONSEQUENCES OF AUSTERITY

Aggregate economic performance, however, is only one aspect of the problem. We should also ask if there have been any significant differences in the distributional consequences that followed from Labour and Conservative austerity?

In the first instance we can identify some important similarities in the incidence of austerity under both Governments. Quite apart from the effects of distributive policy, economic recession and rising levels of unemployment tend to reinforce existing inequalities in income and labor-market power. Accordingly, the Gini coefficient measuring inequality in final income (after inflation, taxes, and benefits) rose from 31 in 1975 to 32 in 1979 and 33 in 1983, as a larger proportion of those at the bottom of the social hierarchy found it increasingly difficult to get work (see O'Higgins, 1985). These disparities in final income were exacerbated by the tendency of both Governments to raise expenditure taxes proportionately more than income taxes, perhaps in the belief that the former were politically less visible (table 5.9). Expenditure taxes tend to fall more heavily on the lower-paid; and the bottom income quintile in Britain spent 21 percent of their gross income on expenditure taxes in 1975, 23 percent in 1979, and 27 percent in 1983.

Nevertheless, the distributional strategy adopted by the Thatcher regime has been significantly different from that of its Labour predecessor. The Labour Government made a concerted attempt to orchestrate the distribution of income through a series of tripartite negotiations with producer groups; and it tried to offset the impact of austerity on lower-income earners with higher transfer payments. By contrast, the Conservative approach to austerity has been based on a strategy of reinforcing market mechanisms and the market-led allocation of resources so as to increase work incentives and the flexibility of factor inputs in the economy. The distributional consequences of the two approaches seem to display some important differences.

Under Labour the costs of austerity were spread rather evenly over the population, allowing for the usual ability of the wealthy to avoid the worst consequences of recession. Under the Conservatives, by con-

Table 5.9   Trends in income in the UK, 1974–84

	Gross trading profits* (% change p.a.)	Average earnings – whole economy (% change p.a.)	Consumer price index (% change p.a.)	Real personal disposable income† (% change p.a.)
1974	−6.2	17.9	16.0	–
1975	9.1	26.6	24.2	0.3
1976	25.3	15.5	16.5	−0.6
1977	59.4	9.1	15.8	−1.6
1978	20.6	12.9	8.3	7.3
1979	8.8	15.6	13.4	5.7
1979	8.8	15.6	13.4	5.7
1980	12.2	20.6	18.0	1.0
1981	14.3	12.9	11.9	−2.3
1982	18.3	9.4	8.6	0.2
1983	20.5	8.4	4.6	1.6
1984	23.7	6.1	5.0	2.3
Average, 1974–79	19.5	19.3	15.7	2.2
Average, 1979–84	16.3	12.2	10.3	1.4

Sources: OECD, *Economic Outlook* (June 1985); *National Institute Economic Review* (Nov. 1981, Feb. 1985, Aug. 1985).

*Profits of industrial and financial companies net of stock appreciation, but before provision for depreciation.

†Total income from all sources less income taxes, national insurance contributions and net transfers abroad, deflated by the implied consumers' expenditure deflator.

trast, the costs of austerity have been placed disproportionately on lower-income earners and the unemployed. While Labour policy narrowed income differentials across the population, Conservative policy has widened the disjunction in material well-being between the affluent and the poor, between those in work and those without it, and between those with considerable power in the labor market by virtue of wealth or skills and those without such power.

By far the most significant distributional consequences follow from the Government's toleration of a rising level of unemployment. While 17 percent of the bottom income quintile was unemployed in 1976 and 18 percent in 1979, over 35 percent of that quintile was jobless by 1982. Similarly, the number of people on supplementary benefits rose from 2,675,000 in 1973 to 2,850,000 in 1979 but jumped to 4,340,000 in 1983.

The most obvious cost of the Thatcher strategy has been a massive increase in the number of jobless and poor. The growing number of jobless has divided the nation into regional, racial, and age-related enclaves. For instance, the average unemployment rate in Britain was 13 percent during 1984–85; but it reached 20 percent among those below 20 years of age and 50 percent among black youth in many inner-city areas. Similarly the 1984 unemployment rate in southern England was 8–9 percent versus 15 percent in Scotland, Wales, and the North. Partly as a result, gross weekly earnings (of men over 21) increased by 4 percent in the Southeast and 2 percent in the Southwest over 1979–83, but fell by 3–4 percent in the Midlands and the North. Wages were typically 20 percent higher in the Southeast than wages in the North. Whole communities suffer from the effects of mass unemployment in their area; and current trends are increasing, rather than diminishing, these discrepancies. In 1982–83, 78,000 new jobs were created in Southern England and East Anglia, while 44,000 jobs were lost in the North, Wales and Scotland.

Moreover, this recession has had very uneven effects across the populace. Those in work have done rather well: real disposable income increased as much under the Conservatives as under Labour. The unemployed and the poor have borne the cost of industrial adjustment and the fight against inflation. Not only are jobs harder to find, but many of the Government's tax and expenditure policies have hit them particularly hard.

Whereas expenditure cuts under Labour were at least partially designed to preserve the spending power of the poor, the Conservatives have reduced the real value of transfer payments more substantially. Old age pensions, which rose rapidly under Labour, have fallen slightly in value under the Conservatives. Similarly the average level of child support available to an unemployed couple with two children fluctuated somewhat under Labour but remained as high in 1979 as it was in 1974; under the Conservatives the amount of support has fallen by 20 percent. The real value of most unemployment benefits decreased slightly as the government broke the index-link with earnings, abolished the earnings-related supplement, and subjected them to tax. Although more difficult to document, cuts in the ancillary services provided by local social workers, councils, and the health service may have had an even more dramatic impact on those living below the poverty line (Edgell and Duke, 1985).

One area of particular importance is that of housing. Since low-income families depend heavily on public housing for accommodation, any cuts here tend to have a major impact on disparities in well-being between the affluent and the less affluent. Labour austerity brought some reductions in construction of public housing; but the Conservatives have gone farther to make the sale of council houses and reduction in the public housing stock a keystone of their social program. Funds for the construction, repair, and subsidy of public housing were cut by 55 percent between 1979–80 and 1984–85. As a result the stock of owner-occupied dwellings rose by 1.61 million while the number of public housing rentals fell by 560,000 between 1979 and 1983.

Finally, the Thatcher Government's tax policies have had an important distributive effect (see figure 5.1). The initial three-point fall in the standard rate of income tax was counterbalanced for most people at average earnings by increases in expenditure taxes and the 1981–82 decisions to raise thresholds less than the rate of inflation. But upper-income earners continued to benefit from the large reductions they received in the Government's first budget, while lower-income earners found that increasing portions of their transfer payments were taxed. Between 1979 and 1985 the average rate of tax fell from 52 to 42.5 percent for a person with five times average earnings, and from 30.5 to 30 percent for a person at twice average earnings. However, it rose slightly from 26 to 26.5 percent for a person at average earnings, and from 14 to 16 percent for a person at half average earnings (see figure 5.1). Where the Labour Government's tax and incomes policies tended to squeeze income differentials, Conservative policy has widened them. We can expect the Government to concentrate another set of tax reductions on lower-income earners, but these are unlikely to make up completely for the existing discrepancies (*The Economist*, 23 March 1985: 4).

RECASTING SOCIETY AND THE STATE

Of all British Prime Ministers, Margaret Thatcher may be the most ambitious reformer since David Lloyd George. From the outset one of her principal goals has been to change the nature of state–society relations in Britain. The Government has attempted to reduce the role of the state in economic activity and to allow market mechanisms, rather than public authorities, greater jurisdiction over the allocation of resources. As part of that project it has also been seeking to reorder market mechanisms, by shifting the balance of power away from trade unions in particular.

However, this is a paradoxical project. The reordering of British markets and recasting of state–society relations entails massive institutional change that can be accomplished only by the intervention of a particularly strong state. In order to roll back the role of the state in society, Thatcher has had to strengthen its position and initiate a series of forceful battles with societal actors.

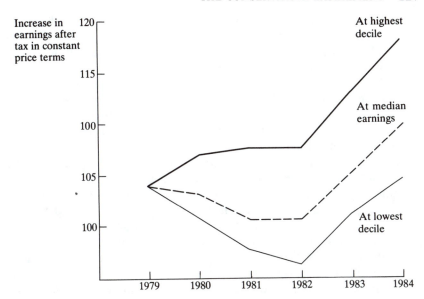

Figure 5.1   Relative gains in earnings after income tax and child benefit of a married couple with two children between April 1979 and April 1984 (earnings of all groups set equal to 104 in April 1979)

If that seems ironic, the Prime Minister perceived the paradoxes from the start. In an early philosophical statement, she (1980: 10–11) said:

the first principle of this government . . . is to revive a sense of individual responsibility. It is to reinvigorate not just the economy and industry but the whole body of voluntary associations, loyalties and activities which gives society its richness and diversity, and hence its real strength. . . . Since Burke's time the activities of the State have penetrated almost every aspect of life. . . . The trouble is that when the State becomes involved in every strike, price or contract affecting a nationalized industry, its authority is not enhanced, it is diminished. . . . In our Party we do not ask for a feeble State. On the contrary, we need a strong State to preserve both liberty and order . . . to maintain in good repair the frame which surrounds society. But the frame should not be so heavy or elaborate as to dominate the whole picture . . . We should not expect the State to appear in the guise of an extravagant good fairy at every christening, a loquacious and tedious companion at every stage of life's journey, the unknown mourner at every funeral. The relationship between state and people is crucial to our economic approach.

Therefore it is appropriate to ask what the effect of her administration has been on state–society relations.

The balance of power within the state has been rearranged under the Thatcher administration. A number of *ad hoc* measures have reinforced the power of the Prime Minister *vis-à-vis* other arms of the state. Thatcher has been remarkably intolerant of resistance from the Cabinet, for instance, and quick to sanction those who stand in her way.[3] She has also been careful to appoint senior civil servants who seem sympathetic to her policies and prepared to execute them without obstruction. Although Thatcher has had to put up with a rising chorus of complaints from "wets" on the Conservative backbenches, the trend toward "Prime-Ministerial government" has accelerated under her tenure (see King, 1986).

More important, several institutional reforms have increased the power of the central government over departments and local authorities that might otherwise have been more potent sources of opposition to public spending cuts and retrenchment. The extension of cash limits on spending to virtually all public programs, along with some more innovations in departmental reporting, severely limited the ability of government departments to evade the Cabinet's controls on public spending. Both the power of the Treasury and its obsession with public expenditure have increased under the Thatcher administration.

Local authorities have been put under great pressure to contain their expenditures; and the complex reforms undertaken with this in mind have gone well beyond measures to control spending totals. The central government has acquired much more influence over the nature of programs administered at the local level (Jones and Stewart, 1983). Initially the Government forced local councils to increase their rates if they wanted extra spending; then it put limits on even this source of finance. In addition, Thatcher moved to abolish the Greater London Council, as much for its capacity to resist her economies as for a tendency to return Labour majorities. Despite stiff opposition from many Labour councils and some financial turmoil, the British state has subjected local authorities to greater central control, just when the French state was decentralizing.

The Government's relations with interest groups have also been heavily mediated by its ideology. The Government's monetarist philosophy has been both a weapon and a screen. If a ruler holds strong beliefs, based on a highly elaborate complex of ideas that prescribe the direction policy should take, he or she is far less likely to yield to the shifting pressure of societal interests than the ruler who has no clear sense of where he wants to go or how to get there. A coherent and technically plausible set of ideas, commanding the support of some body of experts, can confer a degree of independence on the state.

In an era of widespread confusion about appropriate economic policy, the Thatcher Government found and elaborated such a set of ideas. Its monetarist philosophy was then used to reject the representations of many groups as unreasonable. Indeed, the very practice of formulating economic policy through negotiation with the affected interests could be rejected as unnecessary in light of the overriding role of monetarist theory.

One of the groups affected by the development of monetarist ideology was British industry. The Confederation of British Industry has never been a particularly powerful interest group (cf. Leys, 1985; Grant and Marsh, 1978); but Thatcher abolished its favored arena for consultations, the NEDC, and openly flouted the complaints it mounted against stringent fiscal and monetary policies. By virtue of the administration's long-term interest in a renewal of profitability and investment many of its policies were likely to be congruent with the interests of industry; and the Prime Minister showed a special concern for the needs of small business. More than many others, however, this was a Government that preferred to think for itself; and the monetarist philosophy played a major role in dictating which of the CBI's demands would be seen as reasonable and which would be rejected.

By the very terms in which it defines debate, however, every ideology also privileges the interests of some groups over others (cf. Schattshneider, 1960). Whether the bias is intended or not, it can have a subtle influence on policy; and monetarist theories have always reflected the concerns of the City more intensely than those of industry. The monetary and fiscal rectitude they prescribe is very much in keeping with the concerns of brokers about the marketability of government debt and the concerns of bondholders about the impact of inflation on the real value of their investment. Despite the waning of empire, therefore, economic policy continued to favor the interests of the City over those of industry for a slightly different set of reasons.

Even here, however, the role of ideas was central. Thatcher does not seem to have been particularly more susceptible to *ad hoc* pressure from the City than from industry. Monetarist lines of thought convinced her to stick to a tight monetary policy in 1979–82 despite opposition from the Governor of the Bank of England, traditionally an influential spokesman for City interests. Only the most sustained opposition from the Bank persuaded her to give up plans to move toward a monetary base system of credit control. Unless they were able to win over the Prime Minister's own monetarist advisors, officials of both the Treasury and the Bank frequently lost intra-governmental battles over the direction of economic policy (Keegan, 1984; Riddell, 1983).

Nevertheless, it was the political influence of the trade unions that waned most severely under the Thatcher regime. An underlying precondition was undoubtedly the huge increase in unemployment. In a full employment economy the British unions had been powerful enough to force even Conservative Governments into negotiating with them. But the speckled course of economic performance in the 1970s led the British electorate and the Thatcher Government to give greater priority to the reduction of inflation and the improvement of British competitiveness than to the attainment of full employment.

Freed of political constraints that had once seemed to dictate the pursuit of full employment, the Government allowed the number of jobless to rise from 1.2 million in May 1979 to over 4 million by 1985. Even more than its industrial relations legislation, that limited the ability of the unions to mobilize rank-and-file support for industrial action. In addition, popular disillusionment with the former political influence of the unions freed the Thatcher Government from at least some of the electoral sanctions that might once have followed such resistance to industrial action.

Accordingly, the Government carefully orchestrated a campaign of resistance to public sector strikes. After timely concessions on the Clegg awards in 1979 and reorganisation of the coal industry in 1981, it defeated a number of unions in succession. Moreover, Thatcher refused to enter into detailed negotiations with the TUC about economic policy; and what limited influence the unions once had over policy was attenuated. The experiences of the 1920s and 1980s suggest that the power of the British unions is based not simply on the structural features of their organization but on the conjunctural experience of full employment as well.

THE LONG-TERM PROGNOSIS

Will the structural changes in British society effected by the Thatcher Government last? That was certainly the Government's intention. It hoped to alter the operation of British markets, the relation of state to society, and the fundamental attitudes of the British populace to industry and entrepreneurs in order to put Britain on a higher growth path. If that long-term strategy is successful the short-term sacrifices sustained in its behalf can be seen as worthwhile, at least by Conservative standards.

A definitive judgement will have to wait for the long term, but preliminary indications suggest that the changes Thatcher has inspired are still far from permanent. Recent increases in the power of the state relative to society depend heavily on conjunctural factors; and there is a potential contradiction in the Government's strategy. A failure to secure higher levels of employment could discredit the monetarist theories on which much of the Government's independence and electoral success have been based; yet any return towards full employment could strengthen the unions again *vis-à-vis* the state and employers.

The Government's faith in monetarist economic ideas has already faded to some degree. As the money supply proved difficult to control, exchange rate policy appeared problematic, and an economic recovery capable of reducing unemployment proved elusive, disaffection with monetarist ideas rose inside the Conservative Party. If such factors continue to undermine the strategic orientation of the present Government or bring in a more moderate successor to Thatcher, the Party and the Government could again be open to the kind of economic debate that allows societal interests to put pressure on policy.

In addition, we should note the character of the organizational changes that Thatcher has made in the state. They were primarily designed to improve the Government's control over public expenditure, rather than to increase the capacities of the British state to inspire or direct industrial reorganization. Thatcher's attempts to allocate industrial grants more selectively and to impose rationalization on the nationalized industries were steps in this direction, but even they have been limited by an overriding desire to decrease the funds devoted to such purposes. No steps have been taken to enhance the state's control over the flows of investment in the economy; and deregulation has actually diminished the state's leverage over many sectors of industry. Therefore this is a strong state of a particular kind, and not one that succeeding administrations could necessarily use to put selective pressure on industry.

Indeed, Thatcher's industrial strategy has been quite distinctive. A contractionary fiscal and monetary stance intensified pressure on all segments of British manufacturing in the hope that recession and a rising exchange rate would force all firms to become more competitive and weed the weak from the strong in a neo-Darwinian struggle. The market, rather than the state, was to be the instrument that selected the firms to survive, reorganized industry, and rejuvenated the British economy. To that end, product markets were to be made more competitive by deregulation, and the labor market was to be freed of rigidities by measures that weakened the trade unions.

Therefore, it is even more important to ask if the Government has succeeded in effecting a permanent change in the character of British markets and industry. There is no doubt that the strategy has produced short-term results. As a result of government pressure and rising levels of unemployment, the unions have been forced to accept lay-offs, deskilling, and the reorganization of work. An austere economic climate drove many less competitive firms out of business and compelled many large enterprises to reduce levels of overmanning. Industrial output per man-hour increased by over 20 percent between 1979 and 1985. The British economy was put on a diet, and some of its operations are much slimmer (Pratten, 1982).

However, this was a costly strategy: manufacturing output fell by 15 percent in 1980 and 1981 alone, and has yet to return to 1979 levels. It is quite possible that a number of potentially viable enterprises went bankrupt, along with the chronically uncompetitive, during the period. It is also not at all clear that rising levels of productivity can be sustained as Britain moves out of recession. Productivity rose in 1980–84 largely as a result of once-for-all reductions in manning levels; but continuing productivity gains will depend on other factors, such as increases in investment, which the Government's tight macroeconomic policies discourage, and the reorganization of factor inputs for which the Government is offering few positive incentives (Buiter and Miller, 1983: 355; *The Financial Times*, 20 April 1983).

Moreover, the Conservatives' attempts to weaken the shopfloor power of trade unionists so as to reduce real wage rates and facilitate the reorganization of work have not been a complete success. Although strike rates have fallen slightly, especially in the private sector, recent studies suggest that the unions remain very strong at the plant level. Among the employed, levels of union membership have not fallen significantly. Average real earnings are still rising as fast as they did in the mid-1970s; and employment is no longer falling as fast relative to output as it did in the 1980–82 period (Batstone, 1982; Jones and Rose, 1986).

The reduction in trade union power that the Government has been able to secure may depend heavily on high levels of mass unemployment. If that is the case, any return to prosperity could see a resurgence of union power; and the Government's strategy provides little basis for constructive dealings with the unions in such an instance. The unions may be more democratic institutions as a result of Thatcher's rather successful moves to impose secret ballots on their leadership choices and decisions to strike; but similar ballots on political funds reveal continuing militancy, and the General Secretary of the TUC warned that "if and when there is an upturn in economic activity and the balance tilts toward the workers, then do not be surprised if workers remember the scars inflicted on them and are ready to inflict a few scars themselves" (cited in Riddell, 1983: 190).

The Thatcher Government initiated a remarkable break with the pattern of past policies. It rejected the post-war growth strategy built around macroeconomic manipulation of demand. However, it replaced that macroeconomic strategy not with microeconomic intervention but with an approach that depends on normal market behavior to revive the economy. In that respect the British pattern of 'arm's-length' industrial policy remains intact; the reforms have taken Britain back toward an even older tradition of laissez-faire.

If the diagnosis of Britain's long-term economic decline offered in chapter one is correct, the Thatcher experiment does not augur well.

Her strategy is based on the premise that self-regulating markets can be relied upon to revive the British economy and restore its international competitiveness with a minimum of state intervention. However, that diagnosis suggested that market mechanisms have not inspired adequate industrial adjustment in the past. Even with unions at their weakest, British industries do not always move rapidly towards international competitiveness; yet the Government has done little to tackle other sources of obsolescence and rigidity in the British economy, related to outmoded management strategies, distributional systems, and the supply of capital.

In this light it is significant that the Thatcher years have coincided with a substantial increase in North Sea oil revenues, which peaked in 1985–86 and should decline steadily into the mid-1990s (Devereux and Morris, 1983). Although North Sea oil tended to raise the exchange rate and reduce the size of the manufacturing sector, it also increased public revenues and lifted Britain's perennial balance of payments constraint for a temporary period (Forsyth and Kay, 1980, 1981). Therefore the Thatcher experiment was undertaken during a decade of unique opportunity.

Ironically, this was the one period when a sustained reflation (to increase the output of British industry and reduce unemployment) might have been mounted without any need for special measures to correct the balance of payments; but Thatcher chose deflationary policies on the grounds that they were more likely to improve the competitiveness of British industry. Similarly, oil revenues might have been used to increase private and public sector funding of industrial investment; but Thatcher chose to restrain public spending on industry in favor of tax reductions which she hoped would have a more generalized incentive effect on work effort. She also lifted exchange controls so that many of the extra revenues could flow into foreign investment. Between 1979 and 1983 the investment of British nationals in overseas portfolios, net of foreign investment in Britain, was over £23 billion. There is an argument for such a strategy: the returns on this investment will bolster the balance of payments as oil revenues run out. However, the net effect has been to accelerate Britain's transformation from a world manufacturer to a 'rentier nation' dependent on returns from natural resources and overseas assets for its income.

THE POLITICAL SIDE OF THE STRATEGY

In a democracy every economic program also contains a political strategy, and Thatcher's distinctive approach to economic management was designed to forge a new social coalition behind her policies. She took advantage of the changes that economic trends had made in the shape of the British class structure. Over a period of years, industrial restructuring has entailed class restructuring, in Britain as elsewhere (Urry, 1983; Massey, 1980). For instance, the decline of manufacturing and growth of the service sector have increased the proportion of white-collar workers relative to blue-collar workers within the population (Heath et al., 1985: 36). Women have come to play an increasing role in the labor force, with especially marked effects on traditional attitudes and family roles in regions of industrial decline where their husbands no longer hold jobs. A structure of income differentials under which skilled manual workers are paid more highly than many non-manual workers has rendered income-related dimensions of class increasingly incongruent with distinctions based on workplace control. And the growth of dual labor markets in many sectors of the economy has drawn lines through many traditional class categories.

As a result the traditional electoral base of the Labour Party is shrinking; and an increasing number of people are in contradictory class locations (Hobsbawm et al., 1981; Wright, 1979; Dunleavy and Husbands, 1985). An electorate that was once strongly divided along class lines is increasingly fragmented. The waning of traditional party loyalties has led to partisan dealignment and increasing electoral volatility. In short, the voting patterns of many people are not fully determined and seem dependent on the ability of each political party to find issues that are especially salient to them.

In this context, the economic policies of the Thatcher Government were designed, in part, to create new cleavages that would pull segments of traditional Labour support into the Conservative camp. By concentrating resources on those who were well paid, among both the working and middle classes, Thatcher hoped to construct a new social coalition across class lines. She encouraged the sales of council housing, private home-building, and the wide distribution of shares in formerly public enterprises in part because property-owners have been more likely to vote Conservative.[4] The Government's appeals to nationalism, exemplified in the Falklands War, and strong stands in favor of law and order have also been designed to raise the salience of issues that cut across traditional class lines. Hence, the inner-city riots of 1981 and 1985 have been treated as problems of public safety rather than of urban blight. The effect is to relegate blacks, council-house tenants, and the unemployed to the status of an underclass, somehow separate from the bulk of the working populace.

The distinction is also perfectly in keeping with the moral appeal to traditional Victorian values of work, the nuclear family, the British heritage, and property with which Thatcher has suffused her defense of market-based economic strategies. It is exemplified in the speech with which she closed the Conservative Party Conference of autumn 1985:

Come with us then towards the next decade. Let us together set our sights upon a Britain where three out of four families own their own home, where owning shares is as common as having a car, and where families have a degree of independence their forefathers could only dream about . . . A Britain where there is a resurgence of enterprise with more people self-employed. . . . A Britain where savings keep their value. . . . A Britain where standards in our schools are a source of pride, and where law-abiding people go their way in tranquility with their children, knowing that their neighbourhood is safe and their country secure (*The Times*, 12 October 1985: 4).

Similarly, monetarist thought has brought a whole new set of economic targets to public attention. In 1975 one of the Government's senior economic advisors had to ask a colleague what the PSBR was; today, its control is accepted as a priority goal, along with control of the money supply. The market is viewed much more favorably by many people; and longstanding critics of state intervention have received a great deal of encouragement (Rose, 1983).

Despite the power of this vision, however, it is not clear that Thatcher has succeeded in effecting a permanent change in the terms of political discourse. That outcome may depend heavily on the, as yet uncertain, success of the Government's economic strategies. After all, the very similar set of ideas that guided economic policy in the 1930s (with some success) ultimately foundered on persistently high levels of unemployment; and unemployment has again replaced inflation as the principal issue with which the British electorate is concerned.

The evidence suggests that Thatcher has responded to basic demands within the British electorate but has not yet fundamentally reshaped the attitudes that underlie them. In 1979, for instance, only 37 percent of those with an opinion favored increasing government services on health, education, and welfare and an equal number preferred tax cuts; by 1985 almost two-thirds of British voters were willing to accept higher taxes to improve these services, and only 17 percent of those with an opinion preferred tax cuts (*Gallup Political Index*, May 1979; February 1985). After 7 years of neo-conservative rule the center of the British electorate seems as moderate as ever: still committed to the welfare state and increasingly concerned about unemployment.

These findings suggest that those who characterize the Thatcher regime as "authoritarian populism" may overstate both the authoritarianism of the government and its popularity (Hall and Jacques, 1983; cf. Jessop et al., 1984; Longstreth, 1985). Thatcher's victory in the 1983 election depended heavily on the appearance of schisms within the opposition and the unpopularity of Labour policies (Crewe, 1985). In the context of the post-war period as a whole, the more striking characteristic of the Thatcher regime has been its divisive character.

As we have seen, post-war economic policy-making had generally been consensual and inclusive. Keynesianism embodied a kind of implicit class compromise that both parties endorsed and, as problems arose, the further evolution of policy became the subject of detailed negotiations between the state and the relevant producers groups. In the meantime, demand stimulus was a tide that floated all boats.

By contrast, the strategy chosen by Thatcher Government has been more exclusionary and conflictual. By relying on austerity to weed out the least efficient, and intensifying the degree to which resources are allocated through market mechanism, it imposed special hardships on those with the least market power. In a very uneven recession the costs of measures designed to raise profits at the expense of wages were borne primarily by the increasing numbers of unemployed. There is a very real sense in which Britain is again a country of 'two nations'.

Higher levels of social conflict were the natural result of policies that renounced bargaining in favor of more unilateral state action; but there has also been an element of deliberate divisiveness in the strategy. The Prime Minister practiced a 'politics of friends and enemies' designed to win support by rallying national opposition to a few groups designated as antagonists. Prominent among the latter were international foes, such as the Soviet Union and Argentina, but several internal groups have also been treated as enemies of the nation, including inner-city rioters, football hooligans, drug dealers, and striking trade unions.[5]

It remains to be seen whether an appeal to nationalistic symbols and material incentives for the working population can counterbalance economic policies that intensify the hardships of a growing underclass. The viability of that political strategy is likely to depend on the capacity of the economic policies to regenerate economic growth and forestall a further period of prolonged mass unemployment. However, its fate will also be decided by the ability of Opposition politicians to conjure up alternative moral visions that seem to combine a greater measure of compassion with an equal measure of economic promise. As usual, the future of the British polity and economy rest, at least partly, on the ability of competing politicians to employ material incentives and symbolic instruments to construct new social coalitions.

PART III: The Political Economy of France

6

The Political Role of Economic Planning in France

Since World War Two the French economy has followed a pattern of state-led growth. At its heart was a profound transformation in state–society relations. During the Third Republic (1870–1940) the French state stood above society, as the guarantor of social balance. A legislature torn between competing factions of a politically fragmented bourgeoisie and working class could do little more than preside over a fragile social stasis. After a century of bitter conflict and frequent regime-change, it sought political stability above all else. As Stanley Hoffmann has observed, this was a Republic "with plenty of brakes and not much of a motor" (Hoffmann, 1963).

During the war, however, many of the leaders of the Third Republic were discredited by collaboration with the Vichy regime that accompanied German occupation. They were replaced in the immediate post-war period by a new generation of leaders determined to make a break with the past. Many had fought alongside the Communists in the French Resistance or served with the Free French under General Charles de Gaulle. Their agenda was as much economic as political (Kuisel, 1981). In the late 1940s France was still a nation of small producers, heavily agricultural and industrially stagnant. Most French firms were much smaller and less aggressive than their counterparts abroad. The architects of post-war French institutions decided to use the state to stimulate socio-economic change. If the paramount goal of those who survived World War One had been to secure social stability, those who rebuilt France after World War Two aimed at economic growth and prosperity (Maier, 1981).

For this purpose they extended state control over key sectors of the economy and established several institutions designed to reinforce the economic will and capacities of the state. The nationalization of the Bank of France begun in 1936 was completed and state control over the flows of funds in the economy was extended through nationalization of several private banks. The gas, electricity, and coal industries were nationalized, as were Air France and most of the largest insurance firms. Within the state itself, a national planning commission (Commissariat Général du Plan) was created along with a national agency for the collection and analysis of economic data (INSEE). Finally, the Ecole Nationale d'Administration (ENA) was founded to centralize recruitment to the senior civil service and to provide future French administrators with the skills and attitudes appropriate to the task of directing the French economy (Kessler, 1978; Kuisel, 1981: ch. 7). While nationalization of the primary industries, and above all else the centralization of credit control, gave the state new capacities, ENA and the CGP imbued French bureaucrats with the willingness to use those capacities.

With these institutional innovations, key parts of the French state prepared to embark on a strategy of state-led growth. Over the course of the post-war period their approach was characterized by expansion of the nationalized sector, a highly interventionist industrial policy toward the private sector, the extensive use of diplomatic pressure in support of exports, and the development of a system of national economic planning. Although the relative importance of the various components fluctuated, the centerpiece of the French strategy for most of this period was the system of economic planning. The Plans contained the most explicit statement of the government's industrial goals and privileged techniques. For this reason we can best approach the evolution of French economic policy through an examination of planning.

French planning occupies a special place among the economic techniques of the advanced industrial societies. As Aaron Wildavsky (1973: 147) has noted: "When really pushed to show results, somewhere, someplace, sometime, planning advocates are likely to cite the accomplishments of indicative planning on the French model as the modern success story of their trade." Despite its fame, however, the Plan is not easy to describe. Conventional definitions oscillate between the highly abstract and the overly concrete. The Plan is something more than merely a document produced every 5 years but something less than a mechanism for the elimination of social uncertainty.

The purpose of this chapter is to describe the operation of French planning and the role that it plays within the political economy of France. We begin with a straightforward account of the contribution that the Plan has made to the French economy. Within the historical perspective sketched above, however, it should be apparent that planning has also contributed to the evolution of state–society relations in France. Therefore we must go beyond the conventional economic view of the Plan to consider its political role within post-war French society.

THE ADMINISTRATION OF ECONOMIC PLANNING

Planning was initiated in 1946 with the establishment of the Commissariat Général du Plan as an independent agency reporting to the Prime
Minister and charged with the preparation of a national socioeconomic
plan for the ensuing 5 years. Under Jean Monnet, its first Commissioner, a small planning office was established in the rue de Martignac.
It was initially staffed with about 50 civil servants; by 1979 it employed
140 full-time staff but remained one of the smallest French agencies.
The Commission drew on the statistics and economic expertise of
INSEE and the Ministry of Finance to construct a series of plausible
economic scenarios for the coming years. In the 1970s a formal macroeconomic model, FIFI, was used for this purpose; earlier estimations
were based on national income projections and rough input–output
models. These global estimates were employed to establish the broad
constraints within which more detailed economic planning for major
industrial sectors and regions would be conducted.

Given its small personnel, the bulk of the Planning Commission's
work was carried out by a series of committees, known as Modernization Commissions, which brought businessmen, trade unionists, outside experts, and other civil servants together with the planning staff to
discuss the future of key industrial sectors and potential problem areas
within the economy (see figure 6.1). In 1946 there were 10 such
Commissions with a total of 494 members. By 1963 the Fifth Plan
employed 1950 people on 32 Commissions. Those concerned with a
particular sector were often called Vertical Commissions; those discus-
sing a problem area, such as regional policy, manpower or research and
development, were known as Horizontal Commissions. After consultation with the government, the planning staff integrated the reports
from these Commissions into a statement of options that was debated
in the Economic and Social Council and the National Assembly before
being elaborated into a final Plan. It was again submitted to the
Economic and Social Council for advice and to the National Assembly
for approval (see figure 6.2).[1]

THE NINE FRENCH PLANS, 1946–88

We cannot describe the content of a typical French Plan because there
have been nine separate Plans, each with its own character and goals. A
brief chronology is therefore in order.

The First Plan was the Monnet Plan implemented in 1946 initially to
cover the period to 1950 but extended with some revisions until 1953. It
was inspired by the need to allocate Marshall Plan aid and domestic

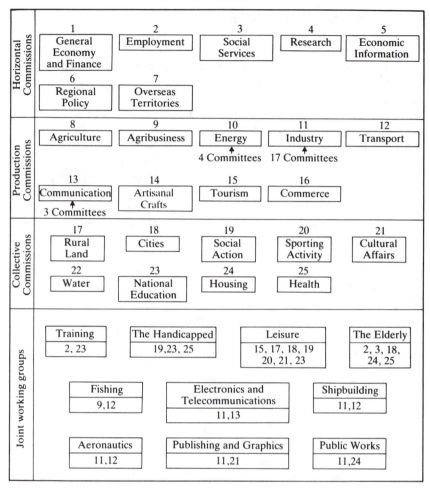

Figure 6.1   The Modernization Commissions for the Sixth Plan
Source: Pascallon (1974), p. 32. Note: the numbers associated with each working group represent its affiliated commissions.

resources (which were very scarce in the years just after the war) to the industrial sectors on which economic growth was most likely to depend. Accordingly, the Plan presented detailed investment programs for the six sectors deemed most crucial for subsequent economic development: steel, coal, transportation, electricity, cement, and agricultural machinery. In 1950 the fuel and fertilizer sectors were added. Not only investment, but import licenses, building permits and price concessions were allocated in accord with the Plan's list of priorities. The principal object of the Plan was to remove impediments to production from the most vulnerable sectors of the economy, and at this it was remarkably successful. Almost all of the Plan's targets for these sectors were attained by 1953 (Cohen, 1977: Pt. III).

The Second Plan (1953–57) continued to give priority to heavy industry but broadened its goals to include the removal of restrictive practices and the stimulation of growth throughout the economy. Accordingly, it set detailed investment and production targets for the whole of manufacturing industry. Its object was a 25 percent increase in gross domestic product (GDP) over 4 years. In fact the economy grew by 30 percent during this time, a striking accomplishment marred only by an accelerating rate of inflation and an unexpected increase in imports that entailed balance of payments problems (Sheahan, 1963).

Accordingly, the Third Plan for 1957-61 concentrated on import substitution in order to correct the imbalance of payments. It presented detailed growth projections (for virtually all sectors of the economy) that interlocked into an overall program for resource allocation. By 1961 the 20 percent growth of GDP anticipated in the Plan had been achieved, but it must be noted that the economy's trajectory toward that goal bore little resemblance to the planners' projections. When General de Gaulle initiated the Fifth Republic in 1958, he followed the advice of Jacques Rueff and the Ministry of Finance to devalue the franc and deflate, precipitating a recession, in order to improve the balance of payments. An Interim Plan for 1961–63 was then drawn up, but the disruption engendered by short-term macroeconomic management rendered the planners' intricate projections virtually meaningless (Cohen, 1977: 282 ff).

The Fourth Plan (1962–65) again presented a detailed set of targets for output and investment in each industrial sector, focusing on steel, telecommunications, chemicals, construction, household electronics and public works in particular. Once again, however, the Plan did not specify which short-term policies would be necessary to attain these objectives; and it was thrown off course by the deflationary Stabilization Plan introduced in September 1963 by the Finance Minister, Valéry Giscard d'Estaing. Nevertheless, several crucial investment programs escaped these financial cutbacks at the insistence of the planners; and although some sectoral goals were not attained, the global target of 24 percent growth by 1965 was fully realized.

The Fifth Plan (1965–70) responded to the experience of its predecessor by emphasizing macroeconomic indicators designed to guide short-term policy, rather than targets for the physical output of sectors. For the first time, projections for prices and incomes figured prominently in the Plan, and more attention was paid to international competitiveness and to ancillary social goals associated with regional inequalities. The social unrest of May 1968 led the Government to devalue the franc and reduce public expenditure so that, although the

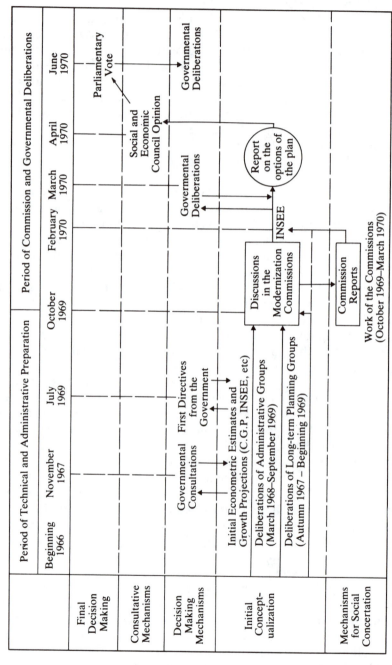

Figure 6.2   The Process of Formulating a National Plan (6th Plan)
Source: Pascallon (1974), p. 37.

Plan's growth projections were more than fulfilled, its public spending targets were not met and the rate of inflation (at 4.4 percent a year) far exceeded the 1.5 percent norm specified in the Plan (Estrin and Holmes, 1983: 68).

The Sixth Plan (1970–75) put renewed emphasis on the growth of heavy industry. It concentrated on six basic policy options elaborated into 25 specific objectives, and introduced a set of indicators, known as *clignotants* or warning lights, designed to direct the government toward corrective action when the goals of the Plan were not being met. While some provision was made for social infrastructure, the basic object of the Plan was to create a more favorable environment for industry. Once again the planners were most concerned about the ability of French manufacturers to compete within the newly liberalized trading regime of the European Economic Community. The ambitious 7.5 percent annual growth rate anticipated in the Plan was largely achieved until the oil crisis of autumn 1973 plunged the world into recession.

The Seventh Plan (1975–81) was primarily concerned with France's adjustment to that recession. It gave priority to the control of inflation, the balance of payments, and the restoration of full employment. Although the Plan projected a return to full employment, it contained no specific macroeconomic targets and few sectoral analyses. Instead, it emphasized 25 'priority programs' designed to direct public expenditure toward key social and economic problems. Most prominent among these was a massive commitment to rebuild the French telephone system and telecommunications industry. Although this last goal was accomplished, most of the other targets, including that of full employment, were subordinated to the deflationary program that Prime Minister Raymond Barre introduced in 1976 to reduce inflation and improve the balance of payments.

An Eighth Plan (1981–85), which concentrated on industrial competitiveness, the reduction of French energy dependence on outside sources, agriculture, employment and housing, was published in 1981 but abandoned immediately when the Socialists under President François Mitterrand won the elections of May and June 1981. The new Government soon introduced an Interim Plan for 1982–83, which gave absolute priority to the reduction of unemployment. Its aim was to generate 500,000 jobs over 2 years, primarily through an expansion of the public sector. By 1983 about 300,000 jobs had been created, but balance of payments problems forced the government to reintroduce an austerity program.

The Ninth Plan for 1983–88 was less sanguine than many of its predecessors about France's economic prospects. It foresaw continuing austerity to correct the balance of payments deficit until 1986, and again made the reduction of unemployment a principal goal.

THE EVOLUTION OF PLANNING

It should be apparent that both the content of the Plans and the nature of the planning process have changed substantially over the past four decades. Four developments deserve special mention. Each was induced in order to strengthen the Plan, yet, curiously, the planning process emerged from each a little weaker.

The initial, and most important, shift came in the move from the limited industrial Plans of the 1940s and early 1950s to the global resource allocation attempted in the Plans of the 1960s. The First Plan, as devised by Jean Monnet, had a single goal: modernization of the supply side of the economy by removing bottlenecks in six sectors of industry. Its targets were clear and the subject of wide consensus. The Second and Third Plans were more ambitious. Their projections extended to a broader range of industrial sectors and became economically more detailed. However, they made no attempt to define broad macroeconomic objectives, and the profile of the Plan itself was lowered in the 1950s to fend off criticism from the feuding politicians of the Fourth Republic. In general, planning remained a small, technical operation with a fairly limited set of objectives.

By 1963, however, the Planning Commission was asked to provide a blueprint for the optimal allocation of resources among all sectors of the economy. The number of people involved in its preparation tripled between the Third and Fifth Plans, and the planners were asked to consider social as well as economic goals. When the Fifth Plan appeared in 1965, it contained detailed macroeconomic projections for the entire economy. Complex appendices described the intricate networks of goods and funds that were supposed to flow from each sector of the economy to the others. Commentators began to speak of "*le Plan comme l'anti-hasard.*"

This development can be attributed, in part, to the growing technical virtuosity of the planners. Through INSEE they began to acquire a substantial body of data about the economy and sophisticated macroeconomic models for analyzing it. The temptation to use this knowledge to realize long-range policy objectives was almost too great to pass up. Equally important, however, was the inception of the Fifth Republic, which strengthened the Presidency and brought General Charles de Gaulle to power. Committed to enhancing France's position in the world, and conscious that her power depended increasingly on economic might, de Gaulle was highly sympathetic to the planners' project. He declared that:

In a nation and under a regime such as our own, change is constantly necessary . . . at my level, the Plan is needed because it covers everything, fixes the objectives, establishes a hierarchy of need and importance and introduces among both officials and even in the public spirit a sense that what is global, ordered and continuous compensates for the inconveniences associated with liberty without losing its advantages. Therefore, I will ensure that the preparation and execution of the Plan take on a profile that they have not had before, giving them the character of 'a burning obligation' (Prate, 1978: 82).

Accordingly, the planners challenged fate; but economic management is rarely a match for the forces arrayed against it. While the early Plans depended mainly on the correct identification of bottlenecks and the judicious application of capital spending, global resource planning required exceptionally accurate predictions of the course that all economic sectors would take. As the Plans became more grandiose they became more fragile. Sudden shocks, such as the strikes of 1963 or the oil crisis of 1973 which earlier Plans might have absorbed, rocked the very framework of the Fourth and Seventh Plans; and while limited Plans encouraged congruent short-term policies, global Plans depended on them.

A second major shift in the nature of planning occurred in the early 1960s when the ambitions of the Plan were further extended from management of the economy to the provision of a social infrastructure. After 15 years the French realized that planning had brought growth without prosperity. French workers still enjoyed the longest working week in Europe, as well as the continent's most unequal distribution of income. France had one of the highest growth rates in the Western world but only one telephone for every seven people and toilets for only half the housing units in Paris (Cohen, 1977b: 263). The planners were asked to redress these problems and, in 1962 "*le Plan de modernisation et d'équipement*" became "*le Plan de développement économique et sociale.*" A widening circle of social actors wanted to see their concerns addressed by the Plan (Hamon, 1966; Hayward, 1973). Accordingly, the Fourth Plan provided for construction of schools and hospitals, and the Fifth Plan was heavily oriented toward social policy. For over a decade the social theme dominated much of the planning process.

By 1970, however, this attempt to improve the quality of life rather than simply expand the quantity of goods in France had produced mixed results. Three crucial programs collapsed, in apparent testimony to the difficulty of achieving reform in French society (cf. Crozier, 1973). The planners' attempts to direct the construction of new public facilities were stymied by the determination of the Gaullist party to retain control over such projects within the traditional Ministries, where they could be manipulated for political purposes; and public construction budgets soon proved to be one of the easiest targets for spending cuts in the face of short-term economic fluctuations (cf. Grémion, 1976). An attempt to rationalize the social security system during the Fifth Plan was withdrawn in response to protests from peasants, trade unionists and shopkeepers (Cohen and Goldfinger, 1975). A widely heralded reform of the university system collapsed when students at the program's prototype campus in Nanterre took to the streets to begin the events of May 1968 (Fomerand, 1975). A decade had been devoted to planning according to *"une idée moins partielle de l'homme"* only to end in the Sixth Plan with a return to the focus on heavy industrial growth.

The third significant transformation in planning came in the late 1960s and 1970s when its focus shifted from economic growth *per se* to the drive toward international competitiveness. That was a response to the opening of the French economy, which began in 1959 when the Treaty of Rome initiated the European Economic Community, and accelerated with the tariff reductions of the Kennedy Round and the final abolition of tariffs between EEC nations on 30 June 1968. These developments meant that French firms, which had been sheltered behind tariff barriers for over a century, would have to compete on an equal basis with foreign firms, not only for world markets but for domestic sales as well. The invasion by American multinationals, drawn to France by the prospect of access to the entire European market, added a further dimension to the threat (Servan-Schreiber, 1969).

During the 1950s the planners' principal task had been to secure high levels of production. Much like Stakhanovites, they showed less concern for the marketability of goods and the efficiency of manufacturing than for the volume of production in basic industries (Scott and Sprout, 1981). The first three Plans sought expansion at any cost. To this end they channelled large amounts of capital toward sectors (rather than to individual enterprises that were the competitive units), depressed the cost of capital in such a way as to encourage over-investment rather than the efficient allocation of funds, and accepted high levels of inflation as a catalyst for industrial borrowing.

In the newly open economy, however, import controls could no longer be used to adjust the balance of payments, and inflation posed a real menace to export growth. Therefore, the side-effects of the old policy became the focus of the new one. The Government began to show genuine concern about the rate of growth of wages and prices. In the early 1960s tentative moves toward an incomes policy were made, and the Fifth Plan deliberately considered the impact of its proposals on the rate of inflation and the wage share. Not surprisingly, profits were projected to increase by 8.6 percent a year, while wage growth was to be restricted to 3.3 percent per capita (Cohen, 1977: 186).

The principal shift, however, came at the microeconomic level. Termed *la nouvelle politique industrielle*, the dominant feature of the new program was a concern for the competitiveness of individual firms rather than the growth of entire sectors. To this end, grants that had once been given to every firm in a sector were now offered only to a few. Funds that once flowed freely to encourage expansion were now tied to schemes for industrial reorganization. The planners sought new tools to replace the broad regulations and open-ended subsidies that characterized earlier policies. They now turned to more selective incentives and the negotiation of bilateral agreements whereby individual firms, in effect, entered into contracts with the state: *contrats fiscaux, contrats de stabilité*, and *contrats de programme* (Debbasch, 1969: 128 ff; MacLennan et al., 1968: 276 ff).

These new forms of intervention were used in the first instance to accelerate the consolidation of many industrial sectors, where small, family firms oriented to a fixed market share were replaced or merged into industrial giants capable of competing aggressively on world markets. The primary objective of industrial policy, in the words of the Fifth Plan, was "the establishment or reinforcement . . . of a small number of firms or groups of international size . . . in most industrial sectors (aluminium, steel, mechanical and electrical engineering, electronics, motor cars, aircraft, chemicals, pharmaceutical products, etc.). The number of these groups should be very small, often even reduced to one or two" (Commissariat Général du Plan, 1965: 68). This policy endeavored to create 'national champions', groomed to carry the colors of France on the battlefield of the new international economic order (cf. Vernon, 1974: ch. 6).

As a result of this initiative, each year between 1966 and 1969 saw a series of mergers with a value twice that of mergers in the entire period 1950–60 (Warnecke and Suleiman, 1975: 27). France did develop a series of national champions in many of the leading industrial sectors: Péchiney-Ugine-Kuhlmann, Saint-Gobain-Pont à Mousson, Thomson-CSF, Agache-Willot, Creusot-Loire, and Dassault were all enlarged in these years. By 1974, however, even the planners were beginning to doubt whether the scale of a firm was the fundamental determinant of its international competitiveness. Several of these ventures, notably in the steel, chemical and computer sectors, proved to be a massive drain on the public treasury without ever achieving the levels of efficiency that would have made them powerful competitors even for the French market (cf. Zysman, 1977). Many of the 'national champions' of the 1960s proved to be the 'lame ducks' of the 1970s (Berger, 1980).

Consequently, an enduring concern for competitiveness led the authorities to look elsewhere during the second half of the 1970s. The government began to take the view that small firms were more likely to secure niches in the international market and retain the flexibility to survive recession (cf. Piore and Sabel, 1984). Some suggested that only full exposure to international market forces could generate and assure the competitiveness of French industry. Exponents of this view called into question the advantages of state-led industrial strategies and of planning itself (cf. Stoffaes, 1978).

As these developments were taking place the planning process underwent a fourth transformation. What had begun as a relatively technical operation, managed by civil servants with some distance from the political parties in power, became increasingly politicized. Throughout the 1950s the planners had skillfully maintained their autonomy from the legislature and from the rather weak political executive of the Fourth Republic. The Modernization Commissions emerged as non-partisan institutions, capable of bridging the social divisions in French society where the politicians had failed. During this period it was unusual for the National Assembly even to review the Plan. By their very success, the planners preserved a certain technical credibility and independence.

With the advent of the Fifth Republic in 1958, however, the political context of planning changed. The Constitution conferred substantial new powers on the political executive. It replaced the legislature as the principal political threat to the planners; and a united Gaullist party under a strong President began to enjoy some continuity in office. The President himself embraced the Plan as if it were his own, and began to give it a high political profile. These developments enhanced the control that the political executive could exercise over the planners, and encouraged both the Government and the electorate to see the Plan as a program for which the Government bore direct responsibility.

Not surprisingly, successive Governments started to take an active interest in the content of the Plans. This first became apparent in a small way when the Planning Commissioner was forced to remove politically embarrassing inflation projections from the Fourth Plan (McArthur and Scott, 1969: xxii). Soon the Prime Minister began appointing close allies to the key post of Planning Commissioner (Ortoli in 1966, Montjoie in 1967 and Albert in 1974). By 1965 the Government did not even bother to let the Modernization Commissions finish their deliberations before it published the Fifth Plan; and the Planning Commissioner opened work on the Seventh Plan by declaring that: "On behalf of the Government, I am undertaking consultations, but the Government will be the sole judge of what it wishes to retain and propose for the approval of Parliament . . ." (Prévot et al., 1977: 54; Hayward, 1973). Ultimately, substantial portions of the Eighth Plan were entirely rewritten by the Prime Minister's office (*Le Canard Enchaîné*, 10 September 1980). The Plan had become a highly political document and the planners began to act as an adjunct to the Government's industrial policy.

THE IMPLEMENTATION OF THE PLAN AND INDUSTRIAL POLICY

From the outset, French planning has been an ideological project. Monnet's strategy was clear: "As great as the weight of its reports, it is by the marshalling of simple ideas, few in number but widely disseminated, that the Plan will become a national reality" (Monnet, 1976: 306). This was, in fact, merely a recognition of necessity. With a small staff in the rue de Martignac the Planning Commission could not hope to direct the French economy by edict. Instead, its persistent arguments for industrial restructuring and policies directed toward growth were meant to persuade industrialists and economic policy-makers alike to pursue strategies in line with the goals of the Plan.

By creating a climate of opinion that emphasized the importance of economic growth and the means to achieving it, the planners hoped the Plans' objectives would become self-fulfilling prophecies. Believing that their customers and the state would act in accord with the Plan to increase output, businessmen would expand their own capacity in anticipation of rising demand. Accordingly, demand and capacity would rise. The prophecy, once promulgated and made credible, would be fulfilled.

In most respects the ideological project of the planners was highly successful. In the otherwise stagnant 1950s they were able to create a climate of opinion conducive to economic growth. To some extent, optimistic growth projections could become self-fulfilling prophecies because they built the business confidence on which corporate expansion depended. During the 1960s and 1970s the planners also warned policy-makers and industrialists about the imminent threats posed by intensified foreign competition and domestic energy costs. Many commentators believe that the provision of more accurate sources of information and the improvement of business confidence were the principal contributions of the planners to the French economy (McArthur and Scott, 1969).

The attention drawn to this aspect of planning, however, tended to convey a slightly misleading picture of French planning and industrial policy in general. Many Britons, in particular, viewed French planning as a purely "indicative" exercise, namely "a system which relies on pointing out desirable ends rather than on giving orders to achieve them" (Shonfield, 1969: 84). The National Economic Development

Council and the National Plans of the 1964–70 Labour Government, for instance, were largely indicative instruments, adopted in the belief that they would emulate the French system of planning (Leruez, 1975).

As the British belatedly discovered, however, the French strategy of state-led growth did not depend entirely on the persuasiveness of the planners' ideas. On the one hand the bureaucrats could not monitor the behavior of more than a small proportion of French business. Many firms were barely influenced by industrial policy-makers, taking their cues instead from the market (McArthur and Scott, 1969). In that respect the French system never resembled the mechanisms for central planning employed in Eastern Europe. On the other hand the state paid considerable attention to the largest enterprises in key sectors and, when necessary, could bring a substantial range of material sanctions to bear on firms whose cooperation with the goals of the Plan was sought.

There are multiple ways in which the French state exerts influence over the private sector. As a buyer its goodwill is vital to many firms. In 1978, for instance, the state bought goods worth 128 billion francs from the private sector (Lougovoy, 1981: 371). Many of the nationalized industries virtually control subsidiary sectors, such as the electrical equipment industry (Cohen, 1977a: 26). As a seller, through the nationalized firms, the state controls raw materials – including most forms of energy and transportation – important to many industrialists.

Public investment has always been a mainstay of French industry. In its first 4 years the Plan provided 50 percent of the nation's total capital investment; and public funds still account for almost half of the gross fixed capital investment in France. In many cases these have been allocated to private enterprises in return for their consent to "*quasi-contrats*" that require investment to accord with the goals of the Plan. The system of price control, in force continuously since 1945 (with the exception of 1976–81) gave the state the ability to regulate the prices most firms charged for their products or, more important, to demand compliance with national industrial strategy in exchange for exemption from price control (Bonnaud, 1970).

Various forms of regulation confer additional power on the government. For example, for many years the Ministry of Finance had to approve all new bond issues and any issues of capital stock in excess of 250,000 francs.[2] The taxation system has also been used to influence the behavior of industry (Lutz, 1963: chs. 5 and 6). There is strong evidence, for instance, that the surge in French exports after 1958 was a direct by-product of new depreciation allowances granted to firms which export more than 20 percent of their sales (MacLennan et al., 1968: 164). And in the 1960s the government employed a series of '*contrats fiscaux*' that conferred privileged tax treatment in return for a firm's agreement to undertake certain operations.

By far the most powerful weapon in the arsenal of the French state, however, is the preponderant role that the nationalized banks and the Bank of France play in the allocation of private investment. Since the Paris *Bourse* is quite small, most French firms depend on long-term loans for their capital needs. By 1950 many of the lending institutions to which business might have turned were already under state control, including the Crédit National, Crédit Agricole, Crédit Hotêlier, Société Générale, and the Banque Française de Commerce Extérieur. Some of these rank among the largest banks in the world. Even before President Mitterrand nationalized the banking system in 1981, over 70 percent of French lending was under the control of the public sector (Lougovoy, 1981: 219).

More important yet, the French banks have traditionally redis-counted their large loans at the Bank of France. In other words they tended to seek approval and a partial guarantee for the loan from the central bank. The Bank of France, in turn, is controlled by the Ministry of Finance, through the National Credit Council. For much of the post-war period the rate of growth of the money supply in France has also been set by a system of direct quotas on bank lending, known as the *encadrement du crédit*; and the state often exempted certain industrial sectors from its lending limits. At one point, for instance, all requests from private firms for medium-term credit over 500,000 francs and long-term credit over 2.5 million francs had to be approved by the Crédit National, the Planning Commission, and the Bank of France. Through these kind of mechanisms the French state has been in a position to control the allocation of credit to French industry. It has often used this power to enforce an industrial strategy (Zysman, 1983, 1977; Morin, 1974; Cohen et al., 1982).

The other remarkable aspect of French industrial policy has been its reliance on what might be called 'exceptionalism'. Tocqueville (1955: 66) first identified the practice under the *Ancien Régime*. He observed:

> In point of fact, there were no royal edicts or decrees, no letters patent duly embodied in the code book that did not lend themselves to a host of differing interpretations when they were applied to particular cases. Letters from the Controller-General and the Intendants show that government was always ready to countenance deviations from the orders issued by it. . . . There we have the old regime in a nutshell: rigid rules, but flexibility, not to say laxity, in their application.

The post-war French state followed a similar practice of burdening firms with such a multitude of restrictive regulations that few could survive without selective exemptions that rendered them dependent on the goodwill of the industrial policy-makers (Stoléru, 1969: 148 ff).

In the 1950s, for instance, the planners took advantage of a tight credit situation, made worse by the French peasant's traditional prefer-ence for highly liquid assets, to consolidate their control over bank lending (MacLennan et al., 1968: 167; Bauchet, 1964: 105). In the 1960s the planners were happy to encourage a measure of inflation because it rendered the system of price control even more constricting for most firms, and thereby enhanced the power implicit in their ability to grant exemptions. This is what makes French price control such a deceptive operation. Apart from short periods when a temporary price freeze was utilized to halt the spread of inflation, the main function of the system has been to facilitate the granting of relief through *contrats de stabilité, contrats de program*, and *contrats anti-hausse* with indi-vidual firms. In the 1960s these were awarded by the thousands, each entailing cooperation with some aspect of government policy (Gré-mion, 1974: 182; Franck, 1964). Taxation has been used in the same way. As the Rueff Report of 1958 observed, "French finance is honey-combed with special exceptions and exemptions" (McArthur and Scott, 1969: 286; Shonfield, 1969: 165; Pascallon, 1974: 103–4).

Exceptionalism accords well with the two-tier operation of French economic policy. At one level the explicit general rules, such as corpor-ate taxation or price control, assure the electorate that the government is enacting popular legislation; but the existence of these rules simulta-neously enhances the ability of the planners to reach bilateral agreements with business. Moreover, when negotiating with individual companies in this environment, the state can offer them positive inducements, in the form of exceptions, rather than penalties for non-compliance. This encourages closer working-relations between business and government, enabling the state to portray itself as an angel of mercy rather than the prince of destruction, and ultimately enhances the ease with which it controls many aspects of business activity (Wildavsky, 1973: 97).

Control over these sanctions, of course, does not rest exclusively with the Planning Commission. In order to implement the Plan the Commission depends on the cooperation of several other agencies. The *Fonds de développement économique et social* (FDES) established in 1955, for instance, has been responsible for allocating up to 4 billion francs a year (1968) in subsidies to encourage firms to undertake projects in line with the Plan. Similarly, subdivisions of the Ministry of Industry often bear responsibility for the development of particular industrial sectors in conjunction with subcommittees of the FDES. In most cases the planners have representatives on the inter-ministerial committees that allocate subsidized funds or grant exceptions to regula-tions, in return for appropriate behavior from a firm. Their task is to persuade these committees to act in accordance with the Plan. Figure 6.3 identifies the networks that connect the institutions. The evidence suggests that the planners are particularly dependent on cooperation from the Ministry of Economics and Finance, whose officials chair many of the key committees and control access to the banking network. Thus, the industrial strategy that the state ultimately implements is a hybrid of actions taken by many different agencies. The Ministry of Finance occupies the central position among them, but the Plan was designed to be the template against which the appropriateness of these actions would be measured. The Plan has never been entirely synonymous with French industrial policy, in part because its influence depends on the planners' persuasiveness within a myriad of inter-ministerial committees.

In this light it should be apparent that a simple dichotomy between 'indicative' and 'coercive' planning does not capture the character of the French experience. While the formal aspects of the Plan's operation emphasize its purely indicative character, planning was actually coupled with a more dirigiste industrial policy to form a pattern of state-led growth. French policy-makers made skillful use of the difficulties facing industry, wearing the blandishments of the Plan with material incentives and market stimuli into a rope that pulled French business from a position of economic backwardness to the forefront of the European economy.

THE POLITICAL FUNCTIONS OF ECONOMIC PLANNING

The successes of planning were as much political as economic achievements. Any project whereby the state attempts to transform society must have a significant political dimension. Without endorsing the full-blown causal analysis that functionalist terminology sometimes implies, we might say that the planning process performed several crucial political functions for the project as a whole. However, this is a case in which Robert Merton's (1969) classic distinction between manifest and latent functions can usefully be applied. Many accounts of the Plan, including those written by its own officials, suggest that it was designed to perform three basic functions. These are often described as: the development of participation, the achievement of transparency, and the enforcement of rationality. However, we need to separate the manifest functions of the Plan from a set of latent functions which gradually became the more important tasks it performed within the overall project of social modernization. By separating rhetoric from reality in this way, we can also identify the most important political dimensions of planning.

From participation to alliance-building

Since its inception in the famous memorandum of 5 December 1945 from Monnet to de Gaulle, the Plan has been presented as a mechan-

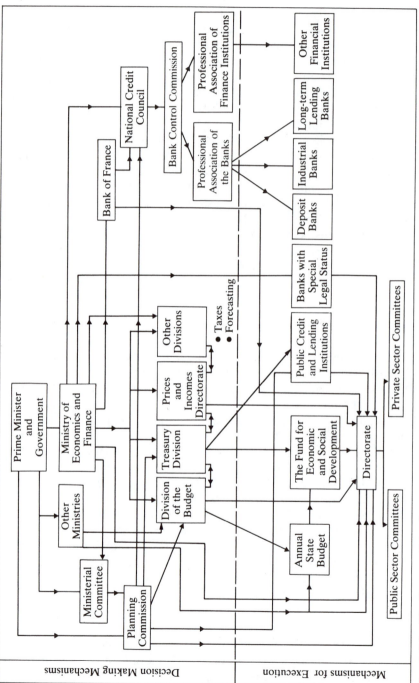

Figure 6.3   The Process of Implementing a National Plan (6th Plan)

ism for ensuring wide participation in the determination of economic goals and priorities (Monnet, 1976: 282). "The spirit of the Plan" was said to be "the agreement of all economic and social forces in the nation" (Massé, 1965: 152). Formal discussions of the Plan were supposed to be "a means of providing the citizens with effective participation in the exercise of political power" (Club Jean Moulin, 1961).

Initially the Plan did draw a variety of social actors into the process of industrial policy-making. At this time the affected groups were concentrated in six sectors of heavy industry where there was general agreement on the need for growth. But as planning became more ambitious and its decisions less clear-cut, the question of who was to bear the sacrifices of reorganization became increasingly controversial. Just as full citizen participation raises difficulties when determining the site of airports – everyone wants them in someone else's community – so too can it impede industrial rationalization (Milch, 1976). The public revelation of economic strategy encouraged those who would lose from it to begin protests at an early stage in the deliberations.

At the same time the planners found that their state-led strategy required increasingly close cooperation with the managers who controlled the means of production in key sectors and firms. In the 1960s the move toward a new industrial policy concerned with enhancing the competitiveness of individual firms brought about important changes in the structure of relations between business and the state. This policy depended on the negotiation of bilateral agreements between the state and individual enterprises that could be negotiated only behind closed doors. Moreover, the planners were no longer interested in feeding resources to entire sectors, favoring instead increased support for individual firms selected as the new "national champions."

These developments had profound implications for the planning process. The planners dealt with them by developing a private side to the process, operating in tandem with the public side of the Plan but hidden from public scrutiny and involving a much more restricted group of participants. It was here that the most crucial decisions were taken. Therefore, while the number of participants in the formal deliberations of the Plan increased dramatically from 1946 to 1970, the locus of power within the planning process shifted to a set of private discussions between state officials and small groups of enterprise managers who bargained over an industrial strategy.

Planning became "a rather clandestine affair" or "a conspiracy in the public interest between big business and big officialdom" (Shonfield, 1969: 128, 137). By 1969 outside observers could note that "government strategy formulation for a sector such as the industrial sector of the economy has very little to do with the discussions of the vertical Modernization Commissions"; instead "strategic plans for all the industrial sectors were decided in private and outside the official institutions and procedures associated with the planning process" (McArthur and Scott, 1969: 74, 26; Friedberg, 1974; Gournay and Viot, 1963: 81).

To an increasing extent, then, planning was transformed from a widely participatory process into one through which the state could forge a series of alliances with selected industrial managers in the interest of economic reorganization. Since their own personnel lacked the information and enforcement facilities to impose reorganization on industry unilaterally, the industrial policy-makers needed some forum for securing the advice and acquiescence of industrialists. The Plan provided legitimacy for talks between the two parties, an agenda of issues, a context in which the representatives of an isolated business community could accustom themselves to dealing with the state, and an organ for coordinating the incentives used to secure acquiescence in the overall strategy (cf. Crozier, 1965). A set of institutions capable of legitimating such relations was doubly necessary in a society where "it was orthodox republican doctrine to deplore and denounce intermediary bodies which came between the citizen and the state" (Williams, 1966: 375).

The social actors most completely excluded from this process were the trade unions. According to one unionist's account of the Modernization Commission meetings: "It seems that everything happens as if the procedure was arranged beforehand in such a way that a certain number of decisions are taken by direct agreement between the employers' representatives and the civil servants." Another had "the very definite impression that our meetings are half-serious. Many parts seem to be agreed in advance between the representatives of the employers and the chairmen . . . of the groups, and the most interesting information supplied outside the official meetings" (PEP, 1960: 349; Hayward, 1967).

In response to this, two of France's largest unions, the Confédération Générale du Travail and Force Ouvrière, withdrew from participation in the preparation of the Second Plan and virtually boycotted the proceedings until the Eighth Plan. The Confédération Française Démocratique du Travail continued to participate in the formal sessions until the preparation of the Sixth Plan, when it withdrew with similar complaints. As a result, only 82 of the 615 individuals who met in the Modernization Commissions of the Third Plan, for instance, were trade unionists (PEP, 1960: 349; MacLennan et al., 1968: 348). For over 30 years the representatives of labor have played little role in the planning process.

In this respect the planning process replicated and reinforced the general balance of power in the French polity where labor occupied a position subordinate to capital. During a brief period of strength, resulting from their participation in the Resistance, the Communists and Socialists contributed to the nationalizations and establishment of planning itself in such a way as to fortify the position of the state *vis-à-vis* society immediately after the war. However, the Communist Party was expelled from the governing coalition in 1947 and remained out of office until 1981. Just as in Japan, a succession of conservative Governments administered the dirigiste policies of post-war France.

To some extent the organizational weakness of labor may have contributed to its political inefficacy. Barely 15–20 percent of the labor force was unionized in France, and membership was split among four major confederations. Of these, the CGT was affiliated to a politically isolated Communist Party that was unable or unwilling to form a common front with the Socialists; and the latter found that occasional participation in the conservative Governments of the 1950s tended to weaken their ties to the CFDT and FO. As in the preceding century, the right continued to draw on a reservoir of support from the large agricultural sector in France. Therefore there was little the unions could do to prevent the state from using the Plan to forge an alliance with the dynamic sections of capital.

FROM ECONOMIC LIGHT TO POLITICAL SHADOW

The second function normally associated with planning might be called the achievement of transparency. The Plan "spells out the nation's economic choices and illuminates these choices by the consistency of its methods" (Bonnaud, 1966). In so doing it is supposed to "bring a greater clarity to the social debate and to political choices" (Ullmo, 1974: 22–4; Atreize, 1971: 353–4). By completely enumerating the policy choices and their implications, the planning process enables the nation to agree on the best one.

This notion has been closely tied to the concept of 'indicative planning'. Behind it lies the familiar assumption of contemporary economics that there is an essential harmony of interest among the actors in the socioeconomic field: conflicts among these actors arise primarily because they lack full information about their options and interests. By providing the missing information – about hidden interdependencies of interest and potential collective gains – the Plan was expected to turn this underlying harmony of interest into an *économie concerté*. It was as much in his capacity as an economist as that of a violinist that Etienne Hirsch coined the latter term (Monnet, 1976: 306).

But herein lies the inadequacy of transparency as a goal. The process of choosing is one of those peculiarly antinomic processes fundamental to human existence. It first entails a widening of options followed by a narrowing of these down to one. When a whole society selects an economic path, massive involvement in the widening of options only makes the subsequent narrowing down more difficult, because there are genuine conflicts of interest behind most policy options (cf. Dahrendorf, 1969). Political leaders face hard choices even after technical data about the options have been provided. As a result the achievement of real transparency intensifies social conflict, rather than reducing it. It calls all existing policies into question once again, shines a harsh light on the inadequacies of the regime, and threatens the ability of the government to win consent for its policies.

Successive French governments have understood this quite well. As a result the 'transparency' sought by most of the Plans resembled a strong light that illuminates certain aspects of a room, but leaves others in deliberate shadow (Nizard, 1973: 201). Schattschneider (1960: 71) called this phenomenon the 'mobilization of bias': a deliberate attempt to set the terms of a national discussion in such a way that the conclusion is predetermined without appearing to be so. The real purpose of the Plan became to narrow the choices being actively considered – by excluding proposals held to be unfeasible in a market economy, incompatible with high levels of growth, or antagonistic to the intensive development of advanced sectors of industry – while appearing to widen them. This capacity to maintain the appearance of doing one thing while actually doing its opposite was what ultimately accounted for the Plan's great effectiveness as an agency for the mobilization of bias.

The Plan accomplished this task by modifying the symbolic vocabulary with which the French make sense of their economy and society. The planners set out to construct "a specific symbolic representation of the medium-term constraints which could not be ignored without risk" (Nizard, 1973: 14). Although political choices were often presented as economic necessities, the terms of the Plan became the prism through which French officials and citizens viewed the economy. The Plan virtually defined what progress would consist in (cf. Hayward, 1967: 452; Fourastié, 1955). The intention was not only to facilitate the coordination of programs, but also to minimize social conflict. Planning operated at a deep level "to homogenize the conceptual terms of reference and therefore simultaneously to unify the administrative apparatus and through it the social sub-systems that it manages" (Nizard, 1973: 18).

At times the planners even resorted to a less subtle technique for the mobilization of bias: the alteration of forecasts to downplay the adverse effects of government action. The Fifth Plan deliberately underestimated the rate at which coal was likely to be displaced as a national energy source in order to obscure the socioeconomic problems that mine closings would entail; and estimates of productivity gains in the same Plan were understated to disguise the rate at which unemployment was likely to grow (McArthur and Scott, 1969: 142). In sum, planning involved the production of norms more than the delineation of choices. The nominal independence of the Planning Commission lent an air of technical credibility to proposals that might otherwise be politically suspect.

FROM AGENT OF RATIONALITY TO APPRENTICESHIP IN SOCIAL CHANGE

The third function often ascribed to French planning is to maximize the role of rationality in economic decision-making, in the dual sense of increasing the extent to which policies are chosen according to rational calculation and of improving the degree to which policies are coordinated with one another (cf. Wildavsky, 1973: 144; Gruson, 1968: 367; Ullmo, 1975: 24; Masse, 1965: 166). Thus, one analyst defined planning as "the periodic reexamination of the assignment of means to ends and of the manner in which the ends fit together" (Ullmo, 1974: 231). In practical terms that meant the coordination of policies synchronically, so that they complement rather than contradict each other, and diachronically, so that short-term policies fall into congruence with medium- and long-range goals.

To some extent the planners have served these ends. They forced several other organs of the French state to address the long-term economic problems facing the nation. Through participation on a variety of inter-ministerial committees, planners improved coordination among certain policy agencies. Their accomplishments, however, have been limited by the central role played by the Ministry of Finance in policy-making. That Ministry often saw itself as the guardian of fiscal stability and refused to alter short-term stabilization policies to correspond to the Plans' projections for long-run growth (Bauchard, 1963; Mariano, 1973).

At the microeconomic level, inter-departmental rivalry and the planners' dependence on other agencies to implement their projections often produced an industrial policy that resembled "a fire-fighting approach: the timing of state actions, the remedial measures, and the industries selected for attention . . . all seemed related to special crises rather than to a pre-developed plan" (McArthur and Scott, 1969: 471). This may be an overly harsh judgement. In comparative terms France still seems to have succeeded in developing a 'strategic state'; and the planners deserve some credit for enhancing the capacity of the state to think and act strategically (Cohen, 1982). However, there is no doubt that French policy remains far from fully coordinated.

In view of this it would be more accurate to describe the primary function of planning as socialization. Planning has provided what Crozier (1965: 65) terms 'an apprenticeship in social change'. If the Plans failed to bring all policies into congruence, they did change the outlook of key actors in both the public and private sectors. A population formerly oriented to the values summed up in that peculiarly French expression *"malthusianisme"* (which emphasizes preservation of the status quo, small-scale enterprise, and jealous protection of existing turf) were inculcated with a new set of attitudes favoring economic growth, large-scale enterprise, international competitiveness, and the pursuit of innovation. This was no mean achievement.

Moreover, the key social actors in a society where face-to-face negotiation was scorned were taught to sit down with one another and negotiate agreements on a host of issues, ranging from industrial renovation to collective bargaining. Into a polity which had been "absolutely closed to any discussion of social problems in rational terms because questions of ends were debated with great ideological intensity in complete isolation from questions of means," the Plan introduced pragmatic forms of debate about how to pursue the nation's collective goals (Crozier, 1973: 159). The Planning Commission's accomplishment was not so much *"la réduction de l'incertitude"* as *"la réduction de l'intransigeance"* (Hamon, 1966: 210–12).

Nowhere was this more apparent than in the operation of the early Plans. In many cases their detailed projections of inter-industry resource transfers were completely vitiated by intervening events; yet their overall growth targets were attained. We can account for this by noting that the most important component of the planners' message to industry was not its blueprint for the reallocation of resources but its enthusiasm for and faith in the possibility of growth. As Charles Kindleberger (1963: 155) observed, the most useful aspect of planning was that which had ". . . a faint resemblance to a revivalist prayer meeting."

CONCLUSION

This review suggests that in order to understand the role of the Plan we must appreciate the political dimensions of its task. Behind the motif of 'indicative planning' lay an apparatus with the capacity to put real pressure on private sector actors to conform to the government's economic strategy. Behind the rhetoric of the planners concerning participatory democracy, economic enlightenment, and rationality, French planning performed several latent functions even more crucial to the success of the overall project as its professed goals. The Plan provided an institutional framework within which the state could build alliances with key sectors of industry to effect industrial reorganization. As an agency for the mobilization of bias it helped secure consent for the government's economic policies; and it led the nation through an apprenticeship in social change.

We might summarize the role of the French Plan by saying that it served two basic purposes. Its primary task was the modernization and reorganization of the nation's productive apparatus. In that respect it was the centerpiece of a strategy of state-led growth. This entailed a measure of economic triage, letting the more inefficient sectors of French industry die – in some cases from exposure to the global market – and strengthening the sectors with apparent competitive potential in manufacturing and agriculture. However, this kind of activity inevitably generated social dislocation and resistance. Accordingly the Plan also served a second purpose – to prevent social conflict – a task that was accomplished in three ways: by masking individual loss with the veneer of common interest, by presenting industrial execution as economic euthanasia, and by tying present sacrifice to future gain. These functions were especially important in such a fragmented society.

Individual Plans occasionally took on additional tasks, but these two broad purposes remained central to planning throughout its development. As it happens they also define the problematic within which the eventual evolution of planning can be understood. It should be apparent that these two missions stand somewhat in contradiction to each other: the reorganization of production to attain greater efficiency tends to intensify the social conflict that planning is also supposed to prevent. How can two contradictory tasks be performed by the same institution? This dilemma plagued the operation of planning from the beginning. The next chapter will consider the subsequent evolution of the Plan as a process determined in large measure by attempts to resolve the tensions that these conflicting missions generated.

7

The State and the Evolution of Planning

Economic planning is a dynamic process that not only epitomizes state–society relations, but is also capable of reconstructing them. The preceding chapter examined the role that the planning process played in the broader strategy of state-led growth. It was deliberately employed by the managers of the French state to facilitate the reconstruction of the French economy. However, this is not the end of the story. As in the case of many public programs, the development of planning had several unintended consequences. In this instance those consequences led first, to a largely unanticipated alteration in the position of the state within French society, and secondly, to the decline of planning itself. By tracing the further evolution of French planning we confirm that state–society relations in a nation are not fixed but open to change.

For this purpose it will be useful to introduce the concept of étatism (*étatisme*). It is employed here as an ideal-type often used to refer to several putative features of the relationship between French society and the state. Those features are usually associated with France but need not be found exclusively there. The concept of étatism can be broken down into four dimensions.

The first involves the extent to which the state is a cohesive unit. The political and administrative apparatus of a state may be more or less unified or fragmented. Virtually all democratic theories favor some separation of powers between the executive, legislature and judiciary; but nations diverge considerably in the degree to which their institutional arrangements reflect such a separation. In America, for instance, the legislature and executive enjoy much greater independence from each other than has traditionally been the case in Britain or France. Similarly, the administrative agencies of government themselves may be closely coordinated by a superordinate institution or a powerful political executive, as in Fifth Republic France, or they may be left to follow more independent courses of policy, as in Fourth Republic France.

Closely related to this is the second dimension of étatism, namely the extent to which the state is insulated from the demands of other social actors. An étatist state stands somewhat apart from the society in which it is located. If a state is highly centralized, its points of contact with other societal institutions or groups are minimized, and the initiatives for policy are consequently more likely to come from within the state itself. This is a 'state above society' characteristic in some measure of many French regimes, ranging from the *Ancien Régime* to the Fifth Republic (cf. Hoffmann, 1978).

Although this kind of insulation provides the state with some freedom from social pressure, it does not necessarily mean that the government can impose its policies on resistant social groups. In the case of the Third Republic, insulation was symptomatic of a degree of impotence. There, a National Assembly so far removed from societal concerns that it was known as '*la chambre sans fenêtres*' could do little more than preside over a fragile social stalemate (Hoffmann, 1963). Therefore, the third important dimension of étatism consists in the capacity to implement policy, if necessary over the objections of key social groups. Only then does *l'état arbitre* become *l'état actif*. A state acquires this capacity when it controls a set of policy-related levers, providing access to critical information and expertise, control over domestic and international capital flows, influence over private investment and incomes, and successful recourse to force if necessary. These instruments are the substance of constructive power.

Finally, there is a more ideological dimension to étatism associated with the political authority of a state. It might be described as the recognized ability to speak for the public interest. This has always been a crucial component of French étatism. Since the days of the Revolution the state has usually been seen as the only institution capable of acting in the general interest of the nation, and as such, it alone has a monopoly on political virtue. The roots of this view may lie in Rousseau's understanding of the general will, but it is reaffirmed regularly in contemporary political discourse. President Georges Pompidou tapped this well-spring of legitimacy in 1970, for instance, when he told the Conseil d'Etat that:

> All our law stemmed from the conception of a strong state, stronger perhaps for limiting its intervention to the most characteristic functions of public power: justice, defence, order. In these spheres the state alone expressed the general interest and alone took the decisions to ensure it prevailed. . . . Only the state . . . can have a complete and disinterested vision of the general interest (Hayward, 1973: 116).

A natural corollary to this view holds that aggregations of individuals and formal organizations outside the state cannot pretend to speak for the general interest. Their political status is suspect. How can the spokesmen for special interests legitimately contribute to public policy? This view carries the implication that the public interest is something to be discovered, a special form of knowledge accessible only to those in public positions, rather than the outcome of a process of partisan mutual adjustment (cf. Lindblom, 1959). *La loi le Chapelier* of June 1791 (quoted in Goguel and Grosser, 1970: 172) announced that "the destruction of every kind of corporation of citizens of the same state is one of the fundamental tenets of the French constitution." Almost 200 years later, similar views were described in a public blueprint for French development:

> Every power relationship within society is defined in terms of its relation- ship with the state and can only really be accepted once recognized by the state. Because it alone is invested with authority and is confronted with a multitude of special interests the state and those who personify it have come to consider themselves as the sole trustees of the general interest. From this comes a definite reluctance to delegate authority and associate groups with the exercise of power (*Plan et Prospective*, 1972 cited in Hayward, 1976: 349).

The complement to a strong state was supposed to be a weakly organized society, composed of an aggregation of individuals rather than strong secondary associations. The ability to summon up this image of legitimacy remained one of the principal assets of the French state well into the post-war period.[1]

In the literature on France, étatism has been heavily identified with planning (cf. Shonfield, 1969; Hayward, 1975, 1976). As chapter six indicates, that was entirely appropriate in the early years of planning. As we shall see, however, the relationship between the evolution of planning and that of étatism was ultimately curvilinear. As planning evolved it first enhanced, but then began to undermine, the étatism of the French state.

Three facets of this development are of primary importance. The first concerns changes that planning induced in the independence of the state. Secondly, we should consider the impact of planning on the unity of the state. Finally, we can examine the relationship between planning and the legitimacy of the state. Each of these components corresponds to one of the dimensions of the étatist ideal.

THE INDEPENDENCE OF THE STATE

The conventional association of planning with socialism should not be allowed to obscure the fact that French planning was designed to enhance the operation of the market rather that supersede it (cf.

Griffiths, 1977: 40). The planners realized early on that "they would succeed only if they placed themselves at the service of the business world and civil service and sought, in return, to secure their help, instead of trying to compel their obedience" (Crozier, 1965: 154). Accordingly the planners concentrated their efforts on forging what was in effect an alliance between business and the state for the direction of the economy.

With the opening of the economy at the outset of the Fifth Republic, however, this relationship began to change. The planners realized that if the French economy were to compete effectively in the new European market, many of the isolationist, small, family firms that had hitherto dominated French industry would have to be abandoned in favor of larger and more competitive units. This resolve was reinforced by the new President. "Nobody . . . insisted more than General de Gaulle on the need for France to be 'a great industrial power' so as to be *'une grande puissance tout court'*" (Hoffmann, 1963: 77).

The industrial policy-makers therefore began to use the Plan to forge what might be called an alliance, no longer with business in general, but with the largest enterprises in the fastest-growing sectors of the economy in order to rationalize the structure of French industry. For this purpose, *la nouvelle politique industrielle* was introduced. The Plan shifted its emphasis from programs oriented to business in general to more selective measures aimed at individual firms. Through various forms of bilateral contracts, most of the tax advantages, export assistance, price control exemptions, and investment funds available in the 1960s were channelled to large, dynamic enterprises. The banks were directed to pursue policies that "favored the development of large enterprises rather than the accession of medium-sized enterprises to the level of the big ones" (cited in Warnecke and Suleiman, 1975: 38; Friedberg, 1973, 1974; Gremion, 1974; Priouret, 1968). In return, these companies were to provide the productivity gains and exports that would propel France to even higher levels of economic growth.

At the heart of the program was a set of policies encouraging industrial concentration. By 1965 France had the highest rate of mergers in Western Europe; and hidden forms of cartelization brought her largest firms into an average of twenty joint ventures each by 1967. In the chemical industry, for instance, "all major companies were in joint ventures to the point where the concept of a firm as a management entity had lost much of its meaning" (McArthur and Scott, 1969: 204, 210). The particular beneficiaries of this policy were the large petrochemical, electronics, aeronautics, pharmaceutical and data-processing enterprises identified in the Fifth Plan. The planners were also delighted since they found it easier to reach planning agreements with firms that controlled a large sector of the market. They frequently used the expression "80–20" to indicate that planning is most effective in sectors where 20 percent of the firms control 80 percent of the market (Friedberg, 1974: 101).

With its merger policy the state essentially created the new social partners with whom it was to ally; and it changed its industrial interlocutors. During the 1950s trade associations and professional groups had served as the major spokesmen for industry. To implement the new industrial policies, however, the planners often had to negotiate directly with the managers of the firms they were intending to support, without the mediation of trade associations, who frequently opposed rationalization in order to protect their weaker members (cf. Friedberg, 1974: 135). During the 1960s representatives from advanced sectors and the state engaged in an almost continuous round of bargaining. To a degree present in few other nations, the management of French industrial strategy became a cooperative endeavor between civil servants and industrialists.

That process brought the managers of large industry and government officials closer together, and distanced both from other social actors. The interchange reinforced the like-mindedness and mutual dependence of the two sides. The most dramatic consequence to follow from this was the growing interpenetration of private management and the civil service. It became increasingly common for civil servants to move on to positions in business, sometimes to return again to public employ, and even for business managers to move into civil service positions. The practice became known as *pantouflage*. In 1954, for instance, 4 percent of the heads of the private banks in France came from the public service; by 1974 that proportion had risen to 30 percent (Birnbaum, 1978: 69). By 1973, 43 percent of the heads of the hundred largest corporations in France had at one time been civil servants (Birnbaum, 1977: 141). The very idea would be almost unthinkable to British or American businessmen. Government policies were creating a kind of technostructure in France, a new social group at the pinnacle of private and public sector management with a distinct set of shared attitudes, backgrounds and interests.

Moreover, the interchange was predominantly with the advanced sector of industry: "not only do the members of the Grands Corps occupy, as indicated, key positions in the private sector but they occupy these positions almost exclusively in the most dynamic sectors of the economy" (Warnecke and Suleiman, 1975: 40). Pierre Lalumiere agrees:

The Inspectors of Finance who leave [the corps] gravitate toward the most active sectors of the economy. They maintain a very strong position in the area of finance capitalism whose principal institutions they direct. At present, they are infiltrating the chemical and automotive industries which are experiencing expansion. They tie their fortunes to the most dynamic sectors of the economy (Warnecke and Suleiman, 1975: 39).

The new focus on bilateral agreements negotiated between the state and individual firms also enhanced the importance of the private side of planning. Such agreements could only be reached behind closed doors. Planning itself became a kind of cartel and the planners' task was made much easier by "the key fact . . . that the same type of men are sitting in both the management and civil service posts in the cartel" (Granick cited in MacLennan et al., 1968: 346). As Bourdieu and Boltanski (1976: 54) observe:

> One could not overestimate the role played in this common circulation of information by the similarity of those accustomed to it. Associated with a common educational background, products of the same schemas of thought, of perception, and of taste, the directors of the banks (almost all of whom come from the Inspectorate of Finance), of the nationalized industries, and of a number of private enterprises think and want what those in charge of the policy decisions think and want, which indirectly produces the conditions of success for their decisions.

The developing alliance between planners and advanced industries gradually politicized the private sector and privatized much of the public sector (see Birnbaum, 1977, 1978).

This alliance reached its culmination during the preparation of the Sixth Plan. The story begins with the reorganization of the Confédération Nationale de Patrons Français (CNPF), which had been the peak association of French business since the war. Until the mid-1960s the CNPF maintained an ambivalent posture toward the Plans in an effort to placate both the larger enterprises, who approved of it, and the small firms, who felt threatened by it but made up a majority of the association's members (Atreize, 1971: 57; Bonnaud, 1966: 313). As usual, however, shifts in political context initiated changes within the major secondary associations of society. Under the influence of the new industrial policies, the larger and more dynamic firms began to agitate for a greater voice in CNPF policies.

A rift developed within the organization in 1966 when Paul Huvelin, the former managing director of Kléber-Colombes, and a man closely acquainted with the problems of the advanced sector of the economy, was elected to the Presidency of the CNPF to succeed Georges Villiers, a former Résistant and the owner of a small family firm in the provinces who had led the organization since 1946. Tension within the Patronat continued until the organization split over a dispute about the Grenelle accords signed with labor after the events of May 1968. The bitter struggle which followed lasted until October 1969, when Huvelin forced through a series of reforms that, in one stroke, established the CNPF as the definitive voice for French industry, oriented the organization to the new industrial policies, and brought it effectively under the sway of large enterprises, where it remained through the 1970s under the tenure of its next President, François Ceyrac (Parodi, 1971: 305 ff).

When the large corporations gained the upper hand in 1968, the CNPF suddenly reversed itself and embraced the concept of planning. It even took the initiative in the preparation of the Sixth Plan (Reynaud, 1975: 38–9). Its first step was to convince the government that the existing Modernization Commissions should be downgraded and subordinated to a new Commission of Industry, headed by two of the leading spokesmen for large enterprise, André Benard and Roger Martin of Pont-à-Mousson. The government acceded over the opposition of the CNPF's own membership (Nizard, 1972a: 383; Atreize, 1971). Then, at the urging of Benard and Martin, the CNPF issued a stream of statements calling for the government to give priority in the Sixth Plan to exports and advanced industry rather than the social goals identified in previous Plans. The object of these moves was to consolidate support for a policy of national champions and to direct resources into industrial investment rather than private or social consumption. Few expected the government to heed these statements since the formulation of the Sixth Plan took place just after the events of May 1968 amidst a rising chorus of demands that industrial investment should be cut back to make room for private consumption and the construction of new social infrastructure.

When the Sixth Plan was published, however, it appeared to conform to the demands of the CNPF almost exactly. It opened with a declaration that: "The pattern of growth presented in the Sixth Plan is based on three principles: the achievement of a strong external trade balance; the priority of investment over consumption; limitation of the share of national resources going to the public sector, and moderation in the growth of transfer payments" (Commissariat Général du Plan, 1971: 51). The state had committed itself to an allocation of resources that heavily favored the advanced sections of capital.

There was an immediate outcry. The CFDT, the only major union still involved in the planning process, withdrew with this explanation:

> What is in question is the role and conception of the Plan. By accepting the "rules of the game" of the "market economy" in compliance with the wishes of the Patronat, the Plan is completely abandoning its voluntarist mandate to construct a model of civilisation orienting the economy toward the satisfaction of the most important needs of the population (Atreize, 1971: 60–1).

Even the Director of Econometric Research for the Plan was hard put to explain the outcome. When forced to do so, he observed:

The motive invoked politically is the historical legacy of the French economy which does not allow any lessening of economic effort; the deep reason is without doubt the pressure that one part of business – the large enterprises – exerted, notably through the Industrial Commission, on the elaboration of the Plan (Delange, 1973: 379).

The furor over the publication of the Sixth Plan was acutely embarrassing to the government, which appeared to have abdicated responsibility for socioeconomic management to one segment of industry. The Plan had been captured by its clientele and *l'impératif industriel* had become *l'impératif des industriels* (Atreize, 1971: 29). The Ministry of Finance tried to regain control over the planning process by transferring responsibility for the final reports from the industry-dominated Commissions to financial planning groups under the Ministry's domain, but even this maneuver failed. The problems were more fundamental. Increasing interpenetration between the higher civil service and the management of large enterprise had created a powerful elite with interlocking careers and mutual interests that rendered it less responsive to other social groups. At the same time the planners' dependence on the cooperation of enterprise managers to implement the new industrial policies forced them to respond to those managers' concerns.

The state had entered into an alliance with the advanced sector of capital to rationalize the French economy and accelerate its growth. In this effort it was relatively successful. However, the unintended consequence was to increase drastically the state's dependence on this sector of capital. Under the aegis of the planning process, some segments of industry acquired a degree of influence over the nation's industrial policy that bordered on control. The regime began to lose room for policy maneuverability and the independence from social groups that is one of the hallmarks of an étatist state.

THE COHESION OF THE STATE

For significant periods in its history the French state has been used by various elites to impose their goals on society. In many cases institutional reforms were employed to enhance the cohesiveness and capacities of the state. The intendants of the *Ancien Régime*, the administrative reforms of Napoleon Bonaparte and Napoleon III, the creation of the grands corps, and the channelling of the post-war elite through ENA and the Polytechnique were all means toward this end. The Planning Commission was also designed to enhance the ability of the state to formulate and implement a coordinated economic policy.

Its mission was to devise an overarching economic strategy and ensure that the various agencies of the state worked together to implement it.

In some respects the planners were quite successful. They were able to promulgate a strategic vision of the potential implicit in the French economy. Simply to survive through the internecine political quarrels of the Fourth Republic, which saw 25 governments come and go, was an accomplishment. In Monnet's (1976: 308) words: "*Les gouvernements changeaient, nos idées s'incrustaient.*" However, the Plan never succeeded in imposing a genuine cohesiveness on French economic policy; and in the end it contributed to the further fragmentation of the state.

The French state is often perceived as an ideal bureaucracy, composed of well-coordinated agencies with considerable power, expertise, and independence from civil society. It is said to have governed a divided society with unity, impartiality, and efficiency when feuding politicians were unable to do so. A closer study of the impact of planning on the French bureaucracy, however, suggests that this traditional view should be revised. We find, first, that the bureaucracy has always been susceptible to division. Second, it should not be seen as a completely impartial arbiter or even as a neutral agent of the political executive, but as a crucial intermediary that brings pressure from society to bear on the state as well as vice-versa. Finally, the bureaucracy generates conflicts within society that are subsequently reflected within itself.

As the planning process evolved, it contributed to the development of conflict within the state and to the fragmentation of its policy actions in three broad ways. In the first instance the effect of the Plan was to render interdepartmental competition substantially more intense (cf. Grémion, 1974). Its principal antagonist was the Ministry of Finance. With control over macroeconomic management, the flows of funds and all forms of public spending, the Ministry of Finance was a kind of citadel within the state, exercising a *tutelle* over the other Ministries. Virtually no other agencies were informed about the sources of funds available to the Ministry and the uses to which they were put. Its own civil servants described the Ministry as a temple surrounded by "a halo of mystery and esotericism" (Alphandery et al., 1968: 52; Bonnaud, 1975: 102).

The divergent mandates of the Ministry and the Plan made conflict inevitable. The Ministry of Finance was responsible both for preparing an annual budget that would meet immediate demands for resources and for imposing deflation when necessary to correct inflationary pressures in the economy. By contrast, the tasks of the Plan were to resist immediate demands on resources in favor of a longer-term investment strategy and to oppose deflation in the interest of sustained growth (cf.

Delange, 1973). In the early years of the Plan, any conflict between these two organs was fairly easily managed by senior officials because the Plan's purview was restricted to a few industrial sectors. When the activities of the Planning Commission were expanded to include global resource planning over a 5-year period, however, the two organizations found themselves in direct conflict (see Lautman and Thoenig, 1966: 40). At stake was both the distribution of power within the bureaucracy and the allocation of resources in the French economy.

The contestants in this bureaucratic struggle began from highly unequal positions. The planners were formidable publicists, and from time to time they could call upon real support at the political level (Delange, 1973: 383). At the outset they also controlled the funds being channelled into France from the Marshall Plan. The Ministry of Finance, however, controlled all direct public investment, most of the banking system, and virtually all the financial incentives used to implement the Plan (Bonnaud, 1975; Cohen, 1977a). Not surprisingly, it was able to impose deflation over the objections of the planners in several famous instances, including the interruption of the Third Plan in 1960, the stabilization policy of 1962, and the Barre program of 1976. The post-war period was divided into periods of open conflict between these institutions and periods of *entente cordiale*.

The broader significance of this battle lay in its impact on policy, which oscillated to some degree from one pole to another according to adventitious shifts in bureaucratic power. The contest institutionalized a conflict between short- and long-term economic goals; and the formulation of economic policy was ultimately split between institutions that spoke for different interests and pursued divergent goals.

A second dynamic soon appeared with equally significant consequences for the internal unity of the state. For many years French economic and industrial policy-making had been based on a traditional pyramid. At the top of the hierarchy stood the Ministry of Finance, which presided over the grand design of policy. However, it rarely dealt with individual cases, and left the detailed implementation of programs to specialized Ministries. Each of the Ministries assumed responsibility for certain sectoral interests (Jobert, 1973). By nourishing their own sectors on a selective basis with the programs of the state in return for behavior responsive to their particular recommendations, the specialized departments acquired a measure of authority over the actions of their client groups. Departments exercised a *tutelle* over their clientele that was the envy of other nations (see Grémion, 1973; Nizard, 1972a).

The planning institutions tended to disturb the foundation on which this *tutelle* rested, as well as its traditional hierarchy, by providing industrialists with an alternative conduit to the state. As relations between planners and industrialists grew closer, the latter could appeal via the Plan to the Ministry of Finance or the Prime Minister when they were frustrated at the departmental level. The introduction of the new industrial policy in the 1960s accelerated this process. It meant that the planners themselves had greater influence over the disbursement of industrial subsidies, putting them in direct competition with the departments for influence over industry. Since the policy focused on bilateral relations with individual firms, those firms were encouraged to deal with the state directly rather than through their trade associations. Because the trade associations were most closely linked with the specialized departments, the influence of the departments suffered as well. Finally, the administration of an increasing number of selective grants drew the Ministry of Finance into more detailed involvement with their administration (Jobert, 1973; Grémion, 1973). That opened up room for greater conflict within the state and made it more likely that firms would bypass the departments to appeal directly to the Ministry of Finance.

The impact on the specialized departments was profound. They found that their authority in the eyes of traditional clienteles came to depend increasingly on how effectively they performed as spokesmen for them in negotiations with the Plan or the Ministry of Finance. If they proved weak or unforthcoming, their clientele had a tendency to go directly to the planners or the officials of Finance. Therefore, departments for whose approval sectoral actors had once competed, now had to compete for influence over their own sectors. The departmental role had been reversed from that of supervisor to that of advocate. The state's control over incentives in each sector had been diluted among competing agencies and the traditional authority of the *tutelle* was eroded.

Hitherto we have been considering the French bureaucracy, but planning also precipitated a deeper division between the bureaucracy and the political wing of the state. The very success of the Plan generated extraordinary rates of economic growth, urbanization, and industrialization that changed the face of French society. One by-product was a level of social dislocation that threatened the remnants of the old economic order and even upset many of those who otherwise benefited from growth.

The groups most adversely affected by state-led growth were the shopkeepers, peasants, employees and owners of small and medium-sized business, and those in declining sectors of the economy. Eventually they began to organize and express their grievances in both electoral and extra-parliamentary arenas. Peasant cooperatives were transformed into exponents of direct action. At times tractors were used to blockade the borders, artichokes dumped across highways, and warehouses of wine burned to the ground. The Poujadiste movement against tax reform was absorbed into lobbying groups such as the Conféderation Générale des Petits et Moyennes Entreprises which were often bitterly opposed to the proposals of the planners (Berger, 1977; Bauchard, 1963). Occasionally their resistance led to national political fights, such as the battle against the tax reforms mooted in the Fontanet circular of 1961, and the anti-supermarket campaign that culminated in the 'Royer law' of 1974.

These groups turned to their elected representatives in the legislature and political executive for help in opposing the proposals of the planners. The two groups, peasants and shopkeepers, who had traditionally been the most anti-statist in their beliefs and reluctant to deal with the authorities, suddenly turned to the state to protect them from the effects of socioeconomic change. Moreover, they sought out one arm of the state, the legislature and political executive, to forestall social change which another arm of the state, the Planning Commission and industrial policy-makers, was instigating. Here we have another instance of a familiar process, observed as long ago as the sixteenth century, when the Tudor monarchs intervened to delay the Acts of Enclosure passed by the English Parliament (see Polanyi, 1944).

In the early years of the Fifth Republic the politicians were able to resist the demands of these aggrieved groups. The organizations of the traditional sector were weak, and the Gaullist majority in the National Assembly was broadly based. Toward the end of the 1960s, however, the base of electoral support for the governing coalition shifted away from industrial workers and cadres. It came to depend much more heavily on the votes of farmers, pensioners, shopkeepers and others sympathetic to the traditional sectors (Berger, 1980). Since the Gaullists (RPR), of the two principal parties in the legislative Majority during the 1970s, were growing increasingly dependent on this vote, and the Independent Republicans were being transformed from a party of local notables into a party of technocrats, this conflict between modernizers and nostalgics was becoming institutionalized in the division within the Majority (see Birnbaum, 1977: ch. 7).

Consequently, the politicians felt compelled to limit the ability of the planners to pursue economic policies that antagonized their constituents. The President did so initially by appointing close associates, rather than more independent experts, to the position of Planning Commissioner (Ortoli in 1966, Montjoie in 1967, etc.). Secondly, the Prime Minister insisted that the Seventh Plan should give priority to small, medium-sized, and artisanal enterprise rather than heavy industry. It was made a *programme d'action prioritaire*, for which 816 million francs was budgeted.

Finally, the President took the unprecedented step in June 1978 of cutting the immensely powerful Ministry of Finance in half. With

171,000 civil servants spread over 3000 locations in France, the Ministry of Finance had become a state within a state (*Le Point*, 10 April 1978: 54). Its division into a Ministry for the Economy and one for the Budget was designed to subject it to more direct political control (*Le Nouvel Economiste*, 17 April 1978: 30). As if to ensure that the new emphasis was understood, the man appointed to be the new Minister of the Economy was not a graduate of ENA or a member of the grands corps, like many of his predecessors, but a local politician and a former car dealer from the provinces.

These initiatives cut short the experiment in coherence that the Plan had been designed to perform. Like the other developments outlined here, they eroded the coordinated approach to policy associated with an étatist state. However, there was an implicit logic to these measures.

Conventional wisdom holds that a state divided against itself cannot stand; but there is a sense in which precisely the opposite is true. A state faced with multiple tasks and well-defined conflicts of interest among the social classes it governs, or among sub-groups within them, may find it useful to maintain a degree of deliberate malintegration among its various policy-making arms. In this way each arm can mobilize consent among its particular constituencies by pursuing policies which, even if never fully implemented, appear to address the needs of those groups. In many cases, the pursuit of incompatible policies renders most of them ineffective, but this technique prevents any one group from claiming that the state has come down on the side of its opponents. Such has been the behavior of the French state within the economic sphere in recent years.

THE LEGITIMACY OF THE STATE

These changes in the relations between state and society in France also had ideological reverberations. The French have traditionally believed that the state should remain independent from the pressure of social groups in order to guard the public interest. In 1960 one commentator rather lightly suggested that the French conceive of politics "as a kind of morality play, with the Public Interest defending the castle against a horde of savage, ruthless mercenaries of the selfish interests" (Schubert, 1960: 93). But Thoenig (1973: ch. 9), among others, has shown that French civil servants shared this conception of their role. The state's rationality is assured by its neutrality: *l'état arbitre* has been one of the central beliefs legitimating public policy in France for over two centuries.

During the 1960s, however, the ability of the public to regard the state as an independent entity was eroded by the increasingly close connections between the representatives of capital and the state, which the planning process encouraged. The growing influence of interest groups over economic policy became a subject of widespread concern. In July 1971 six prominent members of the National Assembly issued a manifesto warning that the Fifth Republic had become "a pressure group regime" (Hayward, 1972: 297). Several distinguished observers warned: "There is a danger that the conditions of impartiality necessary if the state is to exercise its public functions and regulate society may not be fulfilled" (Worms, 1974: 197). *L'état arbitre* had become *l'état partenaire*.

The decline in the public's regard for the state as the privileged defender of the public interest accelerated as members of the senior civil service themselves voiced increasing skepticism. Birnbaum (1978: 85) found that many officials no longer saw any difference between the public and private sectors. Grémion (1974: 173) discovered that most members of the grands corps perceived little basis for conflict or separation between the two sectors. As Suleiman (Warnecke and Suleiman, 1975: 40) observed, this was "a remarkable assertion, particularly when one considers the extent to which the agents of the state have traditionally seen themselves as the sole guardians of the general interest."

The extensive use that the new industrial policy made of exceptions to existing regulations in order to influence the behavior of individual firms compounded the problem. Such arrangements violated the long-standing French view, traceable to the enlightenment equation of freedom with rule by law, that legitimate state action must be based on rules. As Friedberg (1973: 107) noted, "from the moment when the industrial actions of the state are no longer mediated by rules but are the result of explicit political choices, the administration, by virtue of that, loses its own legitimacy."

French leaders responded to these changing conditions in several ways. They may not have known that the state's legitimacy was itself threatened by these developments, but they knew that their activities were being judged by old standards that cast them in a rather bad light. So they began to look for new standards with which to justify their policies. The solution that they eventually hit upon was to combine the traditional notion that the state was the guardian of the general interest with the new idea that in a complex society those who can best discern what is in the general interest in any area of policy are the experts in that field. Their specialized knowledge and technical training confer on them an objectivity and professional perspective that others lack (cf. Ellul, 1964; Gilpin, 1968). Disinterestedness becomes associated with expertise; Rousseau is reconciled with Saint-Simon. In this way respect for technocracy was cultivated among civil servants and populace alike.

We see here a classic example of how ideologies change (see Walzer, 1968; Schurmann, 1968). In search of a better justification for their policies, political leaders took the form of the traditional norms (which was built upon the concept of the general interest) and gave it new content (invoking the role of expertise in the modern world). That new content was drawn from ideas that had been germinating in France for many years. One can find roots for a technocratic ideology in Saint-Simon, Comte, and in X-crise and *Esprit*, influential movements of the 1930s which popularized a view of government as a technical rather than political endeavor. After the war, ENA and the Polytechnique gave the idea additional support. One happy by-product of this view was that private and public sector managers, as symmetrical parts of the new technocracy, could be expected to consult with each other on matters of mutual speciality and concern. As Birnbaum (1978: 83) noted, "the notion of a general interest has evolved; from henceforth it is no longer incompatible with the constant ties which link the state to the business world."

The planners became masters of this ideology. They set out to present planning as a search for technical truth rather than as a process of political negotiation. It was typical for Commission chairmen to observe that: "These Commissions are not political organs where various determined interests oppose each other. They are centers of study and reflection where one searches for agreement and not for a majority vote" (Fourastié and Courthéoux, 1968: 96). The approach was epitomized in the way the French set about devising an incomes policy in the early 1960s. They saw the task not as one of bargaining with the interested parties but as a problem to which there must be a technical solution. In this case Jean Toutée, of the Conseil d'Etat, who was appointed to look into the matter, produced a report that skirted the issue of negotiations and centered instead on the need to devise an appropriate statistical formula from which to calculate wage agreements (Hayward, 1966). Inadequate statistics, rather than incompatible interests, were seen as the source of social problems.

For a period the new approach to legitimation was useful. Jack Hayward (1967: 455) noted that

the government succeeded in presenting its policy preferences as the only ones feasible from a technical point of view . . . thanks to this technique a highly politicized Fifth Plan was successfully presented as a non-political accomplishment embodying technical competence and a wide exchange of views.

This device, however, had its limits. Behind a consensual facade, debates within the Modernization Commissions continued to be highly conflictual; and Planning Commissioner Pierre Massé was forced to replace Commission members, who had once sat as individual experts, with spokesmen for particular interests. Attempts to secure an incomes and industrial policy inevitably drew the state into conflict with social groups; and, as Toutée noted, "the State cannot always and completely triumph; in fact it is never entirely triumphant. In each struggle, it loses some part of its authority, its power, the 'aura' of respect which should surround it" (quoted in Hayward, 1966: 186). A backlash began to develop in France, reflected most clearly in the writings of Jacques Ellul (1964) against the appeal to technical expertise.

An additional justification became necessary to legitimize the state's role in the economy. The politicians gradually constructed such an argument around the claim that the dirigiste state was capable of delivering rates of economic growth higher than those of most other European nations and high enough to provide real income gains for all of its citizens. As the French economy took off, a sense of national pride in France's economic and technical accomplishments began to develop. For some this was a simple by-product of the value they attached to rising levels of income, but for others it was part of a growing cult of economic growth and technological development. A certain mystique grew up around the ideas of progress, economic innovation and high technology. In Parisian society the technologically avant-garde became culturally avant-garde. Political leaders encouraged this by associating France's international prestige with the development of the nuclear *force de frappe*, the Concorde supersonic airliner, the Plan Calcul in computers, and such technical achievements as the construction of a uranium enrichment plant at Le Havre (Gilpin, 1968; Cohen, 1982). The Plan itself became the high priest of high technology and the nation's foremost apostle of sustained growth. The idea that France could lead the world in such endeavors was immensely popular, a modern version of the cult of prowess to which the French have always attached such value (see Pitts, 1963; Servan-Schreiber, 1969).

By the 1960s the French state began to base its claim to legitimacy no longer on the impartiality of its economic regulations, but on the results they produced. On one hand that enabled the regime to regain some of the legitimacy that it might otherwise have lost through the decline of étatism. On the other hand it put the state in an increasingly precarious position. By the mid-1970s the performance of the domestic economy had come to hinge on international events beyond any one nation's control. International economic interdependence had grown to the point that France was largely reliant on external sources for its energy supplies, and on the buoyancy of foreign markets for its accelerating rates of growth. Therefore its economic performance was exceptionally vulnerable to the kind of global recession that occurred after the oil crisis of 1974.

French politicians had been happy to take credit for the phenomenal rates of growth France experienced for 30 years after the war. Consequently they found it hard to avoid blame for the poor economic performance that followed 1974. As a result of taking overt control over economic life through the Plan, the French state dispelled the nineteenth-century notion that the economy is essentially separate from the polity and runs according to a market mechanism of its own. As François Pérroux observed, "the Plan cleanses people's minds of the illusion that economic life obeys mysterious natural laws, that it is subject to an order of things to which man should submit and whose secrets are held only by the sorcerers of the tribe" (cited in Hamon, 1966: 206). The evolution of planning inspired a shift in popular conceptions of the economy, and of the state's role within it, that left the regime especially vulnerable to an economic downturn of the sort that followed.

THE CHANGING ENVIRONMENT FOR PLANNING

From this account it should be clear that the relationship between state and society is a dynamic one. Because state–society relations are constituted from a longstanding set of practices that have become institutionalized, they are not likely to change overnight. There is evidence that even the French Revolution failed to transform many aspects of the state–society relationship (Tocqueville, 1955; Skocpol, 1979). Precisely because institutions are ultimately human artefacts, however, it takes positive action to sustain or reproduce them; and incremental adjustments of behavior, in response to new challenges, can bring about broader shifts in the state–society relationship.

In this case the evolution of French planning gradually began to erode the étatism of the French state. To drive the French economy to new levels of productivity and technological achievement, the state forged an alliance with the advanced sector of capital that radically narrowed the distance between itself and society. Although the planning institutions enhanced the capacity of the French state for strategic thinking, they did not ultimately improve its cohesion. Moreover, planning eroded the traditional bases on which the state's claim to authority rested and forced policy-makers to seek new ways to legitimate their actions. Their efforts to do so placed the state in a precarious position during the 1970s. Planning, which at first seemed to be the modern instantiation of étatism, turned out to be an instrument of its supercession.

In some respects these developments may have been salutary. French policy-makers had often been accused of taking arbitrary action, unresponsive to the concerns of various social groups (Peyrefitte, 1980). There is little doubt that, partly as a result of their experience with planning, they began to see some advantages in consulting with the representatives of capital and even labor when difficult decisions were to be made, although these consultations were still far more restricted than in many other nations. The Grenelle accords that terminated the events of May 1968 were approved by both labor and capital, even if a subsequent devaluation nullified many of the benefits for labor. In 1978–79 President Giscard d'Estaing opened a series of bilateral talks with the unions and employers to consider the possibility of trading legislation on the rights of employees, the length of the workweek and the minimum wage for a measure of wage restraint. No real progress was made before the 1981 elections, but the Socialist Government that then took office effectively used tripartite negotiations with labor and capital to resolve the financial crisis facing the social security system. There have been some indications that France is moving toward more frequent consultation with social groups (see Keeler, 1985).

In other respects, of course, the growing intimacy of state–business relations proved to be an albatross around the neck of the regime. The steel industry provides an excellent example. In 1978 its trade association could say with some justification that "there is scarcely an industry in France which has been as subject to planning and as involved in concertation as steel" (Chambre Syndicale, 1978: 7). Anxious to improve this sector, successive governments funnelled massive sums into the industry. Its capacity expanded from 4.5 million tons of steel a year in 1946 to 33 million tons in 1978. However, the indebtedness of the steel companies also increased from 33 percent of sales in 1952 to 112 percent in 1978, until the solvency of the firms became completely contingent on annual transfusions of public money. If you owe enough money to a bank, it is said that you own it. In this case, through well-developed channels of privileged access, the industry trade association was able to persuade the industrial policy-makers that their existing investment could be realized and massive lay-offs avoided only if further aid was allocated to steel. Yet the industry remained inefficient in international terms. As a result, when world orders for steel fell by 31 percent in 1974 and world prices by 50 percent, the French share of world sales fell from 40 percent to 26 percent. Saddled with enormous overcapacity, the industry lost 16 billion francs in the ensuing 3 years (Ministère de l'Industrie, 1979).

French policy-makers gradually became aware of the disadvantages associated with planning. They had forged a close alliance with business, but many of their allies were now heavily dependent on the state. Some industries relied almost entirely on state-controlled sources for their capital investment. The FDES, which administered 16.3 million francs in industrial loans during 1964, gave out 248 million francs in 1968. Despite intermittent attempts to encourage *autofinancement*, the medium and long-term debt of French enterprise reached 74 billion francs in 1976, twice the size of its own capital holdings. The state itself was estimated to have 150 billion francs in outstanding loans to industry (*L'Express*, 8 May 1978: 62). Policy-makers, who found this trend slightly disquieting during periods of prosperity, became worried that they would have to bail out much of French industry during a recession.

Moreover, the strategy of grooming 'national champions' for the international market was not proving particularly successful. As the steel case indicates, the economies of scale that accrued to giant enterprises were not necessarily sufficient to ensure international competitiveness; and continuous expansion could soon lead to overcapacity. In the cases of supersonic transport and the computer industry, poor decisions about the appropriate technology to place on the market led to massive expenditure on projects which did not generate enough sales to recoup the investment. Both Concorde and the Plan Calcul produced white elephants (Zysman, 1977). The planners began to question their own abilities both to judge the potential marketability of projects and to ensure their competitiveness. As early as 1967, for instance, three influential policy review commissions under MM. Nora, Montjoie and Rueff issued reports that castigated the government for confusing economic management with economic supervision, and urged a return to the primacy of the market (Michalet, 1974; Hayward, 1972).

Finally, the high visibility of planning became something of a liability in an era of slower economic growth. The authority of the state had already been compromised by the close relations it developed with industrialists. Yet the state's subsequent claim that it would be able to generate sustained levels of prosperity proved to be a precarious base on which to stake the legitimacy of planning. It drew attention to the failings as well as the successes of the program: in a 1972 survey of the electorate, for instance, when asked to say who was most responsible for price increases, more than twice as many respondents named the government than named any other group (*Sondages* 2–3, 1973: 39). Strains implicit in the growth of the planning system itself contributed to its eventual downfall.

Equally important to the demise of planning, however, were shifts in the international economy during the 1970s. One aspect of particular significance was the increasing interdependence among nations in the global economy. In the face of falling tariff barriers and the expansion of industry abroad, French firms faced increasingly stiff foreign competition. The most obvious threat came from the Third World. By 1975 Taiwan, with a population of only 17 million, was producing 400 million pairs of shoes a year, at an average cost of 3 francs a pair compared with 22 francs a pair in the EEC. Four of the newly industrializing countries, Hong Kong, Singapore, Taiwan and South Korea, alone were exporting 16 billion dollars worth of goods a year to the OECD nations (Lindbeck, 1978; Berthelot and Tardy, 1978). Within France this kind of competition cost jobs. The textile industry lost 110,000 positions in 4 years. Shipbuilding, steel, and leather goods were equally hard-hit in the 1970s (Stoffaes, 1968: 40).

The hidden threat, however, came from across the Rhine. France continued to import more from West Germany than from any other nation. In the consumer durables and capital goods sectors, for instance, a 14 billion franc (bF) improvement in the trade balance between 1973 and 1976 consisted of a 21 bF increase in sales to the Third World, reduced by a 7 bF rise in imports from the OECD nations (Cotta, 1978: 169). With the help of subsidized export credits and aggressive diplomatic pressure, France was still able to export turn-key plants, weapons and infrastructural projects to the Third World, but she was losing the battle for her own domestic markets (Cohen, 1982).

These developments intensified the pressure on industrial policy-makers to enhance the competitiveness of French industry. As we have seen, however, the ability of planning to accomplish this was already in doubt. Even the simple provision of industrial subsidies began to seem counterproductive. One study, commissioned in 1976, concluded that "no correlation existed between the increase in investment in a particular sector and the improvement of its trade balance" (Cotta, 1978: 165).

A second key alteration in the economic environment was the quadrupling of international oil prices, precipitated by the response of the Organization of Oil Exporting Countries (OPEC) to the Arab–Israeli war in October 1973. This was followed by a second substantial increase in 1979. As French industry had grown, so had the nation's dependence on outside sources of energy. Whereas 38 percent of French energy was imported in 1960, 75 percent had to be provided by outside sources in 1974. Therefore the immediate effect of the oil price increase was to throw the French trade balance, which stood at a surplus of 773 million dollars in 1973, into a 3.9 billion dollar deficit for 1974.

All of a sudden the balance of payments became the principal preoccupation of French policy-makers. Because oil purchases were denominated in dollars, any devaluation that reduced the value of the franc relative to the dollar was no longer an effective tool for correcting the imbalance. To lower the exchange rate in such circumstances might improve the competitiveness of exports, but it would increase the cost of imported oil so much as to nullify the export effects on the trade balance. One of the traditional weapons in the arsenal of French economic management was no longer of much use. As if in recognition of this, France entered the European Monetary System in March 1979, agreeing to peg its currency to the deutschmark. From 1975 onwards, then, the government became especially concerned about the domestic rate of inflation. Unable to offset its impact on exports by devaluing the currency, the government had to find new techniques for restraining wage and price increases.

These developments strongly militated against planning, which usually thrived on expansionary macroeconomic policies that encouraged firms to expand at the cost of some domestic inflation. Instead, deflationary policies were needed to reduce domestic incomes and thus consumption of imports as well as other goods. Export growth alone could not correct the huge trade deficit.

Finally, the oil price increases brought with them a global recession. In France, the higher cost of oil in 1973–74 imposed what amounted to a 40 bF tax on French industry. An additional amount equivalent to 4 percent of GDP had to be paid to the OPEC nations, depressing demand and raising the cost of French goods (Amouyel, 1979: 845). Domestic inflation soared, and many firms were forced out of business. As new entrants swelled the labor force by 880,000 between 1976 and 1983, unemployment rose inexorably. After 1974 the French rate of growth fell to half the levels reached earlier in the 1970s. Three decades of prosperity gave way to a decade of recession.

In the first instance the recession of 1974 completely vitiated the optimistic projections of the Sixth and Seventh Plans (see table 7.1). France's growing vulnerability to external economic shocks attenuated the planners' ability to predict – and thus direct – the course of the economy. A weaker balance of payments also made it difficult for them to pursue the expansionary policies that underpinned earlier Plans.

The prominence of the Plan embarrassed the government by implying that policy-makers could be held responsible for the course of an economy now in recession. In this context, planning became a kind of ceremonial désenchantée – an exercise in controlled pessimism (Prévot et al., 1977: 47). As the preamble to the Seventh Plan declared: "It is the thankless task of the Plan to recall that everything is not possible at once." When policy-makers are forced to apportion economic sacrifice – rather than distribute the benefits of growth – they naturally prefer to make their decisions out of the limelight.

Table 7.1   The forecasts of the sixth and seventh plans compared with the economic results

	Annual percentage increase in volume			
	Projections in Sixth Plan	Results 1970–75	Projections in Seventh Plan	Results 1976–78
GDP	5.9	3.6	5.2	3.8
Household consumption	5.4	5.1	4.7	3.7
Government consumption	3.3	3.0	2.0	3.8
Gross fixed investment:				
corporations	6.6	3.4	6.9	2.5
households	4.4	3.4	2.0	−0.9
government	7.6	4.3	4.3	2.2
Imports	9.3	6.9	11.9	8.5
Exports	10.0	8.2	12.0	7.4
Consumer prices	3.2	8.7	7.2	10.3
Net number of jobs created (OCOs)	300	27	792	171

Source: OECD, *Economic Survey: France* (Paris: OECD, 1979), 47; Commissariat Général du Plan, *Dossier Quantitatif Associé au 7ᵉ Plan* (Paris; Documentation Française, 1975).

DEPLANIFICATION

These developments culminated in a process known as deplanification. This term refers to the gradual dismantling of the institutions for planning, the drastic reduction in scope of the Plans themselves, and a well-publicized return to economic liberalism, marked by pledges that the state would reduce its role in the economy. Such were the policies pursued under President Valéry Giscard d'Estaing from 1974 to 1981.

The first portents of deplanification appeared in 1974 when the President hesitated for 8 months before appointing a successor to the outgoing Planning Commissioner. *Le Monde* reported that "The Plan has become completely paralysed. Its team is demoralized and beginning to break up; it is unsure whether or not it will simply be allowed to wither away" (Cohen, 1977b: 25).

The speculation proved premature, but when the Seventh Plan appeared in June 1976 it did little to allay suspicions. Whereas the normal preparation time for a Plan had been 4–5 years the Seventh Plan was prepared from start to finish in 5 months. Over 2500 people had sat on the Commissions of the Sixth Plan and another 2000 had assisted in its preparation. By contrast, the preparation of the Seventh

Plan involved no more than 650 people (see table 7.2). A new, and highly political, Central Planning Council was established at the Elysée to keep a tight rein on the Plan. The Council drew up the key provisions of the Seventh Plan and the Council of Ministers ratified the final document before some of the Modernization Commissions had even finished their deliberations (Green, 1978: 71). The planning process, once an important forum for the mobilization of consent, had become a charade that barely masked its highly politicized content.

The Plan itself was drastically reduced in scope under Giscard's administration. It made no attempt at industrial rationalization or the development of a global investment strategy. Instead, it consisted of 25 *programmes d'action prioritaire* (PAPs) which merely assembled the government's existing spending programs into 25 categories and provided them with a rhetorical overlay. Together, the PAPs accounted for 12.5 percent of government spending, but almost half of this was allocated to one program designed to double the number of telephones in France. From global resource planning the Plan had become primarily a statement of the spending priorities in the state's own budget.

Even the economic predictions of the Seventh Plan were banished to an appendix. The authorities rejected the pessimistic estimates of the Planning Commissions and insisted on projecting a 5 percent annual growth rate to 1980. By 1978, however, all pretense of reaching such targets had to be abandoned, and the Eighth Plan, published in April 1979, finally omitted all quantitative targets, stating: "This technique has been rendered obsolete by the fluctuations of a new era and the growing uncertainties that result from them" (Commissariat Général du Plan, 1979: 23). One observer commented, "navigation by visual aid has been substituted for navigational science" (Delors, 1978: 21).

The Eighth Plan (1981–85) was even more limited than its predecessor. Fewer than 600 people were involved in the deliberations of its Commissions; and most of these were civil servants. The planning process was now heavily dominated by public officials, as if in reaction to the state's loss of control over the preparation of the Sixth Plan. The Plan itself listed only 12 PAPs to be funded by the state; and in this case the amount of money assigned to them was not indicated in the document. Moreover, Parliament approved the budget for 1981 – which should have included appropriations for these programs – 2 weeks before the Plan was even submitted to it (L'Ecotais, 1980).

The Plan's principal argument was that economic growth could be secured only through higher levels of investment; but it did nothing to specify where that investment might come from. As one French commentator observed:

When one reads the proposal for the Eighth Plan which the government

Table 7.2 Number of members on the French Modernization Commissions

First Plan	Second Plan	Third Plan	Fourth Plan	Fifth Plan	Sixth Plan	Seventh Plan
494	604	704	1006	1950	2926	650

Sources: Pascallon (1974); Green (1978).

has just presented to the Social and Economic Council, one wonders what justifies the existence of this text. Let us make no mistake; it is interesting, well-written, full of useful information; all Frenchmen should read it, they will emerge more apprised of the realities. But it is not a Plan. Not only because it fixes no overall objective target – neither for rates of growth, nor rates of inflation, nor rates of unemployment, nor internal financial balance, nor external balance – but rather because the State itself does not make any commitment about how the particular objectives cited in the priority action programs are to be attained. Even these occupy only about 30 pages at the end of a document of 270 (Boissonnat, 1980b: 5).

The Planning Commissioner himself complained that the government had removed all pessimistic projections from the Plan, rendered the document incompatible with measures taken in the 1981 budget, and redrafted the introduction so as to turn the Plan into a letter of recommendation for the government (*Le Canard Enchaîné*, 10 September 1980).

The evisceration of planning was part of a wider strategy to reduce the extent to which French industry was dependent on the state for financial resources and direction. The object was to make greater use of market forces and to reduce public pressure on the state for better economic results. Giscard's Minister of the Economy summed up the approach by saying: "I want to remove the administration from the day-to-day management of the economy" (*London Times*, 10 November 1978). The government sought to re-establish the separation between polity and economy in the minds of the electorate and to shift the burden of responsibility for economic performance from the public to the private sector. In the words of the Minister, "Industrial policy means nothing. What we need is an economic policy permanently oriented to free prices and financial flows. It is not up to the state to choose the way to the future, it is up to the leaders of business" (*L'Express*, 24 April 1978).

The program took off when the President appointed Raymond Barre, a well-known conservative economist, to be Prime Minister in August 1976. The first phase of the Barre program began with a classic austerity plan which raised taxes, reduced the rate of growth of the money supply, and set a 6.5 percent norm for wages. In Barre's words, "my first objective, and I would even say my essential objective, is to maintain France's external balance and to assure the stability of the franc in the European Monetary System" (*Le Nouvel Economiste*, 16 June 1979: 31). The massive balance of payments deficit could not be ignored.

At the industrial level Barre's strategy was to strengthen the resources and autonomy of French corporations so that they, rather than the state, might bear responsibility for adapting industry to increasing foreign competition. As if to dramatize this intent, one of his first acts after the legislative elections of April 1978 was to abolish price controls. For the first time in 100 years the traditional *baguette* could be sold at any price. The prices charged by state-owned enterprise for electricity, rail transport, and postage also increased. At the same time Barre attempted to pressure the unions into limiting wage demands. These two programs sought to increase the share of national income going to profits, as opposed to wages, and to force households, rather than corporations, to pay a larger share of the levy that higher energy costs imposed on the economy. As the Minister of the Economy said:

> What is involved is much more than the removal of controls on industrial prices. As long as employers could not fix their prices, they lost interest. The choice of products, the methods of production were secondary. They did not even know if they could introduce the cost of their investments in the final costing of their wares. . . . In a protected society, people make no effort to adapt to competition. In France, I am sure there are reserves of imagination, creativity and courage, which are untapped because we are conditioned by the society about us, and are made to carry out tasks whose object we do not understand (*London Times*, 10 November 1978).

The Prime Minister spoke of inducing "a profound transformation of structures and of behavior" across France. To this end he turned the old price commission into an anti-trust agency designed to fight cartels, and took several measures to bolster the equity market. A new form of preferred shares and tax deductions for share purchases doubled the number of small shareholders in France within 3 months. The ultimate object was to reduce the dependence of French firms on state banks for capital.

The industrial policy-makers began to make greater use of market mechanisms: first, as incentives for the encouragement of efficiency, and secondly, as indicators of competitiveness. They offered "development contracts," worth about 300 million francs a year, to firms who agreed to raise matching private funds and develop new products in such areas of high technology as robotics, biotechnics, and urban transit. In contrast to earlier programs, however, the idea was to fund several firms which would then compete against each other for the market and any subsequent state aid.

CONCLUSION

Under Giscard, France took a step back towards laissez-faire not unlike that taken by the Thatcher Government in Great Britain after 1979. The endpoint for the evolution of planning seemed to be a program whose ostensible object was to reduce government intervention in the economy. However, we should ask: to what extent did the French state ultimately relinquish its role as an agent of socioeconomic change in the 1970s?

There can be little doubt that the government did attempt to for-swear responsibility for the direction of the economy after 1974. As planning evolved, it was gradually legitimated by the claim to provide superior levels of economic growth and prosperity. When events over which France had no control vitiated that claim, the planning process was gradually dismantled and the Plans relegated to a secondary status within the state's overall economic program. International economic developments had limited the efficacy of the Plans as well as their ability to predict future trends.

Simultaneously, economic policy-makers attempted to distance themselves from industrialists with whom they had once built an intimate relationship. On the one hand they wanted to re-establish control over an industrial policy that had fallen too much under the influence of its clients. On the other hand they hoped to reduce the growing financial dependence of industry on the state, partly because it did not seem to foster competitiveness and partly because it entailed huge financial outlays during a period of recession.

However, the Barre government was not entirely successful at either project. Nor was its behavior consistent with a complete return to laissez faire. Behind the scenes, important continuities between the new policies and the old endured. The state's goal was still to shake French industry out of its lethargy by any means necessary. If the new economic policies made greater use of the market, that was because the market was a sharper tool in France than it had been 30 years earlier.

Most important, behind the rhetoric of the regime, huge sums were still being channelled from the state to industry. In 1978 approximately 20 billion francs of public funds, worth 2.7 percent of GDP, were spent on industrial policy. The bulk was sectoral aid: 3 bF to steel, 3 bF to aeronautics, 1 bF to computers, 1 bF to telecommunications, and 1.5

bF to shipbuilding. A special 3 bF fund was established to aid industry in depressed regions; 1 bF was spent on research and development; and 6 bF went to subsidize exports. These amounts suggest that the state had not completely withdrawn from the industrial sphere.

Through the development contracts extended to high-technology firms and substantial programs to develop the computer and telecommunications sectors, the state was still orchestrating a great deal of industrial activity. Despite the failure of the original Plan Calcul (1967–71), the state created another conglomerate, CII–Honeywell–Bull in 1975 with a 1.2 bF subsidy and 4.05 bF in guaranteed orders for 1976–80 to develop the domestic computer industry. Subsequently CGE was persuaded to cede its equity in this group to St. Gobain-Pont-à-Mousson, which then began joint operations with Olivetti. For 1978–82 another 600 mF in public credits and loans were guaranteed to five enterprises working on semiconductors and integrated circuits (Parodi, 1981: 127; Spivey, 1982: 45).

The ambitious program announced in the Seventh Plan to revamp the French telephone system also received billions of francs and considerable regulatory assistance during the 1970s. It was highly successful. In 1975 one waited 18 months for a new telephone in Paris; by 1980 the waiting period was down to 2 weeks (Hough, 1982: 114; Parodi, 1981: 154). Although these projects did not receive as much publicity in the 1970s as their counterparts had in the 1960s, they were equally interventionist. One could still count 150 separate programs of aid to industry in 1980 (Lougovoy, 1981: 363).

The largest proportion of the state's attention and funding, however, was devoted to industrial rescue operations in the declining sectors. In the face of recession, a new agency, the *Comité interministeriel pour l'aménagement des structures industrielles* (CIASI), was established to mobilize public and private funds to finance industrial bail-outs. At the departmental level, special committees (*comités Fourcade*) pressured the banking sector to make emergency loans, and authorized exemptions from tax and social security payments for troubled firms. In the first 5 months alone they handled over 3000 cases (Berger, 1981; Green, 1983). Emergency plans for steel, textiles, furniture, coal and shipbuilding channelled massive sums to these sectors. The 1978 plan for steel formed a new holding company from the existing firms which came under the control of the banks and the state. In return the state took over 12 bF of outstanding debt and added a new 8 bF loan from the Treasury plus 2 bF from Crédit Nationale. Another 1.8 bF was added in 1979 (Stoffaes, 1982; Parodi, 1981).

The government claimed that it was not involved in these rescue operations "to save endangered species but to provide funds for their mutation" (*Fortune*, 9 April 1978: 68). Therefore state aid was tied to sectoral reorganization. There is no doubt, however, that rising levels of unemployment had frightened the policy-makers into a retreat from strictly market-oriented policies. A state which once groomed "national champions" was now feeding "lame ducks"; and in so doing it was responding to pressure from large and small business (Berger, 1981).

Thus, during the *septennat* of Giscard, the importance of planning declined. However, France did not abandon an overall strategy of state-led growth. Despite a slight increase in the emphasis given to market forces, industrial policy remained dirigiste and continued to be a major part of the government's program. The state retained considerable control over the flow of finance; and increases in public investment were employed as a substitute for stagnating private investment. The experience of recession had altered several dimensions of industrial policy. An expanding share of state aid was directed toward declining sectors; but the state was still playing an active role to orchestrate the direction of economic development.

Unfortunately, in an increasingly interdependent world economy and a global recession, these policies were not adequate to restore French levels of growth or to prevent unemployment from rising. And the government was unable to absolve itself of responsibility for these failures, after years of taking credit for French success. A majority of the electorate indicated that their vote in the 1981 Presidential elections would be determined by the state of the economy (*Le Point*, 2 May 1981: 51). They believed that a Socialist regime might be able to do better, and on 10 May 1981 elected François Mitterrand President of the Republic. That action ushered in a socialist experiment that will allow us to judge whether the broad outlines of French economic policy were altered by a fundamental change in the ideological orientation of the regime.

8

The Socialist Experiment of
François Mitterrand

On 10 May 1981 the French people elected a Socialist President for the first time under the Fifth Republic. A month later they ended 23 years of conservative rule by returning a Socialist majority to the National Assembly, enabling President François Mitterrand to form a coalition government from the Socialist and Communist parties. These elections were a decisive act of political will. They brought into office a Government committed to changing the distribution of power and resources within French society and recasting the relations between state and society itself. France embarked on a Socialist experiment.[1]

The purpose of this chapter is to assess the accomplishments of that experiment. Can a change in the complexion of the governing party effect a broader socioeconomic transformation? Many Socialists expected the new regime to change France as profoundly as had the events and institutions of the immediate post-war conjuncture. As one Socialist campaign brochure boldly declared: "Our responsibility is to invent the future" (*Le Projet Socialiste*, 1980: 141).

Admittedly, a final judgement on the accomplishments of the regime will have to wait; structural reforms take time to bear fruit. At the end of the initial legislative term of the government, however, it has become apparent that state and society are not readily transformed. A reforming regime faces constraints implicit in both the existing organization of society and in the nation's position within the international economy. Such constraints limited the choices facing the French Government, imposing trade-offs that it did not always expect and rendering the outcome of its decisions dependent on forces it could not always control.

The other factor limiting the accomplishments of a government, of course, is its political imagination. One only attains what one attempts. The Mitterrand Government – a coalition of Socialists and Communists

– came to office with a bifurcated imagination. Although the Communist Party (PCF) had only four Ministers in the Cabinet and forty-four seats in the Assembly, its control over about 15 percent of the vote and France's largest trade union (the CGT) gave it considerable influence over the government. More important yet, the Socialist Party (PS) itself was less a unified force than a collection of competing *tendances*, loosely gathered into a new party in 1972.

Within the Socialist Party, three main groups competed for influence. On one side stood the CERES group, a neo-Marxist enclave which tended to favor large-scale nationalizations and an all-out dash for growth behind protective tariff barriers. Led by Jean Pierre Chevènement, its members embraced an étatist conception of socialism according to which the state would impose reform from above. The PCF shared many of these views. By contrast, the other side of the Party was dominated by an anti-Marxist group which favored a decentralized form of socialism. Its members hoped to reduce the role of the state in society and find a new path to growth based on *autogestion*, or workers' control, within a more autonomous civil society. They looked forward to the day when a multitude of independent social actors, ranging from trade unions to local action groups, would reform social life from below. This group was often known as the "second left" or the "Rocardiens."

While one side of the party hoped to reaffirm the longstanding étatism of the French state, the other side hoped to decentralize political life. In the middle stood an eclectic group of social democrats, often drawn from municipal politics, who did not advocate widespread structural reform so much as a renewal of Keynesian economic policies and some measure of redistribution in the form of more generous social policies. François Mitterrand himself came from this group, but he was able to retain the leadership of the Party only by forming a series of shifting coalitions with the other *tendances* (Ross and Jenson, 1981, 1983; Portelli, 1980). Once in power he had to choose between their programs; and the unevenness of the Government's record reflects, in part, the ambivalence of that choice.

THE REDISTRIBUTIVE KEYNESIANISM OF 1981–82

Scarcely before the joyous demonstrations marking the victory of the left were over, Mitterrand began to implement his manifesto. He had promised the electorate that a Socialist Government would restore economic prosperity. Although some of his advisors urged an immediate devaluation and protectionism, those he most trusted suggested that reflation should be possible without isolating France from the international economy (*L'Expansion*, 11 May 1984: 169 ff). Their optimism was based on the widespread view that the world economy was about to expand, a conviction supported by most international forecasts. In such a context France might have been able to expand demand and finance the resulting balance of payments deficit until world recovery improved the trade balance.

Mitterrand favored this policy because it appealed to most currents within the party and spoke directly to the redistributive concerns of his own supporters. Government spending designed to increase the incomes of the low-paid and to provide jobs for the unemployed was supposed to spark off a boom in consumer spending that would lead to the expansion of French industry. Accordingly, the Government embarked on an ambitious program of "redistributive Keynesianism" in the spring of 1981.

Family allowances were raised by 81 percent for families with two children and by 44 percent for those with three children in the two years following May 1981. Housing allocations for low-paid workers were increased by 25 percent in 1981. Health insurance benefits were made more widely available to part-time employees and the unemployed. Old-age pensions were increased by 300 F a month to 1700 F for a single person and 3700 F for a couple. The purchasing power of social transfers rose by 4.5 percent in 1981 and by 7.6 percent in 1982. Most significantly, the minimum wage (SMIC), to which the salaries of 1.7 million workers were tied, was raised by 15 percent in real terms between May 1981 and December 1982.

Drastic measures were also taken to reduce unemployment, beginning with statutory work-time reduction. In July 1981 the work-week was reduced from 40 to 39 hours and the workforce was given a fifth week of vacation. The left wing of the PS and the PCF argued against corresponding reductions in pay, while centrist Socialists favored them. Mitterrand ostensibly left the decision up to enterprise negotiators but ultimately urged them to avoid wage reductions. As a result the policy improved the quality of life for many employees but had little effect on unemployment. Only a fifth of all firms took on new employees, and no more than 28,000 jobs were created by the reduction of the work-week (Marchand, 1983: 11).

A second program, announced in January 1982, encouraged firms to negotiate 'contracts of solidarity' with the government. One provision allowed employees aged 55 to 60 to retire on 70 percent of their salary, which was paid by the state if the firm replaced them with younger workers. That scheme created 100,000 jobs in 1982. Under a second provision, employers who reduced the work-week below 39 hours and hired additional employees as a result were exempted from their social security payments for the new employees. Over 13,000 positions were created in this way during 1982. A third program allowed older employees to go on half-time work at 80 percent of their former salary (with the additional 20 percent paid by the state), if younger employees were hired to replace them. 1500 people gained employment under this program during 1982 (*Le Monde*, 1983: 66).

In March 1982 the Mitterrand Government introduced an early retirement program to take effect in April 1983. Anyone who had paid social security contributions for 37.5 years could retire aged 60 on an amount ranging from 80 percent of the former salary of a smicard (employee earning the minimum wage) to 50 percent of the salary of a cadre (middle manager). While some cadres lost the right to retire at 60 with 70 percent of their salary under this scheme, there were 360,000 potential beneficiaries, of whom a quarter were expected to retire and open up positions for younger employees. To supplement its job creation program, the Government itself hired an additional 200,000 employees in 1981–82.

In distributive terms these measures were a great success. The position of the poor, aged, and lower-paid was substantially improved. Many of the least-advantaged French workers were able to take early retirement and longer vacations without loss of income. When most other nations were trimming transfer programs and workforce privileges, France took a dramatic step forward.

The policies simultaneously cut the rate of growth of unemployment. Although 140,000 formerly illegal immigrants joined the labor force under a government amnesty, unemployment rose only 4 percent in France during 1982 against a rise of 29 percent in Germany and 22 percent in the US. No other Western nation had been able to reduce the growth of unemployment so significantly. The French economy grew by 2 percent over two years, while growth in most other European nations was stagnant.

THE ECONOMIC CONSTRAINTS

Unfortunately the reflation of 1981–82 also had some serious side-effects. By the fall of 1981 it had begun to precipitate a massive balance of payments crisis, marked by growing pressure against the franc on the international exchanges. We can attribute this crisis partly to the delayed world economic recovery. In that respect the dash for growth of 1981–82 was a gamble. Mitterrand later explained why he took it: "I was carried away by our victory; we were intoxicated. Everyone . . . predicted the return of growth by 1983. Honestly, I lacked the necessary knowledge to say they were wrong" (*Le Témoinage Chrétien*, 11 July 1983).

At a more fundamental level, however, the balance of payments crisis resulted from constraints – of which the Socialists were only dimly aware – implicit in the economic situation of France. Some derived from the position of the French economy within an international system of economic regimes, while others were caused by structural trends within the French economy itself, intensified by the policies of the preceding regime. François Mitterrand faced a set of constraints that differed dramatically from those presented to Léon Blum or Charles de Gaulle.

Most important, long-term changes in France's international economic position had placed limits on the government's room for maneuverability. French production was now deeply integrated into the world economy. The trade, energy and monetary dimensions of this interdependence rendered autonomous reflation a particularly risky strategy.

On the trade side, imports and exports, which accounted for 13 percent of gross domestic product (GDP) in 1953, were worth 23 percent of GDP by 1983. Therefore, French industry was more vulnerable to international recession, and domestic expansion was more likely to result in rising imports. With regard to energy, France depended on imports for 80 percent of her requirements, and any increase in international energy prices could throw the balance of payments into immediate deficit. (The 1979 increase, in fact, left the nation with a 60 billion franc deficit even before the Socialists took office.) Since 37 percent of French imports were now denominated in American dollars, the nation could also be hurt by shifting exchange rates. In particular it was no longer possible to rectify a balance of payments deficit by devaluing the exchange rate. For every 10 centimes that the franc fell against the dollar, the French import bill rose by 2.5 billion francs (*Commissariat Général du Plan*, 1983: II, 110). That was almost enough to cancel out its beneficial effect on exports.

Structural changes on the domestic front as well constrained the Mitterrand Government. Some had consequences for the labor market. The industrial shake-out that followed the 1974 oil crisis resulted in the loss of 684,000 jobs at a time when demographic trends were expanding the labor force by 230,000 people a year. Even in the absence of further lay-offs, a quarter of a million new jobs had to be found each year in France simply to avoid rising levels of unemployment. Handed this dire situation, it would have been almost impossible for the Socialists to keep unemployment from increasing.

The corporate sector was also in trouble. The industrial policies that Giscard d'Estaing had pursued channelled resources into diplomatic exports (such as arms, airplanes, and turn-key plants) and massive capital projects (such as the telephone system, nuclear plants, and rapid transit). Such a strategy improved the French infrastructure and trade balance but left the consumer goods sector of the economy vulnerable to import competition. While France sold arms to the OPEC nations, the Germans and Japanese penetrated French markets for automobiles, electronics, and consumer durables. Only too late did the attention of the regime shift from the 'challenge of the Third World' to the 'reconquest of the domestic market'. By this time, small and medium-sized firms producing for domestic consumption were in a weakened position.

The distributional choices made under Giscard intensified these problems. The oil price rises of 1974 and 1979 had imposed a cost on the French economy equivalent to about 8 percent of GDP. This debt had to be paid out of the incomes of some sectors of the economy. However, the Giscardien policies effectively insulated the working population from the principal costs of the recession. Instead, they were imposed on corporate profits and the unemployed.

Household spending was allowed to grow by 3.5 percent a year between 1975 and 1980; and social transfer payments grew by twice that amount. During the same period, however, the rate of unemployment increased from 2.6 percent to 7.6 percent and the real value of unemployment benefits declined. As wages climbed, the French middle classes remained unscathed, while those who were out of work fared badly. There was a peculiarly dualistic quality to the recession of the 1970s, which reinforced a longstanding pattern of inegalitarianism in France (Marceau, 1977).

This left Mitterrand with two problems: one economic and one political. On one hand he had to confront the rising level of unemployment bequeathed to him by his predecessor. On the other, he was likely to have to shift some of the burden to the middle classes, which had been largely insulated from the effects of the recession. Despite Barre's talk of "austerity" they had not been forced to pay for the rising balance of payments deficit or the oil costs.

At a corporate level the problem was equally serious. Between 1975 and 1981, the share of value-added going to wages rose from 6.8 to 7.5 percent, and that of taxes increased from 2.7 to 4.3 percent. However, the share going to profits fell from 17 to 9.6 percent, precipitating an investment crisis. The volume of private investment in France fell 14 percent between 1973 and 1981. At the same time, corporate debt rose sharply and the rate of *autofinancement* dropped (Rosanvallon, 1983). These developments weakened the ability of the French state to stimulate investment by expanding demand. Low profit margins and high debt levels meant that French firms would be slow to respond to a demand stimulus.

The Socialists faced an acute policy dilemma for which conventional economic theory left them only two options. They could use traditional Keynesian techniques to stimulate demand, although this might well cause balance of payments problems before it began to affect investment. Their second option was to raise profit levels directly by depressing wages or cutting corporate taxes, but to do this the Socialists would have to discipline the workforce or cut social spending. The first tactic was economically dangerous; the second was politically unpalatable. In large measure the history of the Mitterrand years is the story of how the Government gradually moved from the first option to the second, all the while seeking a third way out of the dilemma.

THE POLITICS OF AUSTERITY, 1982–83

By the fall of 1981 it became clear to French forecasters that the international economy would not expand sufficiently to prevent France from running a massive balance of payments deficit. The cost of the 1981–82 reflation was proving to be high. Public expenditure rose by 11.4 percent in volume during 1981 and 1982, and the budget deficit increased from 0.4 to 3 percent of GDP in 1982. French industry struggled to remain competitive under the weight of a 34 billion franc increase in wages and social security contributions that the new programs entailed. Real disposable income grew twice as fast as production; and the difference was spent on imports. Imports of autos rose 40 percent, electrical applicances 27 percent and consumer goods 20 percent during 1982. As a consequence the trade deficit ballooned from 56 bF in 1981 to 93 bF in 1982. Inflation remained at 12.5 percent for 1981, 11 percent for 1982 and 9.3 percent for 1983, well above the falling levels abroad. The result was a balance of payments crisis that brought the value of the franc under severe pressure on the foreign exchanges.

The Mitterrand Government suddenly began to see the hidden constraints on its policy. Devaluation of the franc and domestic deflation became inevitable. Mitterrand hoped that the former would restore the competitiveness of French exports, while the other restrained spending on imports by reducing domestic incomes. Both were politically unpopular. After the triumphant expansion of its first year, the subsequent years of the Mitterrand presidency would be marked by austerity. The Government implemented this reversal in stages.

West Germany provided the principal market for French exports, and by 1982 French prices were rising at twice the rate of competing German products. Accordingly, the franc was devalued against the Deutschmark on three occasions – 4 October 1981, 12 June 1982 and 21 March 1983 – for a total decline of 27 percent in 2 years. The French hoped that these devaluations would increase exports by 3 percent,

GDP by 1 percent, create 120,000 new jobs, and improve the trade balance by 24 bF over 3 years (Debonneuil and Sterdyniak, 1982). Although most French exports go to Germany, many of her imports are denominated in American dollars. Therefore, the French state was desperate to maintain the high level of the franc against the dollar in order to cut the import bill. Mitterrand tried to persuade the Reagan administration to lower its interest rates. Instead, rising interest rates in America and speculation against the franc carried the currency from 4.20 against the dollar in 1980 to 5.35 in April 1981 and 8.60 by 1984. The effects on the French economy were catastrophic. It has been estimated that the rise in the dollar reduced the French growth rate by 1 percent in 1982, raised unemployment by 24,000, inflation by 3–5 percent, and the public sector deficit by 36 bF. Its effect on import prices alone lifted the trade deficit by 57 bF in 1982 (*Le Monde*, 24 March 1983). This, in turn, renewed speculation against the franc. The Mitterrand Government found itself in a vicious circle not entirely of its own making (see table 8.1).

Table 8.1   The impact of domestic and external factors on French economic performance in 1982

	Growth (%)	Inflation (%)	Unem- ployment (000's)	Trade balance (bF)	Public deficit (bF)
Domestic expansion, 1981–82	0.9	0.2	−64.7	−27.0	51.5
Other domestic policies, 1981–82	−0.4	−0.3	−106.0	−0.2	−18.4
EMS realignment, 1981–82	0.5	1.5	−15.2	−17.9	2.3
Change in US dollar and interest rates	−0.9	3.5	24.0	−57.4	35.8
Total	0.1	5.5	−161.9	−102.1	71.2

Source: Calculations by Raymond Courbis and André Keller on the MOGLI econometric model reported in *Le Monde* (24 March 1983) and in *Prévision et Analyse économique*, 4.1 (1983).

The Government was forced into domestic deflation to rectify the balance of payments. As part of the realignment of parities within the European Monetary System (EMS) in October 1981, West Germany insisted that France eliminate 15 bF from the 1982 budget. As early as 29 November 1981 the French Finance Minister indicated that "it will be necessary to pause before announcing further reforms" (*Le Monde*, 1 December 1981).

The real break came on 13 June 1982 after the franc was devalued again against the German currency. The Government implemented a drastic austerity plan, whose object was to limit the public sector deficit to 3 percent of GDP and improve the deteriorating financial situation of private enterprise. Public spending for 1982 was cut by 20 bF. All wages, except the SMIC, and most prices were frozen until the end of October 1982. The level of employers' social security contributions was frozen for a year; company tax was reduced by 10 percent; a portion of the cost of family allowances was transferred from employers to employees; value-added tax was removed from tools for 3 years, and accelerated depreciation provisions introduced. In total, these measures meant that the wage and benefits bill facing French industry in 1982–83 would grow at only half the rate of the preceding year.

Within the Government these measures reflected a shift in power toward the economic hard-liners. The Ministry for National Solidarity was renamed the Ministry for Social Affairs, and Nicole Questiaux was replaced as Minister by Pierre Bérégovoy, Mitterrand's right-hand man at the Elysée. Questiaux had advocated the system of retirement at 60 with little concern for its cost. In the following year Bérégovoy engineered a radical reduction in the social security and unemployment insurance deficits through increased charges and reduced benefits.

The measures of June 1982 were significant for two reasons: they marked the end of the fiscal expansion on which the Government initially pinned its hopes for economic recovery, and they reflected a reversal of the Government's distributive priorities. In its first year the Government's primary concern had been to redistribute income to the unemployed and workers on lower incomes. Business bore the costs of this program. In June 1982, however, policy-makers concluded that French employers also needed relief. The government imposed higher costs on workers and social beneficiaries to ease the financial burden on French enterprise.

Unfortunately, the deflationary impact of the 1982 measures was not sufficient to stem the run on French currency. Therefore the Government had to devise a new austerity plan, which it announced on 23 March 1983. The plan took austerity one step further. For the first time, real costs were imposed on the French middle classes. Taxes were raised by 40 bF and public spending was slashed by 24 bF in 1983. Out of 22 million taxpayers, 15 million paid a new 1 percent surcharge on taxable income, and 8 million were forced to make a compulsory loan to the government of 10 percent of their taxes repayable in 3 years. Public enterprise prices were raised an average of 8 percent, along with taxes on tobacco, alcohol and petrol. An 8 percent limit was imposed on wage and price increases over the following years. In addition, French tourists were prohibited from taking more than 2000 F out of the country. Elysée officials argued that to secure an equivalent balance of payments improvement by other means would have required a 1 percent reduction in real disposable income, but this was an enormous psychological blow to a nation which spent 30 bF on foreign travel in 1982.

Serious political consequences followed from these moves. In the first instance, middle-class groups adversely affected by the Government's policies demonstrated in the streets of Paris during the spring of 1983, ironically evoking the famous events of May 1968. Farmers and shopkeepers followed suit. By the summer of 1983 the President's popularity had fallen dramatically; only 32 percent of the electorate approved of his policies.

Within the Socialist Party itself the illusions of Keynesianism in one country had been dashed. The Government's hopes for domestic economic expansion foundered in the face of a rising American dollar and continuing world recession. That inspired a profound reevaluation of France's ability to undertake expansion, perhaps even redistributive socialism, alone. Prime Minister Pierre Mauroy declared:

> Quite simply, a real left-wing policy can be applied in France only if the other European countries also follow policies of the left. . . . I want to change the habits of this nation. If the French resign themselves to living with an inflation of 12%, then they should know that, because of our economic interdependence with Germany, we will be led into a situation of imbalance. France must rid herself of this inflationary disease (*L'Express*, 8 April 1983).

The Government decided to tame the inflationary habits of a nation that had always depended on them in order to generate growth. A Socialist administration, elected on a promise to restore prosperity, imposed austerity instead.

There were those in the party who argued for an alternative strategy, based on neo-protectionism. According to this view, France would unilaterally withdraw from the EMS in order to devalue, free of German demands for spending cuts, and use a system that imposed mandatory deposits on importers to improve the trade deficit without recourse to deflation. (Italy had once employed such a scheme without leaving the EEC). Several Ministers, such as Jean-Pierre Chevènement, Laurent Fabius, and Pierre Bérégovoy, as well as Jean Riboud, the industrialist closest to Mitterrand, showed varying degrees of support for this proposal. They suggested that France could develop a new economic strategy based on monetary independence and economic expansion behind rising trade barriers (*Le Nouvel Observateur*, 30 May 1983).

The critical juncture, at which policy might have turned in this direction, came during the third week of March 1983, between the two rounds of the municipal elections. The Socialists sustained losses in the first round, and Mitterrand considered replacing Prime Minister Pierre

Mauroy, who was the principal advocate of a new round of austerity. By this time it was clear that the franc would have to be devalued against the mark once more, and as the Government spent 40 bF on the foreign exchanges to defend the franc, the President pondered his options.

Two factors seemed to swing the decision against neo-protectionism. Finance Minister Jacques Delors successfully persuaded the Germans to revalue their currency by 5.5 percent in exchange for a mere 2.5 percent devaluation in the franc. No doubt the imminent threat that France might leave the EMS helped persuade the Germans to bear the disproportionate share of realignment. This was a small political coup for the French negotiators and a fillip for the EMS. More important, Elysée studies told the President that even the neo-protectionist option would have to be accompanied by deflation if frustrated demand for imports were not to bring domestic inflation. With this in mind, Mitterrand left Mauroy as Prime Minister and Delors at Finance, and agreed to the deflationary program of March 1983 (see Pfister, 1985).

The strategy underlying this macroeconomic policy was essentially conservative. "We want to have wages rise more slowly than prices in order to curb consumer purchasing power and increase profitability," the Prime Minister explained (*Business Week*, 10 January 1983). The extension of wage control in 1982 and reductions in the corporate tax burden over the following years were deliberately designed to raise profits at the expense of wages. The Government hoped that higher profits would bring higher levels of investment and growth.

The retreat from redistributive Keynesianism to wage discipline took France down a familiar path. Social democratic governments in Britain during the 1960s and 1970s had followed a similar route. However, it contained one pitfall. Investment usually responds as readily to the level of demand as to the rate of profit. By squeezing incomes, such a strategy could also depress domestic consumption enough to inhibit investment, despite slowly rising levels of profit. As the critics of the French 'regulation' school pointed out, instead of regenerating growth, the strategy could lock France into another vicious circle whereby falling levels of consumption would depress investment and profits and lead to pressures for even lower wage settlements (Lipietz, 1983). At the macroeconomic level, both the Keynesian and austerity strategies of the Mitterrand Government ran up against constraints implicit in the organization of the domestic and international economies.

NATIONALIZATIONS

For this reason the Government put a great deal of emphasis on its microeconomic strategy. The essence of that strategy was initially to channel vast sums of money directly from the state to industry. Its object was to increase the rate of capital formation despite the limits that austerity imposed on the stimulation of demand and the truculence of French business under a Socialist regime. In a sense the policy was designed to overcome one of the classic structural constraints of capitalism – the dependence of investment on 'business confidence'. No matter how low that level of confidence, investment would continue because at least half of it would be provided by the state through aid to the private sector and the nationalized industries.

When macroeconomic austerity was instituted in 1982–83 this policy continued. The public spending cuts initially fell on social expenditure and defense rather than industry. As the Minister of the Budget said, the Government had reconsidered its priorities:

> We will hold spending down in 1983 by cutting many social programs. And in coming years, we plan to cut government spending from 46% of gross domestic product to 42% by further cutting on social programs and aid to municipalities. There are maybe 15,000 public swimming pools in French municipalities; we have to ask ourselves if we need 20,000 (*Business Week*, 10 January 1983).

Simultaneously, 30 percent of the military equipment purchases authorized for 1982, worth 15 bF, were cancelled, and manpower in France's conventional forces was severely reduced. Only the nuclear *force de frappe* remained untouched (Laulan, 1983). This approach skewed French defense policy toward the nuclear option.

In the straitened circumstances of the 1980s, most nations were cutting either defense or social spending in order to support the other category; they had to choose between a commitment to national security or the welfare state. France had found a third way. Its Government was trimming both defense and social spending to pass public resources into industrial investment.

The keystone of the Government's microeconomic strategy was the nationalization program completed in February 1982. Although the largest French banks were already under state control, the Government nationalized 36 smaller banks, two investment banks, Suez and Paribas, and the remaining minority of private shares in the Crédit Lyonnais, Banque Nationale de Paris, and Société Générale. It acquired 100 percent of the shares in six industrial conglomerates: the Compagnie Générale d'Electricité (CGE), the Compagnie Générale de Constructions Téléphoniques (CGCT) and Thompson-Brandt in electronics and telecommunications, Rhone-Poulenc in textiles and chemicals, Péchiney-Ugine-Kuhlman (PUK) in aluminum and chemicals, and St Gobain-Pont-à-Mousson in glass, paper and metals. State debt in the two major steel firms, Sacilor and Usinor, was converted into a majority shareholding, and the government acquired 51 percent of the shares of two arms and aeronautical manufacturers, Dassault-Greguet and

Matra, as well as control over the computer firm CII–Honeywell–Bull, and the pharmaceutical house, Roussel-Uclaf (see Délion and Durupty, 1982). The state now owned 13 of the 20 largest firms in France and a controlling share in many other French companies. State holdings accounted for 24 percent of the employees, 32 percent of the sales, 30 percent of the exports, and 60 percent of the annual investment in the industrial and energy sectors of the French economy.

The cost of the nationalizations was not negligible. The state would pay about 39 bF in capital and 47 bF in interest over 15 years for its purchases. In 1983 its payments totaled 9 bF. Most dispossessed shareholders were amply compensated; for instance, each share of Rhone-Poulenc, which had recently traded as low as 45F, was exchanged for a bond worth 126 bF paying 16 percent interest. Ministers Rocard and Fabius had argued that the state could save 30 bF by nationalizing only 51 percent of each company, but they were overruled by Mitterrand, who was anxious to satisfy his Communist coalition partners (*L'Express*, 14 June 1983).

What purpose did the nationalization serve? Prior to the election, the very ambiguity of the project helped unite diverse factions on the left. Each group saw nationalization as a means toward its own end, whether that was the implementation of workers' control, the elimination of private profit, the strengthening of the unions, or the rescue of France's industrial base. Nationalization could be all things to all people, and as such it was a powerful unifying device.

Because the project had to be defined more concretely after the elections, however, it became a source of division within the Government. Those who expected the nationalized firms to spearhead the drive toward workers' control were largely disappointed. The new administrative councils of each enterprise contained six state appointees, six outside experts, and six representatives from the workforce.Workers were given a voice, but not control over the enterprise.

Similarly, contention continued within the administration over the degree of influence it should exercise over the nationalized industries. The rapid turnover in Ministers of Industry reflected this struggle. In the space of 2 years, Pierre Joxe, Pierre Dreyfus, Jean-Pierre Chevènement and Laurent Fabius all held the position. When Dreyfus replaced Joxe, a tight rein was supposed to give way to the arm's-length relationship that Dreyfus had established at Renault. Chevènement, however, reintroduced daily intervention in the decisions taken by the heads of the public enterprises, and their complaints to the President played a role in his subsequent resignation. The appointment of Fabius in May 1983 reflected Mitterrand's new determination that "the nationalized industries should have total autonomy of decision and action" (*Le Monde*, 28 May 1983).

Of course the newly nationalized enterprises would never operate totally autonomously; but it was equally hard for the state to acquire effective control over them. Formal ownership was only the beginning. Real power consists in the ability to direct an enterprise so as to achieve one's ultimate goals. The French state still had to clarify its goals and learn how to use such enterprises to implement them. In 1982–83 these companies had the worst of both worlds: they lacked adequate direction from the state to guide their long-term strategy, yet they were subject to sporadic government intervention into their daily operations. Because the state faced more intense political pressure to avoid lay-offs than did private firms, its capacity to restructure French industry might even have been reduced by the nationalizations.

In effect the measures of 1981–82 simply consolidated the longstanding influence of the French state over industry. The large state banks, which had been important since the Caisse de Dépôts was formed in 1816, and the practice of rediscounting loans at the Bank of France already enabled the state to control the flows of funds in France. In addition, by 1980 the government was the major shareholder in 500 firms and a minority shareholder in 600 others (Hough, 1979: 191). French officials had always been able to put a good deal of pressure on selected industries. As one officer of St Gobain explained, nationalization made little difference: "It is the state who told us to replace CGE in CII–Honeywell–Bull in 1978, and it is the state who told us to get out of it in 1982" (*Le Monde*, 5 February 1983).

Nevertheless, the nationalizations had produced two tangible benefits by 1983. They allowed the state to accelerate the pace of rationalization in several industries, notably chemicals; and they ensured that several sectors of French business continued to invest heavily despite the world recession.

Funds for investment were made available to each enterprise in return for signing a 3–5-year "planning contract" with the Ministry of Industry. On this basis the newly nationalized industries received 20 bF in 1983, of which 12.6 bF came from the budget and the rest from the nationalized banking sector. Additional funds were to be raised through the capital markets and various forms of research and regional aid. In return, the newly nationalized industries had to invest 31 bF in 1983 (22 bF of it within France), equivalent to 50 percent of total industrial investment in France and roughly 20 percent more than the firms had otherwise planned. As table 8.2 indicates, almost half of these funds went to the steel and chemical sectors alone. In addition the older public enterprises received 43.5 bF in 1982 and 56.8 bF in 1983, almost half of which went to the railways (Greffe, 1983; Hall, 1985).

The nationalization of the banking sector reinforced this strategy. Three months after the banks were supposedly guaranteed operating

Table 8.2   Direct aid to nationalized industries, 1983 (billion francs)

Charbonnages-Chemicals	1,000
CGE	870
CIT-Honeywell-Bull	1,500
EMC	250
PUK	2,400
Renault	1,650
Rhône-Poulenc	1,800
Saint-Gobain	750
Snecma	300
Thomson	1,600
Steel	6,450
Chemicals	1,650
Total	20,220

Source: *Le Monde*, 11 February 1983, p. 26.

autonomy, they were instructed to lend 6 bF to the nationalized industries, purchase 7 bF in state debt during 1983, and maintain their industrial lending rates at 14 percent. Small and medium-sized enterprises were also expected to benefit from such loans. In order to use the banks as an instrument of policy their *tutelle*, or traditional supervisory responsibility, was transferred to a new monitoring unit at the Ministry of Economics and Finance, and the National Credit Council was reorganized. The French banks had been subject to the *encadrement du crédit* (government controls on lending above authorized ceilings) since 1972, but loan recipients were now more carefully scrutinized and some banks were expected to supervise the rationalization of entire industrial sectors.

The results of this strategy were mixed but not unpromising. In 1982, the newly nationalized industries lost 16 bF, and the traditional state sector of EDF (Electricity), GDF (Gas), SNCF (Railways), RATP (Paris Transport), Air France and Charbonnages (Coal) lost 27 bF, compared with total losses of 19 bF in 1981 and a small profit in 1980 (Wright, 1984; Hall, 1985). For a period it looked as if the state was simply keeping a set of inefficient firms afloat. However, the losses of the traditional state sector fell to 21 bF in 1983 and 10 bF in 1984; and several of the newly nationalized enterprises, which had been in trouble in 1980, recovered nicely. The aluminum sector was usefully rationalized around Péchiney, chemicals around Rhone-Poulenc, and paper products around Saint-Gobain. All were making profits by 1985. The most worrisome sectors remained steel, which lost 14 bF in 1984, and automobiles, where Renault, once a star performer, lost 12.5 bF in 1984 (*Le Nouvel Economiste*, 3 April 1985: 46).

INDUSTRIAL POLICY: ETATISM RESURGENT

The initial industrial policies of the Mitterrand Government were openly interventionist, reaffirming the etatism that had traditionally characterized the French state. The free market rhetoric of Raymond Barre did not appeal to the Socialists. As we have seen, however, the policies pursued by a Barre Government irrespective of its rhetoric were often quite dirigiste. Therefore, there has been a good deal of continuity between the policies of the two regimes, particularly with regard to aid for the declining sectors.

Under Giscard d'Estaing large firms in financial trouble received aid from CIASI and small firms were supported by the departmental committees of CODEFI. Between 1974 and 1981 these agencies handled 660 corporate rescues where 300,000 jobs were at stake. Mitterrand replaced CIASI with an inter-departmental committee, named CIRI, chaired by the Minister of Finance and staffed by a 20-person secretariat handling over 200 cases a year. Six regional committees (CORRI) have been established to decentralize the operations of CODEFI. While these bodies consult the unions more frequently than did their predecessors, the basic administration of aid has not changed. Within 3–6 months the committees usually arrange an infusion of state aid for a failing firm and often merge it with another enterprise (see Green, 1983).

In 1979 Giscard established CODIS and its analogue for small business, CIDISE, to fund innovative projects in growth areas, such as robotics, biotechnology, electronics, office automation, energy-saving devices, underwater exploration, and synthetic textiles. Selected firms received government subsidies, public orders, export aids or import controls in return for signing a "development contract" that specified performance targets to be met over the 3–5-year life of the contract. In total CODIS spent 3 bF to initiate investment projects worth 20 bF, and CIDISE spent 18 bF to provide equity participation or interest-rate subsidies to over 450 projects.[2]

The Mitterrand Government replaced CODIS with Le Fonds de Modernisation Industriel (FMI). It spent 3 bF appropriated from the Caisse des Dépôts in 1983 and another 5 bF in 1984 raised from a new savings bond, the CODEVI, whose interest was tax-free for 3 years. The FMI provided loan guarantees, long-term debentures, and interest subsidies to growth-sector firms investing in new plant or technologies. Its list of preferred sectors was very similar to that of CODIS, and the Fund was supposed to dispose of all requests for aid within 8 weeks of their receipt.

One agency which Mitterrand retained in its original form was ANVAR, established in 1979 to sponsor research and development.

Over 3 years ANVAR and its 22 regional committees handled more than 4000 cases, and in 1983 it distributed 900 mF, mainly in equity loans. This reflected the Government's continuing commitment to raise French expenditure on research to 2.5 percent of GDP by 1988. Mitterrand took further steps to improve the flow of savings into private investment. Besides the new CODEVI bond, another savings bond indexed to inflation (the *livret d'épargne populaire*) was issued to encourage savings among the 11 million households that pay less than 1000 F tax. To increase investment in the stock market the complicated and heavy system of capital gains tax was replaced by a flat rate of 15 percent. A second market, in which firms were required to issue only 10 percent of their stock, was created to give small business access to equity capitalization. Finally, businesses started in 1983 were forgiven half their taxes for the next 3 years (*Le Nouvel Economiste*, 9 May 1983).

Like their predecessors, the Socialists continued to emphasize the export of arms and turn-key plants. Foreign orders for French arms rose from 22 bF in 1980 to 42 bF in 1982; and exports of major infrastructure projects were set to increase from 20 bF in 1981 to 40 bF in 1986. These sales are heavily dependent on subsidized loans from the French state, such as the $2 billion it lent to Iraq in 1983. As justification, the Government noted that 1 million jobs depended on arms sales alone, and that the trade surplus on arms was greater than the combined total for all other industries in 1982.

At the sectoral level the Mitterrand Government devised rescue plans for no less than eight major industries in 1981–83 including steel, chemicals, textiles, machine tools, furniture, leather goods, toys, and electronics (see Stoffaes, 1982).

In steel, where the unions are particularly strong, the watchword until 1984 was expansion, whatever the cost or projected market. The Government accepted the recommendations of the Judet report to expand production from 19 million tons in 1981 to 24 million tons in 1986, despite EEC estimates that the market would bear no more than 21 million tons. Seventeen bF was to be spent over 4 years to modernize the productive facilities of Usinor and Sacilor. The French steel industry will have received 60 bF in public aid over the 8 years since 1978, although the Government has targeted 1987 as the year when steel is expected to break even.

By contrast the Government's principal object in the chemical sector has been to restructure the industry into a few massive and specialized firms. The heavy chemicals section of PUK was ceded to Elf-Acquitaine, and a series of mergers were enforced to regroup the industry around three large public firms, CDF-Chimie and Elf-Acquitaine in heavy chemicals and Rhone-Poulenc in speciality chemicals. Pharmaceutical production has been concentrated in three firms: Sanofi (tied to Elf), Roussel-Uclaf and Rhone-Poulenc. If size and specialization were the only relevant factors this would be a winning strategy; but the chemical sector is beset by problems – related to the high cost of raw materials – that this plan does not resolve.

In textiles the Government's actions were designed to save jobs at the cost of increasing state support for a largely uncompetitive industry. The two foundering giants, Boussac-Saint-Frères and Bidermann, have been rescued. In total an industry which suffered 8 bF in losses during 1982 was given subsidies and loans amounting to 820 mF a year and a 12 percent reduction in social security taxes worth 3 bF a year, in return for increased investment and the restriction of lay-offs from 8 percent of employees in 1981 to 1 percent in 1982.

The plan for the machine tool sector regrouped 130 firms into larger entities while providing the industry 3 bF in grants and 4 bF in loans over 3 years. Public orders were used to stimulate the production of numerically controlled machine tools and to reduce the rate of imports of machine tools from 60 to 30 percent. Similarly, funds raised from a special tax on home furnishings were invested in the French furniture industry in return for an agreement by distributors to cut imports from 20 to 15 percent of French sales. In these sectors the state was determined to maintain a French industry despite serious European competition.

The Government's most ambitious plans, however, were reserved for the electronics sector, which President Mitterrand described as "our weapon of the future." Over 5 years, 140 bF was budgeted to redress the commercial imbalance in the sector, create 80,000 jobs, and increase production by 9 percent a year. Public orders were used to stimulate technological progress in microelectronics, computers, robots, and office communications. Several firms were forced out of the industry, which was regrouped around four giant public enterprises supervised by a national advisory committee of 50 officials (*Le Monde* 22 January 1983). The jurisdiction of the Ministry of Industry was extended again to cover the profitable Post and Telecommunications Ministry, so that its resources could be used on this project.

Together these programs pumped vast sums of money into French industry, in keeping with President Mitterrand's assertion that "industry is a priority that overrides all others" (*Le Monde* 3 January 1983). In 1981 public aid to industry totaled 100 bF or 3.5 percent of GDP. That included 40 bF spent on research and development, 16.5 bF in export subsidies and insurance administered through COFACE, 13.2 bF for direct industrial subsidies, 11.3 bF to cover losses in sectors such as shipbuilding and steel, 12 bF in tax incentives for investment, 6.5 bF under various programs designed to increase employment, and 1.8 bF in regional aid. The figures for 1982 and 1983 were even higher. Clearly visible loans and grants to the private sector rose from 20 bF in 1980 to 35 bF in 1982 and 45 bF in 1983 (Stoffaes, 1983: 165; *L'Express*, 7 January 1983).

THE EVOLUTION OF INDUSTRIAL POLICY

In 1981–83 the industrial policies of the Socialists broke with those of the preceding regime. Despite an underlying dirigisme, the Giscardiens had moved away from the policies of the Gaullist period in the late 1970s. As we have seen, they began to question the state's ability to identify industrial 'winners' in an era when success followed from competitiveness. Wasted investment in massive projects such as the Concorde and the Plan Calcul led Giscard and his advisors to wonder whether it was wise to concentrate resources on a small number of projects or a few 'national champions'. Instead, they began to see the market as an effective instrument for identifying competitive firms and projects, and they sought ways in which the state might use market signals to inform its own decisions. Industrial policy-makers under Giscard began to provide 'seed money' to several firms in the same sector, making future aid contingent on market performance. They also advocated a *politique de créneaux* which would forsake the declining sectors and direct aid to firms with products of high value-added in fast-growing markets where France was most likely to find a competitive niche. If the Giscardiens did not always stick to these policies, they at least moved in that direction (Stoffaes, 1978; Green, 1984).

In its first years the Mitterrand Government totally rejected this approach, and criticized the very distinction between rising and declining sectors. The phrase of Pierre Dreyfus was constantly repeated: "There are no condemned sectors; there are only outmoded technologies." Even Laurent Fabius declared: "The distinction between leading sectors and those described as traditional is irrelevant. The new technologies should permeate all industrial sectors" (*Le Monde* 24 March, 13 April 1983). In this way the new regime avoided industrial triage in favor of a *politique de filières* whose object was to strengthen the entire range of products in each sector so that no part was lost to imports. According to this view France could produce everything it needed.

The political advantages of such a policy were obvious. It enabled the government to postpone the difficult task of selecting industries for abandonment while it appeased the PCF and CGT, both of which tended to defend all sectors to the point of autarchy. Moreover, the *politique de filières* was another concept sufficiently ambiguous to appeal to all currents within the Government (see Monfort, 1983).

In operation, however, the virtues of such a policy were less clear. It relied on three principal techniques to generate growth: the creation of very large firms specializing in a particular product line with a virtual monopoly over the French market; massive infusions of capital for investment; and the vigorous promotion of new technologies. In these respects the Socialists' initial industrial policy bypassed the Giscardien experiments and returned to the approach of the Gaullists in the early 1970s. Once again, high technology was a magic word; consumption was squeezed to supply investment, and enormous national champions were being groomed in each market. The resemblance to the Sixth Plan was striking indeed.

The approach had many drawbacks. It assumed that future growth would come from high volumes of mass-produced commodities competing on price terms in world markets, when several analysts were suggesting that growth would be generated in the 1980s primarily by smaller firms employing craft-based techniques and short production runs to generate specialized goods that compete on quality terms (Piore and Sabel, 1984). Similarly, increases in capital and the scale of production do not always improve the efficiency of a firm. For many years increasing state aid to the French steel industry simply led to growing overcapacity in world markets and the postponement of effective rationalization (Delatte, 1979). The Government's desire to support all segments of all sectors threatened to intensify the rigidities in French industry and delay the reallocation of resources to growth areas. The policy assumed that France could compete in most sectors; but the growth of international interdependence and specialization meant that a nation had to develop comparative advantage in a few areas if it were to compete on world markets.

Curiously enough, the Government's own policy-makers soon began to recognize some of these problems. Their thinking evolved much as that of the Giscardiens had before them when they encountered the constraints of operating within world markets. Even the nationalized enterprises could not escape market rationality except at great cost.

The principal factor that pushed the Government away from its initial industrial strategy, however, was the financial constraint implicit in its austerity program. In order to render that program credible and slightly less bitter, President Mitterrand had promised both to keep the budget deficit below 3 percent of GDP during the ensuing years of his term and to reduce the tax burden on industry and individuals by 1986. The result was a severe squeeze on public spending. As we have noted, industrial aid was initially spared, but as the nationalized industries and sectoral rationalization schemes continued to consume billions of francs, even they became the object of cutbacks. Growing popular discontent suggested that the electorate might not tolerate the levels of taxation and public spending necessary to channel a major proportion of industrial investment through the state.

The principal break came in the spring of 1984 when the Government announced details of a restructuring plan for steel, shipbuilding and coal that would entail the loss of 60,000 jobs by the end of the decade. Until then the policy-makers had steadfastly resisted schemes that required large lay-offs. Shipbuilding capacity was to be cut by 30 percent over 2 years; coal production was to drop from 18.5 million tons in 1983 to 13.5 million tons by 1988; and one out of every four jobs in steel-making would be eliminated by 1987. These industries were expected to break even by 1987, and the other nationalized industries were given until 1986 to do the same. To underline its seriousness, the Government allowed the massive steel firm, Creusot Loire, to go bankrupt when its management refused to accept a rescue plan that would have ceded control over much of its parent company to the banks. This became the largest bankruptcy in French history.

Initially, many commentators expected a softening of such policies prior to the crucial legislative elections of 1986. However, President Mitterrand acted decisively in favor of continuing austerity in July 1984 when he shuffled his Ministry, appointing Laurent Fabius as Prime Minister and Pierre Bérégovoy as the new Finance Minister. France's youngest Prime Minister in 150 years, Fabius was a Mitterrand protegé and advocate of austerity. Bérégovoy was a fiscal conservative who had already engineered sweeping cuts in social security. Together they were to maintain a stable public sector deficit and reduce taxes on individuals and enterprises. In time for the 1986 elections, the Government moved decisively away from redistributive policies in favor of tax cuts designed to raise private sector investment and middle-class purchasing power.

Bérégovoy abandoned the traditional system of indexing wages to prices and put pressure on the unions to keep wage increases below the state's 5 percent guideline for 1984. At the same time he began to remove price controls on industrial products and reduced employers' national insurance charges. Taxes were cut by about 5 percent in 1985 so that four out of every five taxpayers would pay less than they had in the preceding year. To make room for these reductions, however, public spending had to be cut radically. After no real increase in 1984 and 1985, reductions in total expenditure of 1 percent in real terms were mandated for 1986. These measures became necessary, in part, because France had to pay mounting interest charges on a growing public sector debt and a foreign debt that had reached 525 bF by 1985.

On the industrial side, Fabius's principal goal was to force the nationalized sector to break even. However, his Government was inclined to leave day-to-day operations up to the chiefs of the public enterprises. Fabius had always been an advocate of industrial modernization and the industrial budget remained high, especially for research and development. Instead of turning toward autarchy, however, he reinforced the openness of the economy. Exchange controls were lifted. The nationalized firms were allowed to invest abroad and encouraged to form alliances with foreign producers in the high-technology sectors. Several failing firms were refused industrial aid. France again embraced the international market system.

PLANNING UNDER THE SOCIALISTS

Within the sphere of industrial policy it is most interesting that economic planning played only a minor role since *planification* had been one of the principal themes of the Socialist electoral program. For years planning had been a totem of the left, and many observers expected its renewal under the Socialists. Its absence was added evidence that a change of government could not necessarily remove the broader constraints within which the French state operated.

Upon taking office the Socialists raised the status of the Plan by setting up a Ministry for this purpose under Michel Rocard, one of the leading figures in the Party. The Ministry quickly prepared an Interim Plan for 1981–83 and appointed a new Commission Nationale de Planification, with seven sub-committees and numerous working groups, to draw up a Ninth Plan for 1984–88. Its deliberations culminated in the passage of a global outline plan and detailed financial allocations by the National Assembly in the spring and fall of 1983. For the first time, regional plans to implement the national program were to be negotiated with the new regional governments; this was a striking institutional innovation.

Within a short time, however, it became apparent that the planners were having almost no effect on government policy. As one senior economic official said: "In this Ministry, the Plan has no influence at all. We occasionally use it as a debating point but it does not affect our decisions." The Planning Minister was never influential with his colleagues. He lost successive battles to place a planning official in each Ministry, to gain representation on the administrative councils of the nationalized industries, and to persuade regional leaders to join the National Planning Commission (*Le Monde* 30 July 1983). His pessimistic outline for the Ninth Plan was sent back by the Elysée for redrafting.

In part, the limited influence of the planners can be attributed to the circumstances of the new Government. As a former rival for the Presidency, Rocard was not overly influential with Mitterrand; the PFC and CERES group in the Party also tended to oppose many of his moves. Most significantly, however, real power over the daily decisions that would actuate the Plan belonged to a Minister of Finance, who was preoccupied with the exchange rate, and a Minister of Industry, who was interested in arrogating most planning functions to himself. Because everyone wanted to be a planner in the new Socialist Government, they were unwilling to delegate that function to the planning commission.

Nonetheless, planning was primarily the casualty of long-term developments which the Socialists could escape no more than any other government. Slow and erratic rates of growth meant that the planners had fewer resources to allocate, gloomier forecasts to promulgate, and greater difficulty making accurate predictions. Planning became politically embarrassing. For some time the Plan had done little more than recite the pre-existing financial priorities of the government.

Planning under the Mitterrand Government followed suit. The optimistic projections of the Interim Plan were soon rendered obsolete by austerity. The Ninth Plan reiterated and rationalized the government's decision to give priority to industry and noted that austerity would continue until 1985, but it contained few quantitative forecasts or new observations. The 35-hour week appeared as a distant ideal rather than a commitment. Rocard himself called the Plan "a theatrical exercise in collective psychodrama" (*Le Monde: Bilan* 1982: 56). It received a cool reception in the Assembly, and in March 1983 the Ministry of Planning was abolished. The work of the National Planning Commission continued under Jean Le Garrec at the Prime Minister's office; but the once-central concept of planning became a peripheral element in the Socialist's economic policy. Even Le Garrec expressed the puzzled disillusionment which characterized the Government's abandonment of planning, saying: "Today, given that nothing is predictable any more, one wonders how to plan" (*Le Monde* 30 July 1983).

THE STATE UNDER THE SOCIALISTS

The Socialists took office with the intention of restructuring the state and its relations with civil society (cf. Kesselman, 1983). As we have seen, however, party opinion was split between divergent visions of the alternatives. Those seeking étatist solutions were pitted against others arguing for autogestion and greater decentralization. The result was an uneasy compromise in which étatists retained the upper hand.

One of the less-expected features of the Socialists' reforms was a series of attempts to strengthen their own political base. Not surprisingly, they moved quickly to secure key positions in the state: within the civil service about half the posts at director level changed hands, and a quarter of the new appointees had ties to the political left. The Ministerial cabinets, of course, changed with their Ministers and 60 percent of the new officials were affiliated with the PS. Many also had ties to the union movement. There were few purges once the new team was installed, and those who left generally moved to other influential positions within the state (Dagnaud and Mehl, 1983). This turnover of personnel reflected a long-term trend toward politicization of the French bureaucracy.

Ministerial cabinets looked more heterogeneous under the new government. About half their members came from the prestigious Ecole Nationale d'Administration or Polytechnique, and half were of upper middle-class origin. This is not surprising since many Socialist militants are professionals, and fully 34 percent of the deputies elected to the National Assembly in 1981 were teachers. However, the famous grands corps that supplied 60 percent of the advisors to the previous President filled only 19 percent of the posts in the Elysée under Mitterrand. Instead, the lesser-known corps of *administrateurs civils*, which had often attracted Socialists, rose to new prominence. In short, the left brought not a dismantling of the old elite, but a circulation within it (Dagnaud and Mehl, 1983).

The organization of power within the state remained determinedly étatist. Instead of decentralizing authority to the Ministries, Ministers remained advocates before the President rather than autonomous centers of decision-making. Power revolved around a few of the President's closest economic advisors, such as Alain Boubil, Jacques Attali, and Christian Sautter. As one civil servant explained: "Under the institutions of the Fifth Republic, access to the chief of state is vital for a Minister – but even more in the Mitterrand system where everything depends on the personal relations the President has with a few men" (*L'Expansion* 22 April 1983).

However, several factors undercut the centralized qualities of state organization. One was the fractious nature of the Socialist Party. Although the President insisted on retaining responsibility for most policy decisions, Socialist tradition dictated that the Party should be more involved in the determination of policy than had been the case under Giscard or de Gaulle. In the early years of his term, therefore, Mitterrand took pains to involve the Party's General Secretary, Lionel Jospin, and his colleagues in deliberations about policy. He also tolerated considerable conflict among Ministers who represented the diverse currents of opinion within the Party. Chevènement, Rocard, Fabius, and Pierre Joxe, for instance, frequently let it be known that they were not in complete agreement with Mauroy or Delors over the Government's strategy. As a result, the Government often appeared to be an armed camp of hostile factions over whom the President presided with more sufferance than force.

Mitterrand's attempts to placate various factions within the Party also led the administration to take a number of steps which hurt its electoral popularity. Measures to bring parochial schoolteachers under civil service control, to limit concentration of the press to the detriment of prominent right-wing publishers, and to reorganize professional education were all inspired by factional struggles within the Party. Because these measures contained an element of partisan preference, the Government began to lose its image as a more resolute defender of the public interest against private interest than the opposition.

Second, the very scope and ambition of the Government's economic programs limited the coherence of state action. As Vincent Wright (1984: 298) noted:

> Most major industrial policies require the intervention of several ministries (Industry, Finance, Labour, Social Affairs, Environment, European Affairs), often several divisions within each ministry, the Planning Commission, the DATAR (the state's industrial decentralizing agency), the nationalized banks and credit institutions, and regional or sectoral funding agencies. The Lemoine Report revealed that no fewer than thirty state bodies are involved in decision-making for the electronics industry and none had the legitimacy or authority to impose its views. At present there are some 150 different procedures for aiding industry, being funded by different bodies employing different criteria.

The continuity of policy also suffered from unusual instability at the Ministerial level. In the 4 years between 1981 and 1984, for instance, there were five different Industry Ministers.

In order to deal with these problems, Mitterrand made extensive use of interdepartmental committees. Four hundred and fifty-nine interdepartmental meetings were held in the first 3 months alone of 1982 as against 328 in 1980; and the number of such committees rose from eight in 1980 to 36 in 1982 (Dagnaud and Mehl, 1983: 217). This continues a long-term trend away from the traditional French reliance on rule-based administration and carefully isolated spheres of responsibility and toward governance through a more flexible form of bargaining among interdependent administrators (cf. Hall, 1983a).

Unfortunately, many *autogestionnaires* within the Party remained frustrated. One described the Government's policies as "socialism trapped within the state" (Vivéret, 1983). The one program deliberately designed to reduce the influence of the central state was that of local decentralization.

In 1981 the Minister of the Interior, Gaston Deferre, successfully introduced legislation to transfer authority for the management of French regions, departments and communes from the old prefects to locally elected councils and mayors, who would now supervise the local executives. Regional councils were elected. The prefects, renamed *commissaires de la république*, gave up *a priori* control over local decisions, retaining only *a posteriori* review of the legality of those decisions. New powers over local economic development, town planning, professional training, housing, cultural and social matters were transferred to the localities along with some taxing authority still being elaborated. In the meantime, block grants replaced several programmatic subsidies. The cities of Paris, Lyon and Marseille were also subdivided into arrondissements with their own mayors.

This was unquestionably the most significant reform of local government in France since 1884. It substantially enhanced the powers of many local politicians, removed a variety of obstacles to local planning, and provided more scope for local experimentation. Many Socialists hoped that these measures would transfer responsibility for the regulation of social conflict from the central state to the municipalities. Jean Pierre Worms, floor manager for the proposal, told the National Assembly: "During the crisis, there is a risk of groups directing enormous demands toward the state. . . . It is especially important for the state to find allies in the crisis; that is the aim of decentralization" (cited in Kesselman, 1983: 100).

However, the significance of the reforms should not be overestimated. As Deferre, the longtime Mayor of Marseille, and Prime Minister Mauroy, the Mayor of Lille, no doubt knew, the local politicians in many large cities had already acquired ample room for maneuver around the prefect by virtue of their own ties to Paris and the *cumul des mandats*, whereby many politicians held multiple local and national offices. While many smaller communes received new powers under the law, a large number of these still relied on the local commissaire for administrative staff (Ashford, 1985). In addition, an increasing number of local politicians were themselves already civil servants, including 52 percent of mayors (Meny, 1984: 72). Although it is too early to form a definitive judgement on the reform, there is a good chance that much local power will continue to lie with the civil servants who formerly served the prefect and now serve the local councils. The reform contains no provision for rendering local government itself more participatory. In that respect it, too, stops short of *autogestioniste* goals (Rondin, 1985).

THE REORGANIZATION OF SOCIETY

The French Socialist Party sought the transformation of society as much as it advocated the expropriation of capital. Many of its partisans hoped that Socialist governance would bring a complete renovation of social relations. In this respect the French left was far more radical than most of its European counterparts.

The agenda of the French left contained two projects relevant to this goal. The *autogestioniste* project hoped for the replacement of hierarchical modes of decision-making – which had been particularly widespread in France – with participatory institutions that would allow those affected by the decisions to join in their formulation (cf. Crozier, 1973; Gorz, 1973). The realm of application was to be virtually unrestricted, involving sectors as diverse as industry, the educational system, and politics. The second project was more restricted in scope, but no less radical. Its goal was to change the balance of power in civil society so as to strengthen the position of the trade unions, left-wing political parties, and other organizations that could be said to represent working-class interests. If successful at this, the Socialists would leave a powerful and enduring legacy for future governments.

Except in small measure, however, the Mitterrand Government seems to have been unsuccessful at both projects. In part this is attributable to the difficulty of social reorganization itself; the evidence suggests that reform on such a scale takes a long time. The economic institutions established in France following the war succeeded in altering the shape of the French economy only after they had been in existence for several decades. The Swedish Social Democrats were able to effect broad social change largely because they remained in power for over 40 years (see Scase, 1977; Korpi, 1980). In France the Socialist majority in the National Assembly has lasted barely 5 years.

The more immediate reason for the Socialists' failure to accomplish these projects, however, lies in the existing structure of societal organizations. Deep doctrinal and organizational divisions between the major trade union confederations and left-wing political parties weakened the representation of working-class interests in France. On the one hand, this fragmentation rendered the Socialist project more urgent. On the other hand, it left the Government without an adequate base of support within the country at large, and limited the ability of the administration to use social organizations as instruments of reform.

The first casualty was the program of workers' control that had played such a large role in the Socialist Party's philosophy over a decade. *Autogestion* was another of those ambiguous concepts whose multifaceted appeal had served to mobilize support for the Party. Like the concepts of nationalization and *filière*, however, it had to be defined more clearly to be implemented; and the process of definition itself exposed a series of political obstacles to reform. Accordingly the new Government's steps in this direction were hesitant, and only two concrete policy initiatives were taken: one stipulated that a third of the members on the administrative councils of the nationalized industries had to be drawn from the workforce; and the other required that 15 out of 25 members on the administrative commissions for social security be chosen via elections among those insured by the fund.

In the end *autogestion* fell victim to fragmentation within the left. Many groups claim to speak for the workers in France, and any scheme of workers' control was likely to transfer power from some of these to others. In particular the balance of power within the Government, which favored the Socialists over the Communists, was the reverse of the balance in the workplace where the Communist CGT was far larger than the Socialist CFDT. Union-based schemes of *autogestion* were, then, likely to leave the CGT in control of many industries, especially in the nationalized sector. If a split opened up between the Socialists and Communists the government could lose much of its influence over even the nationalized industries. That was not a prospect Socialist politicians wanted to contemplate; and schemes for workers' councils independent of the unions met opposition from the unions themselves.

The Government made somewhat greater progress toward its second goal, to strengthen the societal position of working-class organizations. The cornerstone of this program was an extensive reform of industrial relations, based on four laws that the Minister of Labor, Jean Auroux, pushed through in April 1982. The first obligated all firms with 50 employees to negotiate each year on wages and working conditions. The second guaranteed workers certain basic liberties and the right to file grievances when these were infringed. The third extended representative works committees to almost all firms, increasing organized labor's access to information and resources. Finally, health and safety committees were amalgamated and strengthened in each plant (Auroux, 1982; *Le Monde*, 24 March 1982).

These reforms were a far-reaching achievement that enhanced the power of the unions at the plant level; but they were designed to extend contractualization rather than *autogestion*. The reforms reinforced the separation of workers from management by identifying two separate sides, defining autonomous spheres of responsibility, and mandating annual negotiations between them. Nothing required that a contract follow from these negotiations, and the reforms stopped short of giving labor contracts a legally binding status. In these respects the Auroux laws did little to reduce the bitter inter-union rivalry that often resulted in further strike activity after a contract had been signed, and their implementation was impeded by that rivalry. The CFDT, in particular, resisted the law. In 1984, mandated negotiations took place in about 66 percent of eligible enterprises, but only 43 percent of these covered the full range of topics envisaged by Auroux (*Le Monde*, 28 June 1985).

At the national level one would expect the election of a Socialist Government to increase the influence of the trade unions over public policy. However, the relationship of the Mitterrand Government with the unions has been highly ambivalent. On the one hand, labor has enjoyed improved access to policy-makers. Twenty-five percent of the members of Ministerial cabinets themselves came from the unions. On the other hand, the Government has not always heeded the trade unions. In keeping with étatist traditions, Mitterrand took great pains to emphasize that the Government alone would determine what was in the public interest; and he often failed to act on a measure until forced into it by strikes and street demonstrations, much as a conservative administration might be.

Jacques Chérèque, a leading figure in the CFDT, described the Government's relations with the unions in these terms:

> We are listened to politely, but are we really heard? During the first phase of the left's arrival in power, in that euphoria when everything appeared possible including the abolition of the laws of economics, the warnings of the CFDT were not understood. They were assimilated to some kind of moderationism. The following year, at the time when wages were frozen, absolutely no prior consultations were held with the trade unions, even though they were the ones most affected . . . As for the austerity plan of last March, it was not preceded by a single sounding among the trade unions. We are invited to tripartite ceremonies often after everything has already been decided. In administrative practice or in concrete cases, there has still been no break with the customs of the right. The officials of our industrial federations often have a great deal of difficulty obtaining serious discussions with their corresponding Ministers (*Intervention*, August 1983: 47).

Thus, the unions remained at arm's length from the Government. Although strike rates in 1981–84 were the lowest in years, and the Mitterrand Government made some attempts to integrate union representatives more fully into policy-making, the extent of union cooperation with the regime was seriously undercut by inter-union rivalry. Torn between a syndicalism that sought isolation from the state and a Marxism that was often more radical than that of the Government, many of the unions lacked a clear strategy for dealing with a Socialist regime. Those unions without strong ties to the left (the FO, CGC, and CFTC) successfully used their opposition to the Government's policies to draw support away from the more sympathetic CFDT and CGT (*Le Monde* 28 April 1983). When the Communists finally left the governing coalition in July 1984, the CGT was freed to oppose the Government's policies; and ultimately, even CFDT leaders felt compelled to criticize the post-1982 austerity programs.

In short, Mitterrand's efforts to strengthen the social forces of the left were largely unsuccessful. This can be attributed in part to rising levels of unemployment, which more than offset the state's attempts to strengthen the trade unions; in part to divisions within the union movement itself which were intensified rather than reduced by the experience of Socialist governance; and in part to the traditional weakness of the Socialist Party's own ties to the unions.

The Government's attempts to weaken social actors on the other side of the balance were also a failure. Early in its term, the Mitterrand Government took steps to weaken the organizations that had traditionally been privileged interlocutors for business and agriculture. It ended the privileged status of the CNPF, for instance, by recognizing several rival associations as equally legitimate representatives of business. The greatest beneficiary was the Syndicat National de la Petite et Moyenne Industrie (SNPMI) under Gérard Deuil, which increased its share of the vote in the prud'homalles elections of 1982 from 2 to 14.7 percent.

Similarly, the Fédération Nationale des Syndicats d'Exploitants Agricoles (FNSEA), which had hitherto been the principal negotiator with the state over agricultural policy, was stripped of this privilege. The Government recognized three other federations – MODEF, FFA, and CNSTP – as equal parties to such negotiations and reasserted the state's responsibility for implementing agricultural policy. Edith Cresson, the Minister of Agriculture, proclaimed: "It is necessary to end the confusion between the role of professional organizations and that of the state. The former must negotiate and contest if they feel it necessary; the state must make decisions" (Keeler, 1985: 69).

In taking these steps the Government's object was to restore the étatist position of the state and to weaken organizations that were potential threats to working-class power. However, the measures backfired. As we have seen, quasi-corporatist arrangements between the state and producer groups had been a means for regulating social conflict and effectively implementing policy (cf. Streeck and Schmitter, 1986). When these arrangements ruptured, farmers and small businessmen took to the streets to air their grievances. Small business organizations led violent rallies in Paris during September 1982 and March 1983. Over the winter of 1981–82 peasants attacked prefectures, ripped up railway tracks, and dumped produce to draw attention to their predicament (Berger, 1984).

In the end, the Government attempted to restore relations with the FNSEA by replacing the Minister of Agriculture, and it moved closer to the CNPF once again, distancing itself from the SNPMI. By this time, however, considerable damage had been done to the Government's image. A politics of the streets had fostered the illusion of ungovernability, increasing the Socialists' electoral unpopularity and weakening the Government's credibility with producers groups.

In sum, far from introducing the kind of neo-corporatism that social democrats had sought elsewhere, the Mitterrand Government reinforced the plurality of contending interests. Instead of fostering social peace, it intensified many of the underlying divisions within French society. And, most important of all, rather than strengthening the position of working-class organizations, 5 years of Socialist rule left many of them weaker than before.

CONCLUSION

The economic record of the Mitterrand Government has been mixed. Although the 1981 expansion intensified the nation's balance of payments problems, its employment effects were substantial, and contractionary measures would have generated legitimate political dismay. Mitterrand gambled on international economic expansion, and lost; but his subsequent problems were at least partially attributable to the inherited trade deficit and rising American dollar. The government probably should have devalued the franc against the deutschmark when it entered office, as the terms of trade dictated. Immediate devaluation would have delivered a faster and greater stimulus to exports than the slow decline that followed, and it might have reduced the subsequent need for austerity. Most important, the nation might have avoided the need to borrow heavily abroad to prop up the currency, a practice that increased the foreign debt from 120 bF in 1980 to 525 bF by 1985. Rising interest charges were soon a weighty component of the balance of payments deficit.

The Government encouraged a pattern of heavy borrowing within the domestic economy as well. The debt–equity ratios of French firms were already rising dramatically when the Socialists came to power. The portion of investment financed from retained earnings fell from 78 percent in 1979 to 34 percent in 1982. Simultaneous increases in interest rates doubled the cost of debt service alone for French firms as a percentage of value-added between 1979 and 1984. In 1982, 24 percent of the value-added of the nationalized industries went to pay interest charges. Many of these firms also borrowed heavily abroad, and as the exchange rate of the franc fell, the cost of their loans multiplied. The SNCF borrowed 8 bF and EDF 12 bF during 1982 alone (Versillier, 1983; *Le Monde*, 21 April 1983). The state encouraged firms to take *prêts participatifs*, or loans that were technically designated as equity, and over 15 bF was allocated to industry in this way during 1982 and 1983 (Barbe, 1983). Enterprises found such instruments attractive because they were tax-deductible and technically decreased debt–equity ratios, increasing a firm's ability to borrow even as it borrowed. As a result of these moves, however, French business found itself with a level of indebtedness that discouraged further expansion.

A large part of the Socialists' economic program was paid for by borrowing. The Government gambled that these funds would make growth possible again, but there was real danger that the economy would be saddled with levels of debt that inhibited further growth. Like several Labour Governments in Britain, the Mitterrand Government spent its last 4 years in office imposing austerity to pay for the spending spree undertaken during its first 2 years.

In aggregate terms, however, the Socialists' economic record was far from the disaster that their detractors claim (see table 8.3). Between

Table 8.3   French economic performance under Giscard and Mitterrand

	Average 1976–80	1981	1982	1983	1984	1985	Average 1981–85
GDP growth (% volume)	3.3	0.5	2.0	0.7	1.6	1.3	1.2
Unemployment (level)	5.4	7.3	8.1	8.3	9.7	10.5	8.8
Price inflation (annual %)	10.5	13.4	11.8	9.6	7.4	5.0	9.4
Investment (GFCF as % GDP)	21.7	21.4	20.5	19.6	19.8	20.0	20.6
Exports (% volume change)	7.1	5.1	−1.7	3.4	6.9	4.3	3.6
Imports (% volume change)	9.3	1.8	5.8	−1.5	2.3	3.1	2.3
Labor productivity (% change)	3.0	1.5	1.9	1.1	2.4	3.0	0.0
Current balance (billion F)	3.5	−26	−79	−34	−0.8	0.0	−28
Budget deficit (% GDP)	0.7	2.6	2.9	3.1	3.2	3.0	3.0
Real disposable income (% change)	2.6	2.9	2.7	−0.3	−0.7	1.1	1.1

1981 and 1986 the economy grew by 1.5 percent a year on average, roughly as good as the EEC average, even if below the 2.6 percent rate attained in 1973–81. Unemployment rose by 4.7 points to 12 percent of the labor force during the Socialists' term, also in line with EEC figures and comparable to the 4.5-point increase since 1974. Corporate profits, which fell from 27.3 percent of value-added in 1974 to 23.7 percent in 1981, rose again to 27.5 percent in 1984. However, productive investment, which had fallen from 14.4 percent of GDP in 1974 to 13.6 percent in 1981, declined further to 12.3 percent in 1984. France's inflation rate remained about a percentage point above the European average during Mitterrand's term, as it had under Giscard (see table

8.4). But the real disposable income of households rose by an average of only 1.2 percent a year between 1981 and 1986, compared with a 2.9 percent average under Giscard (*L'Expansion*, 8 March 1985: 55 ff; *Le Monde*, 19 June 1985: 17).

Table 8.4   The ratio of French economic performance to EEC averages

Period	GDP growth	Level of unemployment	Average rate of inflation	Capital formation as percentage of GDP
Giscard (1976–80)	1.09	0.97	1.09	1.05
Mitterrand (1981–85)	1.0	0.91	0.97	1.06

Note: The figures in the table are the average French performance figures expressed as a ratio of (i.e. divided by) average performance figures for the European Economic Community nations over the period.

In redistributive terms the Government could claim some solid accomplishments. These included: the 39-hour week, a fifth week of vacation, retirement at 60, a 12 percent increase in the purchasing power of the minimum wage, higher family allowances, and slightly more progressive taxation of higher incomes. In an era when conservative governments, like that of Margaret Thatcher, were trimming the welfare state, these measures represented a distinct alternative.

In the eyes of the French populace, however, these initiatives did not seem to be a radical departure from past policies. Although the real value of social transfers increased by 5.4 percent between 1981 and 1983 it had already risen by 6.6 percent a year since 1974. Tax revenues, which rose from 42 percent of GDP in 1980 to 44 percent in 1983, had already grown from 36 percent in 1974. Even the move to a 39-hour week was in line with a long-term decline from 43.5 hours in 1973 to 40 hours in 1981. The promised shift from indirect to direct taxation never really took place.

Perhaps for this reason, the Government's most serious problems occurred at the political level. It had promised more than it delivered; instead of images of redistribution French voters were left with recollections of the drop in purchasing power they suffered in 1983–84. Instead of enjoying social harmony, they watched social and industrial conflict intensify in the face of austerity. In the face of rising unemployment, the Government ultimately enacted a set of austerity policies not very different from those of its predecessor. The Socialist experiment was a disillusioning experience for France; and the Government's popularity plummeted accordingly. In the European elections of June

1984 the PS received only 21 percent of the vote, and the Communists 11 percent, barely more than the neo-fascists under Jean-Marie Le Pen. As a consequence the Socialists were unable to consolidate the social coalition that had brought them to power. For some years they had attempted to unite the traditional working class, now a dwindling proportion of the population, with professionals and cadres (salaried technicians and middle managers in industry) who formed the bulk of the Party's militants, behind a single program. Many analysts saw segments of the latter as a 'new working class' by virtue of their salaried status and gradual unionisation (Touraine, 1971). On the success of this fusion rested most of the Socialists' hopes for the future.

However, the Mitterrand Government could not consummate this political marriage. Many parts of the traditional working class suffered under rising levels of unemployment. The Communists left the governing coalition in the spring of 1984 partly in order to exploit working-class discontent and draw support away from the Socialists. The tax increases imposed under various austerity programs also hit the middle class particularly hard. As the old adage says, even French voters who wear their hearts on the left wear their wallets on the right; and the Mitterrand Government brought them few tangible benefits. Instead of forging a new cross-class alliance, the 1981–86 experience seems to have intensified divisions among the French electorate (Rosanvallon, 1983).[3]

As if in acknowledgement, President Mitterrand took the unusual step, in 1984, of reintroducing a voting system initially utilized during the Fourth Republic and based on proportional representation. In the face of the Government's massive electoral unpopularity, the new voting system was designed to preserve at least a core of Socialist seats in the National Assembly and to make it difficult for the opposition parties to secure an overwhelming majority. At the same time, Mitterrand began to regroup his party around the middle of the political spectrum, as if to keep open the option of forming a center–left coalition after the legislative elections of 1986. This was a desperate strategy, designed to preserve the President's own position and a modicum of Socialist representation in the Assembly at the risk of engendering political stalemate in the National Assembly and blunting the purposive quality of government under the Fifth Republic.

The Mitterrand years revealed the extent to which even a Socialist regime with a firm mandate is constrained by the international economy and the existing organization of society. As the Government ran up against economic constraints that derived from its insertion into world markets, it faced the difficult choice of adapting its strategy to the operation of market forces or of moving down a more radical path than anticipated. In this unenviable position, it chose the former.

Similarly, the experience of the Mitterrand Government demon-strates the limits of étatism. Although the Government had a solid electoral mandate and a firm hold over the state's fiscal and regulatory capacities, it had difficulty mobilizing support for its policies even among the organizations of the left. As a recently formed organization and one composed of many rather separate organizational fractions, the Socialist Party was not a hegemonic machine even within its regions of greatest support (see Lewis, 1986). Longstanding organizational rivalries between the trade unions, local left-wing organizations, and the fractious political parties themselves undercut the Government's ability to rely on ancillary social organizations to implement and build support for its policies. Many new policy initiatives set off local strug-gles for resources and control even among competing left-wing organi-zations. As a result, programs of social transformation that required intensive cooperation at the local level often foundered for lack of consistent support.

These developments suggest that the success of a socialist strategy of economic reform and social transformation may depend, not simply on the assumption of state power, but on the extent to which the left has also been able to build an integrated base of organizational support in society (cf. Lange and Garrett, 1985). In short, even for the left, étatism is not enough. Once again, divisions within French society undermined the initiatives of an étatist state.

The contrast between the Socialist Party's position in 1981 and in 1986 was striking. A Party whose vibrant ideas inspired a wave of euphoria in the days after its election seemed to have lost its mission. As one Socialist deputy said: "When we look in the mirror, we no longer recognize ourselves" (L'Express 3 December 1982). As a conse-quence, if nothing else, the Mitterrand years are likely to inspire a rethinking and redefinition of socialism itself in France.

PART IV: Comparative Perspectives

9

The Institutional Logic of Comparative Political Economy

Our examination of French and British policy indicates that economic policy-making is a quintessentially political process. Even in a field where the correct choice of policies depends heavily on expertise and the instruments for policy implementation are already concentrated in the hands of the state, policy is driven by a dynamic that is as much political as economic. But politics enters the process in a multitude of ways. In some cases its very involvement renders the course of policy more open than it would otherwise have been (cf. Piore and Sabel, 1984). Therefore, it is particularly difficult to construct a general theory that specifies precisely how and when broadly political factors affect economic policy-making. But it is equally necessary to make the attempt. Otherwise, the notion of political variables becomes a catch-all category, too nebulous in meaning to add very much to our understanding of the determinants of economic policy. We need some over-arching conception of what kind of political variables are likely to be most significant for the course that economic policy takes in different nations.

The case-studies in preceding chapters suggest that many prominent models of politics do not zero in on the most important variables. In the introduction to this volume, several of these models were reviewed: systems theory, cultural analyses, public choice approaches and group theory. None seems entirely appropriate for explaining the course of economic policy in Britain and France.

Systems theory generally explains policies as the performance of functions requisite to the maintenance of a given political and economic system. For instance, it is often suggested that economic policies are pursued in order to ensure the performance of two functions in particular: that of accumulation, understood as the maintenance of conditions for the profitable accumulation of capital, and that of legitimation, understood as the maintenance of social harmony and support for the regime (O'Connor, 1974; Gough, 1978). In some general sense this is probably true. Behind the actions of British and French leaders we have often detected such concerns; and even where they were not uppermost in the minds of policy-makers, the minimal fulfillment of some such conditions seems to have been essential to the survival of the regime.

However, what such analyses tell us about the actual course of economic policy is very limited. Even the cases of Britain and France suggest that the range of political and economic strategies available for the performance of such functions is rather wide. Two nations facing similar imperatives adopted quite different macroeconomic and indus-trial policies; and their policies met with widely varying degrees of success. Although the economic policies of France contributed to growing economic prosperity, those of Britain failed to halt a long-term process of capitalist decline. When confronted with the need to account for systematic variation among the policies of different nations, systems theories explain too much.

By contrast, cultural analyses and public choice approaches explain too little. Each has some validity. Our analysis of étatism indicated that the French have traditionally accorded a degree of legitimacy to state intervention that many Britons find more difficult to accept. However, cultural differences of this sort must still be explained. It seems unlikely that memories of Colbert are sufficient to account for prevailing French attitudes; reference must be made to contemporary institutional struc-tures, such as the Plan, to explain the socialization process that repro-duces certain national attitudes; and these are subject to change. Over a period of time the planning process itself undermined the étatism it was supposed to instantiate.

Similarly, public choice approaches, which deduce the likely course of action to be taken by rational actors, can explain some forms of political behavior. The politicians of Britain and France often timed their elections to coincide with upturns in the economy. However, the context of policy-making contains many factors that are not so readily modelled. Edward Heath called the February 1974 election in the midst of a recession in order to deal with an industrial relations crisis; and differences in the policies of Harold Wilson and Margaret Thatcher can only be explained by reference to overarching conceptions of economic and political ideology that supersede any simple conception of political rationality.

Group theory has obviously also been useful for the analysis of economic policy in Britain and France. We have seen organized groups contend for influence over economic policy in both Britain and France. In many respects the history of British policy during the 1970s can be seen as a struggle for influence between the trade unions and financial capital; and the French Plans were ultimately a conduit for the demands that some segments of French business placed on the state. However, group theory alone has a limited purchase on the outcomes to be explained. It points to the important role that coalitions of social groups play in the policy process but, by itself, cannot explain why some groups are more powerful than others. To answer that question we must look at the institutional framework within which the struggle for power takes place. In many respects, for instance, it was the French planning process that generated business power in France, rather than the other way around. And the outcome of the struggle for influence between labor and finance capital in Britain during the 1970s was decided by the broader organizational context in which the two were contending rather than by the degree of effort either side put into the conflict. Indeed, if the trade unions often behaved as normal interest groups, the behavior of finance capital in this case was made up of a set of individual actions aggregated by market structures, in a way that belies the notion of group action most often utilized in group theoretic models of the polity.

We are left with state-centric models of the polity; but these, too, have been of little use for explaining the course of economic policy in Britain or France. One could say that both states acted in the 'national interest', as some state-centric theories would lead us to expect; but that term is too nebulous to predict policy outcomes with any degree of precision (cf. Krasner, 1980). Certainly, both states displayed some ability to resist societal pressures, but the capacity of the French to take a much more strategic view of industrial development must still be explained. And the divergent economic policies of these nations seem to have been closely related to the relative strength of different societal actors.

In short, none of the prevailing paradigms of politics seems to focus on the factors most central to the direction of economic policy in Britain and France. Some explain too much; others too little. We need a middle-range theory that identifies the most salient factors behind the differences in economic policy across these two nations.

AN INSTITUTIONAL APPROACH

The point of this book has been to develop an alternative view of the political determinants of economic policy that links those policies to the structural constraints implicit in the socioeconomic organization of each nation. Equipped with such a view, we could explain the evolution and difference in the patterns of economic policy among the European nations by reference to the distribution of power among the key social groups affected by such policy, since the socioeconomic organization of a nation both conditions and reflects this distribution of power.

The construction of such a view begins with the observation that national economic policy is influenced most significantly, first, by what a government is *pressed* to do, and secondly, by what it *can* do in the economic sphere. To a large extent, the former defines what is desirable in a democracy and the latter defines what is possible. This dualism reflects the fact that implementation is the obverse of the formulation of policy. Governments are frequently prevented from adopting a policy by the absence of any means to implement it.

The preceding case-studies suggest that both the pressures for a line of policy and the possibility of implementing it are most fundamentally affected by five factors. The first three are intrinsic to the socioeconomic structure of a nation; namely, the organization of labor, the organization of capital and the organization of the state itself. The first refers primarily to the organization of the working class in the labor market. The second refers principally to the organizational relationship between financial and industrial capital. And the third refers to the internal organization of the state apparatus, understood as the bodies that perform the legislative, executive and judicial functions of the nation.

In addition, the economic policies of each nation may be affected by two other factors: the position of the nation within the international economy and the organization of its political system.[1] The term 'political system' is used here to refer to the electoral practices and network of organized political parties that dominate the electoral arena. It is by no means the simple 'transmission belt' that many conventional descriptions imply. Like the state itself, the political system is dominated by a given set of organizations that structure the nature of the demands facing the state.

All of these are organizational variables in the sense that they refer to the specific organization of one aspect of the environment facing public policy-makers. In the case of the domestic variables that should be clear; but even the position of a state within the international economy can be construed as a structural variable. It refers to the relative openness of national markets and the position of national producers more generally within international markets. In some instances, that is secured through explicit international agreement and organization, as in the case of membership in the European Economic Community; in others, the claim rests on the postulate of chapter 2 that markets are themselves a form of institutional framework.

Why is organization so important? Four reasons can be adduced. First, policy is generally formed in response to pressures from various groups according to the interests those groups have in the outcomes of policy-making. But the facility with which specific interests can be articulated and the force with which they can be pressed on policy-makers is dependent upon the organization of the structures within which they are expressed. Secondly, and of equal importance, the very interests of the actors themselves are critically affected by the organization of the economic and political structures within which they operate. For instance, interests of the sort relevant to economic policy do not exist independently of the organization of markets. Thirdly, economic policy-making is invariably a collective endeavor. That is to say, economic policy is the output not of individuals, but of organizations that aggregate the endeavor of many individuals in particular ways. Accordingly, the structure of these organizations has an immense impact on the nature of the policies produced. It is an 'organizational intelligence' rather than the intelligence of the individuals that ultimately determines such factors as the capacity of the state for strategic thinking or the quality of policy. Finally, in order to implement economic policy, the state relies on access to organizational resources in both the public and private sectors. Variations in organization among these sectors put significant constraints on the ability of the state to secure acquiescence for its policies from both the electorate and producers groups.

It should be apparent that this approach draws some inspiration from a recent line of analysis in the literature which explains differing economic policies in terms of the broad coalitions of economic interests that converge around specific policy alternatives.[2] However, it regards the process whereby those interests are defined, articulated and aggregated as especially problematic. In particular, the organization of both economic and political arenas plays a critical role in determining which interests will be effectively articulated and what sort of response they will elicit from the state.[3]

Organization does more than transmit the preferences of particular groups; it combines and ultimately alters them. Accordingly, economic policy may not faithfully reflect a struggle among competing economic interests precisely because organization refracts that struggle. Thus, the notion that the state embodies the 'institutionalization of class conflict' or a 'condensation of class forces' (Poulantzas, 1976) must be modified to take into account the fact that the state acts as a distorting mirror to reproduce a highly imperfect reflection of these conflicts and one that imprints its own image on their resolution. In the long run, of course, organization itself is shaped by the conflicts that underlie it. However, this is rarely a rapid process, and in the meantime the institutions that organize intergroup relations act as a kind of social memory, imprinting the conflicts of the present with the institutional legacy of the past.

In line with this approach, the preceding chapters have paid particular attention to the organizational factors that lie behind the evolution of economic policy in each country. The purpose of this part of the book is to integrate their insights into an explicitly comparative analysis. Specifically, we want to ask if these organizational factors can explain the similarities and divergence in economic policies to be found across nations. This chapter is concerned with the discovery and explanation of continuities in economic policy across nations, while chapter 10 considers the broader implications of such an analysis for our models of politics.

First, we will attempt to ascertain if the economic policies of these nations have followed relatively stable and distinctive patterns over time. If so, it is likely that they are affected by a relatively stable set of variables, such as the organizational factors examined here. Secondly, we will review policy-making in some detail to suggest precisely why these organizational variables might be associated with patterns of economic policy.

To be fully validated, such a theory of comparative economic policy should be tested against a large number of national cases. That is clearly beyond the scope of this work; and the analysis must, therefore, remain preliminary. However, we can take two steps to improve the generalizability of the analysis. On the one hand we can add a third case, that of West Germany, to the comparative analysis. Even if considered only briefly, the German case will contribute a great deal to our ability to specify the range along which the relevant factors vary and their modes of interaction. For that reason, a brief discussion of Germany is indispensable. On the other hand, we can also expand the number of cases against which an organizational approach is tested by considering three sub-fields of policy-making – macroeconomic policy, industrial policy and incomes policy – in each nation. That gives us nine cases within which to seek policy continuities and linkages to organizational variables.

Let us consider the national cases. In each instance, the analysis begins by identifying those aspects of the organization of the state, capital and labor that are pertinent to the argument and then turns to the identification of related policy patterns. The roles of the international economy and political system are discussed at further length in a concluding section.

THE FEDERAL REPUBLIC OF GERMANY

The most distinctive features of the German state with relevance for economic policy are the strict division of control over fiscal and monetary policy between the Ministry of Economics, the Ministry of Finance and the Deutsche Bundesbank, the central bank, and the entrenched power of the latter within the German system. Although the Ministry of Finance supervises monetary policy, the independence of the Bundesbank is guaranteed by the German constitution which has given it a mandate to protect the value of the currency and established it as "a special part of the executive, entrusted as an autonomous body with responsibility for monetary and credit policy" (Wadbrook, 1972: 89). Since the majority of its Board of Directors is chosen by the central banks of the German states (or Länder), and those chosen by the Federal Government are given minimum terms of 8 years, the Bank is relatively insulated from the Ministries of Economics or Finance. Most authorities agree that the officers of the Bank are "on a par with the highest federal authorities and not subject to instructions from the federal government" (Wadbrook, 1972: 89). As a consequence, while the operation of fiscal policy remains in the hands of the government, the instruments of monetary policy, which are also potent weapons for influencing the level of economic activity, are subject to an entirely different set of influences than those normally associated with the parliamentary arena.

The organization of capital in Germany is also distinctive in important respects. Among our cases, the most salient feature of that organization is the relationship between the institutions of financial and industrial capital. In Germany this relationship is characterized by the concentration of financial capital itself and by arrangements which permit financial capital, represented primarily by the major banks, to exercise a high degree of detailed control over the operations of industrial capital at the economic level. Although there are over 3000 quasi-banking institutions in Germany, the financial world is dominated by three 'universal' banks – Deutsche Bank, Dresdner Bank and Commerzbank – which work closely together to exert vast leverage over the rest of the banking sector and much of industry (Medley, 1981; Shonfield, 1969: ch. 11). Legal provisions and customary business practices combine to make such leverage possible. German banks, unlike their American counterparts, are allowed to hold equity in other firms. Moreover, almost 85 percent of all shareholders in Germany generally deposit their shares with a bank which, in the absence of specific instructions to the contrary, enjoys the privilege of voting those shares as it likes. In addition, these banks are entitled to lend their voting rights to other banks and are accustomed to doing so. Since, under German law, the votes of 25 percent of shares in a company are sufficient to block any measure coming before the shareholders, the banks are generally in a position to influence the major decisions of a firm. At the most recent count, the banks voted 70 percent of the shares of the 425 largest firms in Germany, accounting for three-quarters of the value of all the shares on the stock exchange; and 318 of the top 400 companies had two bank representatives on their supervisory boards (Medley, 1981: 48).

By virtue of these arrangements, the German banks have both an interest in and influence over the long-term performance of the major firms within German industry. In keeping with their position, the banks have developed considerable technical expertise in industrial matters and the capacity to provide detailed directions to the firms whose shares they hold. Similarly, the banks have become accustomed to collaborating with each other on their plans for industrial sectors (Shonfield, 1969: ch. 11). By contrast, the British and American commercial banks are prohibited from taking shares in companies; competition is more common than collusion in the banking sector; and the debtor–creditor relationship is a more distant one, based less on the assessment of a firm's strategy and more on a mechanical consideration of the creditworthiness of its balance sheet.

The organization of labor in Germany is distinguished by concentration of the labor-market organizations and the highly regularized nature of their collective bargaining arrangements. Following World War Two, the German workers were reorganized into sixteen large unions, each covering entire industries with up to several million members in them. Almost all became affiliated to a central federation, the Deutschegewerkschaftsbund (DGB). In the view of most authorities these two organizational innovations – unions organized along industrial lines and a unitary union movement – set the basic framework for the coordination present in the industrial relations of postwar Germany (Gourevitch et al., 1984). On this framework has also been built a system for collective bargaining which is highly regulated by statute and quasi-judicial procedures. Its principal features include the use of legally sanctioned contracts running as long as 2 or 3 years, regulations which render wildcat strikes illegal, and the employment of a Federal Labor Court as well as arbitration procedures to adjudicate many disputes (cf. Muller-Jentsch and Sperling, 1978). In most of these respects the organization of the German labor market differs substantially from that in Britain or France.

Is there any relationship between these features of the organization of political and economic activity in Germany and the distinctive patterns of German economic policy? To answer this question we must first identify the patterns in German policy which most broadly distinguish it from the policies of Britain and France, and then locate the roots of the differences. For this purpose, it will be useful to break down economic policy into its three major components, macroeconomic policy, industrial policy and incomes policy, and examine each in turn.

Macroeconomic policy in Germany

German macroeconomic policy has been distinguished by two unusual characteristics for most of the postwar period. The first has been the maintenance of the deutschmark at an undervalued level on the foreign exchange markets. The second has been the presence of bias in favor of deflationary macroeconomic policies consistent enough to constitute a repudiation of Keynesian anti-cyclical policy and severe enough to culminate in the artificial creation of recession from time to time (Kreile, 1978; Wadbrook, 1972).

The longstanding undervaluation of the mark was not dictated by economic circumstances. On the contrary, it was a controversial policy with distinctive costs and benefits for different segments of society and real risks for the German economy as a whole. In distributive terms the effect of the policy was to provide an immense subsidy to export sectors and a measure of protection to domestic capital, financed by imposing higher costs on German workers and consumers in the form of higher-priced imports. Over a period of time the policy dramatically strengthened the export sector of the economy. As a percentage of GDP, exports rose from 8 percent in 1955 to 25 percent in 1980. By 1975 exports accounted for 47 percent of sales in investment goods, 36 percent in chemicals, 56 percent in machine tools and 52 percent in automobiles (Kreile, 1978: 201). This brought clear employment benefits, but it caused a series of balance of payment problems and rendered the economy especially vulnerable to imported inflation (Wadbrook, 1972: 251). Since the German populace is generally supposed to be hypersensitive to the risk of inflation (Krause and Salant, 1977: 591), the adoption of such a policy especially requires explanation.

As early as 1955 it became apparent to many observers that the mark was undervalued, and several prominent economic institutes, mindful of the inflationary consequences, began to urge that the mark be repegged (Kaufmann, 1969). In 1966 even Ludwig Erhard, the Minister of Economics known as the 'father of the social market economy' and a man of considerable influence, began to urge revaluation. Throughout the late 1950s most of the senior economic officials in the unions and both major parties, the CDU and the SPD, also began to advocate *de facto* or *de jure* revaluation (Kaufmann, 1969: 199–200). Nothing was done, however, until 1961, and then a halfhearted revaluation of 5 percent continued to keep the mark below its natural parity. Two forces converged to sustain an undervalued deutschmark. The first was the power of the Bundesbank which, while unable to initiate a revaluation, could effectively veto one. The second was the singular relationship between financial and industrial capital in Germany, which meant that they could combine to oppose the move.

Since undervaluation shields the profit levels of both export and domestic sectors, industry tends to support it in most countries. However, while financial capital in Britain supported an overvalued exchange rate, the German banking community joined with industry against revaluation. In part this may be attributed to the natural aversion of central banks to exchange rate movements, but it is also apparent that the German banking community had an equity interest in the industrial sector and thus an immediate concern for its welfare. Because of this, the two segments of German capital interpreted their interests as congruent, and together they were a potent political force. Accordingly, the president of the German Federation of Industry (the BDI) once announced that "an open or concealed revaluation of the mark could result in a catastrophe for the entire economy" (Kaufmann, 1969: 205), and the president of the Bundesbank, acting on behalf of the banking community, opposed revaluation, declaring that "exchange rate parity is sacrosanct" (Kaufmann, 1969: 191). The president of the BDI and the influential leader of the Deutsche Bank both put pressure on the Chancellor, Konrad Adenauer, who vetoed the plans of his Minister of the Economy for revaluation (Kreile, 1978: 214).

Throughout the 1950s and 1960s this combination of Bundesbank influence and pressure from a coalition of industrial and financial capital effectively maintained the mark at an undervalued level. The revaluation to which Adenauer consented in 1961, in the face of overwhelming inflationary pressures, was barely half that which had been expected, and revaluation was secured again in December 1969 only after it had been made a central issue between the two major political parties in the preceding election. Only by means of an election were the interests of consumers and workers able to prevail over those of capital and the central bank. This situation prevailed for 25 years during which the pattern for postwar German economic policy was largely set. It changed only in 1973, with the floating of the mark, because the Bundesbank itself switched sides in the face of a new international monetary regime which meant that without a floating exchange rate it lost virtually all control over monetary policy (cf. Kreile, 1978: 216).

The second noteworthy feature of German macroeconomic policy was that it remained relatively contractionary. On the fiscal side the federal government tended to run a budgetary surplus, and a comparative study of the 1955–65 period chides the German authorities for failing to use fiscal policy as a countercyclical device (Hansen, 1968: 233, 254). The Keynesian experiment of 1967–72 came late to Germany and was very brief. In it we can see one of those rare instances in which a shift in governing party influenced the course of German economic policy. The move toward Keynesianism was largely made possible by the entry of the Social Democrats into office in 1966 (see Riemer, 1983).

To a certain extent the longstanding bias against countercyclical policy in Germany can be explained by the anti-Keynesian doctrines of her early economic leaders, who believed that a 'social market economy' would stabilize itself (Zinn, 1978). However, the relative power of the Bundesbank played an important role here as well. For most of this period it countered any laxity on the fiscal side with tight monetary policies. Its officials tended to regard recession as "a necessary purge which restored labor discipline as well as confidence in the currency" (Kreile, 1978: 209), and their ability to counteract expansionary fiscal policies with monetary action may well have acted as an implicit restraint on the central government's behavior.

This *pas de deux* became explicit in 1965–66 when the Bundesbank helped create the first real recession Germany had experienced since the war. Angered by increases in public expenditure which preceded the 1965 election, and concerned that the accompanying expansion would lead to inflationary wage increases, Bank officials introduced a restrictive monetary policy in August 1964 and strengthened it during the following 18 months. In the words of the president of the Bundesbank:

> As late as May 1966 the Bundesbank felt obliged to raise the discount rate from 4 to 5 percent although private capital spending was already stagnating. It did so because government expenditure was still too high at that time . . . The bodies responsible for the public budgets did not see reason until the capital market, and later also the money market, failed them (Kloten et al., 1978: 31).

As a result GDP fell by 1.5 percent and unemployment rose from 140,000 to 600,000 in the space of a year (Lieberman, 1977: 207). Germany was the only European nation to experience a recession at this time. Although German fiscal policy took on an anti-cyclical aspect with the enactment of the Stability and Growth Act of 1967, the powerful Bundesbank continued to act as a restraint on expansionary policy in the following years, most notably in 1973–74 when it adopted a restrictive monetary stance in the wake of the oil price increases of that year.

Industrial policy in Germany

In the area of industrial policy the German experience has been distinguished by relatively limited forms of state intervention, which often leave the details of industrial organization up to the financial sector. For instance, regional development aid in Germany has often been distributed through a system in which the banks "play an active part in helping to choose the recipient" (Shonfield, 1969: 263). Applications for aid must first be approved by one of the banks. If granted by the

Ministry of Economics, aid is then administered in the form of a subsidized loan by the bank, which pockets a portion of the subsidy as a fee for service. A number of schemes for sectoral rationalization, such as those for the steel industry in 1962–63 and 1971–74, were orchestrated almost entirely by the three big banks. In each case the government facilitated the reorganization when requested, but left the banks to play the directing role (Shonfield, 1969: 255; Medley, 1981: 53). This contrasts strongly with the techniques used by both French and British governments for rationalization of the same sectors.

The consistent German approach has been possible only by virtue of the unusual relationship between finance and industrial capital in Germany. It ensures that the banks have had the interest, expertise and influence to make such an approach work. In Shonfield's words (1969: 261): "The big banks have always seen it as their business to take an overall view of the long-term trend in any industry in which they were concerned, and then to press individual firms to conform to certain broad lines of development." The banks were especially effective because their equity in many firms meant that they could plan for an entire sector and impose cuts where necessary, powers that individual firms or even trade associations lacked. They were also free from many of the political pressures to safeguard regional interests and employment that the government would have faced if it were seen as the instigator.

Incomes policy in Germany

Finally, in the sphere of incomes policy, German policy-making has been characterized by a pattern that might be described as one of 'tacit tripartism'. The unions exercise a substantial degree of restraint in wage negotiations, but they usually do so without extensive state efforts to secure a centrally negotiated bargain to tie their acquiescence to the delivery of policy goods in return. Once again Germany stands in contrast to both the French and British systems.

Some have suggested that Germany is different because of the unusual fear of inflation that was Weimar's legacy to the Bundesrepublik or because of the establishment of a procedure for 'concerted action' (*Konzertierte Aktion*) in the years following 1967. But neither of these is entirely convincing: workers in many countries have reason to fear inflation, and a pattern of 'tacit tripartism' characterized German wage agreements long before the procedures for concerted action were established. Indeed, many knowledgeable observers have suggested that concerted action is a facade for something with deeper roots (Vogel, 1973: 186).

We should look for those roots in the organization of German labor, which makes it rational for individual German workers to accept wage restraint, in a way that labor organization in Britain and France does not. Wage restraint can be seen as a public good – just as inflation is a public 'bad'. It is a 'good' to the extent that, if achieved, it reduces subsequent price inflation and so raises real income, but it is 'public' in the sense that the benefits of restraint accrue to everybody (rather than only to those who pay for it with restraint, see Olson, 1971). However, wage restraint can be an especially vicious public good because it must be exercised by almost everybody for any benefits to accrue; and if it is not, then those who exercise restraint not only fail to receive any benefit, they also suffer disproportionately greater income losses in the subsequent inflation.

In the face of this logic, the most effective way to secure wage restraint is to turn it from a vicious public good into something approximating a private good – that is, a good of the sort that can at least be counted on to bring benefits to those who pay for it. This is what incomes policies do. By enforcing a measure of restraint on everyone, they provide assurance that a corresponding reduction of inflation will follow for everyone. They also guarantee that others will not make disproportionate gains at the expense of those who exercise restraint; and they may offer certain key actors, such as union leaders, an additional set of goods in exchange for their acquiescence in restraint. These can range from organizational goods, which enhance the power of union organizations, to other sorts of public goods, such as fiscal or social policies of the sort that union leaders value (Pizzorno, 1978).

In the terms of this analysis, the organization of German labor is particularly conducive to the achievement of wage restraint. The centralized character of the German unions, and the legal procedures available to enforce a particular wage bargain, increase the likelihood that, once restraint is agreed upon, it will be widespread and thus pay off for rank-and-file workers. From their point of view, the risks associated with restraint are consequently lower, and the returns likely to be higher, than they would be under a system where the reduction of inflation was conditional on the acquiescence of many more unions competing within a less regularized set of bargaining procedures. In terms of game theory, this case is rather like a prisoner's dilemma, and these organizational changes alter the probabilities associated with each kind of pay-off in such a way as to conduce to cooperation (cf. Axelrod, 1983).

In addition, since the leadership of the German unions is relatively concentrated, the achievement of a wage norm entails securing agreement from a relatively small number of people whose subsequent compliance is also relatively easily monitored. Similarly, the availability of alternative leaders is restricted, and any challenge to an agreement must go through the difficult process of finding alternative leadership before it can be expressed in an organized way. As the events of the 1969–71 period illustrate, this does not eliminate challenges, but it inhibits them (Muller-Jentsch and Sperling, 1978).

Once a reasonable wage norm has been identified, a series of organizational factors also help to give it force with little need for an elaborate and intensely negotiated bargain at the center. Attention focuses on the correct determination of a wage norm rather than on political manipulation to secure consent for it. This has, in fact, been the German pattern. Here it is termed 'tacit tripartism', but it has also appropriately been called an "incomes policy from below" (Kindleberger, 1965: 248).

In the early 1960s, when inflation first became a problem, the Bundesbank took the lead in suggesting a norm; but when its conservative biases became suspect, a Council of Economic Experts was established in part to perform this function (cf. Roberts, 1979). The operation of policy in this sphere has not been entirely unproblematic for the Germans, and from time to time other instruments, including the occasional induced recession and the union's relationship with the SPD, have been used to bolster support for wage restraint. Overall, however, the distinctiveness of the German pattern of incomes policy, especially in contrast to the experiences of the British and French, seems most attributable to factors associated with the organization of labor.

FRANCE

Turning to France and initially to the organization of capital there, we find that relations between industrial and financial capital are such as to give the banking institutions associated with financial capital a detailed knowledge of the affairs of many firms in the industrial sector and considerable influence over their strategies. Whereas real and proxy shareholding by the banks leads to such an outcome in Germany, however, the linchpin of relations between industry and banks in France is the heavy dependence of industrial firms on long-term debt for finance. French industry has traditionally had one of the highest debt–equity ratios in Europe and one of the most underutilized stock exchanges. In 1977 for instance the debts of French industry were worth almost 140 percent of its assets, while the market value of equities listed on the French *Bourse* was barely 12 percent of GDP compared with Britain and the USA, where the corresponding figure was over 40 percent (Commission de l'Industrie, 1980: 6).

As a result of this, the French banks are in a position to exercise a proportionately greater influence over the affairs of industry; and because most of the debt is medium- to long-term, these banks generally take an active interest in the production and marketing strategies of the firms they support (cf. Morin, 1974; Zysman, 1980: 266).

In contrast to Germany, however, the organization of French capital is further distinguished by strong state influence in the banking sector. The history of state intervention in banking in France can be traced back to the reconstruction of the banking system under Napoleon III and to the efforts of the Front Populaire to take control of the Bank of France in the 1930s. But its immediate origins lie in the establishment after World War Two of a series of state-controlled institutions for the collection of savings (Caisse des Dépôts, Banque Nationale de Paris, Société Générale and Crédit Lyonnais), and for the provision of funds to industry (Crédit National), agriculture (Crédit Agricole), housing (Crédit Foncier) and tourism (Crédit Hôtelier). Together these institutions collect and dispose of two-thirds of all the deposits in the French banking system (Morin, 1974: 175). In recent years they have been joined by an additional set of state institutions, such as the Fonds de développement économique et social (FDES), which provides as much as 2 billion francs (bF) a year to industry, the Institut de développement industriel which administers another 1 bF and the Banque française du commerce extérieur which, along with several other agencies, makes available up to 10 bF a year to facilitate exports (Ministère de l'Industrie, 1979). By using these funds to enter into joint ventures with the private banks of France and to rediscount their bills, the state has been able to exercise substantial leverage over the activities of the private banking sector as well. For many years, that leverage was further enhanced by the system of quantitative controls used by the Bank of France to govern lending. The result is that finance capital exercises a detailed purview over the affairs of industry and the state exercises substantial control over finance capital itself (Zysman, 1980; Caron, 1979).

At the same time, the post-war French state has also had a distinctive organization. Three features are particularly striking. First, officials at the Ministry of Finance are able to exercise considerable influence over the actions of the Bank of France (Adam, 1980). The central bank of France is far less independent than its German or even British counterparts. Secondly, the Ministry of Finance in charge of fiscal and monetary policy is also closely involved in the supervision of industrial policy (Adam, 1980). This means that industrial concerns are likely to receive greater consideration in the formulation of macroeconomic policy than they do in Britain, where responsibility for fiscal and industrial matters is clearly divided between departments. Thirdly, a set of institutions was embedded within the French state immediately after the war for the purpose of inculcating its personnel with the notion that they were to be the grand stategists for French industry. Most prominent among these were the Ecole Nationale d'Administration (ENA) and the Commissariat Général du Plan. The former, which became the principal source for recruitment into the civil service, imbued its charges with a sense of their own distinctiveness and a feeling of responsibility for the performance of the French economy (cf. Stevens, 1980; Suleiman, 1980). The latter attempted to fulfill that responsibility by generating and coordinating a strategy for the evolution of French industry (cf. Gruson, 1968; Monnet, 1976). Together, these facets of the French state gave its personnel a capacity to influence the activities of industry and a willingness to do so that their counterparts in Britain and Germany generally lacked.

The organization of labor in France is equally distinctive. Barely a fifth of the workforce belongs to a trade union, and many of those who do have only a nominal affiliation. French unions have notorious difficulty collecting membership dues and maintaining regular organizational relations with the rank and file (Schain, 1980; Reynaud, 1975). Moreover, the union movement is divided into several confederations – the CGT, CFDT, FO, CFTC, and CGC – whose bitter rivalry for members and influence often undercuts their ability to mobilize support or to take a united front on policy matters. Until recently, collective bargaining was largely unregulated by law, and the unions had a very limited legal status in the workplace. In the anarcho-syndicalist tradition, French unions are masters of the mass demonstration and one-day general strike, but only rarely can they mount sustained industrial disruption.

Macroeconomic policy in France

What is the relationship between these organizational factors and the patterns of French economic policy in the post-war period? In the macroeconomic sphere, French policy under the Fourth and Fifth Republics fits a pattern that can be described as one of stimulating investment above all else, usually through the stimulation of demand. Fiscal policy played a role. With the exception of 1958 and 1965, when the government ran a slight surplus, demand was stimulated almost continuously over 1954–74 by a series of public sector deficits averaging 1 to 2 percent of GDP (Hansen, 1968: 193; Salin and Lane, 1977: 550). Monetary policy, however, was the driving force behind the French stimulus. Despite brief periods when credit was tightened in 1963–65, 1968–70 and 1972–73, the money supply was allowed to grow rapidly in France, reaching an average increase of almost 14 percent per annum in the 1960–68 period (OECD, 1974; Salin and Lane, 1977: 578). In general, the monetary aggregates were allowed to grow substantially faster in France than in either Germany or the UK; and lest one think that demand factors alone were responsible, it should be noted that the French state generated much of that demand by subsidizing the rate at which funds were made available. As late as 1980, it is estimated that 44 percent of all business loans in France were at subsidized rates of interest (*The Economist*, 14 March 1981: 62). The first two pillars of French macroeconomic policy were the rapid expansion of demand and the provision of large quantities of relatively cheap credit to industry.

The impact of this policy, of course, was highly inflationary. During 1950–75 the French cost of living rose by 6 percent more than the British and by 42 percent more than the German. From time to time this threatened the growth of French exports and precipitated balance of payments crises. The government was then faced with a choice between the pursuit of less inflationary policies, which would slow the rate of growth, and devaluation of the currency. The British often faced a similar choice; but whereas the British strenuously resisted devaluation during the era of fixed exchange rates (1947–72), the French devalued frequently. They lowered the exchange rate of the franc five times in a 25-year period: by almost 40 percent in 1948, by 22 percent in 1949, by 20 percent in 1957, by 17.5 percent in 1958 and by 11 percent in 1969 (cf. Lieberman, 1977). Devaluation was the third leg of the triad on which their macroeconomic policy was based.[4]

The French policies – expanding demand, subsidizing credit, devaluation – subordinated macroeconomic management to the pursuit of industrial investment. When forced to choose, the French authorities opted consistently for industrial growth.[5]

This order of priorities and the consistency with which it has been pursued can be traced to several features of state and capital organization in France. In part, the emphasis on growth reflects the socializing effects of the ENA and the persistent pressure of the Plan on the Ministry of Finance. Planning officials concede that their principal object was to convert both state and business managers to the need for growth (Monnet, 1976; Crozier, 1965). As chapters 6 and 7 indicated, they were largely successful. The Planning Commission was widely recognized as an effective conduit reinforcing the voice of industrial capital within the state and articulating its demands for expansionary economic policy (Hayward, 1972).

The task of the planners was made easier by a post-war reorganization of the Ministry of Finance vesting it with ultimate responsibility for industrial matters. In the inter-war era the Ministry had been known as a bastion of fiscal conservatism (Cohen, 1977a: 37–8). Like the British Treasury, it resisted a series of attempts to use alternative departments of economic affairs to reorient economic policy. Under the influence of *énarques* and vested with new responsibilities for industry, however, the post-war Ministry became committed to economic rationalization and rapid growth. The success of French industry became the responsibility of the French Ministry of Finance in a way that British industrial success has never been the task of the British Treasury.

With the concurrent reorganization of the financial sector, the Ministry of Finance also gained greater control over many fiscal and monetary levers – control that was denied to the German Minister of Economics, who had to face a separate Finance Ministry and a highly independent central bank. It became possible for the French Ministry to pursue growth through an easy money policy punctuated by periodic devaluations, and through selective exemptions from restrictive policies for critical industrial sectors. Monetary reorganization reduced the independence of finance capital while the Plan was enhancing the influence of industrial capital.

Industrial policy in France

In contrast to Britain and Germany, the French state has been able and willing to intervene forcefully in the affairs of the private sector. The state develops a strategy for individual industrial sectors, puts pressure on individual firms to comply with its strategy, and funds profitable enterprises rather than simply declining sectors.

In the reconstruction following the war, the Planning Commission and Ministry of Finance channelled scarce funds to six key sectors. A system of national planning drew up detailed plans for the division of production within these sectors. During the subsequent two decades, the state fastened on a strategy of creating 'national champions' that would carry France's banner against the multinationals. To this end it encouraged mergers and transferred resources to high-technology industries in growth sectors. The Airbus, Plan Calcul, Concorde and nuclear programs were products of this attempt. The details of French industrial policy are described at length in preceding chapters. Of our three cases, the French state has played the most active role in the rationalization of key industrial sectors.

Both the will and capacity behind this approach can be traced to the organization of French capital and the state. Just as the socialization provided by ENA and the Plan dictated a macroeconomic policy fixated on economic growth, so it encouraged the managers of the state to undertake an activist industrial policy. They were designated the pilots of the 'strategic state'. The failure of French industry would be their failure. Of even greater importance, the reorganization of capital after the war provided them with the tools with which to exercise extensive influence over industry. These were enumerated in chapter six. The most important derive from the dependence of French industry on the banks and the state's control over the banks – crucial features of the organization of capital in France. In short the organization of the state made possible a certain orientation to industrial policy and the organization of capital facilitated its realization.

Incomes policy in France

In the sphere of incomes policy the French experience has again been unique – distinguished from the German and British cases by the failure to develop any form of tripartism whether tacit or explicit. Instead, the French state has relied primarily on price controls to stiffen employers' resolve against workers' wage demands and on periodic devaluation to neutralize the effect of sporadic wage increases on export prices. From time to time groups of officials, often within the Plan and supported by some union leaders, attempted to open tripartite negotiations; but these attempts were never fully successful. In each case the state agreed to such negotiations only when pressed by national crises of the sort generated by the steel strike of 1963 and the events following May 1968. On each occasion, while some of the parties favored a settlement, others acted to sabotage it.

Thus, the Incomes Policy Conference of October 1963 was scuttled by the government's passage of anti-strike legislation in July 1963, by its deflationary moves of September 1963 and by the refusal of the CGT and FO to trade wage restraint for contractual agreements covering social policy, minimum wages and public sector settlements. Similarly, although the government resorted to the tripartite Grenelle Agreements of 1968 to restore order after the events of May–June, the wage gains these offered were immediately undercut by the devaluation of the franc; and the *contrats de progrès* that were supposed to regularize public sector bargaining in this period functioned for barely a year before union resistance intensified and the Chaban–Delmas government that devised them was dismissed (Hayward and Watson, 1975). Indeed, for most of the post-war period the state's efforts have been directed at weakening the union movement rather than at attempting to strengthen and co-opt it by encouraging participation in national bargaining. Over a period of years, union delegates were systematically excluded from the most sensitive negotiations at the Plan (Hayward, 1967). All attempts to secure legal recognition for unions at the workplace were frustrated until 1969, and industrial relations legislation was almost invariably contrived to strengthen alternative workers' committees rather than unions at the plant level (cf. Schain, 1980).

The strategy adopted by the state, and the failure to develop any form of tripartism, can both be related to the organization of the French labor market. The weakness of the unions restricted their ability to secure extravagant wage increases or to disrupt the economy for a sustained period, making it less necessary for the government to resort to tripartite bargaining to limit real wage gains. Union leaders' limited authority over the rank-and-file made tripartite bargaining more difficult and less attractive. As one observer puts it, "The employers and the state . . . can expect few benefits of social order from union organizations that have so little authority over their strike action" (Schain, 1980: 233). The presence of competing union federations also made the achievement of a tripartite bargain difficult. There was a great temptation for unions to score gains among rank-and-file militants by accusing other unions of selling out if they bargained; hence, the attractiveness of entering into a bargain was limited by the fear that a union's rivals might outflank it on the left, while it was immobilized by the agreement.

For individual workers, these factors and the unregulated character of collective bargaining in France meant that there were few guarantees that any national bargain would be universally observed and, thus, there were high risks associated with restraint. At the levels of the state, union leadership, and rank-and-file, organizational factors militated against the achievement of a tripartite incomes policy in France. A strategy that utilized pressure on employers and the occasional devaluation to depress wages was more likely to succeed; and such a strategy has been much more common in France.

GREAT BRITAIN

Turning to Britain, we can see the impact of organization on policy once again. In the organization of the British state two factors are especially significant. First, as in Germany, there is a strict separation between the organ responsible for fiscal policy, the Treasury, and that responsible for monetary policy, the Bank of England. Although its independence is not as constitutionally entrenched as that of the Deutsche Bundesbank, the Bank of England enjoys considerable autonomy and substantial influence over policy, as preceding chapters have demonstrated. This derives from its virtual monopoly of expertise about monetary policy and its position within Whitehall as the spokesman for the financial markets. When issues of confidence in sterling or the government's monetary policy arise, the Bank can both contribute to the definition of the conditions on which 'financial confidence' is deemed to rest, and interpret these conditions directly to the government of the day. As successive Prime Ministers have testified, in the face of such powers, formal limits on the Bank's authority dwindle into insignificance (Keegan and Pennant-Rae, 1979: 99).

Secondly, in contrast to both the German and French cases, where the central economic ministry has been charged with responsibility for industrial performance, the British Treasury's main responsibility since the war has been the control of public expenditure. Until 1962 the internal organization of the Treasury was geared almost exclusively to this function; and the National Economy Group, which was established at that time to oversee the real resources of the nation, was still oriented to the management of aggregate consumption and investment rather than to the sectoral organization or performance of British industry (see Shonfield, 1969: 104). Until 1975 the Treasury had virtually no capacity for assessing the detailed impact of its measures on industry.

Indeed, for most of the post-war period British governments lacked a Cabinet-level Minister of Industry as well. The first steps to remedy this were taken in 1962 when the Board of Trade was given increased responsibility for regional development. Not until the late 1960s, when the Ministry of Technology began to assemble a staff of industrial experts, did the British government develop a capacity for the coordination of industrial policy. Moreover, the Treasury continued to exercise a kind of bureaucratic hegemony over economic policy-making within Whitehall despite the short-lived experiment with a Department of Economic Affairs (Shanks, 1977; Budd, 1978).

The organization of British capital is already quite familiar. It is notable for the international orientation of financial capital and the relatively strict division of interest and operations that persists between the managers of financial and industrial capital. As the home of the first industrial empire, Britain developed a financial sector with worldwide interests as early as the 19th century; and the City of London remained the principal international banking center of the world long after the empire disappeared. As a result, British financiers were far more likely to use their political influence against devaluation (which for most of the period was seen as a threat to their international business) than the German or French bankers. Here is an instance in which the nation's position within the international economic system impinges on its macroeconomic policies.

The outcome is also related to the structure of industrial finance in Britain described in chapter three. On the one hand, UK firms generally rely on internally generated funds and equity for capital investment. As a result, industrial capital in Britain has been much less dependent on the banks for finance than its continental counterparts. On the other hand, what capital the banks do provide to British industry is generally channelled through short-term loans that do not involve the banks so deeply in the management of industry.[6] As a consequence, the British banks appear to have more limited knowledge about the operations of British industry and less of a stake in the profitability of particular industrial sectors than their continental counterparts. British finance capital is thus more likely to define its interests in a way that is separate from those of industry.

The organization of labor in Britain is also distinctive. In contrast to France, Britain has a central Trades Union Congress (TUC) to which most organized workers are affiliated, and which exercises considerable moral authority over them; but it is a loose confederation with limited bureaucratic resources and few sanctions to apply against its members. In contrast to Germany, over 100 separate unions are affiliated to the TUC, many of them still organized along craft lines. Within many of these affiliates a contest for control over union policy also continues among frequently autocratic leaders and an influential network of shop stewards (Clegg, 1979; Taylor, 1978).

In broad social terms, however, this is a powerful union movement. At the economic level, over 50 percent of the workforce is unionized, and in such key sectors as coal, railways and road transport over 95 percent of the workforce belongs to a trade union. In the face of inflation most of these unions have been able to secure real wage gains for their members (cf. Sachs, 1979). In the political arena, the Labour Party has been able to control the left of the political spectrum so as to secure office for almost half of the post-war years; and the trade unions have special influence within the Labour Party, whose funds and annual conference they dominate.

Macroeconomic policy in Britain

How are these factors related to the patterns of British economic policy? As chapters three and four have demonstrated, the most notable feature of macroeconomic policy in post-war Britain has been the recurrence of a 'stop–go' cycle of reflation and deflation (Hansen, 1968; Caves et al., 1968; Brittan, 1970). From 1950 to 1980, each brief period of expansion was all too quickly followed by restrictive fiscal or monetary measures. These sudden fluctuations in policy were also linked to the defense of a high exchange rate.

The expansionary policies pursued during the 'go' side of these cycles can be traced to a desire to stimulate economic growth. However, this sort of stimulus invariably sucked imports into the economy, threw the balance of payments into deficit, and precipitated an outflow of the foreign exchange reserves. Confronted with this situation, British policy-makers faced a choice between letting the exchange rate decline or deflating the economy so as to reduce expenditure on imports relative to exports. In similar situations the French devalued. But for almost 30 years after the war, British policy-makers refused to devalue, except when forced to in 1948 and 1967. They consistently defended an exchange rate which by the end of the 1950s was seriously overvalued, and in the process, generated a disruptive series of 'stop–go' cycles (Brittan, 1970: 299).

In short, for most of the post-war period the British pursued a policy that served the perceived interests of finance capital rather than industry. The consequences for British industry were adverse in two respects. The increasingly frequent and severe deflations entailed by this policy discouraged capital investment which might have improved productivity and growth. The policy also saddled industrialists with particularly high export prices while subsidizing the price of competing imports. British export prices rose by 145 percent more than the average price of world exports in the decade after 1953 (Pollard, 1969: 44). Until the 1970s, however, the representatives of the British financial community believed that the maintenance of a high exchange rate was essential to the survival of London as an international financial center. At each turning-point spokesmen for the City and the Bank of England pressed the government to deflate rather than devalue (Brittan, 1970), and in each instance their views prevailed.

To a large extent this pattern of policy must be attributed to the organization of British capital and the state. The arms-length relationship between financial and industrial capital in Britain led finance capital, in particular, to define its interests in terms that were quite separate from those of industry. As one British industrialist observed: "There is a false assumption that all businessmen have common interests. Yet to me it is patently obvious that the interests of manufacturing business and the City are sometimes not coincident" (Grant and Marsh, 1978: 69). In France and Germany, by contrast, the banks' direct stake in the profitability of industrial enterprise and their familiarity with its needs led the two sides toward a convergent defense of devaluation or undervaluation.

At the same time the organization of the British state privileged issues of international confidence. As we have seen, such issues were primarily in the hands of the Bank of England, which spoke for the interests of the financial community. Preoccupation with the control of public expenditure predisposed many Treasury officials to deflationary episodes so that public expenditure might be cut back. The organization of Whitehall was conducive to the formation of a consensus on the desirability of deflation over devaluation (cf. Blank, 1978); and even growth-minded politicians were influenced by Britain's extensive international obligations. Here the country's international economic position also played a direct role in policy-making.

Industrial policy in Britain

British industrial policy has been described extensively in chapter three. A coordinated policy aimed at the rationalization of key industrial sectors was not developed until late in the post-war period, and even then it relied too heavily on tripartite consensus to effect any kind of controversial reorganization schemes. The degree to which the state actually put pressure on industrial actors was very limited.[7] Its industrial activities were primarily oriented to the maintenance of employment in economically depressed areas rather than to the reorganization of industry; and in the 1970s especially, the vast majority of funds went to firms in declining sectors of the economy (Peacock et al., 1980: 59; McCrone, 1969: 119).

This pattern of policy was strongly influenced by the organization of British capital and the state. The British state simply lacked the means with which to enforce an active policy of sectoral reorganization, even if it could have formulated one. In contrast to the French or German banks, financial capital in Britain has been relatively independent of the state. The Bank of England attempts to influence the total quantities of credit extended in the economy and has occasionally suggested that the banks give priority to export industries in their lending, but the state lacks the detailed control over the flows of funds in the economy which the French state enjoys. Morever, British industry itself has been less dependent on the banking sector for finance than continental firms. Thus, even if the British state had nationalized the banks, its leverage over industry would still have been limited. The tax allowances on which many British governments relied to stimulate investment cannot be focused on individual firms in such a way as to enforce a rationalization program; and the subsidies that several governments have made available to industry do not substitute for more extensive control over an industry's sources of external finance.

As we have seen, the division of responsibility within the British state also tended to limit the willingness of its most powerful officials to develop an industrial strategy. Power over the direction of economic policy remained with a Treasury that had little industrial expertise or explicit responsibility for British industry. Without a powerful apparatus committed to sectoral planning in Whitehall, the British state proved attentive to sectoral problems only in crisis situations. Initiative in this area remained at the political level where concerns naturally focused on the short-term alleviation of unemployment, rather than the long-term reallocation of investment toward growth sectors of industry.

Moreover, even the position of British labor tended to militate against an interventionist industrial policy. Despite some support for economic planning from union circles, many unionists associated it with threats to the autonomy of collective bargaining that was a longstanding ideal of the British union movement. Their influence in the Labour Party, then, could put some limits on the actions of the one party most likely to consider an interventionist industrial policy.

Incomes policy in Britain

The British approach to incomes policy has also displayed three distinctive characteristics. First, successive governments made extensive efforts to implement an incomes policy. Second, each case entailed a lengthy attempt to bargain with the TUC and CBI over the content of policy. Finally, after one or two years under a wage norm, rank-and-file resistance forced the union leadership to withdraw its support for such a policy, and impelled the government to return to free collective bargaining. Thus, the British pattern has been one of alternation between an incomes policy negotiated from above and free collective bargaining (Dorfman, 1979).

Once again, the roots of this pattern can be traced to the organization of the British labor market. The British state found it necessary to attempt to reach agreement on an incomes policy because of the power of the union movement. Their industrial strength rendered the British unions a potentially inflationary force that could not be ignored. Moreover, the unions were sufficiently powerful to maintain real wages through a devaluation so as to render that strategy less useful than it was in France. Successive governments looked to a negotiated incomes policy as an alternative.

If these negotiations were made necessary by the power of unions, however, they were also made possible by the existence of a single union confederation. In both respects Britain stands in contrast to France where the weakness of the union movement limits the need for negotiations, and the multiplicity of unions discourages any one of them from reaching an agreement with the state.

It has also been difficult to secure adherence to an incomes policy in Britain without extensive negotiations and some formal bargaining arrangements. In the centralized union movement of Germany, the acquiescence of a few major leaders is sufficient to assure all concerned that restraint will be widespread. In Britain, however, consent must be secured from a relatively large number of union leaders if a policy of restraint is to have any chance of success. For this purpose, the British have had to develop formal institutional arrangements for bargaining with the unions. In the absence of such arrangements, the generalized distribution of positive incentives proved ineffective at securing restraint. An institutional framework, of the sort the NEDC or TUC–Labour Party Liaison Committee provided, made it possible for the state to demand a *quid pro quo* for each of the goods it distributed, to exact the maximum returns in exchange for those goods, and to monitor any ensuing agreement.

Although the TUC has been able to strike some bargains with the state, however, there have also been organizational limits to how long those bargains could be kept. Because the TUC is such a loose confederation, an enormous expenditure of effort has been required to secure agreement to each incomes policy from the member unions and their rank-and-file. In each case, the organizational resources of the TUC were eventually exhausted, and a rank-and-file backlash began to find alternative leadership with which to challenge prevailing personnel and policy. The existence of a large number of unions and a powerful shop stewards movement has made alternative leadership more available in Britain than in France. Thus, any tripartite arrangement was bound to break down, and a period of free collective bargaining, often under more militant leadership, ensued before another tripartite bargain was attempted. Hence, the alternation between incomes policy and free-for-all which has characterized the British experience in the post-war period.

THE RECENT EVOLUTION OF POLICY

For most of the post-war period, then, the economic policies of Britain, France and Germany seem to have followed distinctive patterns; and these, in turn, can be related to organizational features of their state and society. Although there was some variation in each country's policies over this period, the persistence of broad patterns differentiating the policies of one country from those of the others is striking. In a world of flux, it is underlying continuities which most merit explanation; and the parallel persistence of both these patterns and specific organizational forms strongly suggests that the two are related. The organization of capital, labor and the state seem to have been especially important to policy outcomes.

At this point, however, we must say a little more about the role of each nation's political system and position within the international economy. The impact of these two factors on each nation's policies in the three decades after the war can be charted briefly; but both became especially important factors in the policy changes of the past 15 years.

We see the impact of international economic position most clearly in the case of Britain. As chapter three indicated, the experience of empire left the nation with extensive international obligations and a financial sector heavily oriented to the international provision of services. To some extent, then, the effect of international position has been discussed above as part of the account of the nature and organization of British capital. It contributed to the limited concern that the British banks displayed for domestic industrial interests, as they were pressing successive governments for deflation rather than devaluation.

As we have seen, however, the British state itself had international obligations in the form of overseas sterling balances and extensive military commitments. These clearly had an independent impact on the tendency of policy-makers to resist devaluation, as preceding chapters have demonstrated.

Largely for these reasons, the shift in Britain's international position of greatest consequence was marked by the change from a fixed to floating exchange rate regime. When America left the gold standard in 1971, British policy-makers accepted a floating exchange rate, and their fixation on that policy target was reduced. Nevertheless, the famous 'stop–go' cycles continued for another decade, as successive governments again pumped up the economy only to encounter further exchange rate crises that seemed to dictate deflation even under a regime of floating rates.

In France and Germany, however, the impact of international position became more intense in the early 1970s with the culmination of three decades of change. As noted in chapters six and seven, the French economy became progressively more integrated into the European Economic Community. As a result, many of the traditional tools of the planners were weakened, and they began to realize that the object of industrial policy had to be international competitiveness rather than growth *per se*. Hence, a change in the position of France within the international economy produced a gradual shift in the tenor of industrial policy. That shift became even more pronounced after 1974 when the global recession that followed the oil crisis began to vitiate the planners' projections for growth. As we have seen, the prospect of continuing recession contributed to the process of deplanification described above.

Even in the 1970s, however, there remained broad continuities in French economic policy. Despite the free market rhetoric of the Barre administration and some attempts to reduce the visibility of the state's role in a recessionary economy, the French state continued to play a commanding role in industrial reconstruction. It still orchestrated the reorganization of industrial sectors; and the total amount of state aid to industry in the 1975–80 period was substantially greater than it had been in the first half of the decade. (Cohen, 1982; Commissariat Générale du Plan, 1979; Commission de l'Industrie, 1980.)

The German story is one of self-fulfilling prophecy. The strategy of export-led growth pursued by successive German governments bore fruit. West Germany's share of world exports of manufactures rose from 7 percent in 1950 to 21 percent in 1977. However, that success brought inflows of foreign currency and pressure for the upward revaluation of the deutschmark. As the preceding analysis would suggest, the Bundesbank displayed considerable resistance to revaluation with the interests of German industry in mind; but it gave way at several points in the 1970s, partly because inflows of foreign currency would otherwise have vitiated its efforts at monetary control. The last 15 years, then, have been a period in which the German authorities were cross-pressured as the results of their own success altered the position of the nation within the international economy.

To some extent, the global recession that followed 1974 also inspired adjustments in German industrial policy. As in France, pressure to bail out the increasing number of failing firms intensified to a point that the state could not resist. Both nations provided aid to such declining sectors as coal, shipbuilding and steel. However, there were many respects in which the German rationalization schemes of the 1970s continued to follow longstanding patterns of policy. Most German aid took the form of grants for manpower retraining, research and development or regional development assistance, all of which involved little state intervention in the direction of rationalization itself.

Responsibility for many German reorganization schemes remained with the firms themselves or their bankers. Thus, the shipbuilding and steel industries managed to alter their basic product lines and shed thousands of workers without much government direction; and when Volkswagen ran into difficulties, the government again refused to interfere with the closure of plants, choosing instead to step up regional development aid to the areas most affected by its layoffs (Medley, 1981; Peacock et al., 1980). In 1979 a government commission recommended very little change in the relationship between the banks and industry (Anderson, 1980: 15).

Figures compiled from an important study of industrial reorganization schemes by Jeffrey Hart indicate that the differences observed in national styles of industrial policy have persisted into the 1980s (see table 9.1). His survey of major schemes for the whole 1962–85 period indicates that the most prominent actors were still the banks in Germany and the state in France, while the state and the trade unions were the principal actors in Britain.

Turning to the organization of the political system in these nations, we find that it seems to have played only a subsidiary role in economic policy-making for much of the post-war period. This is, of course, somewhat difficult to assess. British governments tended to follow broadly similar policies, regardless of their partisan complexion, in such a way as to suggest that the organization of labor, capital and the state was more important to the overall shape of policy.

In France, conservative majorities were in office almost continuously since 1950 partly as a result of serious organizational divisions within the left, intensified by the presence of a strong Communist Party, of whom large portions of the electorate were suspicious. In that sense, the organization of the French political system may have had some

Table 9.1   State, union, and bank involvement in sectoral reorganization, 1962–85

	Percentage of sectoral reorganization schemes in which each played a major role		
	Germany	France	Britain
Banking institutions	80	23	30
Trade unions	30	23	40
State agencies	40	77	60
(N)	(10)	(13)	(10)

Source: derived from data presented in Jeffrey A. Hart, "Crisis management and the institutionalization of corporatist bargain mechanisms". Paper presented at the Conference of Europeanists, Washington, DC, 19 October 1985.

consequences for economic policy. The French style of dirigisme, in particular, was characterized by a concern for the profitability of industry that came more easily to the right; and the exclusion of the trade unions from active participation in economic policy-making may be partially attributable to conservative governance. On the other hand, the policies of the Mitterrand Government did not modify either of these characteristics of French policy very profoundly.

Similarly, the entry of the German Social Democrats into the Grand Coalition of 1966 and their subsequent electoral victories did not bring major changes in German economic policies. As noted above, the Social Democrats added a touch of Keynesianism to policy-making in the late 1960s and expressed renewed concern for a *strukturpolitik* that implied a more interventionist industrial policy; but many of the Social Democrats' expansionary instincts were frustrated by the Bundesbank, which insisted, for instance, on tempering their fiscal relaxation of 1974 with a restrictive monetary policy (Anderson, 1980: 21).

In this period, as before, the organization of the German political system around proportional representation and a party system in which the Free Democrats played a critical centrist role may have contributed to the market orientation of German economic policy. As virtually omnipresent coalition partners for each Government, the Free Democrats tended to insist on moderate fiscal policies and clear limits to state intervention. Similarly, the important role played by the Bundesrat, or upper house, in the German parliament tended to give the Christian Democrats, whose state representatives dominated it, influence over the economic policies of even Social Democratic administrations.

In sum, it would not be correct to say that the complexion of the governing party (and hence those aspects of the organization of the political system that tended to bring different parties to office in different nations) had no effect on economic policy; but the organization of capital, labor and the state seems to have been more important for most of the post-war period. One indicator is the extent to which conservative and social democratic parties alike pursued quite different patterns of policy in each of these nations. The differences between Conservative and Labour policy in Britain, for example, were usually far less great than those between the policies pursued by Conservatives in Britain and Gaullists in France or between Labour in Britain and the Social Democrats in Germany.

In the very recent period, however, as successive governments failed to restore 1960s levels of growth, the voting patterns of disillusioned electors have become more volatile, and political parties have begun to search more widely for new economic policies. Hence, the potential has increased for political parties to become the agents of economic innovation, as they seek platforms around which to build new social coalitions. As we have seen, both the Thatcher and Mitterrand Governments made something of a break with past patterns of policy.

Even in these cases, however, reforming regimes have encountered obstacles rooted in the international system and longstanding organization of capital, labor and the state. Behind a similar response to the economic conditions of the 1970s and 1980s, there still lie distinctive patterns of national policy, as the capacity of each state to effect the rationalization of industry or to depress wages continues to depend on various features of socioeconomic organization. Thus, Germany has still been able to depend on the banks to reorganize many sectors. The French state has consolidated its control over the financial instruments central to industrial reorganization and continues to try to use these to achieve competitiveness in the open European economy. And in the absence of instruments with which to enforce state-led rationalization, the British state has moved from the *ad hoc* tripartism of the 1970s to a market-based strategy in the 1980s. Each nation has had some room for experimentation, but the strategies of each still reflect the influences of longstanding patterns of socioeconomic organization.

There are many aspects of this comparison that still remain to be explored; and the next chapter will take up some implications for our models of politics. On the basis of this comparison, however, an organizational approach seems quite promising. It provides us with one way of understanding why rather similar advanced capitalist democracies nevertheless pursue quite different policies in the face of similar economic circumstances. Indeed, it gives us a concrete basis for thinking that differences in the policies of capitalist states may be more than contingent variations. There seem to be persistent patterns to national policies that can be traced back to fundamental differences in the organization of the socioeconomic relations which surround and encompass each state.

10

The Organization of State–Society Relations

The principal theme of this book has been its insistence that we must consider the political dimensions of economic management if we are to understand why nations pursue certain economic policies and why those policies change. A purely economic account will not suffice. However, this account also has important implications for conventional models of the polity itself. In particular it is designed to extend an approach to political analysis that stresses the way in which institutions structure state–society relations and the direction of policy.

The cases of Britain and France suggest that five sets of structural variables will be most important for the course of a nation's economic policy: the organization of labor, the organization of capital, the organization of the state, the organization of the political system, and the structural position of the country within the international economy. Some might like a shorter list of independent variables, especially since each of these varies along several dimensions; but economic policy-making is a complex process, and a careful consideration of the French and British experience suggests that any further reduction would fail to capture the full range of factors affecting their policies.

Conversely, some will say that even this specification misses some determinants of policy. From time to time that may be true: some decisions seem to have turned on contingency or the unpredictable judgement of one or two powerful individuals. Would a Prime Minister other than Harold Wilson have devalued in 1964? Would a President other than Charles de Gaulle have moved away earlier from French planning? The analysis does not rule out hypothetical outcomes of this sort. However, the kind of explanatory variables emphasized here refer to precisely those features of the political scene that are likely to have weighed most heavily in the minds of such decision-makers. If they do not eliminate the free will of policy-makers, they seem to have been consistently important factors in their judgements.

Moreover, it is important to remember that the organizational variables on which this analysis focuses interact with each other. That is to say, their impact could not be modelled by a regression equation in which each figured as a separate independent variable, even if the relevant dimensions of organization were entirely susceptible to quantitative expression. The policy impact of a powerful central bank, for instance, will also be affected by the organizational relationship between industrial and finance capital. Similarly, effects that follow from the ability of trade unions to mobilize the workforce will be mediated by another dimension of labor organization, namely the degree to which unionists are under unified confederal control.

With the case of economic policy-making in mind, therefore, we should consider the overall image of the polity that emerges from this analysis. What is the general nature of organizational interaction within this model? What are its implications for the distribution of power among social groups? Where does this model locate the sources of continuity and change within the polity? What is the general picture of the relationship between institutions, interests, and ideas that emerges from it?

STRUCTURAL INTERDEPENDENCE

We can begin with the nature of interdependence in an organizational model of the polity. As a result of interaction among institutional variables of the sort outlined above, the polity appears as a complexly inter-related system. However, we should be clear about the nature of its interdependence. It has two sides, both the effects of interlocking institutional arrangements. On the one hand, the matrix of incentives facing most political actors is shaped, not by a single set of institutions, but by a combination of interlocking institutions. On the other hand, each policy is likely to have consequences, whether intended or unintended, beyond the initial sphere of action as a result of institutional linkage.

This concept of interdependence should be distinguished from that proposed by systems analysis. One of the central insights of systems theory is its insistence that the polity be viewed as an inter-related system. However, systems analysts generally accord the 'system' an overarching causal priority that it does not deserve. That is to say, they see the polity and economy as organic wholes whose very nature specifies the nature of the action that is taken within them. In general, they imply that such action should conduce to the maintenance of the system as a whole and can be explained in these terms.

By contrast, an organizational approach suggests that the actions of individuals will be affected by the institutional structures within which they operate; but neither institutions nor action are dictated by the existence of any superordinate 'system' with a status beyond that of the institutions themselves. There is no teleology here. Hence, it is quite possible for actions and institutions to have consequences that may be either beneficial or detrimental to the long-term survival of the system. Indeed, we have seen many respects in which the economic policies of Britain and France have been harmful, rather than conducive, to the success of capitalism, if not democracy. It is very difficult to explain the decline of the British economy in systemic terms. In other words, we can recognize the complex interdependence of the polity and economy (within themselves and between each other) without having to say that they are systems of a sort that generate superordinate imperatives for action.

This analysis suggests that structure should take priority over function in any explanation of political behavior. It might best be illustrated by reference to one of the central tenets of neo-Marxist theory. Many theorists argue that, in a capitalist society, the state will act so as to protect the interests of capitalists and to limit the influence of the working class. They base this argument on the view that capitalism is a system whose needs render such an outcome imperative (cf. Poulantzas, 1976).

In French and British economic policy-making, we have found such an outcome. The influence of capital, over economic policy at least, seems to have been greater than the influence of the working class. Equipped with an organizational analysis, however, we can see that this outcome derives from similar features of the institutional structure in both nations rather than from some systemic imperative *per se*.

During the post-war period, both Britain and France have had a capitalist economy and a liberal democratic political system. In a capitalist economy, the owners and managers of capital retain control over the allocation of most of the economic resources associated with production. In the course of a century, trade unions gained some influence over the remuneration and working conditions of the labor force, but capitalists still sit at the top of a corporate hierarchy.

Beside this, however, both Britain and France have erected democratic political systems that subject those at the apex of the political hierarchy to periodic re-election. Within these polities workers have been given a status of formal equality with capitalists: each has one vote apiece. Hence, workers receive a measure of political equality, as citizens, that is supposed to compensate for inequalities that remain within the capitalist economic system (Marshall, 1966). Since there are many more workers than capitalists, they also seem to hold the lion's share of power in the political system, even if capitalists and managers still retain control over the system of production. Initially, many socialists believed that this numerical superiority in the electoral arena would allow the working class to transform relations in the economic arena as well.

However, several factors continued to limit the electoral power of the working class. Cross-cutting cleavages, based on religious, ethnic, regional or ideological differences that became institutionalized within party systems, weakened the institutional expression of pure class interests in the political sphere; and the need to form electoral coalitions, as the size of the manual working class shrank under the impact of economic change, undercut the ability of parties that spoke only for working-class interests to secure power (Przeworski, 1985; Offe, 1985). A variety of institutional factors, ranging from the important role played by funding and access to the media in election campaigns to the inter-electoral impact of interest intermediaries on policy, also tended to offset the numerical advantage of workers in the political process (Miliband, 1969; Lindblom, 1977).

In the context of a capitalist economy, however, the organizational conjunction of political and economic systems has had the most important consequences for economic policy. Politicians who sit at the intersection of a democratic electoral system and a capitalist mode of production face strong incentives to avoid policies that might discourage the owners of private capital from investing and expanding production (Block, 1977; Lindblom, 1977). In order to attain re-election, politicians must generally secure economic prosperity. However, this entails an expansion in levels of investment and production that are under the control of private capital in a capitalist economic system. To pursue policies that so damage the interests of capital as to discourage investment and the expansion of production is to court electoral defeat. Regardless of the role of businessmen in electoral campaigns, then, the political leaders of a capitalist democracy are likely to be especially sensitive to the concerns of private capital.

Thus, the conjunction of a liberal democratic polity and a capitalist economy confers an unusual degree of systemic power on capital. Their power is systemic in the sense that capitalists need not take concerted action to actualize it. Timely reminders from the spokesmen for business are never remiss, but structural incentives, already apparent to politicians, tend to discourage them from pursuing policies that might endanger investment, even in the absence of collective action on the part of capital.

By contrast, the political power of labor depends more heavily upon its ability to form voluntary organizations and then mobilize the members of those organizations to threaten widespread disruption of production or public services. That, in turn, can be effected only through the kind of concerted action that requires extensive effort, organization, and sacrifice on the part of many people (Offe, 1985). In this respect, capital is better placed than labor to influence economic policy in most nations.

Our review of economic policy-making in Britain and France confirms this point. Social democratic governments provide the hard cases: their electoral platforms often contained planks that business-men perceived as hostile to their interests. If those with the highest electoral salience were subsequently implemented, however, many others were quietly dropped, as British Labour Governments and the French Socialists reneged on electoral promises in order to avoid antagonizing capital. In general, there was no mystery to this. Social democratic leaders, from Harold Wilson to Laurent Fabius, confirmed that these revisions in policy were made in order to maintain levels of profitability high enough to encourage investment.[1]

In this case, then, one of the central outcomes postulated by a popular version of systems theory can be explained by reference to the institutional structure of Britain and France and the matrix of incentives that they construct for politicians there. There is no need to postulate a systemic imperative or the existence of a system in any other sense than a particular collection of interacting institutions. The actions that we observe are artefacts of existing organizational structures rather than the dictates of superordinate systemic imperatives.

ORGANIZATIONAL VARIATION AND THE BALANCE OF CLASS POWER

The structural features that characterize the conjunction of capitalism and democracy have generated certain similarities in the economic policies of Britain and France. As we have seen, however, additional variations in state–society relations also influence economic policy. Fundamental differences in the organization of capital, labor and the state combined with differences in the organization of the political system and position within the international economy to generate important divergences in the economic policies of the two nations. Moreover, such an organizational analysis allows us to link patterns of policy to the distribution of power among social groups. Just as the structural features of democratic capitalism affected the overall balance of power between capital and labor, the organization of capital, labor, the state and the political system in each country has also tended to favor the interests of some social actors over others.

The interests of industry, for instance, received much greater attention in post-war France than in Britain as a consequence of the organization of capital and the state. The central organs of economic policy-making in France were vested with more direct responsibility for the prosperity of industry than their counterparts in Britain; and the structural relationship between finance and industrial capital inclined the banks to protect the interests of industry. In Britain, by contrast, an internationally oriented banking community in less intimate contact with domestic industrial sectors was less likely to defend their interests. The spokesmen for industrial concerns were also more marginalized within the British policy apparatus, as a Treasury preoccupied with public spending and a powerful central bank, oriented to finance capital, dominated policy-making.

Similarly, the voice of labor was consistently weaker in France, largely because of the organization of the trade unions and the political system. In both the industrial and political arenas of France, working-class representation was split among competing organizations whose rivalry frequently undercut their ability to press a unified message on employers or the state. By virtue of its ideology, one important agent of working-class representation, the French Communist Party, was marginalized within the political system; yet none of the other working-class institutions in France was able to build such a powerful organizational base. By contrast, even the British Trades Union Congress seemed strong. It had some central organization, much greater coverage of the working population, and tighter organizational ties to its base. In the political arena, the absence of a strong communist party left the Labour Party in control of the left of the political spectrum until the 1980s; and it enjoyed long periods in office.

By now, these features of the two political systems and their consequences for economic policy are familiar to us. However, the ways in which organization tends to privilege the interests of some social actors over others should be emphasized, along with its implications for the nature of political power. In particular, the degree to which the interests of any one social group will be influential within the policy process does not seem to depend entirely on the concerted representations of that group or on the political give and take that most pluralists associate with political power (cf. Dahl, 1970; Polsby, 1963). Instead, some interests will be privileged as a result of the overall organization of interlocking institutional frameworks, while others will receive less attention no matter how loudly their spokesmen scream or how many members their formal interest associations mobilize behind them.

For instance, the internal organization of the state vests the most powerful economic policy-makers with specific sets of responsibilities; and these responsibilities entail a greater concern for some interests than others. The British Confederation of Industry is at least as well organized as the French Patronat and it has excellent contacts in Whitehall, but the British Treasury has simply not been organized in such a way as to render the key economic decision-makers especially sensitive to industrial interests. The presence of an internationally oriented banking system with great influence over the British Government by virtue of the organization of the gilt and foreign exchange markets has been a feature of British society that the CBI cannot alter. There is no French equivalent.

Conversely, while one could imagine the French unions deciding to form a unified confederation, that would be a difficult project to accomplish. Hence, working-class interests in France have had to find expression through existing institutional arrangements, which, as we have seen, tend to diminish the force with which they are pressed on the French state. The elaboration of a planning system that largely ignored the views of labor was made possible by labor's weakness but its operation then reinforced that weakness.

Moreover, the view from the Elysée is not the same as the view from Whitehall. The range of customary policy instruments at hand and the kind of societal resistance to be expected in the face of a given policy vary according to organizational differences that affect the perceived costs and benefits of policy in many issue areas. Hence, policy-makers in both countries have a set of perceptions about how they can act *vis-à-vis* certain interests that is somewhat independent of what the spokesmen for labor or capital say. It is based instead on the opportunities and limits that underlying institutional arrangements pose to the alternative courses of action they are considering.

This is one reason why it is often difficult to locate some set of actors who have the 'real power' over any issue. To the degree that power consists in the ability to realize one's projects, even actors at the very top of the political hierarchy often feel heavily constrained by limitations on the flow of information, the absence of readily available instruments, and competing responsibilities in the political and economic arenas of the sort that interlocking organizational networks impose on them (cf. Giddens, 1979). State and societal organization entails a parcellization of power that is somewhat at variance with the conventional dichotomy between 'powerful' and 'powerless' actors. Rather, everyone partakes in an (admittedly uneven) distribution of power; and the organizational structures that allocate influence also tend to impose certain perceptions, responsibilities, and interests on the actors that simultaneously limit their use of that influence.

In these respects, power does not depend primarily on the exertions of individuals or formal associations of individuals. Their behavior is not irrelevant to the outcome; but within many national institutional settings, some actors are swimming upstream. Whether consciously or not, policy-makers will act with a bias against their interests. This phenomenon is similar to that which E. E. Schattschneider (1960) called the 'mobilization of bias' and Clarence Stone (1980) labelled 'systemic power'. Each national set of interlocking organizational structures tends to lead policy-makers into some courses of action and away from others; and each course of action tends to favor the interests of some social groups over others.[2]

Once again we should be clear that the bias does not derive from the organic need of a system to reproduce itself but much more contingently from the institutional structure that a society has assumed over time. If something like the 'negative' and 'positive' selection mechanisms described by Claus Offe (1984) do exist in capitalist states, their presence is the result of the historical development of particular institutional structures rather than of a functional imperative; and their operation is probably far less systematically directed towards the survival of capitalism than he postulates.

THE INTERACTION OF STATE AND SOCIETY

Given the longstanding continuities that we have observed in national patterns of economic policy and their organizational correlates, we can say that many of the most fundamental organizational features of state and society are not readily susceptible to change. Much of their political influence stems from resiliency in the face of the exertions of individual actors. However, it should be apparent to the reader of the preceding chapters that this is not an entirely static analysis. The economic strategies of Britain and France changed to some degree over the course of the post-war period. Moreover, these changes were accompanied by alterations in the nature of state–society relations.

In short, the dynamic component of the polity should also be described here. This is no contradiction in terms. While they exist, institutional structures exercise a profound impact on the action of those who operate within them, and such structures are not particularly open to dramatic change except in the critical conjunctures of a nation's history, often associated with war or prolonged recession, that call into question existing societal arrangements. Nevertheless, incremental structural change is a familiar feature of politics and also a component of this analysis.

Moreover, such change involves a complex dynamic between state and society. Each sphere acts on the other. On the one hand, the state itself is a product of cumulative social struggles. Those struggles influenced the development of democratic institutions, the balance of power between legislature and executive, and even the instruments for economic planning present in each state. On the other hand, the economic strategies of each state respond to the organization of society, but those strategies then have an impact of their own on societal organization and the relative balance of power between social groups or classes. The consequences of policy can gradually alter the societal organization of a nation, just as the shape of policy is in the first instance heavily influenced by that organization.

Only a few examples of the way in which the state is shaped by social conflict need be cited here. Barrington Moore (1966) has argued that both Britain and France owe their democratic institutions to a series of struggles that weakened the grip of the landed aristocracy on the state and opened the way for shifting coalitions of workers, capitalists and peasants to demand a share of political power (cf. Andersòn, 1966). Similarly, we have seen that the fate of economic planning in Britain and France during the period immediately after World War Two depended on the outcome of conflict between the spokesmen for labor and capital. In France, business organizations were unable to prevent the initial development of planning mechanisms partly because they had been discredited by association with the Vichy regime. However, business organizations remained powerful enough after the war, in Britain, to block implementation of the National Economic Development Act of 1947.

Similarly, the organization of capital and the working class has complex historical roots, linked to the economic trajectory of each nation; but the state also played an important role in their development. The weakness and persistent division of the French unions is connected to the harshness with which the French state repressed left-wing movements in 1848, 1870 and succeeding decades (cf. Vichniac, 1986; Bunel and Saglio, 1977; Shorter and Tilly, 1974; Adam and Reynaud, 1972). Similarly, the strength of the British union movement may be attributable to the relative tolerance with which the British state treated the unions at early points in the industrialization period, just as its peculiar defensiveness is related to attempts by the state to limit union operations later in the century (Geary, 1979; Cronin, 1980).

Following Gerschenkron (1962), we can link the configuration of capital in Britain and France to differing styles of state intervention, associated with the timing of economic development. Although both nations began to industrialize in the eighteenth century, the slower rate of French growth inspired state initiatives to accelerate industrial development, under Napoleon III, the Popular Front, and the post-war regime. Partly as a result, France acquired powerful investment banks, and French industry became more dependent on public institutions than the British. Simultaneously, however, the British state was developing an empire that reinforced the international orientation of the financial sector and the emphasis of British industry on colonial markets.

Some may think that these relations were then frozen over the succeeding century. However, the preceding chapters have suggested that the interactive dynamic between state and society continued after World War Two. They suggest that the nature of societal organization had an important impact on each state's choice of economic policies. And those policies, in turn, affected the organization and the distribution of power among social groups.

In France, for instance, economic planning entailed the development of an alliance between the state and advanced sectors of industry. By channelling resources to such sectors, the state virtually created its own interlocutors. Over time, the actions of this alliance diminished the power and prosperity of more traditional segments of French capital, and accomplished a kind of modernization from above that had costs for many other groups. At the same time, the virtual exclusion of the trade unions from the private side of planning tended to preserve the weakness and isolation of labor in France.

In Britain, the state's pursuit of Keynesian policies initially strengthened the labor movement by providing the kind of full employment conditions under which union bargaining power is greatest. The transmutation of Keynesianism into an intermittent tripartism, however, had mixed effects on the labor movement. It is difficult to find any evidence for Offe's (1985) contention that participation in such neo-corporatist arrangements gradually weakened the trade unions' ability to mobilize their base. If anything, it weakened the unions' capacity to discipline their base and intensified the militancy of the rank and file. However, the gradual politicization of industrial relations that accompanied tripartism generated a reaction against the unions amongst the electorate and contributed to the election of a government determined to break the power of the unions.

Therefore, the relationship between state and society, while crucial to the determination of economic policy, is not static. Many economic policies are designed to alter some dimensions of societal organization, and others have unintended consequences for both societal organization and the relative power of social groups.

NEO-CORPORATISM AND POLICY-MAKING

This account of state–society interaction in Britain and France raises disturbing questions about one of the central concepts developed to describe national patterns of economic policy-making: the concept of neo-corporatism. Since the pioneering work of Schmitter and Lehmbruch (1979, 1982), a vast literature has appeared on this topic (see Cawson and Ballard, 1984).[3] It draws our attention to the impact of societal organization on public policy. Hence, this book and the neo-corporatist literature share many themes. At the same time, however, this account of economic policy-making in Britain and France calls into question some of the fundamental distinctions implicit in neo-corporatist analyses.

Although it is replete with competing definitions, the literature tends to associate neo-corporatism with a particular pattern of policy formation, characterized by extensive bargaining between the state and hierarchically organized associations of functional interests, and the participation of those associations in the implementation of policy (cf. Cawson, 1985: ch. 1). The concept was originally inspired by an attempt to identify the distinctive style of policy-making in such nations as Sweden, Austria, Switzerland, Belgium and the Netherlands.

However, the case of economic policy-making in Britain and France suggests that it is much more difficult to draw rigid distinctions between neo-corporatist and non-corporatist policy systems than the literature implies. In particular, policy-making in both Britain and France has been characterized by a great deal of bargaining between peak associations of producers and the state, and these associations have often been drawn into policy implementation. British tripartism was nothing if not an attempt to persuade the trade unions to implement an incomes policy in exchange for other policy concessions; and French planning pulled the Patronat and many sectoral business associations into the formulation and implementation of industrial strategy. Yet most of the literature sees Britain and France as non-corporatist.[4]

In order to exclude Britain and France from neo-corporatist categories, one has to insist on a very strict interpretation of its definition, but there is plenty of evidence that even the most 'neo-corporatist' nations like Sweden and Austria do not fit a strict definition of the ideal-type. Neither have entirely monopolistic or fully centralized interest associations and neo-corporatist bargains have been known to break down there, as in Britain and France (cf. Neibergs, 1983; Esping-Andersen, 1985).

One might react to this finding by rejecting the concept of neo-corporatism itself. More fruitfully, however, we can look for variations in neo-corporatism. Katzenstein (1985) has already gone some distance in this direction. He distinguishes between two kinds of democratic corporatism: social corporatism, marked by centralized and concentrated labor organization and decentralized business associations, and liberal corporatism, characterized by centralized business organization and a more decentralized labor movement. Each results in a different strategy for industrial adjustment. We have seen analogous developments in the two 'non-corporatist' cases studied here. The divided nature of capital and the presence of a relatively concentrated labor movement in Britain tended to press that nation into a particular pattern of policy, just as the converse was instrumental to a different pattern of policy in France.

If some, but not all, elements normally associated with neo-corporatism are present in Britain and France, we may need a finer set of categories to describe the phenomenon. Neo-corporatism might be seen as a multi-dimensional variable, whose dimensions are continuous rather than dichotomous. In disaggregated form, the bargaining process associated with neo-corporatism might be characterized according to: its degree of centralization (does the state bargain primarily with peak associations or lower-level entities, such as firms or individual unions?); its frequency (how continuous or intermittent is such bargaining?); its inclusiveness (does the state bargain with labor and/or capital?); and the role of the state within it (to what degree is the state a co-equal rather than the most forceful of the participants?).

Similarly, we might characterize the nature of the bargains that are struck according to their scope (what range of issues do they cover?) and their durability (how long do the bargains generally last?). In table 10.1 Britain, France and an ideal-type of neo-corporatist nation are described according to these dimensions; and it should be possible to place other nations on the same kind of chart, perhaps adding to our understanding of variation within the neo-corporatist model.

Table 10.1   The dimensions of neo-corporatism

	Britain	*France*	*Ideal-type*
Bargaining process			
Degree of centralization	high	moderate	high
Frequency of bargaining	episodic	intermittent	continuous
Inclusiveness	mainly labor	mainly capital	both
Role of the state	co-equal	director	co-equal
Nature of bargains			
Scope	moderate (incomes, industrial relations, economic policy)	moderate (industrial, industrial relations, social policy)	
Durability	low	high	high

This exercise reminds us that the kind of bargaining associated with neo-corporatism is present to some degree in all highly industrialized democracies. As Samuel Beer (1969) pointed out some years ago, many of the interventionist economic policies of the modern state can be implemented only with the active cooperation of producer groups.

Indeed, most states have actually encouraged the organization of producers for this purpose. However, it also confirms one of the fundamental insights of the neo-corporatist literature: that the nature and durability of the bargains struck will be limited by the nature of societal organization in the industrial arena. We simply need to extend the analysis of societal organization that the neo-corporatist literature has begun.[5]

THE CONSTRAINTS OF THE POLITICAL SYSTEM

A state–society framework of the sort adopted here has the virtue of redirecting our attention to several factors whose effect on policy has often been underrated: the administrative configuration of the state and the nature of societal organization. However, many analysts of state and society stop here. They posit a dualism between the two spheres that ignores the role of the political system in the construction of policy. The study of political parties has not been fashionable of late; and this analysis suggests that parties do not deserve the principal role accorded them in some group models of political explanation. However, the effect of the political system on economic policy cannot be ignored.

Accordingly, even a state–society model of the polity should leave room for the political system, understood as the complex of political organizations that compete for office or the right to represent the views of social groups and the rules under which they operate. We can think of the political system as an arena, close to but slightly separate from the state, in which a constellation of political organizations compete for electoral support. Like the state, each political system has distinctive organizational features. Each country has a particular set of political parties of varying character, operating within the context of national electoral laws and customary political practices (see Sartori, 1979). Perhaps this organizational space is more subject to change than others; but most national political systems have evolved relatively slowly (see Lipset and Rokkan, 1967; Daalder and Mair, 1984).

The configuration of a political system is important because it is the principal avenue through which the electorate can influence the direction of economic policy. The nature of electoral competition renders the government more or less responsive to certain economic demands. Moreover, the expressive capacities of a nation's electorate will be limited by the nature of the party organizations already established for this purpose. Eventually, the existing organizations will respond to grassroots pressure or new parties will form and acquire influence in response to evolving political identities, but this can be a slow process (cf. Pizzorno, 1978; Sabel, 1981). It takes some time for alternative leadership to find organizational outlets. In the meantime, national political parties present the populace with a limited set of 'ideological packages' from which they must choose in order to express their views in the political arena.[6]

Parties also respond to changing conditions with varying degrees of flexibility. Like all organizations, they become attached to a particular ideology because ideology is central to organizational life. Ideology provides a political organization with an identity over time, tying present activities to past ideals. It links leaders to followers, functioning as a mechanism of accountability to ensure individuals at different levels within an organizational hierarchy that they speak with one voice. And ideological appeals are used to bind individuals to organizations, despite the temptation to free-ride, by tapping their emotions or conscience (Olson, 1971). Therefore, the historically developed ideology of an organization will lead it to speak with a particular tone for groups whose interests another organization might present entirely differently. And even many reforming politicians, like officials, will tend to build their programs on ideas and policies with which they are already familiar.

As a result, there is often a certain stasis to the economic policies pursued in one nation, even by different parties. For over 30 years the British electorate was faced with a choice between two parties, both of which advocated a Keynesian approach to economic management. The convergence of opinion was attributable partly to the peculiar structural conditions of the British economy and partly to the power and persistence of certain ideas within the British party system. However, one effect of the latter was to limit the options facing the British electorate in a particular way.

Similarly, the inertial qualities of the existing party system can limit the possibilities for new electoral coalitions to form. Successive attempts by Joseph Chamberlain and others to forge a British coalition around protectionism and a more active industrial policy were stymied, in part, by existing party alignments founded on cross-cutting issues, like Ireland and Empire. We have also seen how the organizationally entrenched position of the French Communist Party divided the left side of the French party spectrum for most of the post-war period, in such a way as to limit the left's chances of electing and forming a coalition government until 1981.

In a more general sense, the electoral arena can also constrain a government's range of action somewhat independently of the party system. Successive Labour Governments backed away from nationalization partly because support for it waned within the British electorate; and even the austerity-minded regime of Raymond Barre postponed any serious deflationary measures until after the French legislative elections of 1978. In these respects, public choice analyses of the political business cycle have some validity (see chapter 1): the need to secure re-election acts as a broad constraint on government action. As a result, the governments of Britain and France sit in a position that can be somewhat uneasy. They are engaged in coalition-building in two arenas. On the one hand, a government is often called upon to construct coalitions with producer groups in order to implement its economic policies. On the other hand, it needs to maintain an electoral coalition in order to stay in office. However, the bases around which these two kinds of coalitions can be built are not always the same, and contradictions may arise between the two tasks (cf. Beer, 1969). As we have seen, the alliance that the French state constructed with big business in the late 1960s, through planning, began to have adverse effects on its political popularity and the public legitimacy accorded its economic policies. Similarly, the intensive negotiations between many British governments and the trade unions in the 1970s eventually began to erode their electoral popularity.

INNOVATION AND THE POLITICAL SYSTEM

A discussion of the political system is also useful for reminding us that political action is not only a matter of constraint. There is a dynamic element to state–society relations; and from time to time a measure of innovation in economic policy-making breaks through some of the conventional constraints. At such moments the political system is also revealed as one of the principal sources of innovation in economic policy.

Political parties, in particular, have played a crucial role in the introduction of new economic policies. In one respect that is not surprising: contending political parties have an incentive to search for new solutions to old policy problems. The ability to offer such solutions is an important source of electoral appeal; and, as we have seen, the leaders of Britain and France were often mindful of the need to build coalitions within the electorate. Many have not been reluctant to experiment with new policies or tailor existing policies to this purpose. Margaret Thatcher's privatization program, for instance, was partly designed to create a nation of share-holders and home-owners, who might be inclined to vote Conservative; and the redistributive Keynesianism of François Mitterrand's first year in office was partly an attempt to find a policy with broad appeal for all sections of the French working class.

Both the importance and limits of such experimentation can be seen in the many U-turns that French, and especially British, governments took over the past 20 years. Although these sudden changes in the direction of policy, away from a government's avowed intentions on taking office, have been the object of ridicule, they are highly revealing. As Richard Rose (1984) has pointed out, they reflect the importance of longstanding constraints on any attempt at policy innovation; and this analysis has taken some pains to identify those sources of constraint. Nothing reminds us of the impact of state and societal organization on policy more than the sight of a new government's attempts at innovation crashing against such barriers. On the other hand, those very attempts also tell us something important about the political system: it may be the single most important source of policy innovation.

This is a controversial point. An influential line of theorizing suggests that the bureaucracy is the principal source of policy innovation (Heclo, 1974; Sacks, 1980). In this view, powerful public servants, like William Beveridge and Ernst Wigforss, play a much greater role than party politicians in securing the acceptance of new directions in policy. If there is policy field where this theory should apply, it is that of economic policy. Here is a field dominated by experts; the formulation process is a technically complex one, and the correct choice of policy often turns on highly specialized sorts of knowledge. It is precisely the kind of policy area in which civil servants should be most influential.

However, the cases examined in this volume suggest that innovations in economic policy owe as much, if not more, to politicians than to officials. If Keynes played a crucial role in the development of the system of economic management that bears his name, full acceptance of his ideas depended heavily on the advantages that politicians saw in them for effecting a class compromise as well as managing the economy. Thirty years later, it was a set of Conservative political leaders, rather than economists, who turned the British state away from Keynesianism to monetarist economic policies. At the time they did so, most official British economists were still personally opposed to the move. In France, Jean Monnet designed the institutions of the French planning process, but it was Charles de Gaulle who commissioned them and later made planning the centerpiece of economic policy under the Fifth Republic.

The innovative role of political parties was equally evident in Mitterrand's 1981 experiment with redistributive Keynesianism. Such a policy would have been less likely if Keynes had never lived; in that respect, of course, experts do play a role in the policy process. However, the Socialist Government bore responsibility for the adoption of Keynesian policies of 1981 in more than a formal sense. Expert economists were seriously divided on the appropriate course of action; and, as we have seen, it was the combination of economic promise and political advantage that rendered redistributive Keynesianism such an attractive alternative to the Government. Similarly, the nationalization program of the Mitterrand Government was a quintessentially political act, melding longstanding party policy with careful bargaining among the Government's coalition partners. Although the attempts of political parties to initiate radical departures in policy have often failed, they have been an important source of innovation in economic policymaking.

As in a complex tort case, it is difficult to apportion responsibility for innovations in economic policy precisely. Initially, of course, new systems of macroeconomic management are usually devised by economists, as one of Keynes' most famous phrases suggests.[7] But this is an instance in which we must distinguish between invention and dissemination. Just as the invention of new machines was not as important to the industrial revolution as their dissemination, so the crucial step here is the one which popularizes a new economic idea and translates it into policy. Politicians not only exercise de jure control over that step; in many cases they take a much more active role in policy development.

This role has important implications for the policy dynamic, because politicians respond to a somewhat different set of incentives than civil servants. In particular, they are much more mindful of the potential political consequences of policy for public authority and their own capacity to build social coalitions within the electoral arena. To the extent that politicians play a greater role in the process, new policies are likely to be selected as much for their social implications as for their technical proficiency.

These cases suggest that we might want to revise our understanding of how social learning takes place within the policy process. Social learning should not be seen as the preserve of the bureaucracy. It involves both officials and politicians. And if officials tend to learn from the technical success and failures of past policies, politicians are more concerned with the implications of policies for the broader moral visions of equity and efficiency that they present to the electorate. In that respect, two kinds of social learning take place within the polity: administrative learning, driven by a concern to find technical solutions to policy problems; and political learning, characterized by the evolution of collective moral visions.[8]

After all, not all politics is bureaucratic politics. In the wider arena, politics is intimately bound up with governance. And governance is a fundamentally normative matter. One of its principal tasks is to convince the citizenry to give a measure of allegiance to the regime that they would not give to any other social institution – an allegiance that is sustained even when the citizen prefers a losing party or is asked to fight and die for his country.[9] In times of prosperity and distress, politics is also about social justice. Either explicitly or implicitly, politicians are winning the support of the electorate for a particular distribution of material resources. Hence, economic policy is always a normative matter; and it is not surprising to find that many politicians are especially concerned with the moral visions that underlie the more prosaic details of policy-making.

The rise of monetarism in Britain provides a nice example of the role of moral vision in economic innovation. In 1979, monetarism was forced on the official economic machine by Conservative politicians. And the appeal that monetarism had for those politicians did not turn primarily on its technical superiority to Keynesianism for dealing with the economic problems at hand. Because the policy prescriptions of the two theories were based on incommensurable economic models, the technical superiority of monetarism could not be established in a scientific manner. Monetarism appealed to many Conservative politicians because it rationalized a social vision that had long been in their minds (Hall, 1982b).

Moreover, monetarism was an economic ideology with the political potential to forge a new social coalition.[10] It spoke to growing discontent among the electorate with inflation and the political influence of the trade unions. Sir Keith Joseph and Margaret Thatcher were able to present the doctrine as a set of policies capable of disciplining those who sought extravagant wage settlements without according undue influence to the trade unions. It seemed to provide a path toward economic growth without the inflation and increasing state intervention that Keynesianism had entailed. In short, monetarism triumphed in Britain primarily because of its attractions as political ideology rather than because of its persuasiveness as economic science.

Once the Conservative Government took office, however, monetarist ideas continued to play an important role in policy innovation. As we have seen, the 1979 Conservative Government was able to resist many of the conventional pressures to revise its innovative economic policies precisely because it possessed a coherent economic philosophy. The monetarist vision provided a rationale for dismissing the pleas of businessmen, civil servants and trade unionists for economic mercy. The independence that these ideas conferred on the Government could not have lasted for ever. As high levels of unemployment and relatively low rates of economic growth continued, the promise of monetarism to restore prosperity after a period of sacrifice began to wear thin. In the political world, however, even brief periods of independence from political pressure and institutional constraint are valuable.

INSTITUTIONS, INTERESTS AND IDEAS

These considerations force us to confront the role of ideas in politics and their relationship to the organizational analysis that is developed here. We have seen two respects in which patterns of societal organization have an impact on the thinking of the relevant social actors. On the one hand, organizations can structure the very logic associated with rational action from a particular social position; and on the other hand, organizations are indispensable to the diffusion of ideologies among multiple social actors.

The point of much of the analysis in preceding chapters has been to show that organizational relations can alter the basic logic of political rationality for many actors, by altering their relationship to other actors. Not only does organization alter the power of a social group, it can also affect the interpretation they put on their own interests, and thus the direction of their influence. In this case, the ideas or perceptions of the relevant actors are not an exogenous variable but a component of their rational action as it is situationally determined.

To take one example, a British railway worker stands in a different position relative to other workers and the state than his German counterpart. The British worker is likely to be a member of a craft union with only loose organizational ties to workers in other industries or even in other crafts within his own industry. The German worker will belong to a union that unites not only railworkers, but most other transport workers as well. While these two individuals may have rather similar interests, by virtue of holding the same job in the same sector of a capitalist economy, the course of action that it is most rational for the one to take in pursuit of his interests may not be the most rational for the other, because of differences in their organizational position.

To be assured of a real wage increase in the face of inflation, for instance, the German railworker might be best advised to adhere to a moderate wage settlement, since he can be fairly certain that the rest of the organized workforce will do so as well and thus successfully limit the rate of inflation. Rebellion would have costs, in terms of union sanctions, that outweigh the benefits likely to accrue. The British worker, by contrast, faces far fewer organizational assurances that a moderate wage settlement will stick across the economy. It might be more rational for him to propose that his union employ its craft-based industrial leverage to secure a wage settlement above the national norms, despite its inflationary consequences. Given the loose structure of the British union movement, other unionists are likely to take similar action whose inflationary effect will leave the railworker even farther behind if he exercises moderation (see Lange, 1985).

Game theory teaches us that the most rational strategy for any player will vary with the likely response of other players (Hardin, 1982; Axelrod, 1983). Since organizational context can alter the probabilities associated with each value in the range of likely responses of other actors, as well as the players' perceptions of those probabilities, it can alter the calculus of an actor, quite apart from its impact on his political ideas more generally. Organization can be part of the definition of interest itself.

Similarly, the attitudes of the banks towards economic policies with important consequences for industry are likely to be affected by the organizational relationship of the banks to industry. As we have seen, in nations such as France and Germany where financial institutions usually have a direct stake in the profits and long-term growth of industry, as opposed simply to their current creditworthiness, those institutions are more likely to have favorable attitudes towards policies of expansion and devaluation that speak to the needs of industry. One could say that this is a simple matter of interest, but it is really a matter of the perception of interest – since the British banks might also have benefited in the long run from policies more favorable to industry – and perception of interest seems to be deeply affected by organizational position.

It should be apparent, however, that this does not exhaust the range of ideas that play a role in politics. Some attitudes have a more exogenous character in the sense that they derive from fundamental beliefs about politics or economics whose origins are not to be found in any immediate institutional situation. We might call these 'ideologies' to refer to any well-developed network of ideas that prescribes a course of economic or political action. In this sense, ideology comprehends not only various political points of view, which specify what sorts of public activities are possible and desirable, but also economic theories of the sort associated with monetarism or Keynesianism, which specify what economic consequences will follow from the pursuit of particular policies. Ideologies of this sort can be held by individuals in a wide variety of social positions and their presence cannot be associated determinatively with any given institutional location. Thus, the obvious role of such political ideas places a natural limit on the extent to which the attitudes of political actors can be entirely attributed to their organizational position in society or the state.

At the same time, however, the power of ideology is related to modes of organization. Ideas may not be created by organization, but they are certainly disseminated by them. And, while congruence between ideas and interests will not always explain why particular ideas are held, it can go a long way toward explaining the appeal of certain ideas to various social groups. Thus, many French planners espoused ideals of economic growth primarily because they were planners, even if others became planners because they began with such ideals. And monetarist theories of the economy, dictating high exchange rates and high interest rates, gained a popularity in the City that they never enjoyed among British industrialists. In these instances, key groups were not only gripped by particular ideologies; they also gripped them to use as weapons against those with divergent interests.

The effects of organizational structure on the diffusion of ideas are evident, for instance, in the case of the British and French states. Heclo and Wildavsky (1979) found that the British civil service nurtured a 'village culture'. As long as the upper echelons of the Treasury were still staffed by senior civil servants accustomed by their experience to concentrating on the control of public expenditure, and its most central divisions remained responsible for this task, the Treasury was likely to give priority to expenditure control over industrial concerns. Although organizational reforms that brought the National Economy Group to more prominence within the institution raised the position of macroeconomic issues on the Treasury agenda in the early 1960s, other reforms, which turned a public spending review (PESC) into the centerpiece of annual budgetary policy, also tended to perpetuate the Treasury's preoccupation with public expenditure control.

Similarly, the most significant contribution of the French Planning Commission lay not in the manipulation of any economic aggregate, but in its effect on the bureaucratic culture of the state. It was responsible for *"la puissance d'une idée en marche"*, as one Planning Commissioner put it, which persuaded French policy-makers to think strategically about the direction of industry (Massé, 1965). Along with the Ecole National d'Administration, whose socialization of virtually all senior civil servants worked in broadly similar directions, the Planning Commission succeeded in generating and reproducing a particular approach to policy-making. French civil servants felt responsible for the direction of industry, generally capable of undertaking it, and entitled to do so, when their British counterparts were far more hesitant.

It is not convincing to explain the prevalence of these attitudes among French officials primarily by reference to a longstanding interventionist tradition in France, as some cultural analyses have tried to do. Although antecedents for these attitudes can be found in the actions of Colbert and others, plenty of twentieth-century precedents can also be found for public inaction (see Hoffmann, 1963). The operation of a specific set of institutions was central to the perpetuation of one approach rather than the other (see Armstrong, 1973).

Today French policy-makers of all political persuasions are more likely to approve of a dirigiste style of intervention than their British counterparts. And, as a result of years of intense collaboration through the mechanisms of planning, even French businessmen have been socialized into such views. When a sample of French employers was asked 'who should be the decision-makers for very large investments', two-thirds chose the state, either alone or in conjunction with corporate management, and only one-third chose the market or corporate management alone (*Le Nouvel Economiste*, 22 March 1985). The presence of such attitudes can legitimately be seen as a cultural trait of

French society today; but that describes the finding rather than explaining it. For the explanation, we must turn to the nature of French institutions outlined above.

The rise of monetarism in Britain further confirms the point that ideas acquire force when they find organizational means of expression. Most ideas have some power on their own: a number of people will be persuaded by them. But the social power of any set of ideas is magnified when those ideas are taken up by a powerful political organization, integrated with other ideological appeals, and widely disseminated. The likelihood of this happening may depend partly on the congruence between a new set of economic ideas and other facets of the longstanding ideology of an organization. We have already seen such congruence between one strain of Conservative Party thinking in Britain and the implications of monetarist economics.

The point of this discussion is not to reduce ideas to artefacts of social structure. As we have already seen, this cannot be done. It is to suggest, however, that there is room within an organizational analysis for the notion that ideas play a role in politics – indeed, one that reaffirms rather than contradicts the importance of organizational setting for the determination of policy.

RETROSPECT AND PROSPECT

This book has joined an account of economic policy-making in Britain and France with an argument for an institutional or organizational approach to political economy. As we look back over the policy experience of these two nations, we can ask what lessons might emerge about the challenges that they currently face and their prospects for meeting them.

In the first instance, we find that many of the conventional dichotomies used to analyse the political economy need reappraisal. Rigid distinctions between politics and economics, state and market, or domestic and international economic spheres no longer stand up to close scrutiny. As analytic distinctions such concepts have some value and they have been used in the preceding discussion, but the broad effect of an institutional analysis is to underline the degree to which each of the social spheres associated with these concepts interpenetrates others and to identify the commonalities of action and motivation that we find in each sphere.

In these nations, for instance, economic problems are also always political problems. Contemporary economic difficulties and the attempts to find solutions to them cannot be analysed in isolation from associated political dilemmas. To be pursued effectively, any policy must be politically, as well as economically, viable. Indeed many of the most intractable difficulties facing French and British policy-makers in recent years have been as much political as economic.

During the 1970s, both Britain and France witnessed a growing divorce of power from responsibility in the economic sphere. During the high tide of Keynesianism and economic planning, the governments of both nations took on increasing responsibility for the direction and progress of the economy. Whether they were actually able to exercise much influence over the rate of economic growth is a moot point; but the state was seen to have a degree of control commensurate with the growing extensiveness of its intervention. In the 1970s, officials of both states found that their influence over the direction of the economy was now severely limited. Increasing economic openness and global stagnation rendered national economic strategies less effective. But the perceptions of the electorate were slower to change. Whomever they put into office seemed incompetent at the most urgent of economic tasks. As a result, the citizens of both nations have become increasingly disillusioned with their governments, regardless of political perspective. In this way economic recession contributed to an erosion of political authority.

During the same period, inter-group conflict intensified in both nations. Competition for a share of national resources grew as the increment of new resources available each year shrank. Moreover, the conventional techniques of each state for managing economic conflict also broke down under the strain. French planning and British tripartism were techniques for economic consensus-building based on a kind of hegemonic illusion that, through consultation, policy paths of benefit to all social groups could be found. But, over time, both planning and tripartism had unintended consequences. They broadened the number of issues on the public agenda, sharpened the public perception of interest group conflict over economic resources, and rendered the alliances that governments entered into more transparent. As a result, both gradually deprived each state of the ability to claim that its policies spoke to an amorphous public interest, rather than to the interests of particular groups. The state has been forced to find other mechanisms for managing economic conflict.

Finally, both states have also had to find new ways to reconcile their citizenry to short-term sacrifice in the interest of longer-term benefits. This is not a new problem. In his last speech to the House of Commons, Aneurin Bevan described "the central problem falling upon representative government in the Western world as how to persuade the people to forgo immediate satisfactions in order to build up the economic resources of the country . . ." (Wilson, 1971: 19). Whether it is called 'austerity' or 'rigeur', the imposition of economic sacrifice has been a central feature of economic policy in Britain and France for over 10 years now.

Both economic planning and tripartite negotiations might once have been viable instruments for this task. French planning was a deliberate attempt to render the concerns of the future relevant to the politics of today. But the long-term rewards which it promised soon seemed too remote to command the attention of the day. Similarly, British tripartism was an attempt to apportion economic sacrifice through a bargaining process that directed the attention of the participants away from short-term conflicts toward long-term, common interests. However, it collapsed under challenges from those who were left out of the bargains and those who believed it undermined the traditional sovereignty of the British state.

In response, the governments of both nations have turned back towards greater reliance on the market for the management of economic resources and the apportioning of economic sacrifice. In Britain, a Conservative government entered office with this in mind. In France, even a Socialist government followed Raymond Barre's moves in this direction. At a time when public officials have come to doubt their own ability to find a suitable industrial strategy, they have decided to reinforce market signals in the hope that those indicators will lead firms toward greater international competitiveness. As social conflict intensifies, they also hope that market mechanisms will take the pressure off the state to manage economic triage.

However, the institutional analysis presented here suggests that some aspects of the distinction between state-led economic direction and a market strategy are also illusory. Markets are themselves institutions whose effectiveness varies with their configuration, just as the effectiveness of public policy does. Moreover, many markets depend on an ancillary network of social institutions, often generated and sustained by state action, in order to function effectively. Just as the labor market is affected by the nature of national educational institutions and export markets often depend on international economic policy, so capital markets can be strongly affected by taxing and spending policies. Hence the withdrawal of the state can never be complete, and precipitate attempts to accomplish it may impair national markets more than they help them. If markets tend to move toward a state of equilibrium, political initiatives may well determine whether that equilibrium is at high or low levels of productivity and output.

Moreover, there is some evidence that market strategies may intensify the level of social conflict with which any government will ultimately have to deal. Many contemporary states have taken advantage of the kind of class decomposition that seems to be occurring in most nations to impose austerity with less regard for working class unrest than they might have shown 20 or 50 years ago (cf. Hobsbawm et al., 1981; Goldthorpe, 1985). Economic sacrifice as apportioned by the market has fallen predominantly on those who lack the market power to protect themselves – young school-leavers, immigrants, the unskilled, and older workers in declining sectors – and many governments have calculated, perhaps correctly, that an underclass of this sort cannot pose a serious challenge to social order or their own electoral fortunes. Nevertheless, the political dimensions of a market strategy remain uncertain in view of potential social unrest.

Partly for these reasons, the ultimate success of the Thatcher and Mitterrand experiments is still subject to some doubt. Both experiments indicate that the political system remains an avenue for innovation in economic policy. However, each has encountered some obstacles implicit in the longstanding organization of state, society and international system. Serious economic experimentation entails long-term institutional renovation whose design is difficult and whose effects may take some time to emerge.

Institutional analysis of the polity and economy underlines the obstacles that stand in the way of reform. But it also reminds us that economic performance is not entirely a matter of fate or the product of iron laws in economics. The institutions that affect the performance of the economy and distribute power in society are ultimately artefacts of political action. They were constructed out of political struggles, and from time to time, we may recast them.

Notes

PREFACE

1. The words are those of Sir Alec Douglas-Home quoted in Keegan and Pennant-Rae (1979: 60).

CHAPTER ONE: ECONOMIC POLICY AND THE PARADIGMS OF POLITICS

1. We can imagine 'hard' and 'soft' versions of functionalism. The soft version is primarily a mode of description utilized to identify the consequences that a phenomenon has for the broader polity. In this case, function simply refers to the anticipated or unanticipated consequences of the phenomenon for the operation of the political or economic system. It is in that sense that chapter six discusses the manifest and latent functions of planning. The object is to separate its real from rhetorical results. Here the prior existence of the institutions is determined not by their functions, but by a more complex and intrinsically historical process. The hard version of systems analysis reverses this formulation to assert that function specifies structure. Thus, it uses functionalism as a mode of explanation rather than description, and encounters the problems outlined above.
2. A supplementary model assumes that the ideological complexion of the government will alter the relative response to these two variables.
3. A certain level of inflation encouraged firms to expand by assuring them that prices for their products would continue to be buoyant. Since most French firms relied on debt rather than equity for capital investment, they were not unhappy to see the value of the francs they had to pay back decline; and a little inflation gave the planners greater leverage over the firms because they were using exemptions from price controls to secure their cooperation. It is not surprising that Giscard d'Estaing would say: "La planification, c'est l'inflation" (Lord, 1973: 132). The organization of the French tax system, which depended heavily on sales taxes, and the mone-

tary system, which made much use of quotas and subsidies on bank lending, also rendered the fiscal balance and interest rate changes less important indicators or instruments for economic management.

4. I owe this point to Robert Keohane.
5. For reviews of this literature see Held and Krieger (1983), Gold et al. (1975) and Carnoy (1984).
6. The distinction between 'normal politics' and radical institutional change is analogous to that drawn between normal science and scientific revolutions by Thomas Kuhn (1969).
7. This formulation can be seen as another way of making Poulantzas's critical point – that the actions of the state should be understood largely as the product of a set of objective relations rather than the result of more contingent social interactions – while avoiding the excessive functionalism of Poulantzas's own position. See Miliband and Poulantzas (1974).

CHAPTER TWO: MARKETS AND THE STATE IN BRITISH ECONOMIC DECLINE

1. As Aldcroft (1967) points out, of course, these figures obscure the fact that British performance improved somewhat in both absolute and comparative terms during the 1930s.
2. It should be noted that there are significant differences among the cultural theories that this discussion does not treat. In particular, several neo-Marxist analyses, such as those of Anderson (1966) and Nairn (1977) go to some lengths to ground their description of current British culture in a structural account of the historic class struggles that brought the nation to this point. By contrast, others make less of an attempt to explain these cultural traits other than by reference to contemporary accounts of their incidence.
3. On this point I have been greatly influenced by the work of Elbaum and Lazonick (1986) and the analyses of the French 'regulation' school (Boyer and Mistral, 1983; Lipietz, 1984). See also Williams et al. (1983), who move somewhat in this direction.
4. Throughout the text, the term billion is used to refer to 1000 million.

CHAPTER THREE: PATTERNS OF BRITISH ECONOMIC POLICY

1. As we shall see, the relevant counter-case is that of France. There the long-term lending practices of the banks gave them considerable leverage over industry; and the detailed control that the Ministry of Finance exercised over the flows of funds in the financial sector through the subordinate Bank of France allowed it to orchestrate the investment strategies of entire industrial sectors long before President Mitterrand came to office. These institutions, rather than those of the Planning Commission, were the real key to the économie concertée.

CHAPTER FOUR: THE EVOLUTION OF KEYNESIANISM

1. Although there are substantial differences in our analyses, this aspect of my argument has been influenced by that of Frank Longstreth (1983).
2. Britain left the war with foreign reserves of only £250 million and overseas liabilities over fifteen times that, as well as a prospective balance of payments deficit of £1000 million over the next 3 years. The premature termination of the 'lend-lease' program, and America's insistence that Britain try to restore sterling to full convertibility shortly after the war, put further pressure on the reserves.
3. The impact of industrial relations on the Government's electoral popularity is a complex subject that deserves a fuller treatment than is possible here. However, it may be worth reporting some preliminary statistical results that bear on this subject. I constructed an equation to explain the Government's electoral popularity, as measured by Gallup data at quarterly intervals for the period 1959–79, of a sort conventionally used to estimate the impact of economic factors on electoral popularity. When a variable for the number of workers involved in work stoppages over the quarter was added, it proved statistically significant and improved the overall predictive power of the equation. The equation and relevant coefficients are:

$$Y = 6.61 - 2.18(U) - 5.47(I) + 5.64(R_t - R_{t-4}) -$$
$$(2.71) \ (1.08) \quad (2.56) \quad (2.81)$$

$$3.01(N) + LEV - 7.48(CYC) + e$$
$$(1.37) \quad\quad\quad (1.75)$$

In this case: U = the level of unemployment; I = percentage increase over a year earlier on the retail price index; R = personal disposable income at 1975 prices, seasonally adjusted; N = number of workers involved in work stoppages in progress during the quarter; LEV = a set of dummy variables, one for each Government in office during the period, designed to capture any Government-specific effects on the overall level of Government popularity over the period; CYC = a linear trend increasing by one unit over the term of each Government to capture the popularity effects associated with length of tenure in office; e = the usual error term; and Y = the difference between the percentage of voters indicating an intention to vote for the Government and the percentage indicating an intention to vote for the opposition parties, averaged from monthly surveys conducted for that quarter. The signs of all coefficients are in the expected direction. The total R-squared for the equation is 0.58 and the figures in parentheses beneath each coefficient are the standard errors.
4. The precise contribution of Keynesian policies to British economic performance in this period is, of course, a subject of contention. See Matthews (1968).

CHAPTER FIVE: THE CONSERVATIVE EXPERIMENT OF MARGARET THATCHER

1. When some intemperate remarks eliminated Joseph's chances for the leadership, Thatcher challenged Heath in his stead, and although disaffec-

tion with Heath played a more important role than ideology in Thatcher's successful campaign for the leadership, she came around to the same set of views as Joseph, using her position as leader to sell them to the Party. For a good account of the process see Keegan (1984: chs 2, 3). For other excellent accounts of the Thatcher government see Riddell (1983), Krieger (1986), Bruce-Gardyne (1984), Holmes (1985), Thompson (1986), and Buiter and Miller (1981, 1983).

2. It is often difficult to assess the degree to which economic performance should be attributed to the impact of public policy; and it is clear that governments should not always be held responsible for the course of the economy during their term in office. In this case, however, we are dealing with two periods when world economic activity was roughly congruent (OECD, 1977; Bruno and Sachs, 1985). That makes it somewhat more plausible to attribute differences in the British outcome to government policy. To control for factors beyond the influence of the state, however, we will consider Britain's performance relative to the OECD nations in the two periods (rather than her absolute performance) whenever possible.

3. The observation of one dismissed Minister, that "it does no harm to throw the occasional man overboard, but it does not do much good if you are steering full speed ahead for the rocks," is indicative of the strong feelings within the moderate wing of the Conservative Party which Thatcher has had to suppress (Gilmour, quoted in Keegan, 1984: 173).

4. The proportion of owner-occupied housing in Britain rose faster under the Thatcher Government than at any other period in post-war Britain. Crewe (1985) found that of those who had recently bought their council houses, 56 percent voted Conservative and only 18 percent Labour in the 1983 election; but this group might initially have included a disproportionate number of Conservatives.

5. The Government's response to riots in poor and predominantly black areas of Liverpool and London during 1985 is indicative. Although the rioters were demonstrating against police harassment in settings of widespread unemployment, the Government replied by reinforcing the police presence in these areas and intensifying the crackdown on drug dealing that provided the immediate stimulus for the London demonstrations. It rejected suggestions that unemployment or racism played a major role in the revolts in favor of an approach that labelled the unemployed black youths who were involved as simply criminals.

CHAPTER SIX: THE POLITICAL ROLE OF ECONOMIC PLANNING IN FRANCE

1. The Economic and Social Council, a body consisting of representatives from labor unions and trade associations as well as independent experts, was established after the war to provide advice to the government on the direction of the economy (see Hayward, 1966a). The above account approximates the Plan's procedures in its peak years of operation during the 1960s and early 1970s. In earlier years, the Plan did not produce a statement of options and it was considered only rarely by the Economic and Social Council or the National Assembly. Much more important in that period

were the sectoral discussions that took place in the Modernization Commissions, because the Plan concentrated resources on only a few sectors.
2. In this and succeeding chapters, I refer to the principal Ministry responsible for French macroeconomic policy as the Ministry of Finance; however, it should be noted that its name was changed to the Ministry of Economics and Finance in the 1970s. The division with most influence within the Ministry is the Trésor.

CHAPTER SEVEN: THE STATE AND THE EVOLUTION OF PLANNING

1. Together, these dimensions contribute to what has recently been described as the relative autonomy of the state (cf. Poulantzas, 1978; Miliband, 1977; Nordlinger, 1981). However, that term was originally intended to describe the independence of the state *vis-à-vis* capital. Etatism refers to a more general kind of independence and power relative to a broader range of social actors.

CHAPTER EIGHT: THE SOCIALIST EXPERIMENT OF FRANCOIS MITTERRAND

1. For other useful overviews of this period see: Hoffmann (1982), Beaud (1983), Belassa (1982), Simonnet (1982), Lauber (1983) and Kesselman (1983). More complete references for the data cited in this chapter can also be found in Hall (1985).
2. CIASI: Comité interministériel d'aménagement des structures industrielles; CODEFI: Comités départementaux d'examen des problèmes de financement des entreprises; CIRI: Comité interministeriel de restructuration industrielle; CORRI: Comités régionaux de restructuration industrielle; CODIS: Comité de développement des industries stratégiques; CIDISE: Comité interministériel pour le développement industriel et le soutien de l'emploi.
3. See the debate in *Le Monde* from 23 July 1983 initiated by Max Gallo's contention that the intellectuals had deserted the Government.

CHAPTER NINE: THE INSTITUTIONAL LOGIC OF COMPARATIVE POLITICAL ECONOMY

1. The addition of these two factors represents a refinement of the analysis initially proposed in Hall (1983b) where their importance was implied but not made so explicit.
2. Maier (1978) has examined the coalitions which lie behind inflation policy in these terms. Gourevitch uses a similar approach to explain tariff policy in

the late nineteenth century (1977a) and economic responses to the Great Depression (1984). And Esping-Anderson and Friedland (1982) suggest that changing economic coalitions underlie the contemporary economic crisis in Western Europe. The antecedents for this work are analyses which have stressed the impact of the evolving power of the working class on public policy (cf. Martin, 1975; Gough, 1975). The formulation of this approach has also been influenced by two recent works which pay particular attention to organizational factors but are otherwise very different. These are Samuel H. Beer's seminal reassessment of the operation of pluralism in Britain (1982), and the analysis of New Deal legislation in America prepared by Kenneth Finegold and Theda Skocpol (1983). Peter Gourevitch's thought-provoking work finally forced me to grapple with these issues, and the work of Peter Katzenstein (1978) and John Zysman (1980) was helpful in doing so.

3. The impact of different modes of organization on class struggle has been a central theme of the growing number of theorists writing about the appearance of 'corporatism' in the contemporary state (see Panitch, 1981). These theories share the concern of this chapter with the impact of variations in organization on the activities of the state, but the forms of organization which they consider most salient differ from those emphasized here.

4. This is not to say that the French never adopted slightly deflationary policies. The periods of tightening in 1952, 1958, 1963–64 and 1974 have been noted. But each of these pauses was less severe than the one that preceded it, and each was mitigated in important respects (Carré et al., 1972: 491). In the midst of the credit squeeze of 1963–65, for instance, the Conseil national du crédit sent a letter, drafted by the Planning Commissioner, to all the banks, declaring: "If the basic conditions for expansion are to be respected, our credit policy must be selective. In particular, as far as medium-term credit is concerned, there is a case for giving privileged treatment to the most dynamic firms serving foreign markets and to sectors especially hard-hit by foreign competition and for giving privileged treatment to the financing of projects for the reorganization of production" (cited in MacLennan et al., 1968: 165). The letter was accompanied by instructions that these recommendations were to be implemented. Similarly, President de Gaulle, possibly under the influence of Jacques Rueff, opted for deflation rather than devaluation in the 1963–65 period, but he followed it with highly expansionary policies, and his successor reverted to devaluation very soon after taking office.

5. Even Giscard d'Estaing, who had been one of France's more conservative economic managers, reflected this sense of priorities when he announced in 1969: "I consider that my mandate at the Ministry of Economy and Finance runs until 1976. My objective is, by that date, to bring France to an industrial level about equal to that of Germany and England. I would prefer to attain this objective without inflation. But if I have to choose, I would opt for industrial development and regard the fight against inflation as secondary" (cited in Suleiman, 1978: 262).

6. During 1950–72, 76 percent of gross capital formation in Britain was funded

from earnings, compared to 62 percent in Germany and 49 percent in France; and the average ratio of fixed interest capital to variable dividend capital of British firms in 1972 was only 0.55, compared with 0.74 in Germany and 0.92 in France (Thompson, 1977: 196; Lever and Edwards, 1980). In 1972, 73 percent of borrowing by non-financial enterprises in the UK was short term, compared with 49 percent of the borrowing in France and 30 percent in Germany (Thompson, 1977: 263; *The Economist*, 9 October 1976). This is significant because when a bank grants short-term credit it does not usually look closely at the details of a firm's performance or market strategy, as it might in connection with a long-term loan. Instead, it extends funds on more mechanical principles of credit-worthiness associated with balance-sheet figures such as the ratio of liquid assets to liabilities (cf. Thompson, 1977: 196).

7. Even Britain's principal attempt at planning, associated with the NEDC in the 1960s, was a tripartite exercise based on mutual persuasion. As Hagen and White (cited in Blank, 1978: 113) note, the British government approached producer groups "not as a representative of the public interest seeking the recommendations of groups with special interests before it exercised its authority, but as one association approaching two other associations to ask them what they would be willing to do."

CHAPTER TEN: THE ORGANIZATION OF STATE–SOCIETY RELATIONS

1. Of course, there are some limits to the systemic power of capital. As Block (1977) has pointed out, a government can act with more impunity during depressions, when investment is already so depressed that the threat to reduce it further is less weighty, or during international crises, when considerations of national security seem more important than levels of investment (cf. Krieger and Held, 1978). In addition, politicians occasionally pursue a policy that depresses investment because they do not perceive its consequences, as the British budget of April 1974 did. Alternatively, many nations developed schemes of regulation and taxation that ultimately depressed corporate profits enough to restrict investment; but they did so in increments over such a period of time that the full impact was not apparent to politicians. When it became clear, many of these programs were scaled back.

2. Whether we want to call the operation of such factors an exercise of power may be a matter of semantics. To the extent that organizational structures enforce an asymmetry in the capacity of actors to secure policies that are in their interests, they may instantiate what Steven Lukes (1970) has called a 'third dimension' of power.

3. A slightly different line of analysis, which associates neo-corporatism with increasing state control over the economy, was developed by Pahl and Winkler (1974).

4. Of course, Samuel Beer (1969) identified a pattern of 'quasi-corporatism'

in Britain some years ago. See also Middlemas (1979). And John Keeler (1985) has argued that we can find cases of corporatist relations in France (see also Wilson, 1983).

5. In the past 2 years, neo-corporatist analysts have themselves taken some steps in this direction. Some have extended their analysis to an investigation of 'meso-corporatism' at the sectoral level; others have begun to see 'private interest government' as a more widespread mode of social order juxtaposed to 'state-' and 'market-based' models (cf. Cawson, 1985; Streeck and Schmitter, 1986). Both lines of enquiry begin to see neo-corporatism as a broader social phenomenon appearing in many nations, including Britain and France.

6. In many elections, the viable choice facing the electorate is rather limited. For instance, those who were frustrated by the fact that neither major party in the American elections of 1968 opposed the Vietnam War went so far as to describe Hubert Humphrey, the Democratic candidate for President, as 'the used car you wouldn't buy from Richard Nixon', the Republican candidate.

7. Keynes' (1936: 383) words were: "The ideas of economists and political philosophers both when they are right and when they are wrong are more powerful than is commonly understood. Indeed, the world is ruled by little else. Practical men, who believe themselves to be quite exempt from any intellectual influences, are usually the slaves of some defunct economist. Madmen in authority, who hear voices in the air, are distilling their frenzy from some academic scribbler of a few years back."

8. My thoughts on this point owe a great deal to a conversation with Samuel Beer.

9. On this point, a conversation with Judith Shklar was very helpful.

10. Throughout this book, the term 'ideology' is used to refer to any coherent set of ideas that have a bearing on the motivation of the relevant social actors, rather than to particularly dogmatic or extremist beliefs (see Shils and Johnson, 1972: VI, 76).

Bibliography

Aaron, H. 1979: *Politics and the Professors*. Washington: Brookings.

Abernathy, W. and Hayes, R. 1980: "Managing our way to decline," *Harvard Business Review*, 80 (July–Aug.), 67–77.

Adam, N. 1980: "L'Etat, c'est nous," *Euromoney* (Oct.), 110–24.

Adam, J. and Reynaud, J. D. 1972: *La Négoçiation Collective en France*. Paris: Editions Ouvrieres.

Albert, M. 1979: "Sur la planification française." Lecture delivered at the Institut d'Etudes Politiques de Paris, 15 Nov.

Aldcroft, D. 1964: "The entrepreneur and the British economy 1870–1914," *Economic History Review*, 17, 113–34.

Aldcroft, D. 1967: "Economic growth in Britain in the interwar years: a reassessment," *Economic History Review*, 2nd series, 20(2), 11–26.

Aldcroft, D. 1968: *The Development of British Industry and Foreign Competition 1875–1914*. London: Allen and Unwin.

Aldcroft, D. 1970: *The Inter-War Economy: Britain 1919–1939*. London: Batsford.

Aldcroft, D. 1982: "Britain's economic decline 1870–1980." In G. Roderick and M. Stephens (eds), *The British Malaise*. London: Falmer Press, 31–64.

Aldcroft, D. and Richardson, H. W. 1970: *The British Economy 1870–1939*. London: Macmillan.

Allen, G. C. 1951: *British Industries and their Organization*. London: Macmillan.

Allen, G. C. 1976: *The British Disease*. London: Macmillan.

Allen, U. L. 1951: *Trade Unions and the Government*. London: Longman.

Allison, G. 1974: *The Essence of Decision*. Boston: Little Brown.

Alphandéry, C. et al. 1968: *Pour nationaliser l'état*. Paris: Seuil.

Alt, J. 1980: "Political business cycles in Britain." In P. Whiteley (ed.), *Models of Political Economy*. London: Sage, 155–76.

Alt, J. 1985: "It may be a good way to run an oil company, but . . .". Paper presented at the Center for European Studies, Harvard University.

Alt, J. and Chrystal, K. 1983: *Political Economics*. Berkeley: University of California Press.

Altvater, E. 1973: "Some problems of state intervention," *Kapitalistate*, 2, 76–83.

Amouyel, P. 1979: "L'Avenir énergetique de la France," *Project*, 844–55.

Anderson, D. D. 1980: "Germany: the uncertain stride of a reluctant giant." Harvard Business School Case. Boston: Intercollegiate Case Clearing House.

Anderson, P. 1966: "The origins of the present crisis." In P. Anderson and R. Blackburn (eds), *Towards Socialism*. Ithaca: Cornell University Press, 10–52.

Armstrong, J. 1973: *The European Administrative Elite*. Princeton: Princeton University Press.

Amott, T. and Krieger, J. 1981: "Thatcher and Reagan: state theory and the 'hyper-capitalist' regime," *New Political Science*, 8, 9–37.

Artis, M. J. 1965: *Foundations of British Monetary Policy*. Oxford: Blackwell.

Ashcroft, B. 1979: "The evaluation of regional economic policy: the case of the United Kingdom." *Studies in Economic Policy*, 12. Glasgow: Centre for the Study of Public Policy, University of Strathclyde.

Ashford, D. 1983: *Policy and Politics in France*. Philadelphia: Temple University Press.

Ashford, D. 1983: "Recasting the French état: progress of the loi Deferre," *West European Politics*, 6(3) (July), 263–70.

Assemblée Nationale 1976: "Projet de Loi portant approbation au VIIè Plan de développement économique et social." Second Session 1975–76 (June).

Atreize, 1971: *La planification française en pratique*. Paris: Les Editions Ouvrieres.

Auroux, J. 1982: *Les droits des travailleurs: rapport au Président de la Republique et au Premier Ministre*. Paris: Documentation Française.

Axelrod, R. 1983: *The Evolution of Cooperation*. New York: Basic Books.

Bacon, R. and Eltis, W. 1976: *Britain's Economic Problem: Too Few Producers?* London: Macmillan.

Bain, G. 1966: *International Differences in Industrial Structure*. New Haven: Yale University Press.

Ball, R. J. and Burns, T. 1976: "The inflationary mechanism in the U.K. economy," *American Economic Review*, 66 (Sept.), 467–84.

Ball, R. J. et al. 1977: The role of exchange rate changes in balance of payments adjustment – the United Kingdom case. *Economic Journal*, 89, 1–29.

Barbe, Daniel 1983: "Prêts participatifs: les limites du succès d'une innovation financière," *Chroniques d'actualité de la SEDEIS* (Apr.), 162–70.

Barker, T. 1980: "The economic consequences of monetarism: a Keynesian view of the British economy 1980–90," *Cambridge Journal of Economics*, 4, 319–36.

Barkin, S. 1977: "The total labour package: from wage bargain to social contract," *Journal of Economic Issues*, June, 339–51.

Batstone, E. 1982: *Working Order*. Oxford: Basil Blackwell.

Bauchard, P. 1963: *La mystique du Plan*. Paris: Arthaud.

Bauchet, P. 1964: *Economic Planning: The French Experience*. London: Heinemann.

Bealey, Frank 1970: *The Social and Political Thought of the British Labour Party*. London: Weidenfeld and Nicolson.

Beaud, M. 1983: *Le mirage de la croissance*. Paris: Syros.

Beckerman, W. 1972: *The Labour Government's Economic Record 1964–70*. London: Duckworth.

Beckerman, W. 1985: "How the battle against inflation was really won," *Lloyds Bank Review* (May), 1–12.

Beer, S. H. 1959: *Treasury Control*. London: Oxford University Press.

Beer, S. H. 1969: *Modern British Politics*. London: Faber.

Beer, S. H. 1974: *Patterns of Government*. New York: Random House.

Beer, S. H. 1982: *Britain Against Itself*. New York: Norton.

Behrens, R. 1980: *The Conservative Party from Heath to Thatcher*. Farnborough, Hants: Saxon House.

Belassa, B. 1982: "Une année de politique économique socialiste en France," *Commentaire*, 415–28.

Bellon, B. 1980: *Le pouvoir financier et l'industrie en France*. Paris: Editions de Seuil.

Bellon, B. and Chevalier, J. M. 1983: *L'Industrie en France*. Paris: Flammarion.

Benn, T. 1980: "Manifestos and Mandarins." In *Policy and Practice: The Experience of Government*. London: Royal Institute of Public Administration, 57–78.

Bentley, A. 1908: *The Process of Government*. New York: Harper and Row.

Berger, S. 1977: "D'une boutique à l'autre: changes in the organization of the traditional middle classes from the Fourth to the Fifth Republics." *Comparative Politics*, 10(1), 121–36.

Berger, S. 1980: "Reflections on industrial society: the survival of the traditional sectors in France and Italy." In S. Berger and M. Piore (eds), *Dualism and Discontinuity in Industrial Societies*. Cambridge: Cambridge University Press.

Berger, S. 1981: "Lame ducks and national champions: industrial policy in the Fifth Republic." In S. Hoffmann and W. Andrews (eds), *The Fifth Republic at Twenty*. Brockport, N.Y.: SUNY Press, 292–310.

Berger, S. 1984: "Protest Under the French Socialists," *Stato e Mercato*, 12(3) (Dec.), 363–84.

Berthelot, Y. and Tardy, G. 1978: *Le défi économique du tiers monde*. Paris: La Documentation Française.

von Beyme, K. 1980: *Challenge to Power: trade unions and industrial relations in capitalist countries*. London: Sage.

Birnbaum, P. 1977: *Les Sommets de l'état*. Paris: Seuil.

Birnbaum, P. 1978: *La Classe dirigeante française*. Paris: Presses Universitaires de France.

Bispham, J. and Boltho, A. 1982: "Demand management." In A. Boltho (ed.), *The European Economy: growth and crisis*, London: Oxford University Press, 289–328.

Black, S. 1981: "The use of monetary policy for internal and external balance in ten industrial countries." Paper presented to the American Political Science Association, New York.

Blackaby, F. T. (ed.) 1979: *British Economic Policy 1960–74*. London: Cambridge University Press.

Blank, S. 1973: *Government and Industry in Britain*. Farnsborough, Hants: Saxon House.

Blank, S. 1978: "Britain: the politics of foreign economic policy, the domestic economy and the problem of pluralistic stagnation." In P. Katzenstein (ed.), *Between Power and Plenty*. Madison, Wisc.: University of Wisconsin Press, 89–138.

Bloch-Lainé, F. 1976: *Profession: Fonctionnaire*. Paris: Editions du Seuil.

Block, F. 1977: "The ruling class does not rule: notes on the Marxist theory of the state," *Socialist Review*, 33 (May–June), 6–28.

Boddy, R. and Crotty, J. 1975: "Class conflict and macro policy: the political business cycle," *Review of Radical Political Economy*, 7.

Boissonnat, J. 1980a: "Le budget contre le Plan," *L'Expansion*, 5 Sept., 12.

Boissonnat, J. 1980b: "Le syndrome du plan," *L'Expansion*, 17 Oct., 8.

Boltho, A. 1982: *The European Economy: growth and crisis*. London: Oxford University Press.

Bonety, R. 1965: "Incitation et politique des revenus," *La Planification comme processus de décision*. Paris: Armand Colin.

Bonnaud, J. J. 1966: "Participation by workers and employers in planning in France," *International Labour Review* 93(4), 337–61.

Bonnaud, J. J. 1970: "Les instruments d'exécution du Plan utilisés par l'état a l'égard des entreprises," *Revue Economique* (July), 554–96.

Bonnaud, J. J. 1975: "Planning and industry in France." In J. Hayward and M. Watson (eds), *Planning, Politics and Public Policy*. Cambridge: Cambridge University Press, 93–110.

Born, K. 1983: *International Banking in the Nineteenth and Twentieth Centuries*. London: Berg.

Bourdieu, P. and Boltanski, L. 1976: "La production de l'idées dominantes," *Actes de la Recherche en Sciences Sociales* (June).

Boyer, R. and Mistral, J. 1983: *Accumulation, Inflation, Crises*. Paris: Presses Universitaires de France.

Braunthal, S. 1965: *The Federation of German Industry in Politics*. Ithaca, NY: Cornell University Press.

Breton, A. 1974: *The Economic Theory of Representative Government*. London: Macmillan.

Brittan, S. 1970: *Steering the Economy*. Harmondsworth: Penguin.

Broadway, F. 1969: *State Intervention in British Industry 1964–68*. London: Kaye and Ward.

Brown, C. J. F. and Stout, T. D. 1979: "Deindustrialization: a background paper." In F. Blackaby (ed.), *Deindustrialization*. London: Heinemann, 233–62.

Brown, G. 1970: *In My Way*. London: Macmillan.

Brown, W. 1981: *The Changing Contours of British Industrial Relations*. Oxford: Basil Blackwell.

Bruce-Gardyne, J. 1974: *Whatever Happened to the Quiet Revolution*. London: Charles Knight.

Bruce-Gardyne, J. 1984: *Mrs. Thatcher's First Administration*. London: Macmillan.

Bruce-Gardyne, J. and Lawson, N. 1976: *The Power-Game: An Examination of Decision-making in Government*. London: Macmillan.

Bruno, M. and Sachs, J. 1985: *The Economics of Worldwide Stagflation*. Cambridge: Harvard University Press.

Buchanan, J. 1967: *Public Finance in Democratic Process*. Chapel Hill: University of North Carolina Press.

Buchanan J. and Tullock, G. 1962: *The Calculus of Consent*. Ann Arbor: University of Michigan Press.

Budd, A. 1978: *The Politics of Economic Planning*. London: Fontana.

Buiter, W. H. and Miller, M. 1981: "The Thatcher experiment: the first two years," *Brookings Papers on Economic Activity*, 2: 315–79.

Buiter, W. H. and Miller, M. 1983: "Changing the rules: economic consequences of the Thatcher Regime," *Brookings Papers on Economic Activity*, 2: 305–79.

Bunel, J. and Saglio, J. 1979: *L'Action Patronale*. Paris: Presses Universitaires de France.

Butler, D. and Kavanaugh, D. 1975: *The British General Election of February 1974*. London: Macmillan.

Butler, D. and Kavanaugh, D. 1980: *The British General Election of 1979*. London: Macmillan.

Butler, D. and Stokes, D. 1971: *Political Change in Britain*. London: Penguin.

Butler, R. A. 1971: *The Art of the Possible*. London: Hamish Hamilton.

Buxton, N. K. 1975: "The role of the 'new' industries in Britain during the 1930s: a reinterpretation," *Business History Review*, 49: 205–22.

Cairncross, F. and McRae, H. 1974: *Capital City*. London: Methuen.

Calder, K. 1982: *Japanese Banking Policy*. Boston: mimeo.

Calleo, D. 1978: *The German Problem Reconsidered*. London: Cambridge University Press.

Cambridge Economic Policy Group 1978: *Economic Policy Review*, 49, 205–22.

Cameron, D. 1982: "On the limits of the public economy," *The Annals*, 459 (Jan.), 6–62.

Cameron, D. 1985: "Social democracy, corporatism, labour quiescence and the representation of interest in advanced capitalist societies." In John Goldthorpe (ed.), *Order and Conflict in Contemporary Capitalism*. London: Cambridge University Press, 143–78.

Capie, F. 1984: *Protection and Depression*. London: Allen and Unwin.

Carlson, K. M. and Spencer, R. W. 1975: "Crowding out and its critics," *Bulletin of the Federal Reserve Bank of St. Louis* (Dec.), 2–22.

Carnoy, M. 1984: *The State and Political Theory*. Princeton: Princeton University Press.

Caron, F. 1979: *An Economic History of Modern France*. New York: Columbia University Press.

Carré, J. J., Dubois, A and Malinvaud, E. 1972: *La croissance française*. Paris: Editions du Seuil.

Carrington, J. and Edwards, G. 1979: *Financing Industrial Investment*. London: Macmillan.

Carrington, J. and Edwards, G. 1981: *Reversing Economic Decline*. London: Macmillan.

Castle, B. 1984: *The Castle Diaries 1968–70*. London: Weidenfeld and Nicolson.

Castles, F. 1982: *The Impact of Parties*. Beverly Hills: Sage.

Caves, R. 1969: "Market organization, performance and public policy." In R. Caves et al. (eds), *Britain's Economic Prospects*, Washington: Brookings Institution, 279–323.

Caves, R. et al. 1968: *Britain's Economic Prospects*. Washington: Brookings Institution.

Caves, R. 1980: "Product differences among industries." In R. Caves and L. Krause (eds), *Britain's Economic Performance*. Washington: Brookings Institution, 135–98.

Caves, R. and Krause, L. (eds) 1980: *Britain's Economic Performance*. Washington: Brookings Institution.

Cawson, A. 1978: "Pluralism, corporatism, and the role of the state," *Government and Opposition*, 13(2), 178–98.

Cawson, A. 1985: *Organized Interests and the State*. Beverly Hills: Sage.

Cawson, A. and Ballard, J. 1984: "A bibliography of corporatism." European University Institute Working Paper.

Central Policy Review Staff 1975: *The Future of the British Car Industry*. London: HMSO.

Chambre Syndicale 1978: *La Vérité sur la Sidérurgie*. Paris: Chambre Syndicale.

Chandler, A. 1962: *Strategy and Structure*. Cambridge: MIT Press.

Chandler, A. 1974: *The Visible Hand*. Cambridge: Harvard University Press.

Chandler, A. and Daems, H. (eds) 1981: *Managerial Hierarchies*. Cambridge: Harvard University Press.

Channon, D. 1973: *The Strategy and Structure of British Enterprise*. Boston: Harvard Business School.

Chapman, R. 1968: *Decision Making*. London: Routledge and Kegan Paul.

Chrystal, K. A. 1979: *Controversies in British Macroeconomics*. Oxford: Philip Allan.

Clarke, Sir R. 1973: "Mintech in retrospect," *Omega*, 1, 25–38, 137–63.

Clarke, W. 1967: *The City in the World Economy*. London: Penguin.

Clegg, H. 1971: *How to Run an Incomes Policy*. London: Heinemann.

Clegg, H. 1979: *The Changing System of Industrial Relations in Great Britain*. Oxford: Blackwell.

Club Jean Moulin 1961: *L'Etat et le Citoyen*. Paris: Club Jean Moulin.

Coates, D. 1975: *The Labour Party and the Struggle for Socialism*. Cambridge: Cambridge University Press.

Coates, D. 1980: *Labour in Power*. London: Longman.

Cohen, S. 1977a: *Modern Capitalist Planning: the French model*, 2nd edition. Berkeley: University of California Press.

Cohen, S. 1977b: *Recent Developments in French Planning*. Washington: US Congress, Joint Economic Committee.

Cohen, S. 1982: "Informed bewilderment: French economic strategy and the crisis." In S. Cohen and P. Gourevitch (eds), *France in the Troubled World Economy*. London: Butterworths, 21–48.

Cohen, S. and Goldfinger, C. 1975: "From permacrisis to real crisis in French social security." In Leon Lindberg et al. (eds), *Stress and Contradiction in Modern Capitalism*. Lexington, Ma.: Heath, 57–98.

Cohen, S., Galbraith, J. and Zysman, J. 1982: "Rehabbing the labyrinth." In S. Cohen and P. Gourevitch (eds), *France in the Troubled World Economy*. London: Butterworths, 49–75.

Commissariat Général du Plan 1946: *Rapport Général sur le Premier Plan de Modernisation et d'Equipement*. Paris: Documentation Française.

Commissariat Général du Plan 1965: *Vè Plan de développement économique et social*. Paris: Documentation Française.

Commissariat Général du Plan 1971: *VIè Plan de développement économique et social 1971–75. Rapport General*. Paris: Documentation Française.

Commissariat Général du Plan 1975: *Dossier Quantitatif associé au VIIè Plan*. Paris: Documentation Française.

Commissariat Général du Plan 1979: *Rapport sur les Principales Options du VIIè Plan*. Paris: Documentation Française.

Commissariat Général du Plan 1982: *Plan Interimaire: stratégies pour deux ans 1982–83*. Paris: Documentation Française.

Commissariat Général du Plan 1983: *9è Plan de développment économique social et culturel 1984–88*. Paris: Documentation Française.

Commission de l'Industrie du VIIIè Plan 1980: *La situation financière des entreprises industrielles*. Paris: Documentation Française.

Congdon, T. 1978: *Monetarism: an essay in definition*. London: Centre for Policy Studies.

Conservative Party 1977: *The Right Approach to the Economy*. London: Conservative Party.

Cook, C. 1976: *A Short History of the Liberal Party*. New York: St Martin's Press.

Corden, W. M., Little, I. M. D. and Scott, M. F. G. 1978: "Import controls versus devaluation and Britain's economic prospects." Guest Paper 2. London: Trade Policy Research Centre.

Cotta, A. 1978: *La France et l'impératif mondiale*. Paris: Presses Universitaires de France.

Cottrell, P. 1980: *Industrial France 1830–1914*. London: Methuen.

Cowart, A. 1978: "The economic policies of European governments," *British Journal of Political Science*, 8, 285–311, 425–39.

Cox, A. 1982: "Corporatism as reductionism." *Government and Opposition*, 81, 78–90.

Crafts, N. F. R. and McCloskey, D. C. 1979: "Did Victorian Britain fail?" *Economic History Review*, 2nd series, 32: 533–7.

Crewe, I. 1980: "Why the Conservatives won." In H. Penniman (ed.), *Britain at the Polls 1979*. Washington: American Enterprise Institute, 263–306.

Crewe, I. 1985: "How to win a landslide without really trying." In A. Ranney (ed.), *Britain at the Polls 1983*. Washington: American Enterprise Institute, 155–96.

Cronin, J. 1980: *Industrial Conflict in Modern Britain*. London: Croom Helm.

Crosland, A. 1956: *The Future of Socialism*. London: Strauss Farrar.

Crossman, R. 1975: *Diaries of a Cabinet Minister*, 3 vols. London: Macmillan.

Crouch, C. 1977: *Class Conflict and the Industrial Relations Crisis*. London: Heinemann.

Crouch, C. 1978: *The Politics of Industrial Relations*. London: Fontana.

Crouzet, F. 1982: *The Victorian Economy*. New York: Columbia University Press.

Crozier, M. 1965: "Pour une analyse sociologique de la planification française," *Revue française de sociologie*, 6(2) (June), 147–63.

Crozier, M. 1968: *The Bureaucratic Phenomenon*. Chicago: University of Chicago Press.

Crozier, M. 1973: *The Stalled Society*. New York: Viking.

Crozier, M., Huntington, S. and Watanuki, J. 1975: *The Crisis of Democracy*. New York: New York University Press.

Cuthbertson, K. 1979: *Macroeconomic Policy*. London: Macmillan.

Cyert, R. M. and March, J. G. 1963: *A Behavioral Theory of the Firm*. New York: Prentice Hall.

Daalder, H. and Mair, P. 1984: *Western European Party Systems*. Beverly Hills: Sage.

Dagnaud, M. and Mehl, D. 1983: *L'élite rose*. Paris: Editions Ramsay.

Dahl, R. 1970: *A Preface to Democratic Theory*. Chicago: University of Chicago Press.

Dahrendorf, R. 1959: *Class and Class Conflict in Industrial Society*. Stanford: Stanford University Press.

Dahrendorf, R. 1964: "Recent changes in the class structure of European societies," *Daedalus*, 93(1) (Winter), 225–70.

Daniel, W. W. and Milward, N. 1983: *Workplace Industrial Relations in Britain*. London: Heinemann.

David, P. 1971: "The landscape and the machine: technical interrelatedness, land tenure, and the mechanization of the corn harvest in Victorian Britain." In J. R. T. Hughes and D. N. McCloskey (eds), *Essays in a Mature Economy*.

Davies, G. 1985: "The macroeconomic record of the Conservatives." Paper presented at the Center for European Studies, Harvard University, Apr.

Debbasch, C. 1969: *L'Administration au pouvoir: fonctionnaires et politiques sous la Vè République*. Paris: Calmann-Levy.

Debonneuil, M. and Sterdyniak, H. 1982: "Apprécier une dévaluation." *Economie et statistique*, 142 (Mar.), 41–61.

Déchery, B. 1980: *Quelques commentaires sur les politiques industrielles de la France et de la RFA*. Paris: Commissariat Général du Plan.

Delange, G. 1973: "Evolution de la planification française face aux contradictions sociales," *Planification et société*. Grenoble: Presses Universitaires de Grenoble, 374–93.

Delatte, J. 1979: *Crépuscules industrielles 1945–1985*. Paris: Edigeon.

Delion, A. and Durupty, M. 1982: *Les nationalisations 1982*. Paris: Economica.

Delors, J. 1978: "The decline of French planning." In Stuart Holland (ed.), *Beyond Capitalist Planning*. Oxford: Basil Blackwell, 9–33.

Denison, E. F. 1967: *Why Growth Rates Differ*. Washington: Brookings Institution.

Deutsch, K. 1963: *The Nerves of Government*. New York: Free Press of Glencoe.
Devereux, M. P. and Morris, C. N. 1983: *North Sea Oil Taxation*. London: Institute of Fiscal Studies.
Domhoff, W. 1967: *Who Rules America?* Englewood Cliffs: Prentice Hall.
Dorfman, G. A. 1979: *Government versus Trade Unionism in British Politics since 1968*. London: Macmillan.
Douglas, J. 1976: "The overloaded crown," *British Journal of Political Science*, 6(30), 483–505.
Dow, J. C. R. 1964: *The Management of the British Economy 1945–60*. London: Cambridge University Press.
Drucker, H. M. 1979: *Doctrine and Ethos in the Labour Party*. London: Allen and Unwin.
Drucker, H. et al. 1983: *Developments in British Politics*. London: Macmillan.
Dunleavy, P. and Husbands, C. T. 1985: *British Democracy at the Crossroads*. London: Allen and Unwin.
Dyson, K. 1982: *The State Tradition in Western Europe*. London: Martin Robertson.
Easton, D. 1953: *The Political System*. New York: Knopf.
Easton, D. 1957: "An approach to the analysis of political systems," *World Politics*, 11 (Apr.), 383–400.
Eatwell, R. 1979: *The 1945–51 Labour Government*. London: Batsford.
Edelstein, M. 1976: "Realized rates of return on U.K. home and overseas portfolio investment in the high age of imperialism," *Explorations in Economic History* (July), 283–329.
Edgell, S. and Duke, V. 1985: "The perceived impact of the spending cuts in Britain 1980–81 to 1983–84." Paper delivered in Copenhagen, May.
Edwardes, M. 1983: *Back From the Brink*. London: Collins.
Elbaum, B. and Lazonick, W. (eds) 1986: *The Decline of the British Economy*. London: Oxford University Press.
Elbaum, B. and Wilkinson, F. 1979: "Industrial relations and uneven development," *Cambridge Journal of Economics*, 3(3), 275–303.
Ellul, J. 1964: *The Technological Society*. New York: Knopf.
Eltis, W. 1979: "How rapid public sector growth can undermine the growth of the national product." In W. Beckerman (ed.), *Slow Growth in Britain*. London: Oxford University Press, 118–39.
Employment Policy 1944: A White Paper, Command 6527. London: HMSO.
Esping-Andersen, G. 1985: *Politics Against Markets*. Princeton: Princeton University Press.
Esping-Andersen, G. and Friedland, R. 1982: "Class coalitions in the making of West European economics." In G. Esping-Andersen and R. Friedland (eds), *Political Power and Social Theory*, vol. III, Greenwich, Ct: Jai Press, 1–52.
Esping-Andersen, G., Friedland, R. and Wright, E. O. 1976: "Modes of class struggle and the capitalist state." *Kapitalistate*, 4, 5.
Estrin, S. and Holmes, P. 1983: *French Planning in Theory and Practice*. London: Allen and Unwin.
Fay, H. and Young, S. 1977: *The Day the Pound Died*. London: The Sunday Times.

Feinstein, C. (ed.) 1983: *The Managed Economy*. London: Oxford University Press.

Fels, A. 1972: *The Prices and Incomes Board*. London: Cambridge University Press.

Fenley, A. 1980: "Labour and the trade unions." In C. Cook and I. Taylor (eds), *The Labour Party*. London: Longman, 50–83.

Ferguson, T. 1984: "From normalcy to New Deal," *International Organization*, 38(1), 41–94.

Fiegehen, G. C. 1980: *Companies, Incentives and Senior Managers*. Oxford: Oxford University Press.

Finer, S. E. 1973: "The political power of organized labour," *Government and Opposition* 8(4) (Autumn), 391–406.

Fleming, M. 1980: "Industrial policy." In Peter Maunder (ed.), *The British Economy in the 1970s*. London: Heinemann, 141–68.

Fomerand, J. 1975: "Policy formulation and change in Gaullist France," *Comparative Politics*, VIII(1) (Oct.), 59–89.

Foot, M. 1974: *Aneurin Bevan 1945–60*. London: Weidenfeld and Nicolson.

Forsythe, P. J. and Kay, J. 1980: "The economic impact of North Sea oil revenues," *Fiscal Studies*, 1, 3.

Forsythe, P. J. and Kay, J. 1981: "Oil revenues and manufacturing output," *Fiscal Studies*, 2, 2.

Fourastié, J. 1955: *La Prévision Economique au Service de l'Entreprise et de la Nation*. Paris: Presses Universitaires de France.

Fourastié, J. and Courthéoux, J. P. 1968: *La Planification économique en France*. Paris: Presses Universitaires de France.

Franck, L. 1964: *Les Prix*. Paris: Presses Universitaires de France.

Fraser, N. and Sinfield, A. 1985: "The cost of high unemployment," *Journal of Social Policy*, 19(2) (Summer), 92–9.

Freeman, C. and Young, A. 1965: *The Research and Development Effort in Western Europe, North America and the Soviet Union*, viii, 2. Paris: OECD.

Friedberg, E. 1973: "L'Internationalisation de l'économie mondiale et modalités d'intervention de l'état: la politique industrielle." In *Planification et société*. Grenoble: Presses Universitaires de Grenoble, 94–108.

Friedberg, E. 1974: "Administration et enterprises." In M. Crozier (ed.), *Où va l'administration française*, Paris: Editions d'Organisation, 101–40.

Friedman, M. and Friedman, R. 1979: *Free to Choose*. New York: Harcourt, Brace.

Fry, G. K. 1975: "Economic policy-making and planning 1945–70," *Public Administration Bulletin*, 18 (June–Dec.), 3–22.

Gamble, A. 1979: The free economy and the strong state. In R. Miliband and J. Saville (eds), *The Socialist Register 1979*, London: Merlin, 1–25.

Ganz, G. 1977: *Government and Industry*. London: Professional.

Gaventa, J. 1981: *Power and Powerlessness in an Appalachian Valley*. Knoxville: University of Tennessee Press.

Geary, J. 1979: *European Labour Protest 1838–1940*. London: Croom Helm.

Gerschenkron, A. 1962: *Economic Backwardness in Historical Perspective*. Cambridge, Mass.: Harvard University Press.

Giddens, A. 1979: *Central Problems in Social Theory*. Berkeley: University of California Press.

Gilmour, I. 1977: *Inside Right*. London: Hutchinson.

Gilpin, R. 1968: *France in the Age of the Scientific State*. Princeton: Princeton University Press.

Glyn, A. and Sutcliffe, R. 1972: *British Capitalism, Workers and the Profits Squeeze*. Harmondsworth: Penguin.

Godelier, M. 1974: "Structure and contradiction in Marx's Capital." In R. Blackburn (ed.), *Ideology in Social Science*. London: Fontana.

Goguel, F. and Grosser, A. 1970: *La Politique en France*. Paris: Librarie Colin.

Gold, D. A., Lo, C. Y. H. and Wright, E. O. 1975: "Recent developments in Marxist theories of the capitalist state," *Monthly Review* (Oct. and Nov.), 29–43; 36–51.

Goldthorpe, J. 1974: "Social inequality and social integration in modern Britain." In D. Wedderburn (ed.), *Poverty, Inequality and Class Structure*. Cambridge: Cambridge University Press.

Goldthorpe, J. 1985: "The end of convergence: corporatist and dualist tendencies in modern western societies." In J. Goldthorpe (ed.), *Order and Conflict in Contemporary Capitalism*. Cambridge: Cambridge University Press, 344–66.

Goodhart, C. A. E. 1975: *Money, Information, and Uncertainty*. London: Macmillan.

Gorz, A. 1973: *Socialism and Revolution*. New York: Anchor.

Gough, I. 1975: "State expenditure in advanced capitalism," *New Left Review*, 92 (July–Aug.), 53–92.

Gough, I. 1978: *The Political Economy of the Welfare State*. London: Macmillan.

Gourevitch, P. 1977a: "International politics, domestic coalitions and liberty," *Journal of Interdisciplinary History*, 281–313.

Gourevitch, P. 1977b: "The reform of local government: a political analysis," *Comparative Politics* 10(1) (Oct.), 69–88.

Gourevitch, P. 1978: "The second image reversed: the international sources of domestic politics," *International Organization*, 10(32) (Autumn), 881–912.

Gourevitch, P. 1984: "Breaking with orthodoxy," *International Organization*, 10(38) (Winter), 95–129.

Gourevitch, P., Markovits, A., Martin, A. and Ross, G. 1984: *Unions, Change and Crisis*. London: Allen and Unwin.

Gournay, B. and Viot, P. 1963: "Les planificateurs et les décisions du Plan." In *La Planification comme Processus de Décision*. Grenoble: University of Grenoble Press, 55–83.

H.M. Government 1944: *Employment Policy After the War*. Cmnd. 6527. London: HMSO.

Gowland, D. 1978: *Monetary Policy and Credit Control*. London: Croom Helm.

Graham, A. 1972: "Industrial policy." In W. Beckerman (ed.), *The Labour Government's Economic Record 1964–70*. London: Duckworth, 178–217.

Gramsci, A. 1970: *Selections from the Prison Notebooks*. Hoare and Nowell (eds). New York: International.

Grant, W. 1977: "Corporatism and pressure groups." In R. Rose and D. Kavanaugh (eds), *New Trends in British Politics*, London: Sage, 167–90.

Grant, W. 1980: "The last labour govenment's industrial strategy." Paper presented to the Public Administration Conference, York University, September.

Grant, W. 1981: "Business interests and the conservative party," *Government and Opposition*, 143–61.

Grant, W. 1982: *The Political Economy of Industrial Policy*. London: Butterworths.

Grant, W. 1983: "Representing capital." In R. King (ed.), *Capital and Politics*. London: Routledge and Kegan Paul, 69–84.

Grant, W. and Marsh, D. 1978: *The Confederation of British Industry*. London: Hodder and Stoughton.

Green, D. 1978: "The seventh plan – the demise of French planning?" *West European Politics* 1(1) (Feb.). 60–76.

Green, D. 1984a: "Strategic management and the state: France." In K. Dyson and S. Wilks (eds), Managing Industrial Crisis. London: Martin Robertson, 161–92.

Green, D. 1984b: "Giscardisme – industrial policy." In V. Wright (ed.), *Continuity and Change in France*. London: Allen and Unwin.

Greenleaf, W. H. 1984: *The British Political Tradition*. London: Methuen.

Greffe, X. 1983: "Les entreprises publiques dans la politique de l'Etat," *Revue Economique*, 34(3), 496–535.

Grémion, P. 1973: "La théorie de l'apprentissage institutionnel et la régionalisation de Cinquième Plan," *Revue française de science politique* 23(2) (Apr.), 305–20.

Grémion, P. 1974: "La concertation." In M. Crozier (ed.), *Où va l'administration française*. Paris: SEDEIS, 49–100.

Grémion, P. 1976: *Le Pouvoir Péripherique*. Paris: Seuil.

Griffiths, W. (ed.) 1977: *Government, Business and Labour In European Capitalism*. London: Europotentials Press.

Grove, J. W. 1967: *Government and Industry in Britain*. London: Longmans.

Gruson, C. 1968: *Origine et espoirs de la planification française*. Paris: Dunod.

Habakkuk, J. 1962: *American and British Technology in the Nineteenth Century*. Cambridge: Cambridge University Press.

Hadjimatheou, G. and Skouras, A. 1979: "Britain's economic problem: the growth of the non-market sector," *Economic Journal*, 392–401.

Hagen, E. E. and White, S. F. T. 1966: *Great Britain: quiet revolution in planning*. Syracuse: Syracuse University Press.

Hague, D. and Wilkinson, G. 1983: *The IRC: an experiment in industrial intervention*. London: Allen and Unwin.

Hall, A. R. (ed.) 1968: *The Export of Capital From Britain 1870–1914*. London: Methuen.

Hall, P. A. 1981: "Miti culturali e realta economiche: la programmagione francese nel confronto con l'esperienza Brittannica," *Stato e Mercato*, 1(1) (Apr.), 133–71.

Hall, P. A. 1982a: "Economic planning and the state: the evolution of economic challenge and political response in France." In G. Esping-Andersen, R. Friedland and M. Zeitlin (eds), *Political Power and Social Theory*, vol. III. Greenwich, Conn.: Jai Press, 175–214.

Hall, P. A. 1982b: *The Political Dimensions of Economic Management.* Ann Arbor, Mich.: University Microfilms International.

Hall, P. A. 1983a: "Policy innovation and the structure of the state: the politics-administration nexus in Britain and France," *Annals*, 466 (Mar.), 43–59.

Hall, P. A. 1983b: "Patterns of economic policy among the European states: an organizational approach." In S. Bornstein, D. Held and J. Krieger (eds), *The State in Capitalist Europe.* London: Allen and Unwin, 21–53.

Hall, P. A. 1985: "Socialism in one country: Mitterrand and the struggle to define a new economic policy for France." In P. Cerny and M. Schain (eds), *Socialism, the State and Public Policy in France.* London: Frances Pinter, 81–107.

Hall, S. and Jacques, M. 1983: *The Politics of Thatcherism.* London: Lawrence and Wishart.

Halperin, M. 1974: *Bureaucratic Politics and Foreign Policy.* Washington: Brookings Institution.

Hamon, L. 1966: "Le Plan et sa signification politique." In D. Réynaud (ed.), *Tendances et volantés de la société française.* Paris: SEDEIS.

Hannah, L. 1974: "Managerial innovation and the rise of the large-scale company in interwar Britain," *Economic History Review* 2nd series, 27, 252–70.

Hannah, L. 1976a: *The Rise of the Corporate Economy.* London: Macmillan.

Hannah, L. (ed.) 1976b: *Management Structure and Business Development.* London: Macmillan.

Hansen, B. 1968: *Fiscal Policy in Seven Countries 1955–1965.* Paris: OECD.

Hardach, K. 1980: *The Political Economy of Germany in the Twentieth Century.* Berkeley: University of California Press.

Hardin. R. 1982: *Collective Action.* Baltimore: Johns Hopkins University Press.

Harley, C. K. 1974: "Skilled labour and the choice of technique in Edwardian industry," *Explorations in Economic History*, 11, 391–414.

Harris, N. 1972: *Competition and the Corporate Society.* London: Methuen.

Harrod, R. 1967: *Towards a New Economic Policy.* London: Methuen.

Harrop, M. 1981: "The changing British electorate," *Political Quarterly*, 53, 385–402.

Hatfield, M. 1976: *The House the Left Built.* London: Gollancz.

Hayward, J. 1966a: "Interest groups and incomes policy in France," *British Journal of Industrial Relations* (July), 165–200.

Hayward, J. 1966b: *Private Interest and Public Policy.* New York: Barnes and Noble.

Hayward, J. 1967: "Le fonctionnement des commissions et la préparation du Vè Plan," *Revue française de sociologie*, 8(4), 447–51.

Hayward, J. 1972: "State intervention in France: the changing style of government-industry relations," *Political Studies*, 12, 287–98.

Hayward, J. 1973: *The One and Indivisible French Republic.* London: Weidenfeld and Nicolson.

Hayward, J. 1975: "Introduction: change and choice: the agenda of planning." In J. Hayward and M. Watson (eds), *Planning, Politics and Public Policy*. Cambridge: Cambridge University Press, 1–21.

Hayward, J. 1976: "Institutional inertia and political impetus in France and Britain," *European Journal of Political Research*, 4, 341–59.

Hayward, J. and Watson, M. (eds) 1975: *Planning, Politics and Public Policy*. Cambridge: Cambridge University Press.

Head, J. G. 1962: "Public goods and public policy," *Public Finance*, 17, 197–219.

Heath, Anthony et al. 1985: *How Britain Votes*. Oxford: Pergamon.

Heclo, H. 1974: *Modern Social Politics in Britain and Sweden*. New Haven: Yale University Press.

Heclo, H. and Wildavsky, A. 1979: *The Private Government of Public Money*. London: Macmillan.

Held, D. and Krieger, J. 1984: "Theories of the state." In S. Bornstein, D. Held and J. Krieger (eds), *The State in Capitalist Europe*. London: Allen and Unwin, 1–20.

Henderson, P. D. 1983: "Mrs. Thatcher's old-style dirigisme," *Journal of Economic Affairs*, 3(2) (Jan.), 126–8.

Henry, S. G. B. et al. 1976: "Models of inflation in the United Kingdom – an evaluation," *National Institute Economic Review*, 77, 60–71.

Herring, E. P. 1936: *Public Administration and the Public Interest*. New York: McGraw-Hill.

Hibbs, D. A. 1977a: "Trade unions, labor militancy, and wage inflation: a comparative analysis." Cambridge: Center for International Studies, MIT mimeo.

Hibbs, D. A. 1977b: "Political parties and macroeconomic policy." *American Political Science Review*, 71, 467–87.

Hibbs, D. A. 1980: "On the demand for economic outcomes: macroeconomic performance and mass political support in the United States, Great Britain, and Germany." Paper presented to the American Political Science Association, Washington, DC.

Hirsch, E. 1973: "L'Avenir de la planification française." In *Planification et société*. Grenoble: Presses Universitaires de Grenoble, 666–7.

Hirsch, F. 1977: *The Social Limits to Growth*. London: Routledge and Kegan Paul.

Hobsbawm, E. 1968: *Industry and Empire*. New York: Pantheon.

Hobsbawm, E. et al. 1981: *The Forward March of Labour Halted*. London: Verso.

Hodgman, D. et al. 1981: "Determinants of monetary policy in France, the FRG, Italy, and the United Kingdom: some preliminary findings." Mimeo.

Hodgman, D. (ed.) 1983: *The Political Economy of Monetary Policy*. Boston: Federal Reserve Bank.

Hoffmann, Stanley 1963: "Paradoxes of the French political community." In S. Hoffmann et al. (eds), *In Search of France*. New York: Viking, 1–117.

Hoffmann, S. 1978: *France: Decline or Renewal?* New York: Harper and Row.

Hoffmann, S. 1982: "Year One," *New York Review of Books* (12 Aug.), 37–43.

Holloway, J. and Picciotto, S. (eds) 1978: *State and Capital: a Marxist debate*. London: Edward Arnold.

Holmes, M. 1982: *Political Pressure and Economic Policy*. London: Butterworths.

Holmes, M. 1985: *The First Thatcher Government*. London: Wheatsheaf.

Holt, R. 1967: "A proposed structural-functional framework." In J. Charlesworth, *Contemporary Political Analysis*. New York: Free Press, 86–108.

Hough, J. 1979: "Government intervention in the economy of France." In P. Maunder (ed.), *Government Intervention in the Developed Economy*. London: Croom Helm, 190–214.

Hough, J. 1982: *The French Economy*. New York: Holmes and Meir.

House of Commons 1970: *First Report from Select Committee on the Nationalised Industries: Bank of England, Session 1969–70*. London: HMSO.

House of Commons 1980: *Third Report from the Treasury and Civil Service Committee: Memoranda on Monetary Policy*. London: HMSO.

Howson, S. 1975: *Domestic Monetary Management in Britain 1919–38*. London: Cambridge University Press.

HM Treasury 1977: *Evidence on the Financing of Trade and Industry to the Committee to Review the Functioning of Financial Institutions*. London: HMSO.

Hurd, D. 1979: *An End to Promises*. London: Collins.

Ikenberry, J. 1985: "Market solutions for state problems: the international and domestic politics of American oil decontrol." Paper presented to the American Political Science Association, New Orleans.

Imberg, D. and Northcott, J. 1981: *Industrial Policy and Investment Decisions*. London: Policy Studies Institute.

Jenkins, Peter 1970: *The Battle of Downing Street*. London: Charles Knight.

Jenson, J. and Ross, G. 1983: "Crisis and France's 'third way'," *Studies in Political Economy* (Spring), 71–103.

Jessop, B. 1977: "Recent theories of the capitalist state," *Cambridge Journal of Economics*, 1, 353–73.

Jessop, B. 1982: "The dual crisis of the state in postwar Britain: recent developments." Paper presented to the Conference on Representation and the State, Stanford University.

Jessop, B., Bonnett, K., Bromley, S. and Ling, T. 1984: "Authoritarian populism, two nations and Thatcherism." *New Left Review*, 147, 32–60.

Jobert, B. 1973: "Le ministère de l'industrie et la coherence de la politique industrielle," *Revue française de science politique*, 23(2) (Apr.), 321–9.

Johnson, C. 1982: *MITI*. Berkeley: University of California Press.

Joint Economic Committee, US Congress 1981: *Monetary Policy, Economic Growth and Industry in France, Germany, Sweden and the United Kingdom*. Washington: US Government Printing Office.

Jones, F. E. 1978: "Our manufacturing industry – the missing 100,000," *National Westminster Bank Quarterly Review* (May), 8–17.

Jones, G. and Rose, M. 1985: "Redividing labour: factory politics and work reorganization in the current industrial transition." In S. Allen et al. (eds), *The Changing Experience of Work*. London: Macmillan.

Jones, G. W. and Stewart, J. O. 1983: "The Treasury and Local Government," *Political Quarterly*, 54(1) (Jan.–Mar.), 5–15.

Joseph, K. 1974: *Reversing the Trend*. London: Center for Policy Studies.

Joseph, K. 1976: *Monetarism is not Enough*. London: Center for Policy Studies.

Judge, K. 1982: "The growth and decline of social expenditure." In A. Walker (ed.), *Public Expenditure and Social Policy*. London: Heinemann, 27–48.

Kahn, P. 1985: "Economics, politics and the reconstruction of trade unionism in Britain." Paper delivered to the Conference of Europeanists, Washington, October.

Kaldor, N. 1966: *Causes of the Slow Rate of Growth of the United Kingdom*. Cambridge: Cambridge University Press.

Kaldor, N. 1977: "Capitalism and industrial development," *Cambridge Journal of Economics*, 1(2), 193–204.

Kaldor, N. 1984: *The Economic Consequences of Mrs. Thatcher*. London: Duckworth.

Kalecki, M. 1943: "Political aspects of full employment," *Political Quarterly*, 14(4), 322–30.

Kasper, W. 1972: "Stabilization policies in a dependent economy: some lessons from the West German experience of the 1960s." In E. Claassen and P. Salin (eds), *Stabilization Policies in Interdependent Economies*. Amsterdam: Elsevier, 270–86.

Katzenstein, P. (ed.) 1978: *Between Power and Plenty*. Madison: University of Wisconsin Press.

Katzenstein, P. 1984: *Corporatism and Change*. Ithaca: Cornell University Press.

Katzenstein, P. 1985: *Small States in World Markets*. Ithaca: Cornell University Press.

Kaufmann, H. 1969: "A debate over Germany's revaluation, 1961: a chapter in political economy," *Weltwirtschaftliches Archiv*, 103, 181–212.

Kay, J. A. and King, M. A. 1980: *The British Tax System*, 2nd edn. London: Oxford University Press.

Keegan, W. 1984: *Mrs. Thatcher's Economic Experiment*. London: Allen Lane.

Keegan, W. and Pennant-Rae, R. 1979: *Who Runs the Economy?* London: Maurice Temple Smith.

Keeler, J. 1985: "Situating France on the pluralism–corporatism continuum," *Comparative Politics*, 17, 229–49.

Kemp, T. 1969: *Industrialization in Nineteenth Century Europe*. London: Longmans.

Kennedy, W. P. 1974: "Foreign investment, trade and growth in the United Kingdom, 1970–1913: *Explorations in Economic History*, 11, 415–44.

Kenwood, A. G. and Lougheed, A. L. 1983: *The Growth of the International Economy 1820–1960*. London: Allen and Unwin.

Keohane, R. O. 1978: "Economics, inflation, and the role of the state," *World Politics*, 3(1)(Oct.), 108–28.

Kesselman, M. 1970: "Overinstitutionalization and political constraint: the case of France," *Comparative Politics*, 3(1) (Oct.), 21–44.

Kesselman, M. 1983: "Socialism without the workers: the case of France," *Kapitalistate*, 10–11, 14–38.

Kessler, M. C. 1978: *La Politique de la Haute Fonction Publique*. Paris: Presses de la Fondation Nationale des Sciences Politiques.

Keynes, J. M. 1925: *The Economic Consequences of Mr. Churchill*. London: Macmillan.

Keynes, J. M. 1936: *The General Theory of Interest, Employment and Money*. London: Macmillan.

Kilpatrick, A. and Lawson, T. 1980: "On the nature of industrial decline in the UK," *Cambridge Journal of Economics*, 4(1), 85–100.

Kindleberger, C. 1963: "The post-war resurgence of the French economy." In S. Hoffmann et al. (eds), *In Search of France*, New York: Harper and Row, 305–58.

Kindleberger, C. 1964: *Economic Growth in Britain and France in 1950*. Cambridge: Harvard University Press.

Kindleberger, C. 1965: "Germany's persistent balance-of-payments disequilibrium." In R. E. Baldwin (ed.), *Trade, Growth and the Balance of Payments*. Chicago: Amsterdam, 230–48.

King, A. (ed.) 1986: *The British Prime Minister: A Reader*. London: Macmillan.

King, M. A. 1975: "The UK profits crisis: myth or reality," *Economic Journal*, 85, 33–47.

Kirby, M. W. 1973: "Government intervention in industrial organization: coal mining in the nineteen thrities," *Business History*, 15(2), 160–73.

Kirby, M. W. 1981: *The Decline of British Economic Power since 1870*. London: Allen and Unwin.

Kirschen, E. S. (ed.) 1964: *Economic Policy in Our Time*, 2 vols. Amsterdam: North Holland.

Kirschen, E. S. (ed.) 1975: *Economic Policies Compared*, 2 vols. Amsterdam: Elsevier.

Kloten, N., Kellerer, K-H. and Vollmer, R. 1978: "The political and social factors of Germany's stabilization performance." Paper presented to a Brookings Conference on the Politics and Sociology of Global Inflation, Washington, DC (Dec.).

Kogan, D. and Kogan, M. 1983: *The Battle for the Labour Party*. London: Kogan-Page.

Kohl, J. 1981: "Trends and problems in public expenditure development in Western Europe and North America." In P. Flora and A. Heidenheimer (eds), *The Development of Welfare States in Europe and America*, London: Transaction, 307–46.

Korpi, W. 1980: *The Democratic Class Struggle*. London: Routledge and Kegan Paul.

Krasner, S. 1980: *Defending the National Interest*. Princeton: Princeton University Press.

Krause, L. 1969: "Britain's trade performance." In R. Caves (ed.), *Britain's Economic Prospects*. London: Allen and Unwin, 198–228.

Krause, L. and Salant, W. S. (eds) 1977: *Worldwide Inflation*. Washington: Brookings Institution.

Kravis, I. and Lipsey, R. 1971: *Price Competitiveness in World Trade*. New York: Columbia University Press.

Kreile, M. 1978: "West Germany: the dynamics of expansion." In P. Katzenstein (ed.), *Between Power and Plenty*. Madison: University of Wisconsin Press, 191–224.

Krieger, J. 1983: *Undermining Capitalism*. Princeton: Princeton University Press.

Krieger, J. 1986: *Reagan, Thatcher and the Politics of Decline*. Oxford: Polity Press.

Krieger, J. and Held, D. 1978: "Theory of state," *Socialist Revolution*, 40, 189–207.

Kuhn, T. 1969: *The Structure of Scientific Revolutions*. Chicago: University of Chicago Press.

Kuisel, R. 1981: *Capitalism and the State in Modern France*. Cambridge: Cambridge University Press.

Kurth, J. 1979: "The political consequences of the product cycle: industrial history and political outcomes," *International Organization*, 33(1), 1–36.

Kuster, G. H. 1974: *Germany: Big Business and the State*. Cambridge: Harvard University Press.

Labour Party 1976: *Report of the 75th Annual Conference*. London: Labour Party.

Landes, D. 1969: *The Unbound Prometheus*. Cambridge: Cambridge University Press.

Lange, P. 1985: "Unions, workers and wage regulation: the rational bases of consent." In J. Goldthorpe (ed.), *Order and Conflict in Contemporary Capitalism*. London: Oxford University Press.

Lange, P. and Garrett, G. 1985: "Organization and the Political Determination of Economic Performance 1974–80," *Journal of Politics*.

Lange, P., Ross, G. and Vannicelli, M. 1982: *Unions, Crisis, and Change*. London: Allen and Unwin.

Laski, H. 1938: *A Grammar of Politics*. London: Allen and Unwin.

Lauber, V. 1983: *The Political Economy of France*. New York: Praeger.

Laulan, Y. 1983: "Le défense nationale à l'heure de l'austérité," *Chroniques d'actualité de la SEDEIS* (Mar.), 11–146.

Lautman, J. and Thoenig, J. C. 1966: *Planification et administrations centrales*. Paris: Centre de recherches en des sociologies d'organisation.

Lawson, N. 1984: "The Mais Lecture." Presented in London, Oct.

Lazonick, W. 1981: "Competition, specialization and industrial decline," *Journal of Economic History*, 41(1) (Mar.), 31–8.

Lazonick, W. 1983: "Industrial organization and technical change: the decline of the British cotton industry," *Business History Review*, 57(2) (Summer), 195–236.

Lazonick, W. 1985: "Strategy, structure and management development in the U.S. and Britain." In K. Kobayashi (ed.), *The Development of Managerial Enterprises*. Tokyo: Tokyo University Press.

L'Ecottais, G. 1980: "Les deux mondes de Raymond Barre," *L'Express* (20 Sept.), 41.

Lefournier, P. 1981: "Septs ans de malheur," *L'Expansion*, 6, 65.

Leruez, J. 1975: *Economic Planning and Politics in Britain*. London: Martin Robertson.

Lever, H. and Edwards, G. 1980: "Why Germany beats Britain," *Sunday Times* (2 Nov.), 16–17.

Levy, M. 1980: "A predatory theory of rule," *Politics and Society*, 10, 431–65.

Lewis, S. 1986: "The political limits of autonomy: transforming the party-union relationship in France." Paper presented to the Conference on European Studies, Washington.

Lewis, W. A. 1949: *Economic Survey 1919–1939*. London: Allen and Unwin.

Lewis, W. A. 1967: "The deceleration of British growth 1873–1913." Princeton, N.J., mimeo.

Leys, Colin, 1985: "Thatcherism and British manufacturing," *New Left Review*, 151, 5–21.

Lieberman, S. 1977: *The Growth of European Mixed Economics 1945–1970*. New York: Wiley.

Lindbeck, A. 1978: "Economic dependence and interdependence in the industrialized world," in *OECD, From Marshall Plan to Global Interdependence*. Paris: OECD.

Lindberg, L. and Maier, C. 1985: *The Politics of Inflation and Global Stagnation*. Washington: Brookings Institution.

Lindblom, C. E. 1959: "The science of 'muddling through'," *Public Administration Review*, 19(2), 79–88.

Lindblom, C. E. 1977: *Politics and Markets*. New York: Basic Books.

Lipietz, A. 1983: "L'echèc de la première phase." *Les Temps Modernes* (Apr.), 34–57.

Lipietz, A. 1984: *L'audace ou l'enlisement*. Paris: La Decouverte.

Lipset, S. M. 1964: "The changing class structure and contemporary European politics." *Daedalus*, 93(1) (Winter), 271–303.

Lipset, S. M. and Rokkan, S. 1967: *Party Systems and Voter Alignments*. New York: Free Press.

Longstreth, F. 1979: "The city, industry, and the state.' In C. Crouch (ed.), *State and Economy in Contemporary Capitalism*, London: Croom Helm, 157–90.

Longstreth, F. 1983: "The dynamics of disintegration of a Keynesian political economy." Paper presented at the Center for European Studies, Harvard University.

Longstreth, F. 1985: "In place of consensus." Paper presented at the Conference of Europeanists, Washington, October.

Lord, G. 1973: *The French Budgetary Process*. Berkeley, Ca.: University of California Press.

Lougovoy, B. 1981: *L'économie, les français et l'état*. Paris: Presses Universitaires de la France.

Lowe, R. 1978: "The erosion of state intervention in Britain 1917–24," *Economic History Review*, 2nd series, 31(2), 270–86.

Lowell, A. 1908: *The Government of England*. London: Macmillan.

Lucas, A. F. 1937: *Industrial Reconstruction and the Control of Competition*. London: Longman.

Lukes, S. 1970: *Power: A Radical View*. London: Macmillan.

Lutz, V. 1963: *Central Planning for the Market Economy*. London: Longman.

MacLennan, D. and Parr, J. B. 1979: *Regional policy: past experience and new directions*. Oxford: Martin Robertson.

MacLennan, D. et al. 1968: *Economic Planning and Policies in Britain, France, and Germany.* London: Praeger.

Macmillan, H. 1934: *Reconstruction: a plea for a national policy.* London: Macmillan.

Macmillan, H. 1971: *Riding the Storm 1956–59.* New York: Harper and Row.

Macmillan, H. 1973: *At the End of the Day 1961–63.* New York: Harper and Row.

Macridis, R. 1977: "Groups and group theory." In R. Macridis and B. Brown (eds), *Comparative Politics.* New York: Dorsey, 322–7.

Maddison, A. 1977: "Phases of capitalist development," *Banca Nazionale del Lavoro Quarterly Review* (June).

Magaziner, I. 1979: *Japanese Industrial Policy.* London: Policy Studies Institute.

Magaziner, I. and Reich, R. 1982: *Minding America's Business.* New York: Harcourt, Brace Jovanovitch.

Maier, C. 1970: "Between Taylorism and technocracy; European ideologies and the vision of industrial productivity in the 1920s," *Journal of Contemporary History,* V(2) (Apr.), 27–61.

Maier, C. 1978: "The politics of inflation in the twentieth century." In F. Hirsch and J. H. Goldthorpe (eds), *The Political Economy of Inflation.* London: Martin Robertson, 37–72.

Maier, C. 1981: "The two postwar eras and the conditions for stability in twentieth century Europe," *American Historical Review,* 84(2), 327–52.

Maitland, I. 1983: *The Origins of Industrial Disorder.* London: Routledge and Kegan Paul.

Manser, W. A. P. 1971: *Britain in Balance.* London: Longman.

Marceau, J. 1977: *Class and Status in France.* Oxford: Oxford University Press.

March, J. and Olsen, J. 1984: "The new institutionalism: organizational factors in political life," *American Political Science Review,* 78 (Sept.), 734–49.

Marchand, O. 1983: "Des 40 heurs aux 39 heures: processus et réactions des entreprises," *Economie et Statistique,* 154 (Apr.), 3–16.

Mariano, A. P. 1973: *Métamorphose de l'économie française 1963–73.* Paris: Arthaud.

Marsh, D. and Grant, W. 1977: "Tripartism: reality or myth?" *Government and Opposition,* 12, 194–211.

Marsh, D. and Locksley, G. 1983: "Capital in Britain: its structural power and influence over policy," *West European Politics,* 6(2), 36–60.

Marshall, T. H. 1966: *Class, Citizenship and Social Development.* Chicago: University of Chicago Press.

Martin, A. 1975: "Is democratic control of capitalist economies possible?" In L. Lindberg et al. (eds), *Stress and Contradiction in Modern Capitalism.* Lexington. Ma: D. C. Heath, 13–56.

Martin, A. 1979: The dynamics of change in a Keynesian political economy: the Swedish case and its implications. *State and Economy in Contemporary Capitalism.* London: Croom Helm.

Martin, R. 1980: *TUC: History of a Pressure Group.* London: Oxford University Press.

Mason, S. 1976: *The Flow of Funds in Britain.* London: Paul Elck.

Massé, P. 1965: *Le Plan ou l'anti-hazard*. Paris: Gallimard.

Massey, D. 1982: "Industrial restructuring as class restructuring." *Conference of Socialist Economists Working Paper* No. 604.

Mathias, P. 1969: *The First Industrial Nation*. London: Methuen.

Matthews, R. C. O. 1968: "Why has Britain had full employment since the war?." *Economic Journal*, 77, 555–69.

Matthews, R. C. O., Feinstein, C. H. and Odling-Smee, J. C. 1982: *British Economic Growth 1856–1973*. Stanford: Stanford University Press.

Mayntz, R. and Scharpf, F. W. 1975: *Policy-making in the German Federal Bureaucracy*. Amsterdam: Elsevier.

McArthur, J. and Scott, B. 1969: *Industrial Planning in France*. Cambridge, Ma.: Harvard Business School.

McCloskey, D. 1981: *Enterprise and Trade in Victorian Britain*. London: Allen and Unwin.

McCloskey, D. and Floud, R. (eds) 1981: *The Economic History of Britain since 1700*. Cambridge: Cambridge University Press.

McCormick, J. 1985: "Liberalism versus socialism in France: has it made a difference?" Paper presented at the Conference of Europeanists, Washington, October.

McCrone, G. 1969: *Regional Policy in Britain*. London: Allen and Unwin.

McFadyean, M. and Renn, M. 1984: *Thatcher's Reign*. London: Chatto and Windus.

Medley, R. 1981: "Monetary stability and industrial adaptation in Germany." Prepared for the US Congress, Joint Economic Committee (June).

Mellors, C. 1978: *The British MP*. Farnborough, Hants: Saxon House.

Meny, Y. 1984: "Decentralization in socialist France," *West European Politics*, 7(1) (Jan.).

Merton, R. 1957: *Social Theory and Social Structure*. New York: Free Press.

Merton, R. 1969: *On Theoretical Sociology*. New York: Free Press.

Michalet, C. A. 1974: "France." In R. Vernon (ed.), *Big Business and the State*. Cambridge: Harvard University Press, 105–25.

Michalet, G. 1975: "Vote des groupes socio-professionels et variables contextuelles," *Revue française de science politique* 25, 5 (Oct.), 901–18.

Michalski, W. 1972: *Export Trade and Economic Growth*. Hamburg: Verlag Weltarchiv.

Middlemas, K. 1979: *Politics in Industrial Society*. London: André Deutsch.

Middleton, R. 1981: "The constant employment budget balance and British budgetary policy, 1929–39." *Economic History Review*, 34(2), 266–87.

Milch, J. 1976: "Feasible and prudent alternatives: airport development in the age of public protest." *Public Policy*, XXIV (Winter), 81–110.

Milesi, G. 1985: *Jacques Delors*. Paris: Belfond.

Miliband, R. 1961: *Parliamentary Socialism*. London: Merlin.

Miliband, R. 1969: *The State in Capitalist Society*. New York: Basic Books.

Miliband, R. 1977: *Marxism and Politics*. New York: Oxford University Press.

Miliband, R. and Poulantzas, N. 1974: "A debate on the state." In R. Blackburn (ed.), *Ideology in Social Science*. London: Fontana.

Ministère de l'Industrie 1979: *Les Moyens de politique industrielle*. Paris: Centre d'Etudes et de Prévision.

Minkin, L. 1978: *The Labour Party Conference*. London: Allen Lane.

Minnerup, G. 1976: "West Germany since the War," *New Left Review*, 99 (Sept.–Oct.), 3–46.

Mishan, E. J. 1967: *The Costs of Economic Growth*. London: Penguin.

Moggridge, D. E. 1972: *British Monetary Policy 1924–31*. London: Cambridge University Press.

Monfort, J. 1983: "A la recherche des filieres de production," *Economie et Statistique*, 151 (Jan.), 3–12.

Monnet, J. 1976: *Memoires*. Paris: Fayard.

Moore, B. 1966: *Social Origins of Dictatorship and Democracy*. Boston: Beacon.

Moore, B. and Rhodes, J. 1973: "Evaluating the effects of British regional economic policy," *Economic Journal*, 83, 87–110.

Moore, B. and Rhodes, J. 1976: "The relative decline of the UK manufacturing sector," *Economic Policy Review*, 2, 36–41.

Moran, M. 1977: *The Politics of Industrial Relations*. London: Macmillan.

Morgan, K. 1984: *Labour in Power 1945–1951*. New York: Oxford University Press.

Morin, F. 1974: *La Structure Financière du Capitalisme Française*. Paris: Calmann-Levy.

Mosley, P. 1976: "Towards a 'satisficing' theory of economic policy." *Economic Journal*, 86, 59–72.

Mosley, P. 1984: *The Making of Economic Policy*. London: Wheatsheaf.

Mottershead, P. 1978: "Industrial policy." In F. Blackaby (ed.), *British Economic Policy 1960–74*, London: Cambridge University Press.

Mowatt, C. L. 1955: *Britain Between the Wars*. Chicago: University of Chicago Press.

Muller, W. 1983: "Economic success without an industrial strategy: Austria in the 1970s," *Journal of Public Policy*, 3(1), 119–30.

Muller-Jentsch, W. and Sperling, H-J. 1978: "Economic development, labor conflicts and the industrial relations system in West Germany." In C. Crouch and A. Pizzorno (eds), *The Resurgence of Class Conflict in Western Europe Since 1968*, 1, 257–306.

Murray. C. 1984: *Losing Ground*. New York: Basic Books.

Nairn, T. 1977: *The Break-up of Britain*. London: New Left Books.

Neibergs, P. 1983: "Incomes policy in Scandinavia." Senior Thesis for Social Studies, Harvard University.

Nettl, P. 1965: "Conservative or elite dominance: the case of business," *Political Studies*, XIII, 1.

Nicol. W. and Youill, D. 1982: "Regional problems and policy." In A. Boltho (ed.), *The European Economy: growth and crisis*, London: Oxford University Press, 409–48.

NIER, 1984: *National Institute Economic Review*, 108, 70–84.

Niskanen, W. 1971: *Bureaucracy and Representative Government*. Chicago: Aldine.

Nizard, L. 1972a: "La Planification: socialisation et simulation," *Sociologie du travail*, 4, 369–87.

Nizard, L. 1972b: "De la planification française: production de normes et concertation," *Revue française de science politique*, 23(5) (Oct.), 1111–32.

Nizard, L. 1973: "Administration et societé: planification et régulations bureaucratiques," *Revue francaise de science politique*, 23(2) (Apr.), 199–229.

Nordhaus, W. 1975: "The political business cycle," *Review of Economic Studies*, 42, 169–90.

Nordlinger, E. 1981: *On the Autonomy of the Democratic State*. Cambridge, Mass.: Harvard University Press.

Nossiter, B. 1978: *Britain: a future that works*. Boston: Houghton and Mifflin.

O'Connor, J. 1974: *The Fiscal Crisis of the State*. New York: St Martins.

OECD 1970: *The Growth of Output 1960–1980*. Paris: OECD.

OECD 1973: *Monetary Policy in Germany*. Paris: OECD.

OECD 1974: *Monetary Policy in France*. Paris: OECD.

OECD 1977: *Towards Full Employment and Price Stability*. Paris: OECD.

OECD 1978: *Budgetary Indicators: OECD Economic Outlook-Occasional Studies*, July. Paris: OECD.

Offe, C. 1974: "Structural problems of the capitalist state," *German Political Studies*, 1, 31–58.

Offe, C. 1984: *Contradictions of the Welfare State*. Cambridge, Mass.: MIT Press.

Offe, C. 1985: *Disorganized Capitalism*. Cambridge, Mass.: MIT Press.

O'Higgins, M. 1985: "Inequality, redistribution and recession: the British experience 1976–82," *Journal of Social Policy*, 14(3) (Fall), 279–308.

Olson, M. 1971: *The Logic of Collective Action*. Cambridge, Mass.: Harvard University Press.

Olson, M. 1982: *The Rise and Decline of Nations*. New Haven, Con.: Yale University Press.

Opie, R. 1972: "Economic planning and growth." In W. Beckerman (ed.) *The Labour Government's Economic Record 1964–70*. London: Duckworth, 157–77.

Ormerod, P. 1979: *Economic Modelling*. London: Heinemann.

Padgett, J. 1981: "Hierarchy and ecological control in federal budgetary decision-making," *American Journal of Sociology*, 87, 75–129.

Pahl, R. E. and Winkler, J. T. 1974: "The coming corporatism," *New Society* (10 Oct.), 72–6.

Paish, F. W. 1970: *How the Economy Works*. London: Macmillan.

Panic, M. 1975: "Why the UK propensity to import is so high," *Lloyds Bank Review*, 115, 1–12.

Panitch, L. 1975: *Social Democracy and Industrial Militancy*. Cambridge: Cambridge University Press.

Panitch, L. 1981: "Trade unions and the capitalist state: corporatism and its contradictions," *New Left Review*, 125 (Jan.–Feb.), 21–44.

Parodi, M. 1981: *L'Economique et la société française de 1945 à 1970*. Paris: Colin.

Parsons, T. 1951: *The Social System*. New York: Free Press.

Pascallon, P. 1974: *La Planification de l'Economie Française*. Paris: Masson et Cie.

Peacock, A. 1980: "The British economy and its problems." In W. B. Gwyn and R. Rose (eds), *British Progress and Decline*. New Orleans: Tulane University Press.

Peacock, A. et al. 1980: *Structural Economic Policies in West Germany and the United Kingdom*. London: Anglo-American Foundation.

Pelling, H. 1976: *A Short History of British Trade Unionism*. Harmondsowrth: Penguin.

Penniman, H. 1981: *Britain at the Polls, 1979*. Washington: American Enterprise Institute.

PEP 1960: *Growth in the British Economy*. London: Allen and Unwin.

PEP 1974: *Reshaping Britain*. London: PEP Broadsheet No. 548.

Peyrefitte, A. 1980: *Le mal francaise*. Paris: Flammerion.

Pfister, T. 1985: *La Vie Quotidienne à Matignon au Temps de l'Union de la Gauche*. Paris: Hachette.

Phelps Brown, H. 1977: "What is the British predicament?" *Three Banks Review*, 116, 3–29.

Piore, M. and Sabel, C. 1984: *The Second Industrial Divide*. New York: Basic Books.

Pitts, J. 1963: "Continuity and change in bourgeois France." In S. Hoffmann et al., *In Search of France*. New York: Harper and Row, 235–304.

Pizzorno, A. 1978: "Political exchange and collective identity in industrial conflict." In C. Crouch and A. Pizzorno (eds), *The Resurgence of Class Conflict in Western Europe since 1968*. London: Macmillan.

Polanyi, K. 1944: *The Great Transformation*. Boston: Beacon.

Pollard, S. 1969: *The Development of the British Economy 1914–1967*. 2nd edn. New York: St Martins Press.

Pollard, S. 1979: "The nationalization of the banks." In D. E. Martin and D. Rubinstein (eds), *Ideology and the Labour Movement*. London: Croom Helm.

Pollard S. 1982: *The Wasting of the British Economy*. London: Croom Helm.

Polsby, N. 1963: *Community Power and Political Theory*. New Haven: Yale University Press.

Portelli, H. 1980: *Le socialisme français tel qu'il est*. Paris: Presses Universitaires de la France.

Posner, M. (ed.) 1978: *Demand Management*. London: Heinemann.

Posner, M. and Steer, A. 1978: "Price competitiveness and the performance of manufacturing industry." In F. Blackaby (ed.), *Deindustrialization*, London: Heinemann, 141–65.

Poulantzas, N. 1976: *Political Power and Social Classes*. London: Verso.

Poulantzas, N. 1978: *State, Power, Socialism*. London: New Left Books.

Prate, A. 1978: *Les batailles économiques du Général de Gaulle*. Paris: Plon.

Pratten, C. F. 1976: *A Comparison of the Performance of Swedish and U.K. Companies*. Cambridge: Cambridge University Press.

Pratten, C. F. 1982: "Mrs. Thatcher's economic experiment," *Lloyd's Bank Review*, 143, 36–51.

Pressnell, L. S. 1978: "1925: the burden of sterling," *Economic History Review*, 2nd series, 31, 67–88.

Prévot, H. et al. 1977: "La Planification a l'épreuve," *Projet* (Jan.), 47–66.

Price, R. W. R. 1978: "Budgetary policy." In F. Blackaby (ed.), *British Economic Policy 1960–74*. London: Cambridge University Press, 135–216.

Priouret, F. 1968: *Les français mystifiés*. Paris: Grasset.

Le projet socialiste 1980: Paris: Club Socialiste du livre.

Pryke, R. 1981: *The Nationalized Industries*. Oxford: Martin Robertson.

Przeworski, A. 1980: "Social democracy as a historical phenomenon," *New Left Review*, 122, 27–58.

Przeworski, A. 1985: *Capitalism and Social Democracy*. Cambridge: Cambridge University Press.

Przeworski, A. and Wallerstein, M. 1982: "The structure of class conflict in democratic capitalist societies," *American Political Science Review*, 76, 215–38.

Pulzer, P. 1967: *Political Representation and Elections*. London: Macmillan.

Radcliffe Report 1959: *The Committee on the Working of the Monetary System*, Report, Cmnd. 827. London: HMSO.

Ramsden, J. 1979: "The changing base of British conservativism." In C. Cook and J. Ramsden (eds), *New Trends in British Politics since 1945*. London: Macmillan.

Rapport sur les Principales Options du VIIIè Plan 1979: Paris: Documentation Francaise.

Réynaud, J. J. 1975: *Les syndicats en France*. Paris: Seuil.

Richardson, H. W. 1967: *Economic Recovery in Britain 1929–39*. London: Weidenfeld and Nicolson.

Riddell, P. 1983: *The Thatcher Government*. Oxford: Martin Robertson.

Riemer, J. 1983: "Alterations in the design of model Germany." In A. Markovits and G. Romoser (eds), *The Political Economy of West Germany*. New York: Praeger, 53–89.

Rimlinger, G. 1971: *Welfare Policy and Industrialization in America, Europe and Russia*. New York: Wiley.

Robbins, A. 1971: *Autobiography of an Economist*. London: Macmillan.

Roberts, C. C. 1979: "Economic theory and policy-making in West Germany," *Cambridge Journal of Economics*, 3, 83–89.

Roderick, G. and Stephens, M. 1982: *The British Malaise*. Brighton: Falmer Press.

Rogow, A. A. 1955: *The Labour Government and British Industry, 1945–1951*. London: Macmillan.

Rondin, G. 1985: *Le Sacre des Notables*. Paris: Fayard.

Rose, R. 1983: "Two and one half cheers for the market in Britain," *Public Opinion* (June–July), 10–15.

Rose, R. 1984: *Do Parties Make a Difference?*. Brunswick: Chatham House.

Rosanvallon, P. 1983: *Misère de l'économie*. Paris: Editions du Seuil.

Rosanvallon, P. 1985: *Les tendances de la négotiation collective et des relations industrielles en France*. Mimeo, 5.

Roseveare, H. 1969: *The Treasury*. New York: Columbia University Press.

Ross, G. and Jenson, J. 1981: "Strategy and contradiction in the victory of French socialism." In R. Miliband and J. Saville (eds), *The Socialist Register*. London: Merlin Press.

Sabel, C. 1981: *Work and Politics*. Cambridge: Cambridge University Press.

Sachs, J. 1979: "Wages, profits, and macroeconomic adjustment: a comparative study," *Brookings Papers on Economic Activity*, 2, 269–319.

Sacks, P. M. 1980: "State structure and the asymmetrical society," *Comparative Politics* (Apr.), 349–76.

Salin, P. and Lane, G. 1977: "Inflation in France." In L. B. Krause and W. S. Salant (eds), *Worldwide Inflation*. Washington: Brookings Institution.

Sandberg, L. 1969: "American rings and English mules: the role of economic rationality," *Quarterly Journal of Economics*, 83, 25–43.

Sandberg, L. 1974: *Lancashire in Decline*. Columbus: Ohion State University Press.

Sartori, G. 1979: *Parties and Party Systems*. Cambridge: Cambridge University Press.

Saul, S. B. 1960: *Studies in British Overseas Trade 1870–1914*. Liverpool: Liverpool University Press.

Savage, D. 1978: "The channels of monetary influence," *National Institute Economic Review*, 84, 73–89.

Sayers, R. S. 1976: *The Bank of England 1891–1944*. London: Oxford University Press.

Scase, R. 1977: *Social Democracy in Capitalist Society*. London: Croom Helm.

Scase, R. (ed.) 1979: *The State in Western Europe*. London: Croom Helm.

Schain, M. 1980: "Corporatism and industrial relations in France." In P. G. Cerny and M. A. Schain (eds), *French Politics and Public Policy*. New York: St Martin's Press, 191–217.

Schattschneider, E. E. 1960: *The Semi-Sovereign People*. New York: Holt, Rinehart.

Schmitter, P. and Lehmbruch, G. 1979: *Trends toward Corporatist Intermediation*. Beverly Hills: Sage.

Schmitter, P. and Lehmbruch, G. 1982: *Patterns of Corporatist Policy-making*. Beverly Hills: Sage.

Schott, K. 1982: "The rise of Keynesian economics in Britain 1940–64," *Economy and Society*, 11(3), 292–316.

Schubert, G. 1960: *The Public Interest*. New York: Free Press.

Schumpeter, J. 1947: *Capitalism, Socialism and Democracy*. New York: Harper and Row.

Schurmann, F. 1968: *Ideology and Organization in Communist China*. Berkeley: University of California Press.

Scott, B. 1982: "Can industry survive the welfare state?" *Harvard Business Review*, 60(5), 70–84.

Scott, B. and Sprout, A. 1981: *National Industrial Planning: France and the EEC*. Boston: Harvard Business School.

Seldon, A. 1980: *Corrigible Capitalism, Incorrigible Socialism*. London: Institute for Economic Affairs.

Select Committee on Nationalised Industries 1969–70: *First Report*. House of Commons, vol. IV.

Servan-Schreiber, J. J. 1969: *The American Challenge*. New York: Avon.

Shanks, M. 1960: *The Stagnant Society*. London: Penguin.

Shanks, M. 1977: *Planning and Politics*. London: Allen and Unwin.
Sheahan, J. 1963: *Promotion and Control of Industry in Post-war France*. Cambridge: Harvard University Press.
Shils, E. and Johnson, H. 1972: "Ideology." In *The Encyclopedia of the Social Sciences*.
Shonfield, A. 1958: *British Economic Policy since the War*. Harmondworth: Penguin.
Shonfield, A. 1969: *Modern Capitalism*. Oxford: Oxford University Press.
Shorter, E. and Tilly, C. 1974: *Strikes in France 1830–1968*. Cambridge: Cambridge University Press.
Simon, H. 1957: *Administrative Behavior*. New York: Macmillan.
Simonnet, P. 1982: *Le grand bluff économique des socialistes*. Paris: Lattes.
Singh, A. 1977: "UK industry in the world economy: a case of deindustrialization?" *Cambridge Journal of Economics*, 1, 113–36.
Singh, A. 1979: "North Sea oil and the reconstruction of UK industry." In F. Blackaby (ed.), *Deindustrialization*. London: Heinemann, 202–24.
Skidelsky, R. 1967: *Politicians and the Slump*. London: Macmillan.
Skidelsky, R. 1979: "The collapse of the Keynesian consensus." In C. Crouch (ed.), *State and Economy in Contemporary Capitalism*, London: Croom Helm, 55–87.
Skocpol, T. 1979: *States and Social Revolutions*. Cambridge: Cambridge University Press.
Skocpol, T. and Finegold, K. 1983: "State capacity and economic intervention in the early New Deal," *Political Science Quarterly*, 97, 256–78.
Skowronek, S. 1982: *Building a New American State*. Cambridge: Cambridge University Press.
Smethurst, R. G. 1979: "Monetary policy." In D. Morris (ed.), *The Economic System in the UK*. London: Oxford University Press, 339–69.
Smith, D. 1975: "Public consumption and economic performance," *National Westminster Bank Quarterly Review* (Nov.), 17–30.
Spiegelberg, R. 1973: *The City*. London Quartet.
Spivey, W. A. 1982: *Economic Policy in France 1976–81*. Ann Arbor: University of Michigan.
Steinbrunner, J. 1974: *Cybernetic Theory of Decision*. Princeton: Princeton University Press.
Stephenson, H. 1981: *Mrs. Thatcher's First Year*. London: Jill Norman.
Stern, H. N. 1976: "Taxation and labour supply – a partial survey." Paper presented at the Institute of Fiscal Studies, London.
Stevens, A. 1980: "The higher civil service and economic policy-making." In P. G. Cerny and M. A. Schain (eds), *French Politics and Public Policy*. New York: St Martin's Press, 79–100.
Stewart, Michael 1977: *Politics and Economic Policy Since 1964*. Oxford: Pegamon Press.
Stoffaes, C. 1968: *Le Grande menace industrielle*. Paris: Calmann-Levy.
Stoffaes, C. 1982: *Politique Economique de la France*. Paris: Institut d'Etudes Politiques.
Stoléru, L. 1969: *L'Impératif industrielle*. Paris: Seuil.
Stone, C. 1980: "Systemic power in communicty decision making," *American Political Science Review*, 74 (Dec.), 978–90.

Stout, D. K. 1977: *International Price Competitiveness: non-price factors and export performance*. London: National Economic Development Office.

Stout, D. K. 1979: "Deindustrialization and industrial policy." In F. Blackaby (ed.), *Deinudstrialization*. London: Heinemann, 171–95.

Strange, S. 1971: *Sterling and British Policy*. London: Oxford University Press.

Streeck, W. and Schmitter, P. 1986: *Private Interest Government: Beyond Market and State*. Beverly Hills: Sage.

Suleiman, E. 1978: *Elites in French Society*. Princeton: Princeton University Press.

Suleiman, E. 1980: "Administrative reform and the problem of decentralization in the Fifth Republic." In W. Andrews and S. Hoffmann (eds.), *The Fifth Republic at Twenty*, Albany: SUNY Press, 69–80.

Supple, Barry 1977: *Essays in British Business History*. Oxford: Oxford University Press.

Surrey, M. 1982: "United Kingdom." In A. Boltho (ed.), *The European Economy: Growth and Crisis*. London: Oxford University Press, 528–53.

Tarling, R. J. and Wilkinson, F. 1977: "The social contract: postwar incomes policies and their inflationary impact," *Cambridge Journal of Economics*, 1, 395–414.

Tawney, R. H. 1943: "The abolition of economic controls 1918–1921," *Economic History Review*, 12, 1–30.

Taylor, R. 1978: *The Fifth Estate*. London: Pan.

Tew, J. H. B. 1978: "Policies aimed at improving the balance of payments." In F. Blackaby (ed.), *British Economic Policy 1960–74*. London: Cambridge University Press, 304–59.

Thatcher, M. 1980: "The Airey Neave Memorial Lecture," *Commentary*, 1(2), 7–14.

Therborn, G. 1978: *What Does the Ruling Class Do When it Rules?* London: Verso.

Thirlwall, A. P. 1978: "The UK's economic problem: a balance of payments constraint?" *National Westminster Bank Quarterly Review* (Feb.), 24–32.

Thoenig, J. C. 1973: *L'Ere des technocrates*. Paris: Editions d'Organisation.

Thomas, H. 1968: *Crisis in the Civil Service*. London: Anthony Blond.

Thompson, G. 1977: "The relationship between the financial and industrial sectors in the United Kingdom economy. *Economy and Society*, 6(3) (Aug.), 235–83.

Thompson, G. 1986: *The Conservatives' Economic Policy 1979–84*. London: Croom Helm.

Tocqueville, A. de 1955: *The Old Regime and the French Revolution*. New York: Doubleday (orig. publ. 1856).

Tolliday, S. and Zeitlin, J. (eds.) 1986: *Shop Floor Bargaining and the State*. Cambridge: Cambridge University Press.

Touraine, A. 1971: *The Post-Industrial Society*. New York: Random House.

Truman, D. 1951: *The Governmental Process*. New York: Alfred Knopf.

Tufte, E. 1979: *Political Control of the Economy*. Princeton: Princeton University Press.

Turner, H. A. and Wilkinson, F. 1972: *Do Trade Unions Cause Inflation?* Cambridge: Cambridge University Press.

Ullmo, Y. 1974: *La planification en France*. Paris: Cours de l'Institut d'Etudes Politiques.

Ullmo, Y. 1975: "France." In J. Hayward and M. Watson (eds), *Planning, Politics, and Public Policy*. Cambridge: Cambridge University Press, 22–51.

Urry, J. 1983: "De-industrialization, classes and politics." In R. King (ed.), *Capital and Politics*. London: Routledge and Kegan Paul.

Valance, G. 1978: "Le Retour au libéralisme," *L'Express*, 24 Apr., 50.

Verba, S. 1965: "Comparative political culture." In L. Pye and S. Verba (eds), *Political Culture and Political Development*. Princeton: Princeton University Press, 512–60.

Vernon, R. (ed.), 1974: *Big Business and the State*. Cambridge, Mass.: Harvard University Press.

Versillier, Elizabeth 1983: "Aspects financiers des nationalisations," *Revue Economique*, 34(3), 480–95.

Vichniac, J. 1986: "Organization in the French and British steel industries in the late 19th century." In M. Zeitlin (ed.), *Political Power and Social Theory*, VI.

Vivéret, P. 1983: "La gauche piégée dans l'état," *Projet* (June).

Vogel, F. 1973: *German Business and the State*. Cambridge, Mass.: Harvard University Press.

Wadbrook, W. P. 1972: *West German Balance of Payments Policy*. New York: Praeger.

Walzer, M. 1968: *The Revolution of the Saints*. New York: Atheneum.

Ward, T. S. and Nield, R. R. 1978: *The Measurement and Reform of Budgetary Policy*. London: Heinemann.

Warde, A. 1982: *Consensus and Beyond*. Manchester: Manchester University Press.

Warnecke, S. and Suleiman, E. 1975: *Industrial Policies in Western Europe*. New York: Praeger.

Warren, W. 1972: "Capitalist planning and the state," *New Left Review*, 72, 3–29.

Warwick, P. 1985: "Did Britain change? An enquiry into the causes of national decline," *Journal of Contemporary History*, 20(1) (Jan.), 99–133.

Weber, M. 1958: *From Max Weber: Essays in Sociology*. New York: Oxford University Press.

Weir, M. and Skocpol, T. 1985: "State structure and the possibilities for Keynesian response to the Great Depression in Sweden, Britain, and the United States." In P. Evans et al (eds), *Bringing the State Back In*. Cambridge: Cambridge University Press.

Whiteley, P. (ed.) 1980: *Models of Political Economy*. London: Sage.

Whiteley, P. 1983: "The political economy of economic growth," *European Journal of Political Research*, 11, 197–213.

Whiting, A. 1976a: "Is Britain's poor growth performance due to government stop-go-induced fluctuations?" *Three Banks Review*, 109, 26–46.

Whiting, A. 1976b: *The Economics of Industrial Subsidies*. London: HMSO.

Wiener, M. 1981: *English Culture and the Decline of the Industrial Spirit*. Cambridge: Cambridge University Press.

Wildavsky, A. 1973: "If planning is everything, maybe it's nothing," *Policy Sciences*, 4(2), 127–53.

Wildavsky, A. 1975: *Budgeting*. Boston: Little Brown.

Wilensky, H. 1967: *Organizational Intelligence*. New York: Basic Books.

Wilks, S. 1981: "Planning agreements: the making of a paper tiger," *Public Administration*, 59, 399–419.

Williams, F. 1983: *The Times on the Economy*. London: Collins.

Williams, K., Williams, J. and Thomas, D. 1983: *Why are the British Bad at Manufacturing?* Boston: Routledge and Kegan Paul.

Williamson, O. 1975: *Markets and Hierarchies*. New York: Free Press.

Wilson, F. 1983: "French interest group politics: pluralist or neo-corporatist?" *American Political Science Review*, 77, 895–910.

Wilson, H. 1971: *The Labour Government 1964–70*. London: Weidenfeld and Nicolson.

Wilson Committee 1977: *Report of the Committee to Review the Functioning of Financial Institutions*. London: HMSO.

Wilson, T. 1966: *The Downfall of the Liberal Party 1914–1935*. Ithaca, NY: Cornell University Press.

Wilson, W. 1908: *The State*. New York: Harper and Row.

Winch, D. 1969: *Economics and Policy*. London: Hodder and Stoughton.

Winkler, J. 1976: "Corporatism," *European Journal of Sociology*, 17(1), 100–36.

Wolfe, A. 1977: *The Limits of Legitimacy*. New York: Free Press.

Worms, J. P. 1974: "La redécouverte du politique." In M. Crozier (ed.), *Où va l'administration françaose*. Paris: Editions d'Organisation.

Worswick, G. D. N. 1977: "The end of demand management," *Lloyd's Bank Review*, 123, 1–18.

Wright, E. O. 1979: *Class Structure and Income Determination*. New York: Academic Press.

Wright, V. 1983: *The Government and Politics of France*. New York: Holmes and Meier.

Wright, V. 1984: "Socialism and the interdependent economy: industrial policy-making under the Mitterrand presidency," *Government and Opposition*, 19(3) (Summer), 287–303.

Yaffe, D. 1973: "The Marxian theory of crisis, capital, and the state," *Economy and Society*, 11, 186–232.

Young, S. and Lowe, A. V. 1974: *Intervention in the Mixed Economy*. London: Croom Helm.

Youngson, A. J. 1960: *The British Economy 1920–1957*. Cambridge, Mass.: Harvard University Press.

Zeitlin, J. 1980: "The emergence of shop steward organization and job control in the British car industry," *History Workshop Journal*, 10, 119–37.

Zinn, K. G. 1978: "The social market in crisis," In S. Holland (ed.), *Beyond Capitalist Planning*. Oxford: Basil Blackwell, 85–105.

Zysman, J. 1977: *Political Strategies for Industrial Order*. Berkeley: University of California.

Zysman, J. 1980: "The interventionist temptation: financial structure and political purpose." In W. Andrews and S. Hoffmann (eds), *The Fifth Republic at Twenty*, Albany: SUNY Press.

Zysman, J. 1983: *Governments, Markets and Growth*. Ithaca, NY: Cornell University Press.

Index

railways:
nationalization of British, 70
Railways and Canals Commission, 54
rationality:
in French planning, 155, 161–2
bounded (Simon), 12
market, 36
rationalization of British industry:
limitations, 251–2
state pressure to hasten, 53–6
rationalization of French industry:
speeded by nationalizations, 205
rationalization of Germany industry,
240, 256
rationing, 73
RATP (Paris transport), 206
Rayner, Sir Derek, 117
Reagan administration, 103, 199
recession:
British (1980), 105, 115–16
French (1974), 184 (1981), 195–8
German (1965–66), 239
regional development aid,
British, 52, 89, 114
French, 52, 53, 89
German, 239, 256
Regional Employment Premium
(1968), 52
Renault, 204, 206
"rentier nation:"
Britain as a, 133
reorganization, sectoral:
state, union and bank involvement
(1962–85), 256–7 *Table 9.1*
reprivatization program, British,
110–11
research and development:
British spending on, 52–3, 113
resource allocation, global:
in French Plans of 1960s, 146
resource-utilization:
British inefficiency in, 28
"revisionists" in Labour Party, 67, 71
Rhone Poulenc, 203, 204, 206, 208,
209
Riboud, Jean, 201
rigeur, see austerity
riots, British inner-city (1981, 1985),

134, 287n5
Robbins, Lord, 81
Rocard, Michel, 213–15
Rocardiens, 193
Rolls Royce, 53, 55, 90
Rome, Treaty of, 148
Rose, Richard, 274
Roussel-Uclaf, 204, 209
Royer law (1974), 175
Rueff, Jacques, 143, 182, 289n4
Rueff Report (1958), 154

Sacilor, 203, 208
Sacks, Paul, 15
sacrifice, economic, 281–3
St Gobain-Pont-à-Mousson, 149, 190,
203, 206
Saint-Simon, Claude Henri de, 178
Salvadge, Stanley, 66
Sandberg, L, 44
Sanofi, 209
Saul, S.B., 40
Sautter, Christian, 215
Schattschneider, E.E.:
mobilization of bias, 160, 266
Schmitter, P., 268
Schonfield, 240
Schumpeter, J., 10
Scott, B., 9
Sealink, 110
"second left," 193
Second Plan (1953–57) 143, 146
Sectoral Working Parties (SWPs),
55–6, 90
security, national:
or welfare state, 203
"seed money" for firms, 210
service sector:
growth of British, 134
Seventh Plan (1975–81), 145, 147,
150, 175, 185–6
forecast and results, 184–5 *Table
7.1*
Shanks, Michael:
The Stagnant Society, 86
shareholders:
increase in broadening British
base, 110–11

Vickers, 114
Vietnam War, 291n6
Villiers, Georges, 169
Volkswagen, 256
voluntaristic values of British, 91
voting patterns, British:
    not fully determined, 134
wage demands, British:
    public sector, 108–9
wage restraint, German, 240–2
Walters, Alan, 105
Warren, Bill:
    on planning and full employment
    policy of capitalism, 6–7
Weber, M., 19
Weeks, Hugh, 86
Weir, M., 16
welfare state, British:
    costs of, 29, 30
    founding of (1945–51), 70, 71
welfare state or national security, 203
"wets," 106, 128, 287n3
White, S.F.T., 290n7
White Paper of Employment Policy
    (1944), 71
Wigforss, Ernst, 274
Wildavsky, Aaron, 140, 279
Wilson, Harold:
    "bonfire of controls," 73
    Government (1964–70), 51, 79
    promise to reforge Britain in the

white hot heat of the scientific
    revolution, 87–8
Wilson Committee (1977), 39
Winkler, J.T., 290n3
"winter of discontent" (1978–79), 95
women:
    increasing role in labor force, 134
Wood, Kingsley:
    budget (1941), 72
work incentives, 123
work organization, 36
    British inefficiency in, 28, 90
working class:
    in Britain and France, 14
    interests of French, 218–19
    limits to electoral power, 261–2
workmen's compensation (1893)
    (British), 71
World War One (1914–18), 66
Warld War Two (1939–45), 66–7
Worms, Pierre, 217
Wright, Vincent, 216

X-crise, 178

Young Workers Scheme, 113
Youth Opportunities Programme,
    113

Zysman, John, 9, 48, 289n2